Bo Pettersson
How Literary Worlds Are Shaped

Narratologia

Contributions to Narrative Theory

Edited by
Fotis Jannidis, Matías Martínez, John Pier,
Wolf Schmid (executive editor)

Editorial Board
Catherine Emmott, Monika Fludernik, José Ángel García Landa, Inke Gunia,
Peter Hühn, Manfred Jahn, Markus Kuhn, Uri Margolin, Jan Christoph Meister,
Ansgar Nünning, Marie-Laure Ryan, Jean-Marie Schaeffer, Michael Scheffel,
Sabine Schlickers

Volume 54

Bo Pettersson

How Literary Worlds Are Shaped

A Comparative Poetics of Literary Imagination

DE GRUYTER

ISBN 978-3-11-061107-6
e-ISBN (PDF) 978-3-11-048631-5
e-ISBN (EPUB) 978-3-11-048493-9
ISSN 1612-8427

Library of Congress Cataloging-in-Publication Data
A CIP catalog record for this book has been applied for at the Library of Congress.

Bibliographic information published by the Deutsche Nationalbibliothek
The Deutsche Nationalbibliothek lists this publication in the Deutsche Nationalbibliografie;
detailed bibliographic data are available on the Internet at http://dnb.dnb.de.

© 2018 Walter de Gruyter GmbH, Berlin/Boston
This volume is text- and page-identical with the hardback published in 2016.
Printing and binding: CPI books GmbH, Leck

♾ Printed on acid-free paper
Printed in Germany

www.degruyter.com

Acknowledgements

Showing up is eighty percent of life, Woody Allen famously quipped. But the remaining twenty percent is rather important too. Both you who are reading and I who am writing this are lucky to be able to spend some of them on imaginative human artefacts. On the basis of the records we have of when writing first was developed in Mesopotamia some five thousand years ago, about one fourth of everything written was non-administrative, some of it what we today would call literature. It may seem a frivolous activity in the face of the hardships often encountered in life, but still people have never stopped creating, performing and listening to literature and later writing and reading it.

This book aims to pinpoint why we do so: how we use our imagination and combine it with literary representation; how we deal with sorting out whether what we read is fantastic or real, reliable or not; how literary worlds are shaped by different basic modes and themes and varied in all sorts of ways; how we are shaped by literary imagination; and finally why literature matters, and how understanding literary worlds can be useful when studying and teaching literature.

I have spent a great deal of my twenty percent in the last decade or so trying to come up with views on such issues. Most importantly, I had the academic year 2012–2013 off from my chair at Department of Modern Languages, University of Helsinki. During that time I worked under the auspices of The Foundations' Professor Pool in Finland in part funded by The Society of Swedish Literature in Finland, for which I am very grateful. A great number of colleagues and students, conference organizers and participants have kindly acted as sounding boards for various aspects of this study. Let me just single out a few of the most important ones: David Herman (Durham), Monika Fludernik (Freiburg), Anthony Johnson (Åbo/Turku), Paisley Livingston (Hong Kong), Brian McHale (Columbus), Ansgar Nünning (Giessen), Vera Nünning (Heidelberg), Stein Haugom Olsen (Østfold), Anders Pettersson (Umeå – Lund), my brother Torsten Pettersson (Uppsala), Peter Swirski (St. Louis) and Clas Zilliacus (Åbo/Turku) as well as the colleagues and students of The Finnish Graduate School of Literary Studies and my interdisciplinary postgraduate seminar at Department of Modern Languages. Thanks are also due to the editors of the De Gruyter's Narratologia series for graciously accepting this study, De Gruyter's kind and efficient staff, the editors mentioned in the next paragraph and the peer reviewers they engaged. In particular, I would like to single out one of De Gruyter's peer reviewers, whose thorough and constructive statement on this study did much to sharpen my thinking and writing. Finally, I want to extend my gratitude to my colleague and friend Docent Mark Shackleton for graciously polishing my language at short notice.

Some chapters and subchapters of this study draw on previous publications: 1.1–1.4: "On the Study of Imagination and Popular Imagination: A Historical Survey and a Look Ahead", in Sven-Erik Klinkmann (ed.), *Popular Imagination. Essays on Fantasy and Cultural Practice* (Åbo/Turku, Finland: Nordic Network of Folklore, 2002); 2.3: "On the Interrelation of Genre and Mimesis, Especially in Science Fiction and Realist Fiction", in Pirjo Lyytikäinen et al. (eds), *Genre and Interpretation* (Helsinki: Department of Finnish, Finno-Ugrian and Scandinavian Studies and The Finnish Graduate School of Literary Studies, 2010); 3.3–3.4: "Kinds of Unreliability in Fiction: Narratorial, Focal, Expositional and Combined", in Vera Nünning (ed.), *Unreliable Narration and Trustworthiness. Intermedial and Interdisciplinary Perspectives.* Narratologia 44 (Berlin, Munich, Boston: De Gruyter, 2015); 5: "Literary Criticism Writes Back to Metaphor Theory: Exploring the Relation between Extended Metaphor and Narrative in Literature", in Monika Fludernik (ed.), *Beyond Cognitive Metaphor Theory. Perspectives on Literary Metaphor* (New York and London: Routledge/Taylor and Francis Group, 2011); 6.2: "Hypothetical Action: Poetry under Erasure in Blake, Dickinson and Eliot", in Roger D. Sell et al. (eds), *The Ethics of Literary Communication. Genuineness, Directness and Indirectness* (Amsterdam and Philadelphia: Benjamins, 2013); and 6.3: "What Happens When Nothing Happens: Interpreting Narrative Technique in the Plotless Novels of Nicholson Baker", in Markku Lehtimäki et al. (eds), *Narrative, Interrupted: The Plotless, the Disturbing and the Trivial in Literature* (Berlin and Boston: De Gruyter, 2012). For the reuse of text in these papers I am very grateful to the publishers.

Closer to home I have been blessed by Nelo and Oona, Venla and Leevi, four wonderful children who have done their best to raise me, and by my dear wife Marjut, in whose company my heart always listens to the blackbird in our garden sing before sunrise. Marjut, I hope you don't mind if I try to spend as much as I can of what remains of my twenty percent with you – in the company of some of the most spellbinding artefacts created by the human imagination.

Contents

Introduction —— 1

1 Imaginative World-Making —— 9
1.1 Imagine That ... —— 9
1.2 Imagination in the Subjunctive Mood: From Mediation to Creation —— 11
1.3 Imagination as a Shared Frame of Mind —— 20
1.4 Bridging the Study of Imagination and Popular Imagination —— 28
1.5 Literary Imagination —— 33

2 The Imaginative Uses of Mimesis —— 41
2.1 Mimesis as a Basis for Literature —— 41
2.2 The Range of Mimesis: Literary Imagination as Real and Fantastic —— 50
2.3 On the Interrelation between Mimesis and Genre —— 62

3 Kinds of Unreliability —— 78
3.1 From Mimesis to Deception —— 78
3.2 Basic Features of Unreliability and How We Learn Them —— 83
3.3 Narratorial and Focal Unreliability: A Scale of Intentionality —— 88
3.4 Expositional and Combined: Exposition as Manipulation —— 96

4 The Shaping of Literary Worlds —— 110
4.1 The Imaginative Frame of Literary Imagination —— 110
4.2 Literary World-Making: The Basics —— 115
4.3 Modes and Themes —— 121
4.4 Examples of Literary World-Making —— 137

5 Key Combinations: Figures and Narratives —— 150
5.1 Figures versus Narratives, Figures into Narratives —— 150
5.2 From Metaphor to Narrative to Allegory —— 160
5.3 Extended Metaphors in Novels —— 168

6 Other Imaginative Inflections —— 175
6.1 Indirection in Fiction and Drama —— 176
6.2 Hypothetical Action in Poetry —— 185
6.3 Genres and Text Types, Their Hierarchies and Blends —— 198

7 How Literary Worlds Shape Us — 208
7.1   Imagined Selves and Communities in Fiction and Beyond — 208
7.2   Origins of the Modern Hero — 213
7.3   The Literary Spark for a World War (or Two) — 222
7.4   A Chinese Author at the Service of Ideology — 228

8 Why Literature Matters — 235
8.1   Benefit through Delight — 235
8.2   A Sense of Wonder — 242

9 Ten Reasons to Study and Teach Literary Worlds — 253

Conclusion — 267

Appendix 1 — 275

Appendix 2 — 276

Bibliography — 278
   Primary Sources — 278
   Secondary Sources — 285
   Electronic Sources — 315

Index — 316

Introduction

In a brief essay-like short story called "Imagine" the American science-fiction author Fredric Brown (1955/2007: 565) notes how easy it is for us to imagine "ghosts, gods and devils" or "spaceships and the future". Most such things we have been imagining for ages. Then he goes on to ponder what is actually hard to imagine.

> Imagine a piece of matter and yourself in it, yourself aware, thinking and therefore knowing you exist, able to move that piece of matter that you're in, to make it sleep or wake, make love or walk uphill. [---]
> Imagine standing on [a] blob of mud, whirling with it, whirling through time and space to an unknown destination.

This book deals with much that Brown puts his finger on by this little allegory of humankind's life on earth. First, it focuses on the faculty of imagination in humans or, to put it differently, on the human propensity for imagining or imaging, as it comes across in literature. Brown clearly includes in the meaning of *imagine* the sense 'understand', since most humans are well aware that they are conscious and live on a planet in space, even if they may have problems fathoming what this means. I try to show that imagination is central to what it is to be human and that one way of defining *human* is to be able to imagine what could have happened or might happen, including different kinds of creatures – divine, mythical, alive or mechanical, as such or combined – somewhere sometime. We may note that in the above quote Brown seems to hold on to a dichotomy between body ("a piece of matter") and soul or perhaps cognition ("you"), which is one, by now often discredited, way of categorising – that is, in fact, imagining – human existence.

Second, since much of the most interesting imagining beyond religion and myth takes place in literature, it is the primary material of this study. However, just as Brown suggests that what is most difficult to grasp or "imagine" is the most real – the predicament of a conscious species on a planet whirling in space for apparently no purpose and with no destination –, I attempt to show that most of what is imagined in literature is in one way or another based on what is perceived as real. It is this dichotomy between what is and what is not perceived and represented as real that has been given so many fascinating combinations in literature.

Third, in the two quoted sentences Brown pits cognition against the universe, even though of course the latter is mainly understood by the workings of the former in conjunction with five kinds of sense perception. Finally, the

DOI 10.1515/9783110483475-001

way Brown juxtaposes cognition and the universe is through the literary technique Viktor Shklovsky (1917/1998) termed *ostranenie* or *defamiliarization*. That is, when reading the respective sentence, readers come to understand that "a piece of matter and yourself in it" refers to the human body and soul or cognition and "a blob of mud" to earth. In the course of this study we shall consider a number of themes and techniques, by which literature makes use of as well as presents human cognition and the universe it struggles to understand, often delighting in both the findings and shortcomings that endeavour entails.

No lesser authority than Albert Einstein (1931/2009: 97) famously praised imagination, especially its use in science: "Imagination is more important than knowledge. For knowledge is limited, whereas imagination embraces the entire world, stimulating progress, giving birth to evolution. It is, strictly speaking, a real factor in scientific research".[1] If imagination is so central in not only the arts but also science, it may seem rather strange that it has not been studied more in recent years. This study attempts to fill some of that gap by giving a brief account of how imagination has been analysed so far, especially in philosophy and the social sciences, and then goes on to study literary imagination and how its worlds are shaped.

In doing so, I take my cue from one of Erich Auerbach's (1952/2014: 262) last papers, "The Philology of World Literature", in which he calls for synthetic studies of literature that centre on a particular "starting point, a tangible hook" that possesses "an illuminating power that is sufficient to organize and interpret a far broader range of phenomena than the point from which it started". Here imagination, more specifically literary imagination, is the point of departure, and it is by the main themes and techniques that it has employed that I try provide some modest beginnings for the kind of synthetic studies of literature that Auerbach called for.

Since imagination has for centuries been viewed as central in human creativity – at times regarded as a faculty, at times as a mere aspect of cognition –, it is first considered in some detail (chapter 1). In the last few decades we have seen the publication of some fine studies summarizing the history of imagination and popular imagination in various fields, but in effect no major new studies.[2] Since in my view the writing and reading of literature are imaginative

---

[1] Cf. R. G. Collingwood's (2005/2007: 74) point that "imagination is the genus of which knowledge is a species".
[2] A rare exception is Shaun Nichols' (2006) collection of cognitively inspired essays on imagination, which shows how rich an area of research imagination is for philosophers and psychologists alike. Also, there is currently an interest in how literary imagining or imaging works when reading (see 1.5). But of the thirty essays in Lisa Zunshine's (2015) recent major

acts, it is worth studying how they work in terms of what has been termed *literary imagination* (see 1.5). By presenting the makings of a new kind of poetics – that is, a broad view of how literature is shaped – based on a long list of precursors starting with Aristotle, in the rest of this study I analyse how thematic and formal aspects are been blended in literature through the ages. And they are blended, as René Wellek and Austin Warren (1948/1956: 28) note in their *Theory of Literature:* "'Content' and 'form' are terms used in too widely different senses for them to be, merely juxtaposed, helpful; indeed, even after careful definition, they too simply dichotomize the work of art". Even if I heed their point, when need be I make a distinction between themes and techniques, and the more encompassing practices that inform or colour entire literary works I propose to call *imaginative inflections* or simply *inflections*. Inflection, I hope, is an appropriate term, since the fundamentals of world-making, its modes and themes, can be seen as represented by *voice*, if in different ways: in prose fiction, usually one or more narrators and possibly characters too speak (or write);[3] in drama, characters speak; and in poetry, poetic personae or voices speak, even if they may be covert. Also, Mieke Bal (1985: 121–126) and others have maintained that all narratives, even so-called third-person narration, has the implicit frame of (*I say:*). Thus, the term inflection with its reference to voice may be appropriate when describing some of the major modulations of the building blocks of literary world-making, such as unreliability, combinations of narratives and rhetorical figures and different kinds of indirection, hypothesis, genre and text type.

It is my firm belief that literary studies may benefit from an extensive comparative discussion of literature that includes many different kinds of literature across cultures and ages. So many studies about what literature is or why it matters have been written from narrowly Western[4] – or Euro-American – perspectives, often by taking into account only a few centuries (or less) of its history. In order to avoid such myopia, I also discuss works from the beginnings of literature, especially Sumerian, Egyptian, Indo-European (Indian and Greek), Mesoamerican and Chinese, and go from there to the twenty-first century, with many stops on the way. As my multifarious primary material suggests, I make no dis-

---

volume on cognitive literary studies, only one discusses imagination, focusing particularly on the Romantic imagination (Richardson 2015).
3 Some narrative theorists, such as Ann Banfield (1982) and Monika Fludernik (1993), maintain that there at times can be *zero-narration*, that is, narration lacking a narrator, but all theorists agree that most narratives have narrators.
4 I use the term *Western* both for 'the Western world or the Occident' and for 'popular fiction and film set in the Wild West' (especially in 7.2), but the context should make it clear which is meant.

tinction between lowbrow and highbrow, since all literature seems to make use of similar themes and techniques. And you need not worry if you are not familiar with the works, since I try to introduce them in ways that makes it possible for you to get the point whether you have read them or not. At best, this book may even whet your appetite to read and perhaps study some of the works discussed.

Clearly, with my rather encompassing view of literature, some specifications and demarcations are in place. By *literature*, I understand oral or written communication that originally, or in some cases later, has been considered to have significant features that make it pleasing in its own right. That is, I mainly discuss the more or less non-factual and imaginative traditional three main forms of literature: prose (or narrative)[5] fiction (including the epic), drama and poetry, even if much of my focus is on the former. Hence, I do not consider other texts with literary qualities, such as speeches, autobiographies and essays, which a more wide-ranging view of literature would include.

Let me note that I see most literature in the three main forms as *narrative* and that this study on literary worlds aspires to expand cognitive and other narrative studies, which may touch but seldom focus on some of the aspects discussed here. Following the narrative theorist Gérard Genette (1982: 127), narrative can be considered "the representation of an event or a sequence of events", in which – I would add – some (usually human or human-like) agents explicitly or implicitly speak, act or perceive.[6] On this rather generous view of narrative, even nature poetry and nursery rhymes often have narrative features, since they may be about one or several events, but also about what repercussions they have on the perceiver, the very causality of which implies a rudimentary form of sequencing. Some riddles, lyrical poems and aphorisms only have vestiges of narrative through some sequencing in terms of depiction or causality: if *x*, then *y*, even if the *y* may only be implied, as in answer to a riddle or an insight suggested by the poem or aphorism on a perceiving consciousness, whether inside or outside the text. Similarly, haikus consist of three lines, often with a narrative or pseudo-narrative order of premise–action–reaction, in which the latter may be that of the speaker and/or the reader.

However, this study does not primarily aim to enlarge narrative studies as much as to provide an understanding of how the literary worlds that narratives

---

[5] *Prose fiction*, *narrative fiction* and *fiction* are often used interchangeably, even if many narrative theorists understandably prefer *narrative fiction*.
[6] For a discussion of various views of narrative see Ryan (2007). Well aware of the different criteria people apply to narrative, she in fact denies "the importance of *conscious judgments of narrativity*" (Ryan 2007: 31–33, 32 quote).

construct are shaped: by literary representation (on a scale from the fantastic to the real), three main modes (*the oral, the visual* and *the written*) and three main themes (*challenge, perception* and *relation*). They are often combined as well as inflected in various ways by unreliability, genre, text type, (blends of) figure and narrative, indirection and (what I term) hypothetical action. We should remember that the Latin *fingere* (to shape, mould or feign) is the root of both *fiction* and *figure* (meaning 'three-dimensional shape'),[7] which make use of sequencing and spatiality, respectively. This implies the close relation between on the one hand the stretch of imagination and (un)reliability (cf. feigning) in art and beyond (chapter 3) and on the other blends of rhetorical figures and narratives as well as other inflections (chapters 5 and 6), so that form and content go together in such seamless ways.

I do not discuss at length the differences between the three main forms of literature, in part since my main aim is to study literary themes and techniques that occur across literature and in part since Earl Miner (1990) in his important study *Comparative Poetics. An Intercultural Essay on Theories of Literature* has done a fine job in sorting out the main features of these forms (for him, "genres") when comparing literature from the East and the West.[8] He discusses central features in different kinds of literature, but at the same time specifies features that often occur across literature. My interest, however, lies in locating the thematic and formal universals in literature of different times and cultures. I do so by analysing themes across literatures, also in translation, as well as techniques mainly in literature written in English, thus trusting that themes come across better in translation than techniques. And literary techniques are given more or less space according to how much recognition they have received in literary studies, that is, neglected features are dealt with at some length. As for genres, I do not spend much time sorting out their features as such, even though I discuss some generic issues, mainly in 2.3 and 6.3. Nor do I more than touch on interpretive issues (as in 8.2), since I think it requires a separate study.[9]

---

[7] On the etymology and semantic import of *fiction* and *figure*, respectively, see Christine Brooke-Rose (1991/2009: 157) with a focus on fiction, forging and imitation and Auerbach (1938/2014: 65) with a focus on narrative and figure.
[8] Miner (1990: 218 *et passim*) detects specific key features: in lyric (that is, poetry excluding narrative poetry and prose poetry) he finds *presence, intensification* and *matters of moment*; in drama *estrangement, engagement* and *make-up* (or *blatancy*) and in narrative fiction *continuum, fulfilment* and *movement*.
[9] A preliminary account of how to combine narrative studies with hermeneutics can be found in Pettersson (2009a).

Basic for my view of literary world-making is that it builds on an imaginative use of literary representation or *mimesis*. As I see it, all creations of the human mind, whether societies, sciences or arts, are built on material processed by human cognition, largely as reflections on and representations of what has been perceived. It is in this sense that I view this study as a *poetics* (from the Greek *poieîn*, to make), a study of the making of literature as based on mimesis, just like Aristotle's *Poetics*. Needless to say, I do not compare this study with that work in any other sense than that I aspire to cover some key literary aspects of how literary works and their worlds are shaped. In other words, whereas Aristotle goes into some detail concerning the origins and elements of and differences between tragedy and the epic, I try to pinpoint some fundamental aspects of prose fiction, drama and poetry and in what sense such aspects are imaginative, as they draw on and comment on the world as authors know it. I do so not just by analysing particular literary works but also by viewing their features in a *comparative* perspective, in order to determine their theme and form in the light of how traditional, generic and original they are.

As for the notion *world* (in *literary world*), it stems from the Germanic *wer-ald*, meaning 'all' but in fact literally 'man-era'. Thus, even in defining their world, humans – at least in Germanic languages like English – have put themselves in the middle of it in a temporal sense. Thus, originally *world* is doubly specified: by man (according to the patriarchal metonymy for "human") as well as by the time he lives in. Today of course the spatial denotation is the central one. As we shall see in chapter 4, the human-centred view is apposite in the phrase *literary world*, since humankind is the hub of all its major themes. By *literary world*, I mean 'the imagined scenario of a literary work as shaped by thematic and formal means', whether it is a short poem, like a haiku, or an extensive novel or epic, like the *Mahābhārata*. In the same vein, Eric Hayot (2012: 44 – 45, 44 quote) has recently defined the *aesthetic world* as "the *diegetic totality* constituted by the sum of all aspects of a single work or work-part" and has also pointed out that *diegesis* denotes an interior (narrative) world, which implies that there is an extra-diegetic world outside it.[10] Similarly, for me, the imagined worlds in literary works are always related to those of popular imagination and ultimately to the actual world which it represents by imitative and creative uses of mimesis.

Finally, here is an outline of this study. In order to set the scene for the ensuing discussion, in chapter 1 I provide a survey on imagination, popular ima-

---

10 For a discussion of terms relating to literary worlds see Hayot (2012: 42 – 53).

gination and literary imagination.[11] This leads to the grounding of imagination in mimesis, its complex combination of the real and the fantastic in literature, and the interrelation of mimesis and genre (chapter 2). Then I go on to study literary unreliability, whose scope and relation to mimesis have not been duly recognized (chapter 3). Having given a broad overview of the workings of imagination and mimesis and how the latter can be undercut by unreliability in literature, I try to show how literary worlds are shaped by three different modes and three main themes (chapter 4). The formal and thematic variations given to the themes are considered next, from the blend of figure and narrative (chapter 5) to other imaginative inflections, such as indirection, hypothetical action and the hierarchical use of genres and text types (chapter 6). Thus, chapters 2 to 6 outline the shaping of the literary worlds, in part based on how literary representation (chapter 2) is inflected by unreliability (chapter 3) and in part how the modes and themes (chapter 4) are modulated by combinations of figure and narrative (chapter 5) and other imaginative inflections (chapter 6).

In chapter 7 I change focus to how literary worlds in turn shape people and their views of the world in ideological and other ways. This discussion of the interrelation between literary worlds and the real one is developed by spotlighting why literature matters, how we may benefit from it at the same time that we delight in it and how it holds us in its grasp by a sense of wonder of one kind or another (chapter 8). Then I present ten ways in which the analytical tools offered in this study can be of use when studying and teaching literature and apply them to the theme of star-crossed love and the genre of the fable (chapter 9). The conclusion summarizes the arguments made and shows by a few disparate case studies how literary worlds can be studied in greater detail by employing the frame offered in this study.

The nine chapters can be viewed as three groups, which could be termed *general*, *specific* and *world-oriented*. First, I present various views of imagination, including literary imagination and its representations, and how those representations are inflected by how reliable they are (chapters 1 to 3); then show how literary worlds are shaped by modes and themes and some key ways in which they are inflected (chapters 4 to 6); and finally consider how literary worlds inform the real one by examining how they change the world, how they matter in other respects and why they should be studied and taught (chapters 7 to 9). Thus, the argumentative line traces how literary imagination builds on mimesis in forming modes and themes; how various literary techniques are used; and

---

[11] Readers who only want to focus on the literary uses of imagination can gloss over 1.1 – 1.4 and start with 1.5 Literary Imagination.

then how literature, however fantastic, returns to the world by commenting on it, however obliquely. The circle it traces is not vicious, but so rewarding that listeners, audiences and readers have for centuries travelled along it in search of pleasure and benefit, usually well aware of the seductive and mercurial qualities inherent in imagination.

In my view, literary worlds are based on rather limited thematic and formal building blocks, which by various blends produce their infinite variations. I analyse these worlds on the basis of a wide array of literature and scholarship from different times and cultures in a way that as far as I know has not been done before. The point is not just to show that most building blocks have been there from time immemorial but also to study – even celebrate – the profuse variations they have had in literature ever since. The objective is to present and flesh out a comparative view that deepens the understanding of what literature is and does, and thus to benefit, perhaps even revitalize literary studies. That is, I try to express my passion for the web of literature in all of its forms and would be thrilled if some of that enthusiasm might live on and spark new ideas in the readers of these pages.

1 Imaginative World-Making

1.1 Imagine That ...

Thomas Suddendorf, an Australian psychologist working on primate cognition, has recently tried to define what constitutes what he calls *the gap* in cognitive abilities between humans and other animals. He notes that it is due to the development of a number of features – "language, mental time travel, mind reading, intelligence, culture, and morality" – but then goes on to single out "ONE OF THE MOST fundamental aspects of our human mind: we can imagine things other than what is available to the senses. We can picture past, future, and entirely fictional worlds and think about them" (Suddendorf 2013: 44; capitals original). The ability to imagine has intrigued humans for millennia and it is, as Suddendorf points out, the very basis for a number of cognitive abilities, including literary world-making.

Imagination is studied in a number of academic disciplines, such as philosophy, psychology, education, cognitive and evolutionary studies, anthropology, comparative literature and popular culture studies. One reason for the elusiveness of the very notion is the vague or strictly specified and often conflicting usage of *imagination* and its cognates, *image, imagery, imagine, imaginative* and *imaging* in and between various disciplines. Another is that even within a particular discipline, most notably in philosophy, the definitions and approaches vary considerably in the course of its history. A third reason is linguistic divergence: in Greek we have *phantasia* (*phantasma*) and *eikasia*; in Latin *phantasia* and the more prevalent *imaginatio*; in English *fancy, fantasy* and most centrally *imagination* and its cognates (that is, terms drawing on both the Greek and Latin ones); and in German alone there are at least three central terms, *Einbildungskraft* (e.g. in Kant), *Fantasie* (e.g. in Schleiermacher) and *Vorstellung* (e.g. in Brentano and Wittgenstein). In other words, there is linguistic as well as synchronic and diachronic disagreement as to the very notion and its meaning. Below I shall review some of these historical and disciplinary discrepancies.

But let me first note that perhaps the most notable division in the usage of *imagination* is between an individual versus a communal focus, largely conforming to Norbert Elias's (1998: 269–290) juxtaposition of two fundamentally different views of humankind, *homo clausus* (the closed man) and *homines aperti* (the open men).[1] The individual or singular usage, often viewed in the abstract as a

---

[1] For a brief evaluation of the notions see Mennell and Goudsblom (1998: 33–36). Cf. the corresponding views of (the study of) man: cognitive individualism (*homo clausus*) and cognitive

faculty, *(the) imagination*, is most prevalent in disciplines with a focus on the mind (or the way of thinking) of the individual, especially in philosophy, psychology and education, however much the notion might differ in other respects in these disciplines. The communal usage often occurs as the uncountable noun, *imagination*, with a specification that it shares a certain aspect of, for instance, philosophical, national, chronological or social character. Examples are *moral* imagination, *American* imagination, *medieval* imagination and *popular* imagination. This denotation of imagination as a *shared* frame of mind has been neglected by most academic disciplines, although in recent years it has been discussed in anthropology, literary studies and popular culture studies.

But it is symptomatic that even major dictionaries, like *Webster's Encyclopedic Unabridged Dictionary of the English Language* (1989: 711 s.v. imagination), despite offering eight meanings of the word, omits this shared, communal, plural usage. Similarly, the most encompassing survey of imagination, Eva T. H. Brann's (1991) eight-hundred-page tome *The World of the Imagination. Sum and Substance*, covers a wide range of terms and disciplines and their relation to broader and shared notions of imagination, such as theology and imaginary worlds, but includes no chapter on shared imagination as such. On the other hand, one of the leading evolutionary anthropologists, Michael Tomasello (2014) now views the development of human thinking in terms of *shared intentionality* that includes the cooperation of individual, joint and collective intentionality, so that joint intentionality (which makes us surpass our closest primate relatives in cognitive ability) forms a kind of bridge from individual to collective intentionality.

It is perhaps as telling that one of the best brief surveys of imagination, Kieran Egan's (1992: 9–43) dense thirty-five-page review "A Very Short History of Imagination" spends less than one full paragraph on shared or popular imagination. This neglect is all the more evident in six other surveys, all by philosophers: Mary Warnock (1976), Mark Johnson (1987: 141–166), Richard Kearney (1988; 1998 – the most thorough and encompassing studies, excepting Brann 1991), Alan R. White (1990: 1–79) and David L. Norton (1996: 5–19) – have next to nothing to say about it. Yet, as we shall see in 1.4, Johnson, Kearney and Norton present views of imagination that consider the individual in a socio-cultural setting, thus building a bridge between the two main senses of imagination. However, the shared or communal view has traditionally in many ways gone against received academic and other elitist views of imagination,

---

sociology (*homines aperti*), in contrast to cognitive universalism (i.e. the universal man), which, when combined, provide the scope of *cognitive sociology*; see Zerubavel (1997/1999: 20).

and is thus particularly important to establish more firmly on the academic agenda.

Before focusing on literary imagination, let us have a look at the various ways in which imagination has traditionally been viewed in academia (that is, in philosophy, psychology and, to some extent, education), so that we may better understand the divergence in usage in general and the communal and plural meaning that underlies the notion of popular imagination and by extension literary imagination. To my mind, a review of the study of imagination and popular imagination reveals that neither notion can be studied properly if the other is neglected. What is more, it shows that we must have a thorough historical and cross-disciplinary awareness of the discussions of imagination in order better to understand and study actual and potential uses of imagination, popular imagination and ultimately literary imagination.

1.2 Imagination in the Subjunctive Mood: From Mediation to Creation

The notion that imagination is a way of thinking of the possible, as suggested by most literature on the subject, is eloquently epitomized by Ralph D. Ellis's (1995a: 2–3, 79–82 *et passim*) view that imagination as a central element in consciousness is *subjunctive* in mood. Entertaining the idea of the possible may capture most of the varied and amorphous ways imagination has been discussed in philosophical, psychological and pedagogical discussion ever since Plato. In its most encompassing sense, as for instance in Hans Vaihinger's by now classic study *The Philosophy of 'As if'* (1925/2009: 81–97), *fiction* is much like imagination in that it is not only delimited against hypothesis, but as such includes a plethora of human activity, from ideas, methods and schemata to fantasies, conceptual aids and chimera. In fact, to put it bluntly, Plato and Aristotle left us with a rather checkered view of imagination (or, more precisely, *eikasia* and *phantasia* or *phantasma*) whose impact is still seen in contemporary discussions of it.[2] The two most salient facets are its *mediating* role between sense perception and the intellect and its *reproductive* role as a mirror of phenomena in the world (which, in turn, reflect original ideas).

---

[2] For a brief but informative survey of Greek usage see White (1990: 7–13).

Understandably, for Plato, and later for Augustine of Hippo and Descartes, among others, imagination entailed a derivative activity which obscured reason.³ But Aristotle (1986: 186–201; 427a–429a), in *De Anima*, was the first to employ it with positive connotations in a brief chapter conveniently placed between those on sense perception and the intellect.⁴ He gives it two rather separate meanings: first that of an interpretive act and then that of a faculty to produce something approaching (though not explicitly described as) mental imagery (the shift occurs in 428a; see Aristotle 1986: 198). Thus it is safest to agree with one of *De Anima*'s translators, Hugh Lawson-Tancred (1986: 84), that we are, even at this early date, dealing with a "family-concept". In fact, Aristotle (1986: 200, 245n99; 429a) makes the meaning of *phantasia* even more intricate by suggesting what apparently is a specious etymology of it as deriving from light, *phos*. Together with the suggestion in the latter passage on imagination (as well as a later one on thinking in images)⁵ and the etymology of the Latin term *imaginatio*, the emphasis on light may have led later commentators on imagination to what was to become one of its most prevalent denotations (and one that still figures prominently in dictionaries), the act or faculty of forming of mental images.

In the Middle Ages the Platonic-Aristotelian tradition was the central one: Augustine, Bonaventura and Thomas Aquinas still view imagination, with much Platonic suspicion, as a mediating faculty between body and mind (see Egan 1992: 16–17). Among the Italian Renaissance humanists this tradition is as strong, as is evident in *On the Imagination* by Gianfrancesco Pico della Mirandola (c. 1470–1533), the major work by the nephew of the famous Giovanni Pico della Mirandola:

> inasmuch as cognition originates from sense, as in many cases was contended by Aristotle [in *De Anima*], [...] and as has been accepted by a continuous succession of philosophers; and inasmuch as sense itself, when informed with the likeness of a sensible object, immediately has recourse to phantasy, and, so to speak, consigns to it what it has drawn in from without; and inasmuch as these images remain therein for a very long time, and are very like to perpetual sensations; therefore we must infer that the behavior of all animate beings arises from the nature of the phantasy – the imagination. (Pico della Mirandola 1930: 39)

---

3 However, note R. G. Collingwood's (1938/1970: 46–50) argument that such a reading is a distortion, even a misunderstanding, of Plato.
4 Apparently inspired by Aristotle, this is precisely how Gilbert Ryle (1949/1990: 232–263) and Anthony Kenny (1989/1992: 113–122) place their chapters on imagination.
5 See Aristotle (1986: 208–209, 248n121; 431a–431b).

Further on, Pico della Mirandola (1930: 43) warns that imagination is "irrational and devoid of correct judgement, unless aided by the guidance of a superior power" – a caution echoed throughout Western history, even as late as White (1990: 185). More particularly, it is the covert impetus of the rather sceptical view of employing creative imagination in teaching and learning by *careful tutoring*, from Thomas Hobbes's (1651/2008: 11) definition of it as *"decaying sense"* and John Locke's (1690/2004, 1693/1996) disregard of it to John Dewey's (1916/1980: 245) admonition not to foster "mind-wandering and wayward fancy".[6] Another important dimension of the quote from Pico della Mirandola is the stress he lays on imagination as founded on entertaining *images*, which, as I mentioned above, is noted by Aristotle in *De Anima*. In fact, Alan White's (1990: 3–45) survey of the history of imagination from Aristotle to Immanuel Kant (which omits all medieval and Renaissance philosophers) focuses on the centrality of the image in philosophical discussion on imagination.

However, it is an exaggeration to claim that imagination prior to the Enlightenment "was not considered either particularly interesting or energetic in our mental lives" owing to the conclusion that it "was almost entirely a *mimetic* faculty", as Egan (1992: 17) explicitly does, and Johnson (1987) and White (1990) seem to suggest by excluding all discussion between Aristotle and Hobbes. In histories of imagination it is seldom noted that by about 1600, if not before, two major thinkers, apparently unaware of each other's work, widen the concept in ways that point to future Romantic views.[7] In his *Essays on Magic*, completed in 1588, Giordano Bruno (1998: 138, 139) mentions that the "role of the imagination is to receive images derived from the senses and to preserve, combine and divide them" and that this activity can be determined by ulterior agents, such as "a spirit, rational soul or demon". But Bruno (1998: 138) also presents another way imagination occurs: "by the free creative choice of the person who imagines, for example, poets, painters, story writers and all who combine images in some organized way".

Some years later, in *The Advancement of Learning* Francis Bacon (1605/1996: 217, 218) discusses imagination as a mediating faculty, the "Janus of Imagination" facing both Reason and Action, yet for him too it is not "simply and only a messenger; but is invested with or at leastwise usurpeth no small authority in itself". In "matters of Faith and Religion" as well as "in all persuasions that

---

6 As we shall see, there are also some more positive views in philosophy, such as Mary Warnock's (1994: 189) plea to teachers to "educate a child's imagination", indeed to make this a central pedagogical aim.
7 See, however, Kearney (1988: 159–161) on Bruno and Egan (1992: 19) on Bacon.

are wrought by eloquence and other impression of like nature", Bacon asserts, "we raise our Imagination above our Reason", whereas he cannot find "any science that doth properly or fitly pertain to the Imagination". This emphasis on the creative use of imagination points in two directions: to the mythical Hebraic tradition of *yetser*, usually translated as *imagination*,[8] and to the Romantic concept of poetic creation (see 1.5).

The Enlightenment view of imagination is often equated with René Descartes's (1637/1968: 59) stance in his famous fourth "Discourse on Method", according to which "we should never let ourselves be persuaded except on the evidence of our reason. And it is to be observed that I say: of our reason, and not: of our imagination or our senses". However, not all enlightened philosophers were Platonists in this sense. In his *Ethics* Benedictus de Spinoza (1677/1989: 56; II Prop. XVII), although alluding to Descartes and his notion of perceiving images in his *Optics*, emphatically states that "the imaginations of the mind, regarded in themselves, contain no error" and goes on to assert that "if the mind while it imagined things not existing as present to itself knew at the same time that these things did not in truth exist, it would attribute this power of imagination to a virtue of its nature, not to a defect".

As we enter the Romantic period the most important philosopher on imagination is Immanuel Kant, who by emphasis on its cognitive centrality and by broadening of the concept to include three – or, as we shall see, perhaps four – functions simply put imagination at the centre of most philosophical discussion ever since. In *De Anima*, we have noted, Aristotle placed imagination between sense perception and the intellect and claimed that it was both interpretive and productive, a view that has been echoed in philosophy until the late twentieth century. Kant's (1787/1996: 164–68; A 115–21) change to Aristotle's view in his *Critique of Pure Reason* may seem slight, but has major repercussions: imagination is still both productive and reproductive, but it is placed between sense perception and apperception (not intellect).[9] The claim that imagination forms or colours what is perceived even before it is apperceived highlights the immediacy and importance of imagination.[10]

---

8 However, Kearney (1988: 41; see also 37–78) notes that *yetser* originally meant 'to form or create', as it does in *Genesis*.
9 Kant does not mention Aristotle here, but his account on imagination clearly draws on *De Anima* or views based on it.
10 In a neurophysiological account of how emotions work in mammals, including humans, Joseph LeDoux (1996/1998) claims that it is the amygdala in the limbic system of the brain that informs sense perception on its way to the cortex. In such an account – mainly based on

1.2 Imagination in the Subjunctive Mood: From Mediation to Creation

Kant maintains that "only by classing all perception with one consciousness (original apperception) can I say, for all perceptions, that I am conscious of them". This schematizing act must have "an objective basis" and it lies "in the principle of the unity of apperception" (Kant 1781–1787/1996: 169; A 122). Kant's dense rhetoric is not always easy to follow, but at least it is clear that he here adds a classificatory or schematizing element to imagination, which has become influential for later accounts. In short, in Kant we have at least three functions of imagination. Two are more or less traditional (Aristotelian), if more clearly separated and delineated: the *reproductive* and the *productive*. Especially, the latter is now forcefully presented as a unifying consciousness through time, which was to have a major influence on the romantic and phenomenological traditions discussed below.[11] The *schematizing* function, on the other hand, was to be the impetus of cognitive metaphor theory developed by George Lakoff and Mark Johnson (1980, 1999). In fact, in his own research Mark Johnson (1987: 165) explicitly mentions Kant as a precursor and in doing so detects a fourth function in Kant: the *creative*, which seems present in the perhaps most central productive function.[12] This is evident as Kant (1781–1787/1996: 169; A 123) stresses that imagination as "a power of an a priori synthesis" should be named "productive imagination".

Yet Kant's functions would not as such have had such an impact on literary studies, especially in English, had they not been developed by Samuel Taylor Coleridge in his influential *Biographia Literaria*. In fact, Coleridge (1817/2000: 308, 298n) formulates his position as a development of that of the "venerable Sage of Koenigsberg" (Kant) and, as a contrast to Descartes, replaces *cogito* with *sum*, "I AM".[13]

Coleridge (1817/2000: 313) famously prioritized the creative function, which he termed *primary* imagination and consigned the unifying productive and schematizing functions to the *secondary* imagination, and the reproductive function to *fancy*. In other words, the emphasis in the Romantic tradition is on ontology, on a subject who primarily *is* and in his or her imagination repeats, in

---

stress experiments with rats – the mediating role between perception and apperception is taken over by emotions.
11 Of course, in philosophy too Kant's view of imagination has had major influence, see e.g. Warnock (1994).
12 See Nuessel (1998) for a review of Johnson's own broader conceptualization in the light of similar suggestions in Vico's *New Science*.
13 The more active, or, more precisely, *creative* role of imagination in synthesizing sense perception Coleridge champions had already been suggested in the eighteenth century by David Hume (1758/1999: 124, 5.10), who was another central source of inspiration for Kant.

Coleridge's words, in its "finite mind" "the eternal act of creation in the infinite I AM" (Coleridge 1817/2000: 313). This has evident theological connotations, since, as Coleridge knew, Yahweh or Jehovah is often taken to mean 'I am'.[14] Thus, by its creative aspects and aspiration to the divine I AM, Coleridge's stress on the creativity of imagination is not very far from *yetser*, the Talmudic notion of creative imagination mentioned above, which however centres on ethics rather than ontology (see Kearney 1988: 49). In the words of Martin Buber (1952: 38; see also 35–42), one of the most perceptive commentators on imagination in the Hebraic tradition in the twentieth century, imagining the possible can lead to temptation, yet "imagination is not entirely evil, it is evil and good, for in the midst of it and from out of it decision can arouse the heart's willing direction toward [God]". Still, as we shall see in 1.5, it was Coleridge's development of Kant's view of imagination that was to be the most influential in literary studies.

The mid and late nineteenth century is not much discussed in the philosophical literature on imagination, with the possible exception of Kierkegaard and Nietzsche as forerunners of twentieth-century existentialist views (see Kearney 1988: 201–217). For them, imagination is much more circumscribed than the transcendental Romantic tradition would have. Despite Kearney's (1988: 196–197) view of existentialism as "the most influential philosophy of imagination between the mid nineteenth and mid twentieth centuries", in the latter part of the nineteenth-century the Romantic tradition was still to be reckoned with, especially since it merged with the hermeneutic tradition in Germany and the aesthetic tradition in Italy.

Much influenced by Friedrich Schleiermacher, Wilhelm Dilthey, one of the towering German philosophers of his day though regrettably overlooked today, developed the psychological-historical side of the philological tradition and thus gave new dimensions to the study of imagination. The neglect of Dilthey is only in part due to the fact that the philological-historical tradition in hermeneutics has been ousted by the more interpretivist Gadamerian-Ricœurian tradition in postwar philosophy, but also to the fact that latter-day critics, including Hans-Georg Gadamer (1975/1989), have disregarded, slighted or misunderstood Dilthey's contextualist project.[15] In fact, Dilthey's point in most writings on hermeneutic understanding, including creative imagination, must be understood as the combination of an inner, psychological view and an outer, contextualizing

---

[14] Coleridge's intention in making this connection is clear when he gives the fundamental theses of his view: "We begin with the I KNOW MYSELF, in order to end with the absolute I AM. We proceed from the SELF, in order to lose and find all self in GOD" (Coleridge 1817/2000: 300; cf. 298, 707n).

[15] See Makkreel (1975/1992: 414–419), Rodi (1985) and Pettersson (2009a).

historical one. In brief, he emphasizes that "The Poet's imagination is historically conditioned, not only in its material, but also in its technique" (Dilthey 1887/1985: 54). Thus, in early as well as late studies Dilthey (1883/1988: 129; 1910/1985: 235) fuses psychology and history, as when he asserts that "a true poetics [...] must take its concepts and principles from a combination of historical research and [a] general study of human nature" or when he considers the poet's imagination – in this case Goethe's – "in its relations to the material of lived reality, tradition, and what earlier poets have created".

In his *Aesthetic* Benedetto Croce (1902/1922: 155–474, 1 quote) discusses imagination in passing throughout his historical survey of aesthetics, but in fact it also forms an integral part of his aesthetics of intuitive knowledge, since such knowledge is "obtained through the *imagination*". For Croce (1902/1922: 11), intuitive knowledge must be expressed, that is, "intuitive knowledge is expressive knowledge". Later in the twentieth century, this "expression theory" was developed by R. G. Collingwood (1938/1970), and related, more interdisciplinary frameworks on symbolical meaning-making were devised by Ernst Cassirer (1944/1974), Kenneth Burke (1941/1961), Susanne K. Langer (1942/1956, 1953/1963, 1962, 1988), Victor W. Turner (1982), Norbert Elias (1991/1995) and Ellen Dissanayake (1988, 1992, 2000). However, this tradition had a comparatively small influence on the mainstream of philosophy – let alone literary studies and art history – in the twentieth century, perhaps because it was wrongly equated with a naive "ideal" theory (in Collingwood's case).[16] This is in part due to the fact that it is too encompassing for narrowly disciplinarian views and in part because it wars against some central tenets of analytical philosophy and (post)structuralist literary theory. In sociology and anthropology, on the other hand, it has exerted a considerable influence (see 1.3).

Yet in the late nineteenth century philosophy and psychology had a particularly fruitful period of *rapprochement*, also in the sense of developing new views on imagination. Some of this goes back to Dilthey's work, yet surpassing him in influence is the philosopher-psychologist Franz Brentano in Vienna. Randall Collins (1998: 693) epitomizes Brentano's importance by hailing him as "the most influential lecturer at the end of the century", since he tutored many subsequently famous students, among them, Sigmund Freud and Edmund Husserl. It is Brentano's (1973/1995: 88) notion of consciousness as informed by *intentional inexistence* (i.e. "reference to a content, direction toward an object") that is at the basis of Husserl's phenomenology and, via Husserl, of Sartre's psy-

---

16 Ridley (1997) has refuted this view of Collingwood.

chology of imagination.[17] Before considering such twentieth-century philosophers who put much faith in imagination, we should note that for Freud (1929/1961: 28–30; 29, 30 quotes), "the life of the imagination", as in artistic appreciation (as well as creation), is a sublimation that induces a "mild narcosis" in order to bring about "a transient withdrawal from the pressure of vital needs".

Three philosophers as different as Jean-Paul Sartre, Gilbert Ryle and Ludwig Wittgenstein are sometimes grouped together as representing the most important advances on imagination in the twentieth century. For instance, as noted above, Alan White (1990: 47–74) views the "imagining images" tradition the central one in philosophy before the twentieth century and claims that Sartre, Ryle and Wittgenstein share the project of discarding this tradition in a section somewhat drastically termed "The Death of the Image".[18] However, this should be taken with a pinch of salt, since, for instance, when in *Philosophical Investigations* Wittgenstein (1953/1991: 101, § 301) famously claims that "An image is not a picture [Eine Vorstellung ist kein Bild]", he does not leave it at that but goes on to state "but a picture can correspond to it". Still, neither Wittgenstein nor Ryle (1949/1995: 232–263) has much new to offer except insightful analyses of how parochial and sight-centred previous discussions of imagination have been.

But in *The Psychology of Imagination* Sartre (1940/1978), firmly grounded in Husserl's phenomenology, takes the notion of imagination as thinking of the possible to one of its logical endpoints. Imagining an image, he asserts, is "a negation of the world from a particular point of view", even if "'being-in-the-world' [...] is the necessary condition of the imagination" (Sartre 1940/1978: 215). By arguing that this negation helps man comprehend reality, Sartre (1940/1978: 216) renders imagination perhaps the most grandiose role in the entire history of philosophy, very much in the line of the German Idealist Johann Gottlieb Fichte[19]: "imagination is not a contingent and superadded power of consciousness, it is the whole of consciousness as it realizes its freedom". Still, what Kearney (1988: 185) has said about the Romantic imagination is as true of Sartre's view: neither can "possibly deliver on its promises" and, furthermore, the history of the nineteenth and twentieth centuries made it patently clear that neither can "transform *reality*" as such.[20]

---

17 For a survey of this tradition and its aftermath see Kearney (1998).
18 See, however, Warnock's (1976: 131–195) chapter mainly dealing with the three philosophers under the heading "The Nature of the Mental Image".
19 See e.g. Fichte (1797–1800/1994: 28, 95).
20 In 1.4, 1.5 and 7, however, I shall discuss some possible uses of imagination – one of them implicit in Sartre – that can effect such changes. In his later work Kearney (1998: 13) stresses the continuity between German Idealism and phenomenology.

When considering recent views of imagination in sciences such as linguistics, cognitive science, psychology and neurology, we notice the prominence of the study of image, imagery and imaging (rather than imagination, or the imaginary as in Sartre and, later, Lacan and Kristeva). This suggests that if the philosophical warnings of equating visualization with imagination (a central point in White 1990) has been heeded at all, it has led to studies of human image-making, which is closer to visualization than imagination in any of its traditional senses.[21] However, some of the most interesting work conducted in cognitive science and cognitive literary studies, notably by Ralph D. Ellis (1995a, 1995b), Raymond W. Gibbs, Jr. (1994, 2008a) and Alan Richardson (2010: 38–57), is directed to bridging the work on imaging and imagery on the one hand and imagination and understanding (even phenomenology in Ellis 1995a) on the other.

Finally, there is the postmodern view of imagination. In an attempt to summarize the implications of a host of French thinkers of structuralist or poststructuralist inclination (Lacan, Althusser, Barthes, Foucault, Derrida), Kearney (1988: 252) suggests that they all reflect the "crisis of the imaginary", in which the real is supplanted by imaginations of linguistic and technological reproductions. They are sceptical of any original meaning (which is considered a humanist illusion), and so meaning is "deconstructed into an endless play of linguistic signs, each one of which relates to the other in a parodic circle" (Kearney 1988: 252). Hence, explicitly or implicitly, they discard the Romantic concept of creative imagination, even if, at least in Kearney's (1988: 253) view, without the notion of origination (whether exterior or interior to man), "the concept of imagination itself collapses".

Although exceedingly brief, this survey suggests that imagination has been a central concept many philosophically minded thinkers have felt they cannot neglect. In fact, the most recent development seems to be to view human cognition in a broader evolutionary light, as Suddendorf (2013) does. From a notion characterized by entertaining thoughts of the possible in a great number of ways, it has finally been restated in evolutionary terms as a significant feature of human cognition. As a notion extended into many other fields than philosophy, imagination throws light on the entire Western frame of mind, especially in the

---

21 See e.g. Lakoff and Johnson (1980) and (1999), Donald (1991), Esrock (1994), Posner and Raichle (1994/1997), Turner (1996), Posner and Levitin (1997/1999), Gibbs (2008a) and their references. See also recent volumes of *Metaphor and Symbol* (*Metaphor and Symbolic Activity* before 1997). Emphasis on the image is as central in Taylor and Saarinen's (1994) media-focused imagology but it is only one aspect of a kind of imagology based on ideological usages (see Johnson 2005). For a summary of different (if not altogether opposite), largely Hallidayan, language-based approaches to consciousness see Matthiessen (1998).

way it has, even prior to the Enlightenment, so clearly focused on the individual. It is about time, it seems, that communal and (multi)cultural ways of thinking should more prominently be included in discussions of imagination.

1.3 Imagination as a Shared Frame of Mind

Now let us consider the origins of shared or popular imagination, which as an approach, as I have noted, is not particularly dominant either in a diachronic or synchronic perspective. However, in some sense sharing a frame of mind is as old as human communication. This is true, even if Michael Corballis (1999: 139) were right in his reformulation of the old hypothesis that the origins of language are gestural, since even iconic gesturing presupposes one of the prerequisites of language, "the ability to adopt the mental perspective of another individual".[22] What is more, as so many researchers in primatology, psychology and sociology have found, intersubjective attunement in infancy is fundamental to development in humans (see Tomasello 2014; Bråten 1998a; Elias 1998: 60–63; Hutcheon 1999). This is, in many ways, how we become human.

In cultural terms it is of utmost importance, especially in an oral culture, that communication, its crucial features and insights can be coded in some way. This is where myths – along with metaphors and proverbs – come in, since myths are generally considered a fundamental way of sharing a frame of mind. In the literature on myth this connection is often made, but in the literature on imagination I reviewed above, only Egan (1992: 10–12) discusses the importance of myth.[23] Central mythical features, he argues, are captivating images and an emotionally engaging quality, which together ensure that the myth will be passed on. Egan (1992: 11) goes on to claim that "it was the need to memorize things that early stimulated and developed the capacity for imagination. Patterning of sound, vivid images, and story-structuring were, we might sensibly observe, the most important early social inventions". It is precisely social convention that is the basis of classic views of myth in Émile Durkheim and Lucien Lévy-Bruhl, even though the latter erred in making a strict division between primitive and developed thought.[24] In short, according to Richard Chase's (1960/1961: 134) summary of the anthropological view of his day, "primitive man, like civilized man, lives in two worlds, the matter-of-fact workaday world and the

---

[22] For an opposite, speech-centred view of the origins of language see Lieberman (1998), and for an evaluation of both hypotheses see Donald (1991).
[23] See also Goldman (1998: 18–22).
[24] See e.g. Cassirer (1944/1974: 79–83).

magico-religious world and [...] he employs various psychic and social devices for keeping them separate". In his definition of myth Chase (1960/1961: 129) also makes explicit the connection between myth (meaning 'story') and imagination: *"myth is literature and must be considered as an aesthetic creation of the human imagination"*.

I have spent a paragraph delineating myth, since I think myth or, perhaps rather, "mythical imagination" based on belief, as Ernst Cassirer (1944/1974: 75) terms it, merges with what we today term popular imagination. To be sure, in contemporary usage popular imagination is less reliant on belief, more informed by modern – or postmodern, if you like – self-consciousness. But we should note the interaction between myth and imagination: (popular) imagination creates myth, which, in turn, may spawn other creations by (popular) imagination, and so on. It is this realization of myth's – and ritual's – reciprocity with the human imagination that Cassirer, Langer, Elias, Turner and Dissanayake analysed in the twentieth century, and their considerable significance for a host of sciences has not yet been fully understood or explored.

However, this focus on (the role of imagination in) symbolic representation has now been taken up by, for instance, social and political theoreticians on the one hand and neurologists and evolutionary anthropologists on the other. It is symptomatic that neither tradition seems aware of the symbol studies conducted in the humanities. This is evident in Robinson and Rundell's (1994) anthology on imagination in social theory, which includes major names, such as Cornelius Castoriadis,[25] Martin Jay, Niklas Luhmann and Paul Ricœur, as well as in Terrence Deacon's (1997/1998) magisterial treatise on how the co-evolution of language and the human brain has been spurred by the use of symbolic reference: excepting philosophy, no references are made across disciplines and, more specifically, the Cassirer-Langer tradition is almost entirely disregarded.

I think it is important to be reminded of the fact that there is still a spectrum between unquestioned belief and utter scepticism in our understanding of various phenomena relating to shared or popular imagination. What happened in the latter part of the twentieth century, it seems, is that the growth of popular culture and postmodernism in the arts eroded the strict division between what is real and what is imaginary or virtual. Interestingly, as Elias (1983/1987: 49 quote, 56–65) has shown, this was the crucial distinction earlier-stage societies made in order to go beyond their "magical-mythical forms of thinking". Related

---

[25] Much of the contemporary discussion on imagination in social theory seems to draw on Castoriadis's (1975/1987) work, in which the definitions of the symbolic and the imaginary are informed by structuralism and the emphasis on creative imagination draws on Kant and Fichte (see Castoriadis 1975/1987: 127–128, 146n53).

erosion has, of course, occurred due to relativist stances, from Einstein, Werner Heisenberg and Thomas S. Kuhn primarily in the natural sciences to poststructuralism primarily in the human sciences. This does not, for the most part, signal a regression into magical-mythical world views, but playful border crossings in the arts and sometimes an equally playful but often very serious probing into the limits and rhetoric of science and its discourses.

But how did we reach this stage in Western culture where, at times, (supposedly) high and low culture, science and fiction merge?[26] At the start of this chapter I mentioned that Kieran Egan is the only historian of imagination who touches on the shared meaning. With reference to Jacques Le Goff's *L'imagination médiévale* from 1986, Egan (1992: 17) speaks of "the profane imagination in popular culture" in contrast to the official church concept in the Middle Ages: "this intellectual underworld", as he terms it, celebrated and enjoyed "witchcraft, folklore, occultism, and other realms where the body, dreams and magic enjoyed an energetic currency denied them by the church".[27] The fact that the church still kept policing the borders of imagination in 1600 is evident in Giordano Bruno's death at the hands of the Inquisition. However, in post-Renaissance Europe, Peter Stallybrass and Allon White (1986: 193) claim, drawing on Bakhtin, Freud and Kristeva, "the formation of the cultural Imaginary of the middle class [...] involved an internal distancing from the popular which was complex and often contradictory to its effects".

Still, although it is true that much *folk*, later *popular*, today largely *mass* culture has provided alternatives to high or mainstream culture, far from all such culture is dissident, revolutionary or esoteric. One way of schematizing the relation between the terms is to view popular as a category joining folk and mass.[28] Even if mass art has a modern ring to it, Noël Carroll (1998: 172) reminds us that it "has been with us, to a certain extent, since the invention of the printing press". Conversely, we should remember that although mass art statistically is "the most dominant art of our times" (Carroll 1998: 173) – which also proves it is far from dissident –, folk art in various forms (handicrafts, folk music, folk-

---

[26] Of course, such blends do not imply that high and low culture or genres have merged once and for all. Authors and artists, publishing houses, academic disciplines and other institutions, readers, audiences and critics still continue to pigeonhole art forms, genres and artefacts. For an informed discussion of the distinction between high and popular art as a social one see David Novitz (1992: 20–41) and for a critical view of the dichotomy in literature see Swirski (2005).
[27] Elsewhere Le Goff (1977/1980: 157; 1981/1986: 14) has shown how in the early Middle Ages "folkloric culture was *refused* by ecclesiastical culture" in three ways (by destruction, obliteration and adulteration), but that popular culture, nevertheless, was "undoubtedly important" for the birth of the medieval notion of Purgatory.
[28] For a different view see Bell (1982: 443–444).

lore) may have been curtailed by mass art and created a variety of *world* and *tourist* hybrids with it, but is nonetheless still in existence.

As for the study of shared or popular imagination, one might argue that it is what studies in folklore focus on (see e.g. Klinkmann 2002). In anthropology, Clifford Geertz (1983/1993: 53) perhaps most famously has traced the role of Bali "in the history of our [Western] imagination". In fact, as far as I understand, Geertz (1983/1993: 36–54) attempts something much grander by his essay entitled "Found in Translation: On the Social History of Moral Imagination", by the collection in which it is included, and indeed by all of his oeuvre: to devise the best possible hermeneutic circle and contextual frame for anthropological study.[29]

Taking our cue from Geertz (and phenomenology), we could say that since popular imagination must be *about* something, it can be studied in two ways: from a particular topic (say, stand-up comedy) to a population aware of it (say, Americans), or the other way around, from a particular population to their awareness of a topic. This indicates that popular imagination could be studied theoretically as well as empirically, and perhaps most felicitously by combining the two approaches. Popular imagination could thus make use of the broad circles of hermeneutics Dilthey, drawing on Schleiermacher and his exemplary praxis, suggested for textual interpretation (see Dilthey 1900/1972: 243). Even closer to Geertz's aim is Dilthey's late emphasis on *lived experience* (*Erlebnis*) as the basis of the study of man (see Dilthey 1907–08/1985: 223), which in fact has been taken up by another central figure in anthropology, Victor Turner, in his later works (1982: 12–19, 75, 86; 1986). It is interesting to note that Turner (1986: 429) defines the liminal phase in ritual – one of his central anthropological interests – as "being dominantly in the subjunctive mood of culture, the mood of maybe, might be, as if, hypothesis, fantasy, conjecture, desire", thus implying that popular imagination, like imagination, can make use of the metaphor of the subjunctive mood.

But perhaps the most major name Geertz and Turner, like all the above-mentioned historians of imagination, largely neglect is that of Giambattista Vico.[30] There are many reasons for this neglect: one is simply that Vico is often relegated to discussions in historiography or the philosophy of history; another is that his key term is not imagination but primarily *fantasia*. Frank Nuessel (1998: 282) has

---

29 For a critical view of using imagination as a method in anthropology see Sandbacka (1987: 24–46).
30 However, there is a brief reference to Vico in Geertz (1973/1993: 250).

usefully summarized Vico's view on imagination, from perception to verbalization (with reference to Verene 1981):

> the process of transforming the perceived world into the received or conceptual world (percept → concept) involves the Vichian "imagination" which consists of the *fantasia* (the imagination proper), the *ingegno* (ingenuity or invention), and the *memoria* (or memory). [—] The interaction of these three components, *fantasia*, *ingegno*, and *memoria*, converge to create conceptualization, and, ultimately, verbalization of our experienced reality.[31]

Even though Vico's view is simply that, in the words of Marcel Danesi and Frank Nuessel (1994a: iv), "the imagination is the essence of mind", it is not as romantically grandiose as those of German Idealism and Sartre's phenomenology. Vico spent most of his intellectual life attempting to provide a firm basis for this major notion (with some debt to Bacon 1605/1996, among others),[32] and was able to do it so convincingly in his *New Science* (Vico 1744/1984) that it remains seminal and topical for much of the recent research on cognition and culture and their interrelation. Vico is important in terms of the present survey, not only by his effort to go beyond the mediating function of imagination and to subcategorize the concept by including creativity and memory as its components – something that cognitive linguists and scientists, often ignorant of Vico, are attempting today –,[33] but in that he first grasped that it is by imaginative insight that we understand our fellow men (see 4.2).[34]

If such Vichian ideas had more often been included in the discussion of imagination in the last two and a half centuries, the notion would most likely be much broader and naturally include the shared, communal aspect.[35] In Isaiah Berlin's (1979/1998: 353) words, drawing on Vico's insight, in order to compre-

---

31 Cf. Vico (1744/1984: 313–314; § 819).
32 See Vico (1708–09/1990: 3–4 and 1744/1984). For a brief assessment of Vico's view of Bacon see Fisch (1984: xli–xlii).
33 See Nuessel (1995, 1998) on the common ground in Vico and Lakoff's and Johnson's works.
34 See for instance Vico (1744/1984: 21–22; § 34 *et passim*) and Berlin (1979/1998: 352–354).
35 For Western thinkers who have affinities with Vico see Tagliacozzo and Verene (1976), Danesi and Nuessel (1994b) and Danesi (1995). We should nevertheless heed Thomas A. Sebeok's (1994: 115) warning not to make Vico a precursor for all sorts of intellectual movements. A case in point may be Dilthey, who, according to Tuttle (1976: 247), despite some similarities and a few brief references to Vico, does not seem to draw on him. Yet a closer look at Dilthey's (1996) hermeneutic and historical writings suggests that here too Vico's influence should not be overlooked. This is evident in his prize-winning Schleiermacher essay, in which Vico's *New Science* is repeatedly discussed and even termed "one of the greatest triumphs of human thought" (Dilthey 1860/1996: 139).

hend "ways of life [...] remote from us and unlike our own" (in space as well as time, I presume), one must understand that all humans have "minds and purposes and inner lives" comparable to ours. Thus, by virtue of possessing "imaginative power of a high degree, such as artists and, in particular, novelists require", we can approximate an understanding of them (Berlin 1979/1998: 353). We should, for instance, remember that one dimension in Karl Popper's (1945/1983: 44; emphasis added) project of defending rationalism includes this Vichian dimension: "reason, *supported by imagination*", he writes, "enables us to understand that men who are far away, whom we shall never see, are like ourselves".

Similar conclusions are central in some recent evolutionary anthropology. As Michael Tomasello (1999a: 6) puts it, what is "crucial in human cultural learning" is that individuals are able to "imagine themselves 'in the mental shoes' of some other person, so that they can learn not just *from* the other but *through* the other". Intriguingly, brain scans have showed that the area made use of when a subject is trying to gain insight into another person's mind is one of the most evolved parts of the brain, the middle of the prefrontal cortex (see Carter 1998: 235). This implies that imagining being in someone else's shoes is one of the crucial differences between humans and other primates (cf. Suddendorf 2013).

Developmental psychologists tell us that this ability, at least part of which can be termed empathy, develops in infants about the age of eighteen months and that the terrible twos can be understood as the child's way of probing this discovery of individual differences in volition (see Gopnik et al. 1999: 35–39). Furthermore, Paul L. Harris (1998, 2000) argues that the role of imagination in children's cognitive development is more central and positive than most of the literature on the subject has claimed. In contrast to Freud and Piaget, he convincingly outlines a *continuity thesis:* children's imagination does not evolve from the primitive and disorganized to the organized, but imaginative involvement is already in place from early childhood (see 3.2 and 4.1).[36] It is the fusion of language and imagination that enables a broad array of cognitive operations and interactions, such as "to exchange and accumulate thoughts about a host of situations, none actually witnessed but all imaginable: the distant past and future, as well as the magical and the impossible" (Harris 2000: 195).

To return to Vico, what is also worth noting is his realization that imagination developed in peoples as well as individuals:

> poetic [i.e. creative] wisdom, the first wisdom of the gentile world, must have begun with a metaphysics not rational and abstract like that of learned men now, but felt and imagined

---

36 Cf. Collingwood's view (2005/2007: 75), originally written in 1930: "Art is the kingdom of the child: and anyone [...] who wants to enter that kingdom must enter it as a child".

as that of these first men must have been, who, without power of ratiocination, were all robust sense and vigorous imagination. (Vico 1744/1984: 116; § 375)

In literary studies too the study of imagination has been extended from the creative genius of the Romantic-hermeneutic tradition to the sense of life literary works may impart to their readers, thus pointing to a study of their role in popular imagination. Martha C. Nussbaum (1995: 2), for instance, finds that "literature and literary imagination are subversive" by their very presentations of other points of view. Hence, for her, the novel – or, more precisely, a particular kind of novel (see Nussbaum 1995: 124n2) – is "a morally controversial form, expressing in its very shape and style, in its modes of interaction with its readers, a normative sense of life. [– – –] It tells its readers to notice this and not this, to be active in these and not those ways. It leads them to certain postures of the mind and heart and not others" (Nussbaum 1995: 2).

This move from considering what literature *is* to what it *does*, how it lives on in the imagination of its readers, is symptomatic of Nussbaum's work, from her study of imagination in Aristotle (summarized in Nussbaum 1990: 77–79) to her extension of her insights on imagination to pedagogical training and child development (Nussbaum 1997: 10–11 *et passim*, 2001: 236–237, 426–427). A similar, if more marked, move in literary studies from narrative theory to ethical interpretation is to be found in Wayne C. Booth's (1961/1983, 1988) career. In fact, Nussbaum and Booth were central in the so-called *ethical turn* in literary and cultural studies (see Davis and Womack 2001).

Perhaps even more topical is the later Wolfgang Iser's (1989: 276) move from reader response to *literary anthropology*, which seems prompted by Iser's insight that the imaginary "can only be grasped by way of its function and so in relation to contexts". An even more comprehensive view of art and imagination (but with careful demarcations), much like those presented in cultural psychology and anthropology, is afforded by David Novitz (1987, 1992: 59 quote), for whom "the fanciful imagination and its exercise are the province not just of the artist but of all people in their everyday lives". These are only some instances in literary studies of what might be termed a *contextualist turn*, which, together with the acceptance of popular culture studies, suggests that literature and a host of other disciplines – focusing on art, music and film – are now more open to studies of imagination and popular imagination, even though the notions as such may not always be applied.[37]

---

[37] See for instance Scruton (1974/1982: 84–133; 1983: 127–136) on art, music, literature and film; Currie (1995: 141–197) on literature and film; Dewey (1934/1987: 271–279) on

Similar turns, it seems, have taken or are taking place in other disciplines in the human sciences as well, but neither space nor competence permits me to dwell on them. However, let me add a few notes in order to suggest how widely spread the notion of a shared imagination is. In historiography, for instance, Hayden White's (1973) central use of the notion *historical imagination*, often synonymous with historical consciousness, has spawned a wealth of approaches, often without White's anchoring in Vico and R. G. Collingwood (1946/1993), whose influence is only evident in a later work (see White 1978/1987).[38] In geography "postmodern" practitioners, such as Derek Gregory (1994) and Edward W. Soja (1996), study "imaginary" spaces, to some extent drawing on poststructuralist or postcolonialist frameworks.[39] Even the natural sciences, it seems, must take imagination and imagery into account, not just as one of the central means by which scientific creativity works,[40] but, for instance, as Harriet Ritvo (1997: 175–187) has shown, zoological history must be able to account for nineteenth-century research on imaginary animals and, as Stephen Hawking (1988/1989: 151–152 *et passim*; 1993/1994: 74–76) has suggested, future physics must be able to explain what he terms *imaginary time*.

But what, if any, might be the difference between studies in popular culture and studies of popular imagination? Perhaps a simple – and, to some extent, simplifying – answer would be that popular culture studies focuses largely on all kinds of artefact (including those electronically mediated or performed), their creation, mediation and reception. In Charles F. Altman's (1986: 8) view, for instance, "Popular culture may be said to exist when a given text achieves wide dissemination through the efforts of a publishing institution (taken in a broad sense) with a vested interest in survival". One of the most notable names in popular culture studies, John Fiske (1989/1990: 23), argues that popular culture in industrial societies is "contradictory to its core" and thus stresses on the one hand that it is commodified, "industrialized", but on the other that in order to be included in popular culture "a commodity must also bear the interests of the people". In Michael J. Bell's (1982: 443) words, it is, at its simplest at least, "the culture of mass appeal" and can be studied along the lines of Roman

---

the role of imagination in creating and experiencing works of art; Burke (1950: 78–90) on imagination and images in rhetoric; and Wollheim (1984: 62–96) on iconic imagination.
38 Of course, even White's (1973) early use of *historical imagination* as a term may draw on Collingwood's (1946/1993: 231–249) chapter by that title, even though he first discusses it in White (1978/1987: 59–60). On Vico's influence on White see Pettersson (1999a: 4–6, 11).
39 For a critique of postcolonial frameworks with poststructuralist underpinnings in translation theory see Pettersson (1999b).
40 See e.g. Miller (1984/1986, 1996).

Jakobson's model of communication.⁴¹ However, at times popular culture studies is defined more broadly as aiming at "an interpretation of culture" (Rosenberg 1986: 154), and then of course it would more firmly include the non-artefactual dimension in popular imagination studies, by analysing any phenomena that (specified or unspecified) groups of people are aware of.

Thus, popular imagination can be studied at least in two ways: by primarily focusing on culture and its artefacts or on shared (awareness of) concepts and phenomena in particular populations. In many cases either pursuit would be illuminated by the other;⁴² in all cases popular imagination studies should make discriminating use of any array of disciplines and their methodologies that might throw light on their objects of study. In fact, the motivation underlying my forays into a host of disciplines in this chapter is a firm conviction that much disciplinary myopia can be dispelled by going beyond one's primary field.

1.4 Bridging the Study of Imagination and Popular Imagination

I have not been able to refrain from pointing to some useful material for building such bridges within and between the studies of imagination and popular imagination in my discussion of both imagination and popular imagination. Whatever we may think of the methodological differences between the "two cultures" (Snow 1959/1964) – largely what Dilthey (1883/1988), drawing on Johann Gustav Droysen, calls *Geisteswissenschaften* and *Naturwissenschaften* –, we cannot afford to neglect either the inner or the outer view of imagination. To put it another way, whatever we say about imagination should not stand in blatant contradiction to corroborated findings in, say, neurology or sociology – or, if it does, then at least one of the disciplines should seriously reconsider its premises or conclusions.

I have implied above that this is what Ralph D. Ellis (1995a) tries to effect by neurological study of image-making, linguistic study of imagery and phenomenological study of the mind. A related approach is Daniel C. Dennett's (1991/1993: 66–98 *et passim*) combination of inside and outside perspectives on consciousness by what he terms *heterophenomenology*. Certainly, the central relation in human imagination between perception, memory and imagination should be studied from different points of view so that, for instance, Husserl's (1999: 198–

---

41 For a critique of such literary applications of Jakobson's model see Pettersson (1999c: 48–49 and 2009b: 145–147).
42 See for instance Paul Fussell's (1975, 1989) multifaceted studies of the world wars.

199) distinction between *mere phantasy* and *recollection* (according to which only the latter has a relation to the then and the now)[43] could be scrutinized from various disciplinary angles. Perhaps Raymond Gibbs (1994: 5) best summarizes the central insight of the figurative view in cognitive studies in the humanities (see 5.1): "Recent advances in cognitive linguistics, philosophy, anthropology, and psychology show that not only is much of our language metaphorically structured, but so is much of our cognition. People conceptualize their experiences in figurative terms via metaphor, metonomy, irony, oxymoron, and so on, and these principles underlie the way we think, reason, and imagine". Here we can see why Vico is of such seminal importance to much of the fundamental rethinking that is taking place in the human and social sciences today. How we view man in general and human cognition in particular, including imagination and emotions, should, as he implied, have consequences for all human studies. Now at last we must concede that Protagoras was right in asserting that *"Man is the measure of all things"* (quoted in Abel 1976/1997: xxi), not in a narrow, potentially narcissistic humanist sense, but in the sense that this is how human meaning-making has always been effected: as an embodied, contextualized understanding of the surrounding world.[44] It is related rethinking that has led prominent figures in anthropology (Geertz), sociology (Elias), psychology (Koch 1999), neurology (Damasio 1999/2000) and even translation studies (Chesterman 1998) to eschew theory-ridden top-down approaches and insist on bottom-up studies and/or on sociohistorically situated studies.

Also, Vico's (1744/1984: 3; § 2) initial emphasis on human nature as having a "principal property: that of being social" shows that he is a precursor of Elias's *homines aperti* view of the necessary interdependence of individuals, towards which the human sciences as a whole finally seem to be moving.[45] However,

---

43 Note, however, that the distinction is vaguer elsewhere; see Husserl (1999: 193, 208–209).
44 There is a rapidly growing literature on various aspects of this issue: e.g. in psychology and the social sciences Tooby and Cosmides (1992); in philosophy Hertzberg (1991) and Haugeland (1995); in cognitive linguistics and philosophy Johnson (1987) and Lakoff and Johnson (1999); in art history and literary studies Carroll (1995), Storey (1996), Easterlin (1999, 2012), Schaeffer (1999/2010), Dissanayake (2000), Miall (2006), Turner (2006), Swirski (2007), Boyd (2009), Dutton (2009), Burke (2011), Davies (2012) and Collins (2013). Similarly, the tradition in philosophy I have elsewhere termed *ontologico-experiential* focuses on experiential and embodied meaning-making and includes scholars such as Michael Polanyi and Eugene T. Gendlin (see Pettersson 1999a: 9–10, 12).
45 Years ago, Brown (1977/1989: 24–48) pointed the way through his interactional and broadly interdisciplinary attempt to fuse the humanities and the social sciences by maintaining that both are dependent on metaphorical thinking and should thus make use of symbolic realism in the framework of a cognitive aesthetics.

this does not necessarily entail that the phenomenologico-hermeneutical tradition (as, for instance, portrayed in Kearney 1998) must be ousted, since it, like the Vichian heritage, relies centrally on what Brentano (1973/1995) calls *Vorstellungen* (ideas, presentations). Such ideas may be firmly lodged in *homo clausus* in this tradition, but they can, as for instance Gaston Bachelard's (1987/1989) *material* imagining implies (see Kearney 1998: 103–106), be prompted by archetypal symbols and go beyond the self. Whatever one thinks of such approaches to symbolical representation – or domain-specific or connectionist models of cognition, for that matter –, it should be evident by now, on the basis of both archeological and cognitive evidence, that (1) studies of imagination cannot bypass symbolic representation and (2) the brain evinces *cognitive fluidity* (Mithen 1996) and other *dynamical, interactive* properties (Horgan and Tienson 1996) to such a degree that the way mental representation works cannot be adequately described by structural or computational analogies. What is needed, then, are both hedgehogs and foxes conducting more micro- and macrostudies of cognition and culture, respectively, and, in particular, of their emergent nature and interrelation.[46]

To view, in a narrower perspective, ways in which imagination and popular imagination might be jointly studied, let us consider Kearney's (1988: 359–397) call for developing imagination in various directions after the postmodern *cul-de-sac*. Kearney (1988: 361–371, 370–371 quote) pleads for both an *ethical* imagination and a *poetical* imagination, which should include a *social* project that "would nourish the conviction that things *can be changed*. The first and most effective step in this direction is to begin to *imagine* that the world as it is could be otherwise". This is where, as Mary Warnock (1972/1978: xvii) points out, Sartre's study on the imagination was to take him, and it comes close to David Norton's (1996: 2) thesis, according to which "our access to [the] perspectival worlds [of other people] is afforded by imagination". Still, even more topical in the context of popular imagination, Kearney's social project is related to Mark Johnson's (1987: 190) fundamental insight when outlining a theory of meaning on the basis of an embodied understanding of cognition:

> In short, a theory of meaning is a theory of how we understand things (of whatever sort). […] [T]his is not merely a matter of how some *individual* might happen to understand some-

---

[46] See for instance Tooby and Cosmides (1992), D'Andrade (1995), Cole (1996), Cornoldi et al. (1996), Olson and Torrance (1996), Shore (1996), Zerubavel (1997/1999), Fussell and Kreuz (1998), Katz et al. (1998), Tomasello (1999a, 2008/2010), Geertz (2000) and Suddendorf (2013). The notion that writers and thinkers – and people in general – can be divided into hedgehogs (knowing one thing) and foxes (knowing many things) was popularised by Isaiah Berlin (1953/1998), who drawing on Archilochus discussed Tolstoy's view of history on the basis of this dichotomy.

thing but rather how an *individual as embedded in a (linguistic) community, a culture, and a historical context* understands. In other words, we are concerned here with *public, shared meaning.*

Thus, here we have three eminent philosophers (Kearney, Norton and Johnson), all of who consider the history of imagination in some detail and all of who either call for or simply view imagination as a concept of shared meaning, the very basis of the rather neglected project of popular imagination studies. In other words, in this sense, imagination relies on popular imagination and, in the final analysis, on a culture (or cultures).

This brings us to another view touched on above: individuals and their imaginations become attuned to their culture by acting intersubjectively in it. This is the often implicit premise of all pleas for educating children's imagination, whether the admonition is to let it grow unhindered, as in Schleiermacher's (1799/1988: 141–161) notion of religious intuition, or, to tutor it carefully, as is more often the case in pedagogical instruction from Pico della Mirandola to contemporary humanists and sociologists, like Nussbaum (1997) and Pat Duffy Hutcheon (1999: 196). In fact, as Donald Verene (1994: 135) reminds us, this is true of Vico as well: his philosophy is "a circle that begins and ends in pedagogy".[47] Thus, as we take a stand – pedagogically, aesthetically, ethically, socially, politically – as individuals, groups or nations, we do so to a great extent on the basis of how our imaginations are attuned to the surrounding culture or cultures (see 7.1). We make crucial decisions in our lives on the basis of what we accept and cannot accept of the popular imagination in which we are immersed by way of our culture.

The points I am trying to make here is, first, that imagination and popular imagination should to a considerable extent be conflated as objects of study and, second, that studies of them should ideally be conducted along a spectrum of disciplines from biology, neurology, neuropsychology, cognitive psychology and cultural psychology all the way to art history, musicology, aesthetics (empirical and philosophical), comparative literature, comparative religion, history, folkloristics, sociology, ethnography and anthropology. Imagination resides at the very centre of the age-old nature versus nurture debate, which perhaps is solved by the interactional view mentioned above: like human cognition in general, imagination is both innate and learned.[48] Of course, except for putting an

---

[47] On nurturing imagination in academia see Pettersson (1999d, 2011).
[48] See Lakoff and Johnson (1999: 507–508). For a similar argument in cultural psychology see Cole (1996: 214–219); in evolutionary studies see Hundert (1995); and in primatology see Savage-Rumbaugh et al. (1998: 217–218).

end to a futile debate, this realization in fact solves very little. What it does suggest, however, is that the roads to take now are ones in which the intricacies of man's interaction with his or her environment must be studied in detail and with a recognition of its staggering complexity.

Let me briefly make explicit what may be implicit in the above: despite the cultural attunement stressed above, there are major differences in how individual imaginations are constituted. This has always been common knowledge, but perhaps at times so common that philosophers and other scholars have overlooked it. However, in his essay "On the Power of Imagination" Montaigne (1958/1993: 36–48) focuses on idiosyncratic differences between individual imaginations. Similarly, a standard jazz ballad like "Imagination" (with lyrics by Johnny Burke) harps on such differences:

> Imagination is funny
> It makes a cloudy day sunny
> Makes a bee think of honey
> Just as I think of you
> Imagination is crazy
> Your whole perspective gets hazy
> Starts you asking a daisy
> What to do, what to do[49]

In a few words – and the ballad goes on to consider other ways of imagining – this item of popular culture touches on what it took the human sciences more than two millennia to reach: it charts different modes and kinds of imagination, not just as cognitive categories but as ways of thinking of the possible and the impossible. In the early twentieth century we find such preliminary charts in I. A. Richards' (1926: 239–253) six senses of imagination and Gilbert Ryle's (1949/1990: 232–263) chapter on different kinds of imagining. But after Richards and Ryle it has taken more than half a century in the life and human sciences and popular culture studies before we finally have started to grasp the interrelation between imagination and popular imagination. In order to understand how this interrelation comes across in literature, we must go to the notion of literary imagination.

---

[49] Transcribed as sung by Frank Sinatra (http://www.metrolyrics.com/imagination-lyrics-frank-sinatra.html; accessed 14 July 2015).

1.5 Literary Imagination

The term *literary imagination* does not have any one received meaning. Most prevalently it seems to be a kind of useful umbrella term for themes or ideas in literature. A case in point is the broad area suggested by the Oxford journal called *Literary Imagination* in that it defines its field as follows: "a forum for all those interested in the distinctive nature, uses, and pleasures of literature, from ancient to modern, in all languages" (litimag.oxfordjournals.org). A browse on the Internet shows that literary imagination or imagination in relation to literature is used in connection with all kinds of literature, such as American, Roman, romantic, Victorian, detective (fiction), lesbian and postmodern as well as in relation to, among other things, ethics, Freud and slavery, that is, in relation to geographical, historical, generic, sexual, disciplinary and/or cultural modifiers.

However, before discussing Western views of literary imagination, it may be instructive to consider an ancient Eastern, a pre-Columbian and a fairly recent African poetics of literary imagination. The Chinese scholar Liu Xie or Hsieh (c. 465–c. 522) wrote the first book-length systematic treatise of Chinese literary criticism, *The Literary Mind and the Carving of Dragons* (*Wen-hsin tiao-lung*), a kind of poetics not unlike that of Aristotle (Liu Hsieh 1959). In typical ancient Chinese fashion, rather than discussing literary features as such, Liu's chapter on literary imagination or spiritual thought (*shen* or *shen-ssu*) focuses on the originary and normative features of literature, that is, how you become a good writer of imaginative literature by learning to employ literary techniques and genres. The main teachings concern reading Chinese classics, concentrating and contemplating in order to reach a state in which one's imagination is "in operation", with "all possible vistas open before it" (Liu 1959: 155). Liu (1959: 158) ends his chapter with a poem that summarizes his view, which centres on poetry:

> Under the operation of the spirit the phenomenal world becomes articulate,
> But does so responsive to varying emotional situations.
> Things are apprehended by means of their appearances,
> And the mind responds by the application of reason.
> It carves and engraves in accordance with sound patterns,
> Forging metaphors and allegories as it goes.
> It gathers together all its ideas and works them into harmony,
> And [like General Chang Liang] wins victory afar while sitting in its tent.[50]

---

[50] General Chang [Zhang] Liang was famous for his strategic and victorious planning of battles. See Liu (1959: 158n9).

In short, Liu expresses an awareness of the mimetic craft in the making of literature and finding the right techniques, emotion and concentration to render literary worlds.[51] The contemporary sinologist Ming Dong Gu (2005: 410) maintains that "it is Liu Xie [...] who first conducted a systematic inquiry into the conditions of imitation and representation in *fu-* [poetic exposition] style writings". As we shall see in 2.1, much in Liu's view tallies with later Western notions and the views expressed in this study.

In a pre-contact dialogue poem, whose title in translation from Nahuatl is rendered "Poetics: A Dialogue of Flower and Song", the Aztec poet Tecayehuatzin of Huexotzinco (c. 1490/2001: 82) "unfolds the songs of the Giver of Life" and wonders "[i]f there is a place where some truth exists on earth?" In contrast to Liu, here the representation of "some truth" is rather tentative. Rather, in Aztec poetics the very making of "flower and song", a double metaphor standing for art in general and poetry in particular, is in focus (see Léon-Portilla and Shorris 2001: 31). At times the inspiration of the poet's song comes from the Giver of Life, at times "it comes out of the earth, it springs forth" – and perhaps the source does not matter, since the power of the Giver of Life, who is manifest in the Sun, is evident in the blossoming earth (Tecayehuatzin 2001: 89). This divine force produces flowers, bird song as well as songs by humans, who can invoke and give pleasure to the Giver of Life by their metaphorical flowers and in this way also strengthen the friendship between the singer and the audience.

The Nigerian poet and journalist Onwuchekwa Jemie's (1971/1998: 277) poem "Toward a Poetics" (1971) starts out: "The great dark work / has not yet been written / a monument to our age / which is the age of negritude". His poetics, then, is openly ideological, but like Tecayehuatzin's Aztec poetics, it views humankind in relation to nature, if with no reliance on a Creator, and looks to the future with some confidence: "you who have known no God / but forests and waterfalls / and the bitter sun / you will articulate the totality / the embarrassment / pride / despair / and hope" (Jemie 1971/1998: 278). Thus, these Aztec and Nigerian views of literary imagination are grounded in the natural world,

---

51 For another rather literal translation of this *tsan* or supporting verse and a thorough presentation and analysis of *Wen-hsin tiao-lung* see Owen (1992: 210 and 183–298). Owen (1992: 201, 590 *s.v. shen*) translates shen as "spirit thought" and discusses the term in some detail in his glossary. For a freer and more poetic translation of the *tsan* see Liu (2000: 649).

while the Chinese one is closer to Western views in that it is based on the mimetic crafting of literature.[52]

As I have noted above, it was Coleridge, following Kant, who established imagination as a notion in literary studies in his *Biographia Literaria*. The fundamental thesis that paves the ground for Coleridge's (1817/2000: 295) view of imagination reads: "Truth is the correlative to being. Knowledge without a correspondent reality is no knowledge; if we know, there must be somewhat known by us. To know is in its very essence a verb active". Hence, even though he considers himself "an English metaphysician", clearly in the German philosopher's footsteps, his equation of ontology with epistemology seems to be firmly grounded in the British empiricist tradition. This is corroborated by how he defends his position through repeated references to Francis Bacon, and it is this defence that leads him to first define *imagination* and then categorize it into the three types – primary and secondary imagination and fancy – discussed above (Coleridge 1817/2000: 304–306, 313).

In "Lay Sermon I" Coleridge (1816/2000: 660) finds no abstractions in the Scriptures, which are "the living *educts* of the imagination", since they have

> that reconciling and mediatory power, which incorporating the reason in the images of the sense, and organizing (as it were) the flux of the senses by the permanence and self-encircling energies of the reason, gives birth to a system of symbols, harmonious in themselves, and consubstantial with the truths of which they are the conductors.

Here Coleridge summarizes much of his view of imagination: how it mediates between sense perception and reason and produces symbols. Five years later, in 1821, Shelley (1840/2002: 637) in "A Defence of Poetry" presents a related mediatory view, even if he starts from language rather than imagination: especially the poets' "language is vitally metaphorical; that is, it marks the before unapprehended relations of things and perpetuates their apprehension".[53] His point on the slowing down of perception – or perhaps rather apperception – may draw on *Biographia Literaria*, since having defined the various kinds of imagination (including fancy), Coleridge famously goes on to characterize "that willing suspension of disbelief". As its definition is often quoted out of context it may be

---

[52] The classic Indian poetics centring on communicating *dhvanis* (aesthetic suggestions) is implicitly mimetic in that it covers a wide range of denotations and connotations and represents emotions in characters; see 3.3 (p. 94), 4.3 (p. 136) and 8.2 (pp. 244–245).

[53] See also Richards (1936/1965: 90–91) on this passage. As for imagination, the very starting-point of Shelley's (1840/2002: 635) "Defence" is that there are "two classes of mental action", reason and imagination, which function so that the former "respects the differences [...] of things" and the latter their "similitudes".

worthwhile to show that it is based on "the plan of the 'Lyrical Ballads'" that Wordsworth and Coleridge had and makes a number rather significant points:

> [I]t was agreed, that my endeavours should be directed to persons and characters supernatural, or at least romantic; yet so as to transfer from our inward nature a human interest and a semblance of truth sufficient to procure for these shadows of imagination that willing suspension of disbelief for the moment, which constitutes poetic faith. Mr Wordsworth, on the other hand, was to propose to himself as his object, to give the charm of novelty to things of everyday, and to excite a feeling analogous to the supernatural, by awakening the mind's attention from the lethargy of custom, and directing it to the loveliness and the wonders of the world before us; an inexhaustible treasure, but for which in consequence of the film of familiarity and selfish solicitude we have eyes, yet see not, ears that hear not, and hearts that neither feel nor understand. (Coleridge 1817/2000: 314)

As we can see, "willing suspension of disbelief" is not intended to cover all sorts of literature, although it has often been taken as the hallmark of literature as such. It is reserved for supernatural characters so as to endow them with "a human interest and a semblance of truth" – or what could be termed mimetic traits. Moreover, it is clear that the plan Coleridge and Wordsworth devised was chiastic: the former was to move from the supernatural and romantic to the realistic, the latter in the opposite direction. Even more intriguingly perhaps, we see that Coleridge's aspiration to give "the charm of novelty to things of everyday" – later, it seems, echoed by Shelley – was nothing less than a kind of estrangement a century before Viktor Shklovsky (1917/1998) defined that term. That is, not only did Coleridge see various kinds of imagination but also that literature could move in two directions on the spectrum between the fantastic and the realistic (or the empirical, if you like). In broader terms, I would even suggest that Coleridge's suspension of disbelief is related to the notion of suspense, since it makes expositional manipulation possible, which creates much delightful suspense when experiencing literature (see 3.4).

Coleridge's view of the imagination was soon included in literary critical discussion. In fact, so much so that his rather critical view of fancy most likely led to it virtually falling out of use in criticism, except with reference to Coleridge's distinction. When in the early twentieth century I. A. Richards (1926/2001: 224–236, 228 quote) finally set out to define six kinds of imagination, he saves Coleridge's notion last in order to discuss it in some detail, bypasses fancy and discusses how the poet "outwits the force of habit" with no mention of Coleridge's (and Wordsworth's) distinction between the two kinds of movement between the supernatural and the realistic. In his second meaning of imagination he notes that "[t]he use of figurative language is frequently all that is meant", especially metaphor and simile (Richards 1926/2001: 224). He goes on to define metaphor in poetry in a way that anticipates late twentieth-century views: "[Metaphor] is the supreme agent by which disparate and hitherto unconnected things are brought together in poetry for the sake of the effects upon attitude and impulse which spring from their collocation and from the combinations which the mind then establishes between them" (Richards 1926/2001: 225). Here Richards can be seen as a precursor for the view that Paul Ricœur (1983/1990: x) was to champion in that in its plot, narrative, like metaphor, "grasps together", a point Coleridge (1817/2000: 307 *et passim*) already made by his neologism *esemplastic* for how imagination interweaves opposites.

But later Richards saw that Coleridge's view had even larger implications. In *Coleridge on Imagination* he tries to elucidate Coleridge's views in two ways: in part he analyses and classifies poems as either representing Fancy or Imagination and in part he defines imagination as "a descriptive psychological term" relating to how the subject and the object coalesce (Richards 1934/1969: 54–55, 94–96, 96 quote). Of course, Coleridge never really developed his notions in the way he apparently intended to do, but to my mind his *Biographia Literaria* and related writings on imagination and fancy (some of which have been quoted above) seem to point to what we today would term an interest in the cognitive – for Richards, "psychological" – workings of the human mind when creating and reading literature, mainly poetry (see Miall 2006, Richardson 2010, 2011, 2015).

In fact, this remains Richards's (1934/1969: 86–87) main fascination with the terms: in imagination "the parts of the meaning [...] mutually modify one another"; in fancy, they are "apprehended as though independent of their fellow-members [...] and collide or combine *later*, in so far as they do so at all". At the very end of *Coleridge on Imagination* it is this point that for Richards makes Coleridge unique in literary studies: his literary-critical views "unite with the analysis of the ambiguities and confusions that are overt or latent in all cases of metaphor, transference or projection to form one study". In Coleridge's works this view may be "embryonic still", but it has Galilean proportions, since it offers "an immense opportunity for improving our technique of understanding" (1934/1969: 232).

In his next work, *The Philosophy of Rhetoric*, Richards started to draw his conclusions of this view by suggesting a cognitive (if not bodily, as in Lakoff and Johnson 1980) grounding for metaphor and retaining its basis in analogy: "*Thought* is metaphoric, and proceeds by comparison, and the metaphors of language derive therefrom" (Richards 1936/1965: 94).[54] Even though in *Principles of*

---

54 *The Philosophy of Rhetoric* is probably best known as the work in which Richards states his tenor-vehicle view of metaphor, that is, one of the traditional views explicitly or implicitly criticised in cognitive metaphor theory. But as his notion of thought as metaphorical suggests, Richards can also be viewed as a precursor of cognitive metaphor theory.

Literary Criticism Richards (1926/2001: 227) does not make explicit the connection between metaphor and imagination, in his Coleridgean definition of imagination – "imagination ... reveals itself in the balance or reconciliation of opposite or discordant qualities" – he seems to imply that imagination too brings together "disparate and hitherto unconnected things".

I have discussed Coleridge, Shelley and Richards in some detail, since although they seem aware of traditional theories of metaphor – especially those of Aristotle, Longinus and Quintilian – in which analogous and extensive aspects of metaphor are discussed, they go beyond them in pointing to the "synthesis of the heterogeneous" that Paul Ricœur (1983/1990: xi) finds in both metaphor and narrative and even to the foundations of cognitive metaphor theory in Lakoff and Johnson (1980). More importantly for my purposes, their seminal insights are helpful for constructing a poetics that can encompass such a broad spectrum for how imagination and popular imagination are combined by literary imagination; how literature builds on representation; how imagination and knowledge, the real and the fantastic, rhetorical figures and narratives can be combined; and how the effect of literature often is to awaken or stir the mind in different ways. It is Richards' challenge, based on Coleridge, of how to improve our understanding of cognition and language, especially of the workings of literature, that I will take up in chapters 2 to 6.

As for more or less theoretical discussions of imagination in relation to literature during and after Richards, the discussion continued especially as concerns romantic poetry and the romantic world view. Perhaps the major name in at least British letters in the mid-twentieth century, excepting Richards, was D. G. James. His *Scepticism and Poetry. An Essay on the Poetic Imagination* (1937) also builds largely on Coleridge, but is skeptical of Richards' emotive view of poetic language (see James 1937: 30 *et passim*). It is perhaps symptomatic that as early as in the mid-twentieth century James in his other study on romanticism *The Romantic Comedy. An Essay on English Romanticism* (1948) traces the decline of the Romantic view of imagination from Blake to Cardinal Newman.[55]

In a sense, most of Northrop Frye's works also centre on imagination. It is, understandably, frequently discussed in his Blake study *Fearful Symmetry*, since, as Frye (1947/1949: 19) so aptly puts it, for Blake, "a man's imagination is his life". In *Anatomy of Criticism* the term *imagination* may seldom be employed and Coleridge is only mentioned in passing, but much like the romantics before him Frye (1957/1973: 84) equates symbols with images "which show an analogy

---

[55] James (1948/1963: 197–212, 205 quote) also includes a perceptive discussion of how for both Coleridge and Newman "the religious imagination [...] issues into *symbol*".

of proportion between the poem and the nature which it imitates". What is more, the central argument in *The Great Code* is that "the Bible and the person of Christ" should be identified "metaphorically", they are "one thing in two aspects", with a noticeably Christian bias in reading the Old Testament (Frye 1981/1983: 77). Of all Frye's books, the one that most explicitly focuses on imagination is *The Educated Imagination*, which is a collection of six radio talks. Here he pleads for educating people's imagination (mainly through the reading of literature), since "the power of detachment in the imagination, where things are removed just out of reach of belief and action" can teach tolerance (Frye 1964: 78). This is not entirely unlike Richards (1932), who in his study of the Chinese philosopher Mencius made his multiple definitions of words into a scheme to further inter-cultural understanding.

In France in the mid-twentieth century, the major philosopher working on what he termed *imagination* (or at times *poetic imagination*) was Gaston Bachelard. In *The Poetics of Space* he terms imagination "a major power of human nature" and much like Coleridge he claims that it has two co-operating functions, that of reality and that of unreality, and that the latter works in poetry "always to awaken – the sleeping being lost in its automatisms", especially those of language (Bachelard 1958/1994: xxiv–xxv, xxv quote). His other central notion related to imagination is *reverie*, "the binding principle" integrating "the thoughts, memories and dreams of mankind" (Bachelard 1958/1994: 6; see also 1987/1989).

In other words, what seemed to happen before and after the Second World War in the theoretical study of literary imagination was that the concept of imagination, after various related paths of romantic imagery and world view as well as semantic, mythical and religious scrutiny, was in part moving beyond a focus on imagination as such. Still, when the *Critical Idiom* series in the 1960s published brief reviews of key notions in literature, there was one on *Fancy and Imagination*, written by R. L. Brett (1969), centring on Coleridge, his precursors and aftermath. In a sense, this little book could symbolize the end of the study of literary imagination *per se*, despite the fact that works like *The Great Code* with related themes and usages were still to be published. For instance, although there is a *New Critical Idiom* series, with new analyses of age-old and topical issues in literature, there is no new edition dealing with imagination (or fancy). However, David S. Miall (2006: 157–171) and Alan Richardson (2010, 2011, 2015), among others, have recently come to view the romantic poets, especially Coleridge, as precursors of contemporary cognitive literary studies.

The latest trend in the study of literary imagination centres on how literary imagining or imaging works when reading. It deals with how readers engage with literary works and this encounter is usually explained in *embodied, experi-*

ential or *enactive*[56] terms (Kuzmičová 2013, Caracciolo 2013). In a sense, the question is of how the suspension of disbelief functions: whether readers move into the literary world by changing their view of deixis from the real world to the literary world, according to the Deictic Shift Theory (Segal 1995), or are primarily aware that they are reading fiction (Walsh 2007: 36 *et passim*), or – in experimental fiction, at least – blend immersion and self-awareness in ways that go beyond any simplistic duck-rabbit view (Polvinen, in press).[57] It seems to me that there can be quite a scale for how disbelief is suspended when experiencing literary worlds, both between and even in individuals, genres, historical periods and cultures. Just think of reading in bed at night compared to reading with a drill intermittently going on outside, of a ten-year-old girl or a seventy-year-old man reading, of reading realist fiction or experimental poetry, or of various ways of reading, such as silently or aloud, slow reading or speed reading, in the Roman alphabet or Chinese characters. That is, all sorts of studies of reading are more than welcome, since they can provide us with more detailed knowledge of how literary worlds have been and are experienced, but most likely such studies will have rather little to say about how such worlds are shaped in the first place.

As I aim to show, imagination and all the important work it has inspired for centuries should be put into better use in contemporary literary studies. That is, the study of imagination, shared imagination and particularly literary imagination can provide tools for analysing how literary worlds are based on imaginative uses of literary representation.

---

[56] Since the enactive view of reading may be the least well known, let me note that Caracciolo (2013: 81) defines his "enactivist account of the imagination" as "the active exploration of a non-actual environment".

[57] The optical ambiguity in a drawing looking both like a duck and a rabbit was made famous by Wittgenstein's (1953/1991: 193–207) discussion of *seeing that* versus *seeing as* in *Philosophical Investigations*.

2 The Imaginative Uses of Mimesis

2.1 Mimesis as a Basis for Literature

In a thorough exposé of the evolution of imagination Stephen Mithen (2001: 32) argues that fantasy – that is, imagining counterfactual worlds – is the most recent form of imagination to evolve (c. 50 000 years ago), but that all kinds of imagination combines "elements of other-worldliness and the familiar". In other words, not surprisingly, imagination has a basis in the world we know. All of literature and its manifold imaginative worlds are likewise based on representation or rather *mimesis*, an ancient term employed by both Plato and Aristotle, though in different senses. It derives from Greek *miméesthai*, to copy or mime, and broadly speaking, Plato used it about the poet speaking through characters in dramatic representation, whereas Aristotle (1987: 4–5, 48b4–19) in his *Poetics* expanded it to signify representation in the arts. Thus, one of the problems in discussing mimesis is the fact that the meaning of the term varies.

The first point to make, then, is that any reference to mimesis may draw on Plato or Aristotle, and if on the former, it usually does not just stand for dramatic representation, but for 'imitation'. However, Stephen Halliwell (2002: 37–71, 70 quote), perhaps the foremost contemporary authority on classical usages of mimesis, detects a "prolonged and profoundly ambivalent relationship with mimesis" in Plato's writings. What is more, Plato can hardly be held accountable for the simplistic equation of mimesis with imitation and, later, realism. In a historical perspective, one of the most important moves occurred when the Greek notion of mimesis was translated into Latin straightforwardly as *imitatio*, a word that in different forms occurs in Germanic as well as Romance languages.[1] *Imitation* had a broader meaning for some time, as for instance is still evident in William Blake's and John Keats's respective "imitation" of Spenser (both readily available on the Internet), where it retains an imaginative sense in that the young poet seeks to define his own literary profile as against that of his precursor. However, the imaginative aspect of the term has faded in literary studies (at least in English), perhaps to some extent in tandem with the convention of literary imitation.[2]

Still, Plato's sense of mimesis, even if not prevalent in literary studies, lives on. Three decades ago the narrative theorist Gérard Genette (1983/1988: 44, 45)

---

[1] To be sure, even in ancient Greek *mimesis* included the meaning 'imitation' but it also had a much wider denotation.
[2] For a history of the various stages of the view of mimesis as imitation see Gebauer and Wulf (1992/1995), especially chapters 3, 6 and 12.

DOI 10.1515/9783110483475-003

maintained, like Mieke Bal (1977/1985) before him, that mimesis is a "superfluous" category, since "the only acceptable equivalence for *diégésis/mimesis* is *narrative/dialogue*". Thus, by distinguishing between diegesis and mimesis in this way, Genette aligned himself with Plato's view of mimesis (as speech by characters other than the poet) to the extent that he feels that narrative studies can allegedly do away with the notion or "category" of mimesis. But in this case Genette's pronouncement was not heeded, except that diegesis became the central notion for narrative in structuralist narratology.

In recent scholarship on reading in ancient times a similar downgrading of mimesis to mere imitation can be detected. When discussing the growth of the symbol and allegoresis in reading from pre-Aristotelian times to Neoplatonism, Peter T. Struck (2004: 68 quote, 70 – 71) views Aristotle as having spawned a tradition in scholarship in which "mimesis ceases completely to be a problem of linguistic representation", since it allegedly simply stands for imitation. Against it he pits the symbolic and allegorical tradition, in which "great poetic language" is viewed as "deeply figurative" and proceeds on the basis of "the poetics of the enigma" (Struck 2010: 4, 24). As I shall argue in this chapter and chapters 5 and 6, such a dichotomy seems to be untenable in two ways. First, it misses Aristotle's point of mimesis as entertaining ideas of the hypothetical: literature is about what *might* happen, which shows that for him it is not simply imitative (see below). Second, it fails to grasp that literary representation makes use of fantastic, symbolical and allegorical meanings. At times authors and literary critics can focus on imitative or creative aspects in the writing and reading of literature, but that does not mean that literature in fact consists of one aspect at the exclusion of the other.

Still, the view of mimesis as imitation is rather widespread in literary studies, usually based on the premise that realist fiction is imitative. As far as I can tell, two towering works in literary studies did much to cement this view. Erich Auerbach (1946/1991: 554) in his magisterial, if non-theoretical, treatise *Mimesis. The Representation of Reality in Western Literature* defines the subject of his book as "the interpretation of reality through literary representation or 'imitation'". Of course, his rich and diverse chapters on Western literature in fact show that imitation for him can encompass many levels of literary representation. Yet his rather straightforward view that realism – both ancient and modern, in the visual arts as well as literature – "represent[s] the most everyday phenomena of reality in a serious and significant context" (Auerbach 1946/1991: 555) seems to have contributed to the view that mimesis simply stands for imitation. Similarly, in one of the most influential studies in mid-twentieth-century American letters, *The Mirror and the Lamp*, M. H. Abrams (1953/1971: 8) defined the "mimetic orientation" as imitation and as "probably the most primitive aesthetic theory" at that. To be sure, he provides a brief history of the concept and further specifications of this *mirror* view of literary representation, as against the preferred *lamp* view introduced by the romantic poets and philosophers (Abrams 1953/ 1971: 8–14, 30–46).[3] But by his stark division and his downgrading of the mimetic orientation Abrams strengthened the imitative view of mimesis and paved the way for the rather strong condemnation of it in late twentieth-century literary scholarship.

Today we find that the equation of mimesis with imitation is quite prevalent in literary studies, usually in works which do not really engage with the notion or its complex history. For instance, Lilian R. Furst's (1995: 23) account of realist fiction and Brian Richardson's (2006: 6, 12–14, 134–40) "antimimetic" view of experimental fiction take for granted that mimesis is straightforward imitation. In fact, in recent narrative theory there is a trend of "unnatural narratology", which draws on the double distinctions that realism is mimetic and that experimental fiction is anti-mimetic and "unnatural", the latter of which is the subject matter for unnatural narratology. In the paper "Unnatural Narratives, Unnatural Narratology: Beyond Mimetic Models" (Alber et al. 2010) four narrative theorists, Jan Alber, Stefan Iversen, Henrik Skov Nielsen and Brian Richardson launched a manifesto that claims that experimental narratives are unnatural and anti-mimetic, and that they need unnatural narratology to deal with them, in contrast to Monika Fludernik's (1996) "natural" narratology. They base their view of mimesis as tantamount to realism on one of the leading narrative theorists, James Phelan (2005, cf. also 2007), and in a later answer to Monika Fludernik's (2012) critique, on Plato's *Republic* (see Alber et al. 2012: 378). Although I share Alber et al.'s commendable interest in experimental, fantastic and strange fiction, I have published a critique of the manifesto based on a different view of terminology (fantastic or experimental literature is in no way unnatural, hence the kind of narratology that deals with it is not unnatural either), of the origins and kinds of literature (which has always included fantastic elements) and of interpretation (Alber et al.'s view of unnatural storyworlds, minds and acts of narration) (see Pettersson 2012a). In fact, in their answer to Fludernik, Alber et al. (2012: 378) admit that "the unnatural is quite obviously mimetic in the sense of Aristotle because it can be depicted or represented in the world of fiction".

Drama, on the other hand, flaunts the mimetic action by the very fact that actors play characters, whether fictional or real (as in documentary drama). In the most inclusive definition of drama that I am aware of, the drama theorist

---

3 For a reading of Stanisław Lem's collection of comic science-fiction stories *The Cyberiad* (1965) in terms of Abrams's dichotomy see Pettersson (2014: 106–113).

Martin Esslin (1987/1996: 24) maintains that "[d]rama simulates, enacts or re-enacts events that have, or may be imagined to have, happened in the 'real' or in an imagined world. What these different types of representation have in common is that they are all 'mimetic action'". On the other hand, there is narrative and epic theatre of different kinds. For instance, in Bertolt Brecht's (1964/1987: 137, 195–197) view, actors should *show*, not *transform into*, their characters, so that what happens on stage is in some sense an oblique mimetic portrayal of characters. Indeed, one of the most important drama theorists, Manfred Pfister (1977/1993: 7–9, 7 quote), when providing an overview of the codes and channels of drama, bases it on the five human senses, owing to the fact drama as performed is "a synaesthetic text".[4] In short, drama represents the multiple ways that humans perceive and act in the world.

As for poetry, Miner (1990: 87–96) may be right in claiming that "presence" and "intensification" is typical of the lyric, but it still portrays what poets or their speakers have perceived or the feelings they harbour. That is, poetry may not mime action *per se* – even though Miner (1990: 97–120) goes on to show how easily it merges with narrative and drama –, yet it provides literary representations of human sense perception and emotion.

Perhaps the greatest challenge to mimesis as the basis for literature lies in the traditional view of Chinese literature as affective-expressive as against mimetic, that is, in both Chinese literature and poetics there is allegedly little that is mimetic. But this dichotomy has recently been challenged in literary studies by comparativists and sinologists. Even Earl Miner (1990: 74), who argues for a dichotomy between Western (Aristotelian) mimetic poetics and Eastern (especially Chinese) affective-expressive poetics must allow that they both are based on the "presumption of the reality of the world and people". Also, his view of mimesis is clearly narrowly imitative, as when he claims that Zeami's (1992/1994) classic Japanese nō drama *Matsukaze* (c. 1412) has "no mimetic fit between characters and theme, between human misery and its presentation", simply because grief and longing are expressed in stylized and allegorical terms (see Miner 1990: 53–55 , 66–73, 68 quote).

---

4 Thus Pfister leaves out kinaesthetic and inner body feelings, which undoubtedly are seldom central in drama, except for instance as an interest in bowel movement in Beckett's *Krapp's Last Tape* and in feigned ailing in Molière's *The Hypochondriac* (see Beckett 1986/1990 and Molière 1982). More importantly, Pfister's (1977/1993: 26–27) impressive theory of drama suffers from following Roman Jakobson's dated and abstract single-context model of communication, since drama, like all literary forms, has complex contexts of mediation and reception. For a discussion of this "single context fallacy" see Pettersson (2009b: 145–147).

More recently, Alexander Beecroft (2010: 35–47) has shown that Confucius' central notion of transmission (*shu*), "although certainly not identical with Aristotelian *mimêsis* [...] clearly does some of the same work for its culture, acting as the conceptualization of the relationship between narrativized mytho-historical past and ritualized performance in the present". More importantly, Beecroft (2010: 240–277) and Martin Svensson (1999: 31–33 *et passim*) have demonstrated in critical practice that Chinese drama and poetry function mimetically (in the broad sense discussed below) and is not devoid of figures (a related argument). What is more, Miner (1990: 26) points out that the age-old Western view that literature should both profit and delight first stated in Horace's *Ars Poetica* is in fact much like the affective-expressive stance in Chinese poetics.[5] Similarly, in a wide-ranging survey of mimetic theory in Chinese literary studies, Ming Dong Gu (2005: 419) concludes that "we should discard the dichotomous view of Chinese and Western aesthetic thought and become self-consciously aware of the interrelated and interpenetrating nature of such ideas as expressionism and mimeticism". The twain have, if not always met, at least had related notions of how literature communicates.

In short, what has occasioned all the dismissive statements concerning mimesis in both Western and Eastern scholarship most likely has to do with the particularly narrow sense it often has been given. What all equations of mimesis with imitation (and realism) seem to miss is the breadth and depth of Aristotle's concept of mimesis. Central to Aristotle's view of mimesis in his *Poetics* is that "the poet's function is to describe, not the thing that happened, but a kind of thing that *might* happen" (Aristotle 1941/2001a: 1463, 9.1451a; emphasis added).[6] That is, as Stephen Halliwell (2002: 16 quote *et passim*, 2012) has shown at length, mimesis centrally includes a creative imaginative aspect as well as an imitative one: "mimesis amounts to a concept (or family of concepts) of representation, which [...] can be broadly construed as the use of an artistic medium (words, sounds, physical images) to signify and communicate certain hypothesized realities".[7] These realities signify an inclusive understanding of Aristotle's mimesis that for Halliwell (2002: 33) encompasses two aspects: imitative *world-reflecting* and creative *world-simulating*, which have been understood and portrayed in a number of subjunctive or hypothesized ways in the study of imagination and in literature (see 1.2 and 6.2).

---

5 See also Beecroft (2010: 41–43) and 8.1.
6 See also Halliwell (2002: 16) and Ricœur (1977/2003: 44).
7 Cf. Gebauer and Wulf (1992/1995: 56): "Mimesis [in Aristotle's *Poetics*] designates the imitation and the manner in which, in art as in nature, creation takes place".

In fact, since I think that Aristotle's view of mimesis can serve as the very basis for literature – and the kind of poetics of literary imagination I develop here –, it should be spelled out in some detail. Having studied Aristotle's mimesis for some three decades, Halliwell (2012: 8) recently summed up five central aspects of Aristotle's "ambitious and yet, in its execution, [...] incomplete structure of mimetic theory". In short, mimesis stands for

> (1) a philosophical anthropology (man as *homo mimeticus*),
> (2) a classification of mimetic artforms,
> (3) a discursive category (as against, science, philosophy and history),
> (4) a frame of reference (on a spectrum from the actual to the ideal) and
> (5) a judgement of the relation between tragic drama and "life".
> (Based on Halliwell 2012: 6–8)

Let me expound on these aspects – especially (1), (3) and (4) – in some detail, since they pave the ground for a mimetic view of literature. In his *Poetics* Aristotle (1941/2001a: 1457; § 4.1448b) famously claims that "[i]mitation is natural to man from the beginning", just as he starts out his *Metaphysics* by stating "[a]ll men by nature desire to know", which indicates "the delight we take in our senses" and whose sensations in humans are preserved by memory, which forms the basis for their intelligence (Aristotle 1941/2001b: 689; § 1.980a–b). A similar view has recently been suggested about human development. According to Merlin Donald (2001/2002: 263), "[m]imesis must have come early in hominid prehistory because it was a necessary preadaptation for the later evolution of language. It provided the underpinnings of social connectivity and conventionality". The fact that humankind is a sort of *homo mimeticus* has been corroborated by recent psychological tests with newborn infants: show them your tongue and they will respond by showing their tongue, even within an hour after birth (Gopnik et al. 1999: 29–30). And it is by imitation together with "the sense of harmony and rhythm", Aristotle (1941/2001a: 1458; § 4.1448b) goes on to claim in *Poetics*, that humans gradually "created poetry out of their improvisations", later progressing to different kinds of poetry based on noble characters (serious) and ignoble ones (comic). This shows in a nutshell Aristotle's view of the imitative basis of human perception and intelligence and the development of different art forms.

In the above-quoted view of the poet's function to describe "a kind of thing that might happen" Aristotle (1941/2001a: 1464; § 1.1451b) explicitly contrasts this function to that of the historian, who describes "the thing that has been", just as at the start of *Poetics* he maintains that it is subject matter – not, for instance, metre – that is the difference between philosophy and physics on the one hand and poetry on the other (Aristotle 1941/2001a: 1455–1456; § 1.1447b).

Close to the end of his work Aristotle (1941/2001a: 1483; § 25.1460b) notes that as "an imitator" the poet "must necessarily in all instances represent things in one or other of three aspects, either as they were or are, or as they are said or thought to be or to have been, or as they ought to be". As Halliwell (2012: 7) notes, portraying things "as they are said or thought to be or to have been" leaves such a leeway for the imagination that it could be said to include alternative or literary worlds. This is in fact corroborated as Aristotle (1941/2001a: 1484, 1485; §§ 25.1460b, 25.1461b) goes on to accept "tales about Gods", since such were still in circulation, and even "the Impossible", if properly justified. Such views show that for Aristotle the mimetic frames of reference include a spectrum of "hypothesized realities" on a spectrum from the actual to the ideal, from world-reflecting to world-simulating.[8]

Elsewhere Halliwell (2002) has provided a wholesale history of mimesis, which shows its many Platonic and Aristotelian turns in Western history. It is important to note that although the imitative views have been fairly widespread in recent literary studies, they have not prevailed. Rather, Aristotle's broader notion of mimesis has become the more accepted view: *Britannica Online Encyclopedia* simply defines mimesis as a "basic theoretical principle in the creation of art";[9] *Routledge Encyclopedia of Narrative Theory* views it as "a central paradigm in Western art theory since Greek antiquity" (Schaeffer and Vultur 2005: 309); and Peter Lamarque and Stein Haugom Olsen (1994/1996: 265) consider "the mimetic aspect [...] both a central and an ineliminable facet of the concept of literature". Thus, neither Plato's narrowly imitative view (whether of theatrical performance or in general) nor the subsequent equation of mimesis with realism has carried the day. Still, as we have seen, views deriving from or building on Plato are current enough for much confusion to reign in literary studies, mostly owing to the fact that there is not enough awareness of the various traditions relating to mimesis. The most widespread study on the topic, Auerbach's *Mimesis*, is not very helpful either, since neither includes theoretical discussion nor considers the differences between Plato and Aristotle. Perhaps this is the reason why a recent survey on mimesis, by Matthew Potolsky (2006: 161), ends up relativizing the notion of mimesis, finally simply concluding that "for Western culture at least, there has been no way out of it".

---

8 As for aspects (2) and (5) that are not discussed here: according to Halliwell (2012: 5), for Aristotle, the mimetic arts include "principally poetry, painting, sculpture, [most] music, and dance". For the complex relation between the plot of tragedy and "life" see Halliwell (2012: 19–20).

9 See http://global.britannica.com/EBchecked/topic/383233/mimesis (accessed 15 August 2013).

I think most readers would concur with that, for one reason or another. But more to the point, I find that Aristotle's view of mimesis – however sketchy – provides literary studies with the most plausible ground for understanding much of what is central to literature: its origins, development, its relation to the complex ways in which literary communication in general and literary representation in particular function. In fact, it is the ground on which to build a poetics of literary imagination, since "[t]he fact that Aristotle never in this connection uses his own term *phantasia* [...] does not prevent mimesis itself from doing some of the same work in his argument as ideas of fictional imagination do in later theories" (Halliwell 2012: 15; see 1.2). For Aristotle, poetical mimesis is simply "somehow hypothetical or 'as if', not assertoric" (Halliwell 2012: 13). It is this *as if* quality that is based on the real world and comments on it in different ways that this study will explore.[10] Here is a thumbnail sketch of how literary representation works.

Even in infancy humans encounter the fictional and the real in various combinations in literary and literary-related storyworlds and acts of narration as shown, for instance, by Brian Boyd's recent study *On the Origins of Stories*. Although critical of wholesale mimetic theories of art (since they cannot account for much music and abstract visual art), Boyd (2009: 72, 177–187, 162 quote) highlights "the importance of advanced pretend play to the origins of fiction": "Humans [...] begin to understand imitation *as* imitation or representation through play, like the exaggerations of mock chase and peek-a-boo". Just as in most mammals, this is based on an understanding of "this is play" as against "this is real", as the anthropologist and communicative theorist Gregory Bateson (1955/2010: 179–180 *et passim*) puts it. In other words, it is high time that literary studies should start to conceive a fully-fledged developmental view of literary interpretation. An important advance in this respect is Jean-Marie Schaeffer's *Pourquoi la Fiction?*, which in 2010 was translated to English as *Why Fiction?* by Dorrit Cohn.[11] Schaeffer (1999/2010: 140) proposes an ontogenetic view of mimesis: "far from being a parasitical outgrowth of a connection to the real that would be an originary given, the imaginary activity, thus the access to fictional competence, is an important factor in the establishment of a stable epistemic structure, that is, in the distinction between the self and reality". By establishing what is real and what is imaginary, we learn about our world, but at the same time about ourselves. It is important that imagination is not regarded as a mere or late addition

---

10 See for instance 6.2 and Vaihinger's (1925/2009) extensive discussion. Also, Michael Saler (2012) has recently studied *as if* in terms of the "New Romance" from Conan Doyle to Tolkien.
11 Other developmental accounts include Dissanayake (2000), Pettersson (2002) and Oatley (2011).

to the human cognition, but as a fundamental activity by which we navigate in the world and understand who we are. In fact, there is considerable research on counterfactual (cf. fantastic) worlds in literature (see Sanford and Emmott 2012: 45–52), often drawing on Marie-Laure Ryan's (1980) *principle of minimal departure*, which suggests that alternative worlds are construed as closest to the world we know, even if fantastic features are introduced.

This means that readers are first and foremost humans finding their way in the world as they know it in the very real sense of daily conducting various kinds of thought experiment: Did my friend intend to hurt me by what he said? What would happen if such and such policies were implemented? Will there be a war? When encountering literature, one of the first things readers have to decide is whether it is or could be read as fiction (in a broad sense), often on the basis of what conventions it may abide by or flout.[12] Thus, however seemingly realist or fantastic, all literary worlds we create or encounter are in some sense based on the world we know. As Schaeffer (1999/2010: 192) puts it, "[we] can certainly form models asserting nonexistent entities, we can even invent the most fantastic universes, but in all cases these entities and these universes will be variants conforming to what signifies for us 'to be a reality,' because our representational competences are always already relative to the reality that has selected them and in which we live". That is, literature "has, and must have, a mimetic function if we are to be able to make any sense of it", as David Novitz (1987: 19) noted a few years earlier. On this clearly rather Aristotelian view, then, there are no antimimetic literary worlds, only different kinds of more or less imaginative ones, and they are all based on or flout different kinds of convention. Put differently, when humans learn about representation in general, this includes all sorts of imaginative uses, so that when encountering fiction in various guises they have a broad understanding of what representation is and – after some acquaintance with literature (in whatever form) – what literary representation is.

So far I have discussed mimesis as one notion, albeit with two aspects, the imitative and the imaginative. But in order to understand how it functions in detail, it can be useful to subdivide it, as Paul Ricœur (1983/1990: 52–77) and Monika Fludernik (1996: 43–46 *et passim*) have done. The latter draws on the former and they share some features: Ricœur's stages are *prefiguration* (preunderstanding; cf. "parameters of real-life experience" in Fludernik 1996: 43), *configuration* (textualization) and *refiguration* (interpretation; cf. "the reading experience" or "*narrativization*" in Fludernik 1996: 45). Fludernik's levels I and IV

---

12 For instance, the fact that "Row, Row, Row Your Boat" is a children's song (in a major key) suggests that the import of its words may be taken with a pinch of salt (see 3.2).

(narrativization) are much like prefiguration and refiguration, respectively, while her levels II and III add some subdivision to configuration as well as in part to refiguration. In other words, Ricœur and Fludernik both go from referential aspects to the text to the interpretation of the text, whereas Fludernik (1996: 45) emphasizes that on level IV all three other levels are utilized.

What should be noted here is that both only discuss narrative, even though much of it might apply to other kinds of literature. Also, Ricœur clearly thinks of mimesis as a process, since he discusses *stages*, whereas Fludernik's (1996: 45) *levels* of mimesis seem more structural, although her fourth level is expressly dynamic. What is somewhat confusing in both schemas is that they blend the making (*poiesîs*) of the literary work with its reading (interpretation): prefiguration and level I can be seen as the grounding on which authors base their story, or as Ricœur (1984/1990: 64) puts it, prefiguration or preunderstanding is "common to both poets and their readers", although of course it can never coincide (authors and readers differ in knowledge and experience). Configuration for Ricœur (1983/1990: 66) is much the same as plot and level II for Fludernik (1996: 43–44) provides "*access* to the story" (by what she terms TELLING, VIEWING, EXPERIENCING and ACTING). Finally, for Ricœur (1983/1990: 76) the move from configuration to refiguration is "brought about by the act of reading", just as Fludernik's (1996: 44–45) levels III and IV move from narrative and generic considerations to the experience of reading. As perhaps these brief notes on the two views suggest, mimesis for Ricœur concerns how emplotment in narrative works, while for Fludernik it provides the basis for her cognitive and experiential narratology. Despite such differences, they show how central mimesis is for both the creation and reception of (narrative) literature.

Since mimesis in literature is about how reality is represented by making use of both imitation and imagination, the question of how this representation manifests itself is crucial.

2.2 The Range of Mimesis: Literary Imagination as Real and Fantastic

What is considered real and what fantastic is essential for an understanding of mimesis. But let me start with two clarifications. First, the line between fact (or the real or the empirical) and fiction (the fantastic) has been drawn in different ways in different times and cultures. For instance, in Pu Songling's (2006) *Strange Tales from a Chinese Studio* from the seventeenth century, fox spirits and ghosts are not viewed as non-existent creatures but part of the world view of that time in China. As Pu Songling's translator John Minford (2006:

xxv) puts it: "In traditional Chinese thinking the boundary between 'this' world and the world 'beyond' is far more elastic than it is for Western readers today". Pu Songling's stories may expressly be *strange* (based on two extant genres of the fantastic in China), but according to the nineteenth-century explicator Feng Zhenluan they should be read as follows: "Every time one thinks a situation weird, it is in fact very real and true to human nature" (quoted in Minford 2006: xxvii; see also xii–xiv). This is related to another important point: what is portrayed as fantastic may obliquely – metaphorically, allegorically or otherwise – comment on human affairs. In other words, it is not only in (animal) fables that fantastic action comments on human behaviour, at times with serious import. Such observations may seem self-evident, but they have often escaped attention in literary studies in the last century or so.

So far in this chapter we have seen that in twentieth-century literary studies *mimesis* was often understood in the rather narrow sense of imitation. This goes for the notion of *realism* too. One of the most influential books on fiction was Ian Watt's (1957: 9–34) *The Rise of the Novel*, especially its first chapter "Realism and the Novel Form". Its argument of how with the rise of the novel in the eighteenth century centres on "realistic particularity" is usually summarized by Watt's (1957: 17–18) two aspects of realism: "the novel is surely distinguished from other genres and from previous forms of fiction by the amount of attention it habitually accords both to the individualisation of its characters and to the detailed presentation of their environment". What is not always noted is that Watt (1957: 32, 33) is rather careful in making his argument: realism or what he more precisely calls *formal realism* is "only a convention" and the novel – equated with *the realist novel* that allegedly originates in Britain with Defoe, Richardson and Fielding – only includes more such description of character and setting than do Homer and earlier prose fiction, where realist passages "are relatively rare" (see however Olsen 2015). Still, Watt's argument seemed so compelling – perhaps together with the view of the downgrading of mimesis to mere imitation – that it had a major impact on the view of realism entering (Western) literary history in the eighteenth century. Also, Watt's study seemed to corroborate Auerbach's (1946/1991) broader view of literary history as becoming gradually more realist and finally producing the realist novel.

A decade later, another important study of prose fiction – surely the form of literature with the greatest number of genres and subgenres – was published: *The Nature of Narrative* (1966) by Robert Scholes and Robert Kellogg, recently republished in a fortieth anniversary edition with the addition of a chapter on narrative theory by James Phelan (Scholes, Phelan and Kellogg 2006). Central in this work is the view of narrative as divided into "two antithetical types", the *empirical* (cf. the realist) and the *fictional* (cf. the fantastic). The former is subdivided into the *historical* and the *mimetic*, which is seen as "the antithesis of mythic", with the "slice of life" (cf. pure imitation) as its ultimate form. Since the mimetic forms are "the slowest [...] to develop" and ultimately aim to give a "slice of life", mimesis is, in the aftermath of Auerbach and Abrams, clearly viewed as mere imitation (Scholes, Phelan and Kellogg 2006: 13). The fictional is subdivided into the *romantic* and the *didactic* and thus aims to "either beauty or goodness" (Scholes, Phelan and Kellogg 2006: 14). But this is merely the pre-history of fictional narrative in the West, since in *Don Quixote* Cervantes produced "a great and synthetic literary form", the novel (Scholes, Phelan and Kellogg 2006: 15). In claiming that the romance and the novel are combined in *Don Quixote*, the authors went against the rather common view in the mid-twentieth century that the novel has two forms: the mythical, allegorical and action-filled romance-novel and the novel (or the novel of manners) (see e.g. Chase 1957: 12–13). According to the two original authors of *The Nature of Narrative*, the synthesis effected by Cervantes has supposedly gone on and, writing in the mid-1960s, they detected signs of "the grand dialectic [...] about to begin again" in the twentieth century. With the benefit of hindsight, we can now say that this did not occur as such, since magic realism and postmodern fiction have on the contrary included synthetic novels that draw on multiple genres.

These two studies, Watt (1957) and Scholes, Phelan and Kellogg (2006), are instructive in the sense that they were – and in fact to some extent still continue to be – influential not only for students and scholars of narrative fiction but as both theoretically and literary-historically important works with implications for literary studies at large. The first aspect that may strike at least readers with a wide-ranging interest is their Western perspective; another is the narrow view of realism as imitation. For Watt, it is the detailed depiction of character and setting that makes it possible for him to equate the novel with the realist novel. For Scholes, Phelan and Kellogg, mimesis simply aims at a "slice of life". To be sure, they go back to Cervantes and are able to see how complex his great novel is, but view all of prose fiction preceding it as either *empirical* or *fictional* (with dual subdivisions in both), and thus fall prey for the age-old problem of the taxonomist: each work must be in one and only one category: historical, mimetic, romantic or didactic.[13] Throughout history, authors are seldom so formally stringent in their writing that they would only use a single category or genre. Even haiku, one of the briefest forms of poetry, is originally a development of *hokku*, which was the opening stanza of the linked poem called *renga*. Despite

---

[13] However impressive in many other respects, F. K. Stanzel's (1979/1986: xvi *et passim*) *A Theory of Literature* has the same drawback.

some efforts at policing requirements of the form after the Golden Age and its great master, Matsuo Bashō, at the end of the seventeenth century, humour (and other innovations) could not be kept out, so the subgenre *senryu* was formed, so named after the first major humorous author of haikus in the eighteenth century. To be sure, readers and publishers of popular genres often expect strict genre adherence and publishers try to see to it that their authors stick to certain features, but still the push for innovation cannot be kept in check – thus literature changes and genres develop.

Turning back to literary history, we have witnessed something of a global turn lately. As far as I can see, it has still not had a major impact on literary studies, but most likely it will. Here are a few major works that may show the trend – and once again, the study of the novel is the vanguard. Mary Anne Doody's (1996/1998) *The True Story of the Novel* gives the ancient novel its due, shows its complexity and richness and makes some excursions into non-Western works. Frank Moretti's (2006a, 2006b) major two-volume edition *The Novel* draws wider global circles but largely emphasizes the novel after Cervantes. Steven Moore's (2010/2011) *The Novel. An Alternative History. Beginnings to 1600* makes major sweeps into the history of the novel until the Renaissance, including classic Mesoamerican, Indian, Tibetan, Arabic, Persian, Japanese and Chinese novels. In the widening gyre of literary studies the publisher Walter de Gruyter (now De Gruyter) issued a four-volume edition *Literary History: Towards a Global Perspective* (Lindberg-Wada 2006) with one volume on early and oral literatures (I), one on genres (II) and two on modern literature (III and IV). Literary theory has recently taken up the challenge in Richard J. Lane's (2013) anthology *Global Literary Theory*, which like most recent books on literary theory only focuses on the last century or so. Finally, there are two editions on world literature, Theo D'haen et al.'s (2013) *World Literature* and David Damrosch's *World Literature in Theory* (2014), with essays starting from the late eighteenth century and Goethe's famous remarks launching the notion of *world literature* in 1827, respectively, to a wide range of recent topics.

Hence, literary studies are increasingly aware that literature has a much wider history than has been so far recognized. And what this history amply shows, I would suggest, is that the simplistic equation between realism and imitation or the severance between literature that is either empirical (realist) or fictional (fantastic) simply does not hold. By considering some literature from various cultures and ages I now try to show that Watt's focal point in defining formal realism in fiction (the novel) – the detailed depiction of character and setting – are found in much literature that is neither realist fiction nor prose fiction as such and that different kinds of realist literature can also include fantastic features and vice versa. This does not mean that I think that demarcations like the real and the fantastic are pointless, but that they should be employed with caution and always be anchored to particular literary contexts in order to be maximally useful.

To go as far back as possible: What is Sumerian poetry, the oldest extant poetry, about? Certainly it focuses on mythological characters, such as the shepherd Dumuzi who marries the goddess Inanna and then dies, since he represents "seasonal abundance" (see Jacobsen 1987: 1–84, 1 quote). In other words, they represent humans and gods, who by liaison or love produce the crop in the agricultural society of Mesopotamia: the real as combined with the mythical. Sumerian poetry includes myths and epics, royal love songs and hymns to the gods and many of them are dramatic in form. In short, narrative, drama and lyrical poetry are all represented. But what are they about *thematically*? Thorkild Jacobsen (1987: 2), who has made a fine compilation of Sumerian literature, presents the texts relating to Dumuzi "in terms of the underlying pattern of human life in which these powers of nature were understood and the human reactions to them expressed: courtship and wedding, death and mourning". If such themes – in whatever forms they take – do not represent various kinds of "slice of life", I do not know what does.

But, you may say, this does not necessarily mean the character or setting receives detailed accounts. True, but are character and setting really the defining criteria of formal realism? Well, let us suppose they are. What is the earliest Indian and Chinese (folk) poetry about? It deals mainly with love and war, more specifically heartfelt portrayals by various speakers to different situations occurring in relationships and war-making. In the lyrical poem "Bo Is Brave" Bo is depicted as an "outrider of the king", but more importantly in the second stanza we learn that the speaker is a woman longing for him who would don her hair, "But for whom should I want to look nice?" she asks (*The Book of Songs* 1937/1996: 53). Most of the poems represent such key emotional moments, at times portrayed through animal or other nature imagery, but to the same effect – thus portraying character. What about setting? A classic haiku should include a *kigo*, a word drawn from a particular list of words defining the exact seasonal situation of the poem, usually with a surprising change. What is more, this change can be surprising for the speaker but more importantly for the reader (or listener) – that is, there is detailed description of setting as well as a human reaction to it. Thus, character and setting is at least obliquely portrayed even in ancient lyrical poetry.

In a modern narrative poem, such as T. S. Eliot's (1922/2015) *The Waste Land*, there are both recognizable character types dramatized in a particular setting (such as the working-class people in a pub in "II. A Game of Chess") and a plethora of references to London, but what anchors much of the poem in recognizable history are the allusions to literature and myth. The references to literary tradition are also palpably realistic – historiographically speaking, they showcase ancillary evidence of a past culture –, starting with the allusion to the beginning of Chaucer's *Canterbury Tales*. The allusive richness in (however brief) characterization, setting and Western and Indian literary and mythical tradition makes it one of the referentially richest poems of the twentieth century.

In drama we could consider a medieval Chinese Yüan play, such as *The Injustice Done to Tou Gno*, in which Tou Gno's unfair suffering is depicted throughout the play, including her execution (shown on stage), and her resurrection as a ghost wreaking vengeance on her wrongdoers by telling her father what happened (Kuan Han-ch'ing 1972). In this way, the real and the fantastic blend in the portrayal of Tou Gno, and the audience could savour the fact that – in contrast to their experience – the wrongdoers from higher social strata are for once punished. As for setting in drama, one could think of Elizabethan and Jacobean theatre in England, where the lack of setting made playwrights like Shakespeare continuously include references to setting so that the audience in its mind's eye could see and feel what it is like. Just consider how the forest of Arden in *As You Like It* is portrayed by multiple references in Duke Senior's speech at the start of Act II, as he takes "the icy fang, / And the churlish chiding of the winter's wind" as "counsellors / That feelingly persuade me what I am" (Shakespeare 1982/1987: 220; II.i: 6 – 7, 10 – 11). The audience can feel the winter and perceive the Duke's reaction to it.

To take a more recent example, in the theatre of the absurd not everything is absurd. Think of Samuel Beckett: in early plays, like *Waiting for Godot* and *Happy Days*, the very starting-point is bizarre: two characters wait for a third who never shows up and two characters are buried in the sand and cannot get away. But in such extreme circumstances their rather quirky behaviour is rather understandable, even psychologically realistic. In Beckett's later one-act plays the circumstances of the character or characters are not as absurd as their behaviour: a character may walk back and forth in a manically exact manner talking to her ailing mother offstage (*Footfalls*) or rock in a rocking chair speaking to herself (*Rockaby*), but what unfolds are life stories which suggest that the protagonists are – or have become – somewhat deranged (see Beckett 1986/1990). In other words, all characters, however strange at first sight, act in rather plausible, even realistic ways *in their condition or frame of mind*. Understandably, mid-twentieth century audiences found such situations and characters absurd, since they were not used to see them on stage.

As for setting in (prose) fiction before the realist novel, it is easy to find suitable examples. Let me quote one of the most striking ones I know from the first page of Heliodorus's (1989/2008: 353) *An Ethiopian Story* (or *Aithiopika*), a romance novel from the second century CE. A group of bandits have come over a mountain and have a view of the sea:

> But the beach! – a mass of newly slain bodies, some of them quite dead, others half-alive and still twitching, testimony that the fighting had only just ended. To judge by the signs this had been no proper battle. Amongst the carnage were the miserable remnants of festivities that had come to this unhappy end. There were tables still set with food, and others upset on the ground, held in dead men's hands; in the fray they had served some as weapons, for this had been an impromptu conflict; beneath other tables men had crawled in the vain hope of hiding there. There were wine bowls upturned, and some slipping from the hands that held them; some had been drinking from them, others using them like stones, for the suddenness of the catastrophe had caused objects to be put to strange, new uses and taught men to use drinking vessels as missiles. There they lay, here a man felled by an axe, there another struck down by a stone picked up then and there from the shingly beach; here a man battered to death with a club, there another burned to death with a brand from the fire.

The description goes on, but it is rendered in such detail that any director making it into the first scene in a film would have no problem staging it. Furthermore, the scene is focalised by the bandits, so readers are offered this view of carnage by rather stoic men, who as they are viewing the aftermath of a blood-shed can piece together what has happened. As readers we get a detailed description as well as a particular reaction to it by the fact that it is viewed through the eyes – and minds – of the bandits: detailed portrayal of setting and an implicit portrayal of the minds of the spectators. Clearly, this is a powerful passage of realist fiction, even in Watt's sense, although the work in many other respects is a romance.[14] But the opposite can also happen: a realist novel can have a fantastic frame, as in the first Chinese realist novel, *A Dream of Red Chambers*, originally written by the Chinese author Cao Xueqin and published in 1791, in which a stone is given life and becomes the narrator (see Cao and Gao 1978/2008).

Detailed and complex characterization and focalisation is also found at least as early as the eighteen-book Indian epic *The Mahābhārata*, originating in the eighth or ninth centuries BCE and receiving its final form in the fourth century CE. The story of the animosity and war between the two sets of cousins – the heroic Pāndavas and the villainous Kauravas – includes complex characterization of the protagonists, heroes as well as villains. One of the most complex ones is Bhīsma, the self-sacrificing grand old man of the dynasty, who is forced

---

14 No wonder *An Ethiopian Story* became popular in Byzantium and later influenced Sidney, Cervantes and Racine, among others (see Reardon 1989/2008: 352).

2.2 The Range of Mimesis: Literary Imagination as Real and Fantastic — 57

to fight on the side of the Kauravas and finally on his death bed gives a long sermon to Yudhisthira, the Pāndava king. When this "best heir of Bharata", the mythical dynasty that founded India, lets the great Pāndava warrior Arjuna mortally wound him (although he can choose when to die, which he does all of six books later), his reasoning is given in terms of what he "thought to himself" (*The Mahābhārata* 2009: 406; 6.111). But perhaps the most complex character of all is Krishna, both god and man, who lends his aid to both warring parties and acts a kind of middle man in divine and human affairs.[15]

The Tale of Genji written by Murasaki Shikibu (Lady Murasaki) in Japan in the first decade of the eleventh century is often considered the first novel, for some even the first realist novel. Here too characterization entails not only behaviour, action, pronouncements and clothing but also focalisation by multiple characters when interacting. Thus, when Prince Genji has seduced a young girl and they wake up in the morning to voices shouting, he at first perceives what is going on (in Royall Tyler's translation):

> Dawn must have been near, because he heard uncouth men in the neighboring houses hailing one another as they awoke. [...] She was deeply embarrassed by this chatter and clatter all around them of people rising and preparing to go about their pitiful tasks. The place would have made anyone with any pretensions want to sink through the floor, but she remained serene and betrayed no response to any sound, however painful, offensive, or distressing, and her manner retained so naive a grace that the dismal commotion might have meant nothing to her. Genji therefore forgave her more readily than if she had been openly ashamed. [...] She was engagingly frail in the modesty of her soft, pale gray-violet gown over layers of white, and although she had nothing striking about her, her slender grace and her manner of speaking moved him deeply. (Murasaki 2001/2003: 63)

Prince Genji perceives her but his perception enters her so deeply that we learn what she actually feels ("deeply embarrassed"). Then the focus turns back to Genji, who in turn is characterized by his selfish and patronizing view of the girl. And the double characterization goes on: as the girl is described mostly through Genji's eyes, readers learn as much about him as about the girl.[16]

---

[15] For a brief but insightful reading of the complexity in Krishna's character see Smith (2009: xxxiv–xli).

[16] In Edward G. Seidensticker's translation the shifts in focalisation between Genji and the girl are more clearly marked: "He could make out every word. It embarrassed the woman that, so near at hand, there should be this clamor of preparation as people set forth on their sad little enterprises. Had she been one of those stylish ladies of the world, she would have wanted to shrivel up and disappear. She was a placid sort, however, and she seemed to take nothing, painful or embarrassing or unpleasant, too seriously. [...] He much preferred this easygoing bewilder-

So much for proving that central realist features occurred in all kinds of literature well before the realist novel, and even before Cervantes. But in fact even more intriguing is to see how and why realist and fantastic traits have so easily been blended in literature.

The origins seem rather evident. In olden times in, say, Mesopotamia, Egypt, Mesoamerica, India and China humans consorted with or at least were affected by gods and goddesses, mythical characters and beasts and other supernatural creatures, all of whom acted in more or less human ways. One of the most influential literary works ever is surely the first collection of fables, *The Pañćatantra*, originally composed on the basis of oral tales in Sanskrit before or at about the start of the Common Era, apparently by a scholar called Visnu Śarma (1993).[17] The fables about animals may have stereotypical features, such as nobility (Lively) or cunning (Wily), but act in all sorts of ways, intelligently as well as stupidly. According to the frame story, the stories are told so as to educate three ignorant princes – and what they learn is "*how* to think, not *what* to think" (Rajan 1993: xxxiii). This is of course the point of the entire collection – to delight its readers and make them learn something about life at the same time (see 8.1). According to *The Nature of Narrative*, the didactic is part of the fictional, thus far removed from the empirical. But what *The Pañćatantra* and other animal fables have shown for millennia is that the didactic can not only be delightfully playful and fairytale-like, but that its teachings can be about, even mould, the world as we know it. Of course, George Orwell too knew this when penning *Animal Farm*.

In terms of the rather underdeveloped theory of literary characters, I find soundest the views that combine life with literary artifice, which can explain the various sorts of characters discussed above. Baruch Hochman (1985: 59) writes about how we should be aware of the reciprocity and difference between real people and characters (as artifice) or what he terms *Homo Sapiens* and *Homo Fictus*. More recently and inspired cognitive literary studies, Blakey Vermeule (2010: 247–248) shows how readers are *absorbed* by characters (by getting to

---

ment to a show of consternation, a face scarlet with embarrassment. [...] She was pretty and fragile in a soft, modest cloak of lavender and a lined white robe" (Murasaki 1976/1985: 28).
17 Some 200 versions in about fifty languages existed even in the early twentieth century and it – or some of the tales later included in it – is said to have inspired (some of) Aesop's *Fables*, *The Arabian Nights*, *Gesta Romanorum*, Boccaccio's *The Decameron*, Chaucer's *Canterbury Tales*, La Fontaine's *Fables* and even Br'er Rabbit stories (most famously in Joel Chandler Harris's *Tales of Uncle Remus*, 1880–1948) and through them countless others. As Gutenberg had (re-)invented movable-type printing (the Chinese preceded him by four centuries), one of the first books printed was the German translation *Das Buch der Beyspiele* in 1483. For these and other notes on *The Pañćatantra*'s influence see Rajan (1993: xv–xvi, xix).

know their minds) at the same time that they *suspend* their final judgements about them (well knowing that what they are reading is literature). It is this sort of duality that seems to come across in all literature, whether real, fantastic or – as so often – real *and* fantastic. A particularly intriguing blend is to be found in Kurt Vonnegut's (1989/1990) *Jailbird*, where actual politicians figure marginally but the names of many of the main characters draw on corrupt politicians throughout American history, thus strengthening its Watergate theme (see Pettersson 1994: 291–298). And often one is at the service of the other: real elements may substantiate the fantastic and fantastic elements can enliven the real.

The same is true of setting, since fantasy worlds or alien planets often come alive – in a sense, are made real – by detailed description, as in Tolkien's Middle-earth or Lem's Solaris. But the reverse can happen too: after a thirty-page realist description of the main street and the people on it in St. Petersburg, Nikolai Gogol (1835/1998: 278) ends his story "Nevsky Prospect" by the narrator claiming that "everything breathes deceit" there "and the devil himself lights the lamps only so as to show everything not as it really looks". In doing so, together with Gogol's (1998: 243–424) other so-called Petersburg tales, "Nevsky Prospect" started the great tradition in Russian fiction of portraying cities in fantastic terms, as in Andrei Bely's *Petersburg* and Moscow in Mikhail Bulgakov's *The Master and Margarita* – just as London was turned into an unreal city in H. G. Wells's *The War of the Worlds* and T. S. Eliot's *The Waste Land*. On the other hand, William Faulkner's Yoknapatawpha County or Gabriel García Márquez's Macondo (in *One Hundred Years of Solitude*) draw on areas in the American South and Colombia, respectively, but remain fictional, whereas Elsinore in *Hamlet* or Oxford in Philip Pullman's Oxford in *His Dark Materials* resemble the real towns but have evident imaginary features.

As far as fantastic fiction is concerned, one of the foremost scholars of realism J. P. Stern (1973: 129) notes that fantastic fiction makes use of realist aspects in two opposite ways to strengthen the fantastic effect: Poe and Kafka anchor the fantastic "in several areas of experience" by various details, whereas in their satires Swift and Rabelais use fantastic and unrealistic detail at the service of "something as realistic as a critique of our political beliefs or a challenge to our defective moral experience". The above excerpt from *The Tale of Genji* substantiates the portrayal of Prince Genji and the girl, before the chapter moves into a decidedly Gothic mode in its description and characterization as, inexplicably, the beautiful girl suddenly dies. The references to "foxes" – in the sense of fox spirits, the popular Far East trope for ghostly femmes fatales – help to guide readers in their interpretation, as they occur in passages preceding and following this one (Murasaki 2001/2003: 62, 67). Not only magic realist fiction but all realist fiction from Charles Dickens (*Great Expectations*) and Thomas Hardy (*Tess of the d'Urbervilles*) to, say, Toni Morrison (*Beloved*) and Don DeLillo (*The Body Artist*) include exaggerated coincidences and ghostly occurrences, which makes it all the more fascinating.

Ever since realism became central in fiction authors have been aware that the realistic and the fantastic can co-occur. As Robert Louis Stevenson (1883/1925: 100) puts it, "All representative art, which can be said to live, is both realistic and ideal; and the realism about which we quarrel is a matter purely of externals". Even practising postmodern novelists in the heyday of postmodern fiction understood that all literature, however fantastic, has a mimetic basis, in the sense that it combines the imitative with the creative. Christine Brooke-Rose and John Barth saw the real in the unreal from *One Thousand and One Nights* and *Don Quijote* to postmodern fiction.

> [U]ltimately all fiction is realistic, whether it mimes a mythic idea of heroic deeds or a progressive idea of society, inner psychology or, as now. [sic] the non-interpretatibility of the world, which is our reality as its interpretatibility once was (and may return). A fantastic realism. (Brooke-Rose 1981/1983: 388)
>
> [N]ot only is all fiction fiction about fiction, but all fiction about fiction is in fact fiction about life. Some of us understood that all along. (Barth 1984: 236)

How else could it be when the very circumstances that made writing possible in the first place are so amply evident in all literature? When humans started to form communities, from nomadic bands to tribes to chiefdoms and finally to states, no writing existed until the formation of states. The first states were formed about 3 700 BCE in Mesopotamia – and somewhat later in Mexico, China, Egypt and then elsewhere in the Middle East and the Indus Valley –, and they were the ones that invented and/or adopted writing systems. Thus, Jared Diamond's (1997/1998: 236) point is important: "all of the early adaptations of [...] invented systems [of writing] [...] involved socially stratified societies with complex and centralized political institutions" (see also Zarrilli et al. 2010: 3–13). The centralized political institution is implicitly evident in the most widespread formula in literature in the world's largest Indo-European language family: a hero (the king or his emissary) is sent out to slay a dragon (later another hero or a villain) (see Watkins 1995/2001). Why must the dragon be killed? Because it – or the evil forces it stands for – is a threat to the society the hero represents. This plot formula is central in Westerns, detective fiction (especially hard-boiled) and thrillers, even if the protagonist in these more recent popular genres often has a vague position between the heroes and the villains, the line between whom may also be blurred.

To be sure, there were wars between clans (*The Mahābhārata*) and kingdoms (*The Iliad*) that were orally traded for centuries before written down, but they too were about states, their in-fighting or wars. Much early poetry and drama, if at times with mythical connotations, in fact depicts the very life sphere that people were familiar with: love, war and quotidian life. And however fantastic and lacking in moral intent literature may be – with bizarre creatures and ghosts, vampires and fox spirits, magic and murder, false monks and cunning gamblers as in the medieval *Kathāsaritsāgara* by the Kashmiri author Somadeva (1994/1996) or *Strange Tales from a Chinese Studio* by Pu Songling (2006) –, it draws on oral traditions with particular world views and shows how speakers and characters act in such extreme and supernatural circumstances. Finally, readers can be thrilled by such literature and at the same time learn about advantageous or disadvantageous behaviour if faced with weird or horrific events (see 8.1 on how literature benefits through delight).

Why refer to such obscure classics, you may ask – who has read them anyway? The *Kathāsaritsāgara* includes versions of the same stories found in *The Pañcatantra* and has like that collection of fables had an immeasurable effect on literature all over the world. As for *Strange Tales from a Chinese Studio*, Franz Kafka, at times called the most influential author of the twentieth century, was quite taken by Martin Buber's edition of Pu Songling's remarkable stories,[18] about which Buber (1911/1998: 111) said in his foreword: "the Chinese avoid all mystifying, shattering horror; instead, we have the magic of the lucid. Here the order of nature is not ruptured but extended; nothing interferes with the plenitude of life, and everything living carries the seed of the ghostly". This seems to characterize both Pu Songling's and (at least in part) Kafka's (1983/2005) short fiction, some of which Buber also published in his periodical *Der Jude* (see Murray 2004/2006: 254–255) and for which Kafka also drew on Buber's edition of Zhuangzi's classic philosophical parables (Buber 1910/1998). Similarly Mo Yan, the Nobel Prize winner for literature of 2012, speaks in his Nobel lecture of Pu Songling as "one of the greatest storytellers of all time" and of how his own fiction carries on "the tradition he had perfected" (see nobelprize.org). Classics often live on in contemporary literature, even if readers are not always aware of their influence.

Thus, as much as what happens or is depicted in literature, whether close to the life sphere of the recipients or not, the reactions to or depictions of what happens is at least as important. But literature does not just blend the real and the fantastic in seemingly haphazard or idiosyncratic ways, but does so largely building on existing conventions we call genres. Next let us consider the close

---

18 In a letter from January 1916 Kafka describes Pu Songling's stories as "prachtvoll" (formidable); see Minford (2006: xxxi, note 31).

relations between mimesis and genre, that is, literary representation and some of its forms.

2.3 On the Interrelation between Mimesis and Genre

First a few words on how the relation between mimesis and genre has changed in prose fiction since the early nineteenth century. In fact, I feel that this change has been so slow and the perspective on it is so short that its extent has not been duly recognized. What perhaps has amounted to an anomaly in literary history has been taken for a normal state of affairs.

On Western Narrative Genres since about 1800

When Mary Shelley wrote *Frankenstein* and Edgar Allan Poe his short stories about C. Auguste Dupin in the early nineteenth century, they did not intend to start the new genres of science fiction and detective fiction, respectively. Nor did their primary audiences think they did. *Frankenstein* seemed much like a scientifically inspired variation of the Gothic fiction familiar to readers at the time and Poe's "The Murders in Rue Morgue", "The Purloined Letter" and "The Mystery of Marie Roget" had, as Heather Worthington (2005) has shown, ample precursors in both the popular press and in Gothic and Newgate novels. This, of course, is nothing new in genre theory: labels often come after the fact and are based on a number of aspects that vary from case to case. What is important to understand is that although there were different markets and readerships for various kinds of fiction, all through the nineteenth century there was no hard-and-fast distinction between the empirical and the fictional (or fantastic) in prose fiction. To be sure, readers could distinguish between, say, the romance-novel and the novel *per se*, but genre distinctions in fiction were more fluid, for authors, publishers as well as readers. For instance, Hawthorne and Melville and later Dostoevsky and Twain wrote fantastic stories with evident science-fiction features as well as realist fiction (see Franklin 1978). In fact, when H. G. Wells in the 1890s more or less single-handedly pioneered some of the most lasting subgenres of science fiction by *The Time Machine, The Island of Doctor Moreau, The Invisible Man, The War of the Worlds* and *When the Sleeper Wakes* (later renamed *The Sleeper Awakes*), he still thought of them as falling under the then current term *scientific romances*, the former word pointing to its basis in science, the latter signalling the fictional aspect.

For a Western reading public up until the twentieth century, it seems that Margaret Anne Doody's (1996/1998: 15) vehemently argued case against separating romance and the novel would ring true: "Romance and the novel are one. The separation between them is part of a problem, not part of a solution". Doody's point is that the separation that has been taken for granted since the eighteenth century does not hold, and elsewhere I have tried to show that the related simplistic separation of postmodern fiction and realist fiction is not tenable (Pettersson 2007). However, as pulp fiction proliferated and turned into various subgenres in the first decades of the twentieth century when the modernist novel had its heyday, a triple polarisation occurred in Western fiction between

(1) experimental and traditional,
(2) serious (highbrow) and popular (lowbrow) and
(3) realist genres (mainly the mainstream novel) and fantastic genres (genre fiction).

The tendency was for experimental fiction to be serious and (implicitly) aimed at elite readers. If understood broadly, much of it was realist in tendency in the sense that after naturalism the epistemological frontier of fictional exploration moved from society to the human mind (*vide* Proust, Joyce, Woolf). But a widespread simplification, even misconception, during the rest of the century was to equate fantastic genres with the lowbrow, popular and traditional. Symptomatic of these divisions was the celebrated dispute between H. G. Wells championing Life (that is, fiction as an investigation of life) and Henry James advocating fiction as Art (that is, the modernist novel).[19]

By blurring the triple polarisation during its prime between about 1960 and 1990 postmodern fiction did much to prove that such simple dichotomies do not hold. After about 1990 or so postmodern techniques have affected, even shaped, much mainstream fiction to the extent that many novels – by, say, Toni Morrison and Dave Eggers in the United States and Julian Barnes and Jeanette Winterson in Britain – display assorted amalgams of realist, fantastic and self-conscious features. This is why I feel that the point made by Scholes and Kellogg in 1966 and reprinted in the new edition of Scholes, Phelan and Kellogg (2006: 15) about a new division between the empirical and the fictional in fiction is not

---

[19] It should be noted that some mainstream realist authors in the twentieth century, such as E. M. Forster, Graham Greene and John Cheever, did not bother to adhere to this division, since they also wrote science fiction, as Harry Harrison (1971) has shown.

tenable.[20] To be sure, genre fiction thrives in many respects, but often it draws on genres beyond the primary one. In fact, the generic range in contemporary science fiction is so widespread that two recent attempts to define science fiction refuse to do so in terms of genre. Farah Mendlesohn (2003: 1) finds it best to term science fiction "an ongoing discussion" rather than a genre and Istvan Csicsery-Ronay, Jr. (2008: 5) merely calls it "a particular, recognizable mode of thought and art" and proceeds to discuss its varieties. In this way, they not only corroborate the tendency of postmodern fiction informing science fiction and vice versa that Brian McHale (1987: 65, 68) detected a long time ago but also show that innovative genre fiction is becoming as generically varied as much mainstream fiction. In short, despite the fact that many kinds of genre fiction still thrive, innovative fiction has returned to the greater generic openness that fiction often displayed before the twentieth century. Thus, in terms of genre, the twentieth century with its triple polarisations between different kinds of fiction was something of an anomaly, and it seems that all three divisions are largely now on the wane, even though genre fiction of many kinds flourish and keep on multiplying into various subgenres.

On Mimesis and Genre

Understandably, with the proliferation of fictional genres and subgenres in the twentieth century, narrative studies could not do without the notion of genre, often implicitly viewed in relation to the empirical (realist) and the fictional (fantastic) on a kind of mimetic scale (see Scholes, Phelan and Kellogg 2006: 13). This is why it may come as some surprise that the relation between mimesis and genre has not as far as I know been dealt with at length. At times it is dismissed, at times highlighted, but usually only in passing. In her chapter on literary knowledge in *Uses of Literature* Rita Felski (2008: 83) challenges Marjorie Perloff's dismissal of generic and formal features as secondary in some literary texts by stating: "In reality, knowledge and genre are inescapably intertwined, if only because all forms of knowing – whether poetic or political, exquisitely lyrical or numbingly matter-of-fact – rely on an array of formal resources, stylistic conventions, and conceptual schemata". But unfortunately she does not go on to substantiate her view.

---

20 However, Phelan's (2006: 333) additional chapter to the 2006 edition shows a contemporary awareness by pointing out new narrative "instabilities" as "history and culture prompt innovations in narrative form".

In literary theory and criticism the relation between mimesis and genre may seldom have been discussed, but I would suggest this is due to the fact that when studying one, the other is taken for granted. Auerbach (1946/1991) does not discuss the genre of the epic or the modernist novel, but his readings of *The Odyssey* and *To the Lighthouse* clearly build on their generic features. Similarly, one of the classic studies on genre, Alastair Fowler's (1982) *Kinds of Fiction*, may only touch on mimesis in passing (mainly in the sense of 'imitation'), but his analysis of genre draws in many ways on literary representation. In the perhaps most encompassing theoretical study of realist fiction, *Theories of Literary Realism*, Darío Villanueva displays the rather unstable view of mimesis in recent literary studies. At first, in a Platonic manner he straightforwardly equates mimesis with imitation in general and realism in particular, as he states that "*mimesis* was the classical name of the relationship between literature and reality before it was replaced by the relatively recent term 'realism'" (Villanueva 1992/1997: 2). By his short history of the relation of the terms realism and mimesis in literary history, Villanueva (1992/1997: 5–14) shows that he is in good company when doing so. However, he repeatedly stresses that reality is reproduced "creatively" – thus showing a more Aristotelian and inclusive conception of the term (Villanueva 1992/1997: 9). He goes on to discuss two warring assumptions at the root of representation in literary works – their relation to reality and their autonomy – and finds that they can lead to fallacies he terms *mimetic* and *aesthetic*, maintaining that his "ultimate goal is to reach a balanced understanding of literature as an art form and a sign of reality" (Villanueva 1992/1997: 12–13, 13 quote).

It may be symptomatic that when the relation between mimesis and genre is discussed in any detail, it is in relation to particular genres in fiction. For instance, in *Mimesis, Genres and Post-Colonial Discourse* Jean-Pierre Durix (1998: 15–59, 43 quote) discusses whether genres still are relevant in postcolonial fiction and comes to the conclusion that although postcolonial authors have been influenced by postmodernism, they "have also shown a renewed interest in the potential of the realistic mode". He studies realism, fantasy and mimesis in relation to postcolonial fiction and shows how magic realism is a kind of hybrid genre that combines fantasy and realism. In her encompassing study of magic realism in contemporary British fiction Anne C. Hegerfeldt (2005: 320) does much the same, and notes the aptness of Brooke-Rose's (1981/1983: 388) term *fantastic realism* to much magic realist fiction. It is hardly a coincidence that discussions of genre in relation to mimesis have of late occurred in studies of magic realism, but it may be worthwhile to broaden the discussion.

My claim here is that mimesis and genre are closely related in novels, and thus that the analysis of their generic features is implicitly based on mimetic features and vice versa. Let me illustrate the interrelation of mimesis and genre by three different kinds of science-fiction novel and a realist novel with science-fiction motifs. My examples are H. G. Wells's science-fiction classic *The War of the Worlds* (1898), William Gibson's seminal cyperpunk novel *Neuromancer* (1984), the perhaps most acclaimed graphic novel ever, *Watchmen* (1986) by Alan Moore and Dave Gibbons, and Junot Díaz's Pulitzer-Prize winner *The Brief Wondrous Life of Oscar Wao* (2007), a generically complex realist novel.

But first we should briefly consider the notion of genre, which of course with its Latin basis in *genus* is a much more recent notion than mimesis. In his important study on genre, *The Architext*, Gérard Genette (1979/1992: 8–23, especially 12, 23) has persuasively demonstrated that we do not find genres in the sense of worked-out systems of form in either Plato or Aristotle but rather *situations of enunciating* or *modes*. As Genette (1979/1992: 23–60, 66 quote) traces the history of modes and how they turn into main genres, he does not discuss mimesis but shows how in the final analysis "all species and subgenres, genres, or supergenres are empirical classes, established by observation of the historical facts or, if need be, by extrapolation from those facts – that is, by a deductive activity superimposed on an initial activity that is always inductive and analytical". Here Genette indicates how establishing literary genres in general and the genres of particular literary works depend on inductive analysis and observation-based deduction. Similarly, establishing the mimesis of any literary work goes from inductively observing the text to the extra-textual reality or realities it represents, during which process readers make use of whatever knowledge they have of those realities. However, part and parcel of interpreting the mimetic aspects of any literary work is understanding how it relates to the literary genre or genres it employs.

Hence, as I see it, the hermeneutic circle takes into account much more than a straightforward understanding of that notion as the interrelation of part and whole when interpreting. No literary work can be read without a simultaneous understanding of its mimetic and generic aspects. Without understanding what and how it represents, you cannot grasp its (often complex) status on a scale from the empirical to the fictional, just as without knowing the generic status of a work, you cannot grasp what is original about it. But what is more, despite the paucity of literary studies combining mimesis and genre, neither mimetic nor generic analysis can be done in depth, if either aspect is totally disregarded. As the genre theorist John Frow (2006: 101) puts it, "We read, consciously or unconsciously, for those layers of background knowledges which texts evoke and which are generically shaped and generically specific". Thus, even though Frow does not mention the notion of mimesis, his view of genre implicitly entails it (see Frow 2006: 46). What I attempt to do below by discussing science fiction in relation to realist fiction is to show how they can be better understood when their mimetic and generic aspects are studied in relation to each other.

It is well-known that in order for fiction to come alive for readers the what-if premise, or what Darko Suvin (1974/1988: 37) following Ernst Bloch has termed *novum* in science fiction, must be afforded a realist frame, that is, in Suvin's terms, it must be "validated by cognitive logic".[21] This is why the relation between science fiction and realism is especially appropriate for studying the various ways in which mimesis works in fiction. As we saw above, in J. P. Stern's (1973) view, realism in fantastic fiction can be on the level of detail or of overriding import, which I find important when, at the end of this chapter, I suggest that mimesis can also occur on an allegorical level. What is more, one of Stern's (1973: 129) central claims – realism "combines with other modes to form integrated wholes" – is borne home by Brooke-Rose's (1981/1983: 85–102) point that science fiction employs thirteen of the fifteen procedures that Philippe Hamon (1973) has found central to realist fiction. However, since the thrust of her argument seems to have been overlooked, it is important to reassert the rather close connection between science fiction and realist fiction in the more encompassing perspective of mimesis and genre.

Science Fiction and Realist Fiction

Let us now consider how some fiction most readers today would term science fiction and realist fiction, respectively, blend mimetic and generic aspects. H. G. Wells's *The War of the Worlds* (1898) is in many ways *the* seminal novel about alien invasion. In a way that since has become conventional, the narrator (who later announces his presence as a first-person character narrator) voices his and thus the readers' amazement at the what-if premise.

> No one would have believed, in the last years of the nineteenth century, that this world was being watched [...] keenly and closely by intelligences greater than man's and yet as mortal as his own [...]. With infinite complacency men went to and fro over this globe about their little affairs, serene in their assurance of their empire over matter. [---] Yet across the gulf of space, minds that are to our minds as ours are to those of the beasts that perish, [...] intellects vast and cool and unsympathetic, regarded this earth with envious eyes, and slowly

---

[21] In a sense, Fludernik (1996) can be seen as a broadening of Suvin's view of science fiction into a cognitive and experiential account of all kinds of narrative fiction.

and surely drew their plans against us. And early in the twentieth century came the great disillusionment. (Wells 1898/2005: 7)[22]

This excerpt from the first paragraph suggests many features. It starts out announcing the existence of aliens and the narrator's incredulous acceptance of this fact. Then it compares the aliens' superiority to man in terms of man's superiority to other animals in evolutionary terms. But it also mentions how humans go "about their little affairs", thus establishing what could be termed the human perspective. This comparison of scale in human and alien matters announces the theme of the novel: the juxtaposition between aliens and humans and the clash between their intelligences, as evinced primarily by military technology. Perceptive readers may also note that the aliens are described as mortal, thus perhaps anticipating their final defeat. However, from a generic point of view, it is important to note that the clash between aliens and humans is announced as having happened in the early years of the twentieth century. This corroborates the fact that this is fiction, not only for readers in 1898 (or in 1897 when the novel was first serialised) but for literary-historically aware readers ever since.

This what-if premise of the existence of aliens in the present (of readers at the end of the nineteenth century) and the human awareness of them in the future (of the early years of the twentieth century) is not only a fictional but a science-fictional one. However, for that premise to have a maximum effect on readers, Wells knew from Gothic fiction and previous invasion fiction (see 7.3), the "little affairs" of men must be represented in some detail. What the first chapters of the novel go on to describe is the mind, character and erudition of the narrator. He provides contemporary facts on Mars, describes the Martians and compares them to humans (see e.g. the notes in the edition used here; 187–199). Thus, the then received facts that the narrator provides in the first few pages about Mars – such as its distance from the sun, its size and features – paradoxically both substantiate the novel as science fiction and strengthen its realistic portrayal by the narrator's knowledge of science. The narrator goes on to recount some of the current research on Mars in the late nineteenth century, naming the famous astronomers Schiaparelli and Perrotin and their observations of Mars, and then introduces the fictional astronomer Ogilvy as an acquaintance of his (10). Thus, Wells does what would become the staple of "hard" as well as of much pulp science fiction: he introduces the scientific facts as a realistic backdrop against which the fictional premise is developed.

---

[22] The edition of each novel analysed in this chapter is given by year of publication and page number when first quoted. Subsequent references are by page number.

In terms of location and character, Wells goes on to give details of the "little affairs" of men. He vividly evokes small towns (now suburbs) close to London, especially the narrator's hometown Woking in Surrey, where he himself lived when penning the novel. In fact, the first falling star or meteorite (later recognized as the alien spaceship) is most likely first observed by people in "Berkshire, Surrey, and Middlesex" before it lands "on the common between Horsell, Ottershaw, and Woking" (13). Thus, Wells carefully zooms in and names actual locations to increase the realist portent – even actual streets, such as Chobham Road in Woking, are mentioned (19). This specificity also goes for character psychology. The narrator, Ogilvy and a London journalist called Henderson act with plausible realist motivation: they are incredulous and cautiously investigate "the Thing" on Horsell Common (11 *et passim*). The narrator himself notes that at the time he, much like his author, was married and "much occupied in learning to ride the bicycle, [...] and busy upon a series of papers discussing the probable developments of moral ideas as civilization progressed" (12). Such detailed depiction at the beginning of the novel provides a firm realist basis that makes the impact of the subsequent fantastic element (the alien invasion) all the more shocking – the kind of narrative tactics familiar from Gothic fiction and later prevalent in thriller and horror fiction from John le Carré to Stephen King. Moreover, the realist basis of *The War of the Worlds* is provided allegorical levels not only in terms of evolutionary conflict but also of national conflict (see Aldiss 2005: xvi–xvii), as the news of the first Martian cylinder "did not make the sensation that an ultimatum to Germany would have done" (35).[23]

The very title of the novel and the titles of its two books – "The Coming of the Martians" and "The Earth under the Martians" – may signal the science-fiction design, but the narration of the novel perseveres in its realist description. Finally, the narrator underlines his candour without a trace of irony, as he notes that "I set this down as I have set all this story down, as it was" (149). The form of the novel is largely that of a fairly straightforward journal depicting the arrival, assault and destruction of the Martians on earth during about four weeks (see 175). In mimetic terms, the journal is a comparatively open genre, its range spanning factual and imaginative commentary. As the narrator walks towards London, actual locations – such as Richmond, the Thames, Roehampton, Hammersmith, Putney Hill, Lambeth, South Kensington, Fulham Road, Baker Street, Westminster, Hyde Park and the Crystal Palace – are repeatedly mentioned so as to corroborate the realist basis. In fact, so detailed is the description that my edition of the novel includes an appendix of the locations of

---

[23] For an analysis of the development of invasion fiction see 7.3.

the novel, including maps of London and its surroundings (181–185). What is more, the narrator is often at pains to prove his carefully weighed scientific attitude in his rhetoric, as when assessing the cause of the death of the Martians: "it seems to me that [the scientist] Carver's suggestions as to the reason of the rapid death of the Martians is so probable as to be regarded almost as a proven conclusion" (177).

What Wells accomplishes by the end of the novel is that the realist depiction of the Martian assault leads to a complete reversal of literary representation. Entering Byfleet Road in Woking the narrator feels that the people he sees are "vague and unreal" and in London "the busy multitudes" seem "but the ghosts of the past", and finally he notes that "strangest of all is it to hold my wife's hand again" (180).[24] The onslaught of the Martians has shattered his complacent world view, which Wells at the end of the novel (and in later non-fiction writings) underlines, since he and his fellow humans have been robbed of "that serene confidence in the future which is the most fruitful source of decadence" (179). Thus, by the use of both the infant genre of science fiction and realist aspects of literary representation, Wells was able to spellbind not just the narrator with "an abiding sense of doubt and insecurity" (179) but readers of his novel for years to come.

As noted above, Wells in many ways provided templates for science fiction, pulp as well as "hard". Almost a century later, a new departure in science fiction came with William Gibson's *Neuromancer* (1984), which owes much to "the New Wave", especially Philip K. Dick and Ridley Scott's film *Blade Runner* (1982) based on Dick's novel *Do Androids Dream of Electric Sheep?* (1968). The very first sentence in Gibson's (1984 rpt: 3) novel points to a technology-ridden world: "The sky above the port was the color of television, tuned to a dead channel". The depiction of a bleak, not-too-distant future on earth when people commonly use computer technology and hard drugs is detailed: the fictional world consists of characters with drug problems and technological implants, artificial intelligences with human-like features and fictional locations, such as the Freeside space station in France and the Sprawl (North America). However fictional, such characters and locations are based on recognizable traits in contemporary industrialised societies. The protagonist Henry Dorsett Case may not be depicted until the last chapter (excepting the coda), but as he spots himself in the mirror

---

24 Interestingly, the last sentence of Wells's novel is an instance of a novel ending on a defamiliarizing note: the fact that the most quotidian act, such as holding his wife's hand, for the narrator is "strangest of all" shows how the preceding action has entirely changed his view of life on earth – as well as that of the reader. Such a technique could be termed *inverse defamiliarization*.

having entered his girlfriend Molly's perception he sees "a white-faced, wasted figure [---] [with] cheeks [...] hollowed with a day's growth of dark beard, his face slick with sweat" (256), a very realistic portrayal of a character with his lifestyle.

However, the detailed realism of the future society, its humans and humanoid artificial intelligences and their realist character psychology is juxtaposed with a plethora of techniques and rhetoric from genre fiction of all kinds. Much of the dialogue draws on the banter familiar from the hardboiled fiction of Raymond Chandler and Elmore Leonard, as does the relationship between Case (cf. the detective) and Molly (cf. the femme fatale). Case is a streetwise criminal computer hack, a kind of technological hustler, who in the fictional world is termed *cowboy*. In fact, just as Scholes and Rabkin (1977: 171–172) have showed that the plot of pulp science fiction (or space opera) is largely based on the Western, *Neuromancer* can be read as another turn on the space-opera plot with Case as the lone cowboy with a questionable past fighting (corporate) corruption.[25] The plot moves between various continents are familiar from James Bond novels and films, as is the plot climax of the protagonist fighting against the clock to survive. Finally, the very theme of *neuromancer* is explicitly drawn from *neuro* and *necromancer* owing to a variation of the Faustian motif of artificial intelligences using dead bodies to communicate and inhabiting the virtual world in which Case finds his alter ego at the end of the novel (243–244). But *romancer* also seems to be a reference to romance fiction, which is the basis of all pulp fiction genres the novel draws on.

Thus, much of the literary representation in *Neuromancer* makes use of various kinds of genre fiction, despite its grounding in recognizable character psychology (however hardboiled) and geo graphical locations (however futuristic). The complex blend of genre fictional plot devices, motifs and language and the swift, computer-informed narration and theme made *Neuromancer* seem so unique that it was considered the seminal *cyberpunk* novel. Still, most likely, the word *punk* in this subgenre denomination refers not only to the petty criminal protagonist but also to the bleak cyberworld portrayed. That is, the novel has distinct features of dystopia and can as such be read as a caution against life on earth going too far in its fascination with drugs and adulation of technology and corporate power. The fact that in his later works and comments on his novels

---

25 Thus, the name Molly may well be an allusion to the unnamed protagonist's girlfriend Molly in one of the most popular Western novels (and TV series) ever, Owen Wister's (1902/2009) *The Virginian*.

Gibson has included much social commentary shows that the allegorical aspect of *Neuromancer* should not be dismissed.

Similarly, in the graphic novel *Watchmen* the theme *Who watches the watchmen?* is signalled in the title as well as throughout, starting in the first of its twelve magazine instalments (Moore and Gibbons 1986/2005: I: 9). When the quote is finally given in the Latin of Juvenal's *Satires* (VI) after the final instalment, it is noted that it derives from the epigraph of the Tower Commission Report of 1987. Since that report reprimanded President Reagan for not having listened to his National Security Advisor, thus causing the Iran Contra scandal, and ultra-right-wing newspaper men are satirized in the tenth and twelfth instalments of *Watchmen*, the allegorical political edge is evident.

Watchmen, however, thematizes other kinds of watchmen, masked crime fighters inspired by Superman and Batman familiar from graphic fiction bearing their names. But what its author Alan Moore and illustrator Dave Gibbons do is mimetically to reverse this most fantastic of graphic genre fiction. In the fictional world of *Watchmen* the heroes of the 1930s comics instigated actual crime-fighting vigilantes (that is, watchmen) to use masks. One of the aspects that makes this graphic novel commonly considered one of the best ever is that it provides psychological complexity to these vigilantes: they have relationship, drinking and mental problems; find it difficult to accept the political views and sexual preference of their colleagues; and struggle with aging and overweight. Even the life story of Dr Manhattan, the only character with supernatural abilities, is given in some detail and his abilities are explained as having been caused by a nuclear accident. What is more, the notion of *watchmen* receives more meanings than Alfred Hitchcock's film *Rear Window:* the ones who watch and are watched (in the sense of both 'safeguarded' and 'policed') are the man in the street, the vigilantes, the entrepreneurs, the journalists and the politicians, as ultimately readers of *Watchmen* watch and read the graphic novel, perhaps as an allegory of twentieth-century American politics. Moreover, *Watchmen* includes narratives in many different genres: excerpts from a fictitious history of graphic fiction and an autobiography by one of the masked vigilantes, filled-out forms from a psychiatric hospital and the New York Police Department, personal letters, a mock-scholarly article, newspaper articles and interviews. Thus, what graphic fiction usually lacks – psychological realism and narrative complexity – is at the core of *Watchmen*, features which for instance are part and parcel of Fludernik's (1996: 36–38) experiential view of mimesis in fiction. In terms of literary representation, the many genres and their uses add realistic credence to the fantastic story of the masked vigilantes.

Junot Díaz's novel *The Brief Wondrous Life of Oscar Wao* (2007) does the opposite of *Watchmen* in that it intersperses its realist narration with references to fantasy and science fiction, which are the protagonist Oscar Wao's favourite reading. But the novel is also a fictional history of The Dominican Republic and the Dominican immigration to the United States during the latter part of the twentieth century. The point it repeatedly drives home is that real life on both personal and political levels is at least as strange, if not stranger than fiction. The narrator points out Oscar's very real predicament in terms of fantastic genres: "You really want to know what being an X-Man feels like? Just be a smartish bookish boy in a contemporary U.S. ghetto. Mamma mia! Like having bat wings or a pair of tentacles growing out of your chest" (Díaz 2007/2008: 23n). Similarly, for decades Dictator Trujillo ruled his totalitarian regime with a network of police, spies and informers, which makes the evil of J. R. R. Tolkien's Sauron pale in comparison: "At the end of *The Return of the King*, Sauron's evil was taken by 'a great wind' and neatly 'blown away,' with no lasting consequences to our heroes; [...] but Trujillo was too powerful, too toxic a radiation to be dispelled so easily. Even after his death his evil *lingered*" (163).

Surely one of the reasons why *The Brief Wondrous Life of Oscar Wao* received four major international awards is its generic richness. It is a *Bildungsroman* for the narrator (who finally understands the fine qualities in his friend Oscar Wao); it is autobiographical fiction, since many of the fictional names occur in the novel's acknowledgements and the novel is dedicated to Elizabeth de León, on whom Oscar's sister Lola evidently is modelled; it is a double love story, both about how Oscar defends his prostitute girlfriend against Dominican criminals with fatal consequences and how the autobio graphical narrator woos Oscar's "sister" by writing the novel; it is a historical novel of the Dominican Republic; and it is a Latino immigration novel of four generations, intricately told backwards starting from the most recent one. In language and style it employs both Latino street slang and scholarly phrasing, often combined in footnotes whose humour largely derives from the clash between them. Similarly, the historical details of the Dominican Republic and Dominican immigration in the United States are clearly based on both the author's personal experience and research. The many genres blend fact and fiction into what is not magical realism but a kind of fantastic realism, since supernatural events do not inform the action, despite the motif of the Dominican curse or *fukú*.

Furthermore, Díaz shows how in the life of Oscar Wao science fiction informs realism. It is Oscar's reading of science fiction and fantasy (one of his favourites being *Watchmen*; see 341) that finally gives him the courage to stand up against the criminals who are harassing his beloved Ybón, however unrequited his love for her is until the final pages of the novel. Oscar's heroic gesture to face the criminals is informed by similar lone heroes in fantastic literature, but lacking supernatural powers he is killed. Still, in his last words to the criminals he asserts that love and revenge will prevail, at least in his imagination: "Love was a rare thing, easily confused with a million other things, and if anybody knew this to be true, it was him. [---] [H]e told them if they killed him [...], [when they were old and weak,] they would sense him waiting for them on the other side and over there he'd be a hero, an avenger. Because anything you can dream (he put his hand up) you can be" (331–332). Of course, the criminals do not heed his words, and the realism of Oscar's world demands that he must suffer for his fiction-informed world view. Thus, paradoxically, the science-fiction motif strengthens the realist portent of Oscar's fate. What makes the end of the novel so touching is not only the fact that Oscar's largely comic and mostly unrequited love for a prostitute is redeemed but also that by his tragicomic death he shows that ideals in fantastic literature can endure in fiction as well as in real life. As the novel ends by Oscar's exclamation "The beauty! The beauty!" eulogising love and life, his words also form the immigrant Díaz's oblique reversal of Kurtz's famous colonial disgust with the colonised, "The horror! The horror!", in Joseph Conrad's (1902/1976: 100) *Heart of Darkness*.

Mimesis and Genre as Co-Determined

However brief, the above readings show that mimesis and genre interrelate on a number of levels, which I would claim can occur in all kinds of fiction. In fact, Ricœur's refiguration and Fludernik's level IV or narrativization could form the basis of dealing with how mimesis is interpreted in narrative fiction. Evidently, the first level that Fludernik terms that of "real-life experience" is fundamental for how mimesis works, so I would claim that it runs through the entire process of interpretation. Yet even before they start reading a literary work, readers are aware of its genre, on the basis of a number of extra-textual and paratextual features, such as where (for instance, on what shelf) they found the book, who gave it or recommended it, what the front or back cover blurb maintains or the library classification states. As readers go on trying to understand the meaning of the language in which the work is written, they *at the same time* learn about the characters and the action they occur in – *pace* some philosophers and critics who claim that linguistic meaning comes *before* the other meanings (see e.g. Gadamer 1975/1989: 391).[26] That is, as readers start reconstructing the fictional world, they are performing many tasks, some of which go beyond the text in a

---

[26] To be sure, Gadamer here discusses deciphering an inscription, but then goes on to discuss writing and literature in general.

strict sense. As they make sense of the language they read, readers try to understand how the characters, setting and action relate to the genres they are familiar with as well as to real locations, people and their behaviour. There may be markers that suggest that the narration is not to be taken at face value (that is, that irony or unreliability colours the narration as a whole or in part) or that there is an additional intent behind the narration, so that it should also be understood as having allegorical (or other) levels of meaning. To put it another way, readers perform operations that relate to extra-textual, paratextual and textual aspects that inform their respective interpretation of the literary work.

By this simplified account I mean to suggest that understanding mimesis in fiction starts with interpretation, which is a process of comparing fiction to real life (at some point somewhere) and in which generic considerations are included from the very beginning. In many ways, the interpretive decision in what generic terms a novel is read affects the way its mimesis is assessed. For instance, when reading pulp science fiction you are not to expect any developed character psychology, which is one reason why *Watchmen* seems such a new departure, as it draws heavily on pulp science fiction (graphic as well non- graphic) while problematizing the lives of its action heroes. Thus, not only the genre or genres but also the generic innovations affect the assessment of the mimetic aspects of a literary work.

What is more, how you read the language and rhetoric of fiction draws largely on generic parameters. In *The War of the Worlds* the what-if premise of its science fiction is grounded in the mock-serious diction by which the narrator's knowledge of science at the start of the novel is rendered. That is, grasping the more general modal properties of fiction often has to do with readers' familiarity with genres and their history. Take naturalism in fiction. Both Wells's and Díaz's novels can be termed naturalist in that they depict brutality in some detail, but a closer look shows how different they are. Besides portraying the brutality of the aliens, Wells clearly draws on Darwin in his portrayal of man's inhumanity to man as well as to other species, a motif topical in naturalist novels of the late nineteenth century. Díaz, on the other hand, shows how personal and political violence works and draws parallels between violence in fantastic literature and real life. In generic terms, Wells is implicitly within the bounds of a scientific romance and Díaz creates a kind of hybrid of realist and postmodern fiction in employing a wealth of genres. Similarly, Gibson as well as Moore and Gibbons make use of multiple genres and are thus able to create generically innovative novels that enrich their primary genres, science fiction and the graphic novel, by various realist features.

Not surprisingly, since science fiction is often termed an allegorical genre, all three science-fiction novels discussed have allegorical features. Although not as explicit as *The Time Machine*, *The War of the Worlds* has a subtext of evolutionary speculation, as concerns earth as well as Mars. *Neuromancer* extrapolates on the basis of recent developments in computer technology and drug industry when creating a recognizable dystopian extrapolation with moral overtones of technology and commercialism run amok. Published during the Reagan era, *Watchmen* has evident pointers to the dangers of right-wing politics. *The Brief Wondrous Life of Oscar Wao* merely employs science fiction and fantasy as motifs but turns into an allegory of mind (imagination) prevailing over matter (realism), that is, over the brutality inherent in personal life and political history as depicted in the novel. The many generic levels and intentions of Díaz's novel suggest that the traditional view of allegory, such as Angus Fletcher's (1964: 7) "doubleness of intention", is not enough, since there can be multiple allegories, as indeed a more recent definition by Madeleine Kasten (2008: 10) suggests. In sum, it is through the use of fictional and at times factual genres in relation to mimetic import that the allegorical level or levels are crafted.[27]

As far as the division between the empirical and the fictional as a dichotomy of fiction is concerned, the study of the relation between mimesis and genre could help to overcome it. One case in point that seldom has been noted is the interdependence of empirical and fictional narration. This has been in focus in this chapter and is perhaps in part corroborated by Scholes and Rabkin (1977: 19), as they point to the rather neglected aspect of the debate between Wells and Henry James: "Wells had defended himself as a realist, not as a romancer, as a reporter on life, not as a writer of imagination". The readings of Wells, Gibson and Moore and Gibbons indicate that there is much to suggest that genre fiction is mimetically grounded on several levels, not least since it often makes use of realist features – just as realist fiction, as in Díaz's novel, can come alive through fantastic features. Thus, Watt's (1957) classic view that the realist novel turns on detailed portrayals of character and setting is based on features that also occur in genre fiction.

What I hope these readings have suggested is that the mimetic and the generic features of any one literary work are co-determined and also inform the way readers assess its rhetorical and allegorical aspects. Literary representation is not only based on the world and genres authors know and employ but also on what readers consider real in the fictional worlds depicted. Assessing how representation works in literature is fundamental for readers so that they can understand how the real and the fantastic blend in literature. That is, mimesis and genre are often co-determined in interpreting literature: if you do not know the

---

[27] For a discussion of how extended metaphor can turn into allegory see 5.2 and 5.3.

genre, you may misunderstand what is represented and the other way around. Thus, understanding literary representation, how it blends the imitative and the creative, the real and the fantastic in various genres is basic for understanding the makings of fictional worlds.

But how a story is told, how characters act or a poem portrays a setting or a feeling is also crucial, so that listeners, audiences or readers know whether and to what extent to trust speakers in poems, narrators or characters in prose fiction and drama – and ultimately their authors. That is, how reliable narrators, speakers and characters are is discussed next in order to show that literary representation is fundamentally inflected by the reliability of what is represented.

3 Kinds of Unreliability

3.1 From Mimesis to Deception

Mimesis, we have seen, is about how humans represent what they have perceived, by imitation and creation. Such representation is central in human life, but occurs also in other life forms. This suggests that part and parcel of mimesis is the question of how accurate, true or sincere the representation is. In literature this has led to a range of uses of unreliability, which occur in some of the very first written literature and earlier on in oral literature. The centrality of reliability in literature, especially the many forms of literary unreliability, is the reason it is discussed before considering how literary worlds are shaped (chapter 4). That is, *pace* the received view, according to which unreliability only at times colours literary narratives, I aim to show that all literary representation is inflected or modulated on a scale of reliability, which concerns narration, characterization and exposition in various combinations.

But let me first put the phenomenon of unreliability in a wider perspective. In the broadest possible terms of seeming to be what you are not, unreliability is ultimately about survival, of the individual and the species. A common phenomenon in nature is mimicry, by which for instance a palatable insect, weed, reptile or fish by coloration mimics a noxious or dangerous one (defensive mimicry) or a dangerous species mimics an inoffensive one (aggressive mimicry). But mimicry also appears below species level, and in fact cellular and molecular mimicry is a field of research in microbiology. In mammals mimicry occurs comparatively seldom, especially if compared to insects, but there are instances of it (e.g. the defenceless East African maned rat resembles the spiky African porcupine). More familiar are the motion dazzle of the zebra, whose striped coloration in combination with motion apparently furthers its survival when chased by predators, and the way a cat when in danger fakes bigger size by standing in profile with its tail up and fur on end (see e.g. Trivers 2011: 29–48). The broadest view of the relation between rhetoric and deception is probably found in George A. Kennedy's (1998: 18) view that "the principles of veracity, credulity, and induction, the possibility of deceit or misinterpretation of cause and effect [...] seem equally to apply to animal communication and thus can be regarded as grounds for the general rhetoric of nature".

Humans also make use of basic forms of mimicry: posture, facial expression, hair (its length, form and colour), make-up and dress are some central features in most cultures through the ages. All of them can be changed, or seemingly changed, at will so as to impress other humans. And even if people are well aware of such changes, they can be extraordinarily effective. It is well-known that the fact that John F. Kennedy had shaved and Richard M. Nixon had not before their televised debate most likely tipped the presidential election in 1960. Most important for an individual to give a reliable impression is the flexible form of communication humans have developed in all cultures: language. Some forms and genres of language use are especially prone to subjective positioning, bias or deceit, as for instance argument, political speech, advertising and autobiography, but in fact all language use aims to persuade in one way or another. What you say or write and how you put it shows who you are – and often you want to seem better than you in fact are. Still, the very self-consciousness that gave rise to human language in the first place also brought about its manifold creativity, including imaginative and deceptive usages. For instance, most of us are quite adept at acting or speaking insincerely or misleadingly by *paltering*, which includes "fudging, twisting, shading, bending, stretching, slanting, exaggerating, distorting, whitewashing, and selective reporting" (Schauer and Zeckhauser 2009: 39).[1]

Early on, humans learned that you can mould what you are by faking what you seem to be. Perhaps this is why the very notion of what we are – *identity* – is void: its Latin root *idem* simply means 'the same'. Usually the way you show who you are is by proving that you are the same that you have been, that is, by *identifying* yourself, thus comparing your present being with your past one. When laws are enforced, jobs filled and treaties signed, a person's present behaviour – or what the person represents – is compared to his or her past by CV, criminal record or previous conduct. But it is also compared to that of others: the notion of *morals* draws on Latin *mōres*, the plural form of *mōs*, 'usage' or 'custom', just as *ethics* is based on the Greek *ethos*, 'custom', 'habit' or 'character', which is more of an inside view of behaviour, since the *ethos* of a person seems more intrinsic than his or her morals. Even in early studies of rhetoric, the moral component was understood to be crucial. In order to be persuasive, Aristotle (1991: 141; 1378a) reminds us in *The Art of Rhetoric*, speakers should have "*common sense, virtue* and *goodwill*". Yet Aristotle notes that it is sufficient to *appear* to have those qualities,[2] thus leaving the door open for counterfeit or simulated features in language and behaviour. In short, in order to persuade, you may resort to unreliability.

---

1 Note that many kinds of paltering are closely related to the rhetorical operations discussed in 6.1.
2 Similarly, according to Cicero (2001: 292), when speaking, "by nature, every emotion has its own facial expression, tone of voice, and gesture", all of which can be controlled and thus feigned (see Book 3, 213–227 Delivery).

We are so used to behaviour according to social, moral and legal conventions that we might think they are the very basis of our speech and action. But in his collection of short stories set in East Los Angeles in the mid-twentieth century Ry Cooder (2011: 16), better known as a musician and producer, has one of his characters say: "Everyone out there is a mad dog from hell until proven otherwise". Well, you may think, that is just East LA. But is it really? Is this not what happens anywhere anytime when laws and morals are not firmly in place and enforced? In a strange part of the woods where you have never been, in a neighbourhood or country with a different code of behaviour, at night in the city you think you know so well and in which you feel secure during the day – in such circumstances, your conduct, just as streetwise conduct throughout history, is more likely to be: *do not trust anybody at first sight*. A more balanced view is offered by Guido Möllering (2009: 152), for whom trust and deception form an "ambivalent relationship" in which they "enable and prevent" each other in complex ways "by leaps and lapses of faith".

A few tentative conclusions can be drawn on the basis of these few comments on deceptive or unreliable behaviour and communication in nature and humankind. First, despite a widespread view in narrative theory, *reliability as such is not the absolute norm* against which unreliability is to be measured, but in each assessment of reliability the context (in terms of familiarity with species, individual, environment, time and genre, etc.) must be taken into account. Whether the normative expectation is reliability or not varies according to circumstances and it can be reversed by the smallest hint of aggression or deception (cf. Möllering's "lapses of faith"). Second, all reliability is corroborated by *comparison* with familiar phenomena, such as the behaviour or communication by other creatures of the same or other species. It is this act of comparison that suggests whether enough parameters are in place for trust to be the most advantageous reaction. Third, such *parameters are often multiple*, as the English plural forms *morals* and *ethics* for assessing human interaction imply. Fourth, measuring the reliability of an individual in any species has to do with *long-term behaviour and its consistency*. Sustained reliable behaviour in an individual during a long time span can make other individuals of the same or other species override or lessen the effect of one particular act of deceptive behaviour. Finally, coming back to the first point, reliability, however central as glue for social interaction, may be overridden by other considerations, especially among humans. Teflon politicians such as Ronald Reagan or Silvio Berlusconi repeatedly breached promises, but since in their posture and rhetoric they were able to make a majority of voters feel a national pride, they became symbols of a strong nation. What seems to matter most is a comparative assessment of what benefits individuals and their community.

Have my remarks on deception perhaps strayed far from literary worlds? Hardly, since suspending disbelief when encountering literature is a convention of making what Möllering calls a "leap of faith" when deciding to trust somebody.³ When listening to a poem, reading literature or watching a play we let ourselves be immersed in – willingly suspend disbelief as to, that is, take a leap of faith into – its literary world by recognizing that it is not real, but works on the basis of us knowing that we are to interpret it *as if* it were real, as long as our disbelief is suspended. Also, recent research is aware of the positive uses of deception (Harrington 2009, Nünning 2015), including its uses in myth, art and literature (Fields 2009).

In literary theory the study of unreliability started out with a fairly specific focus but has gone on to broaden its scope. Wayne C. Booth (1961/1983: 158) launched the discussion by analysing narrators speaking or acting against "the norms of the work (which is to say, the implied author's norms)". In keeping with the text-immanent study that characterized much of literary studies in the late twentieth century (see Pettersson 2005a), the subsequent focus was on narrators and their relation to their implied authors as well as for some, including Booth and his most illustrious follower James Phelan, by implication the actual flesh-and-blood authors who created them. As far as I know, the only monograph on fictional unreliability so far is that of William Riggan (1981), who presented four categories of unreliable first-person narrators: pícaros (e.g. Apuleius' *The Golden Ass*, Defoe's *Moll Flanders*), clowns (Sterne's *Tristram Shandy*, Nabokov's *Lolita*),⁴ madmen (Gogol's "Diary of a Madman", many of Poe's stories) and naifs (Twain's *Adventures of Huckleberry Finn*,⁵ Salinger's *The Catcher in the Rye*). A somewhat broader typology, but still largely a textual one has more recently been presented by Per Krogh Hansen (2005). It consists of four potentially interrelated types of unreliability, depending on whether it is "marked *in* the narrator's discourse [intranarrational], by *other* narrators relating [internarrational], *by virtue of* the type the narrator as character is modelled upon [intertextual; cf. Riggan's types], and *in relation to* the knowledge the reader brings to the text [extra-textual]" (Hansen 2005: 302). A third typology can be found in Tamar Yacobi's (2000: 713) important writings spanning over three decades advancing five integrative mechanisms of interpretation that "account for apparent

---

3 On the parsing of deception in relation to the suspension of disbelief see O'Sullivan (2009: 90).
4 The category of clowns seems the most questionable one in Riggan's categorization, as is evident by his inclusion of *Lolita*.
5 Twain scholarship usually spells the title without the definite article on the basis of Twain's manuscript and the first American edition rather than the first British edition (which as it happens was published a few months before the American); see Twain (1884/1988: 516–527).

incongruities in the text by reference to transmissional features: to the mediator's (e. g., the speaker's, narrator's, observer's) high *or* low capabilities and performance". Of the five features – *genetic, generic, existential, functional* and *perspectival* –, the first two are concerned with how the work was conceived, the third and fourth with work-immanent features relating to the represented world and the fifth points to Booth's original definition (see Yacobi 2000: 714 *et passim*). Yacobi's integrative mechanisms, then, span much of literary communication and serve an interpretive approach by showing how readers can cope with unreliability in art, mainly fiction.

In short, even before cognitive literary approaches, there have been interpretive as well as text-centred accounts. Thus, the move from classical to postclassical approaches to narrative unreliability has been a rather gradual one, as in narrative studies in general (see Pettersson 2005b: 312–313). What is notable is that the interpretive as well as the comparative focus has become more pronounced. "Unreliable, Compared to What?" is the main title of one of the seminal cognitive accounts of unreliable narration by Ansgar Nünning (1999).[6] In contrast to Booth's and Phelan's rhetorical-ethical views, Nünning (1999: 69) puts forward a "cognitive" approach, much like that of Yacobi: "The construction of an unreliable narrator can be seen as an interpretative strategy by which the reader naturalizes textual inconsistencies that might otherwise remain unassimilable". He present four lists of norms and criteria by which to pin down unreliability in fiction: presuppositions (of readers), grammatical signs, referential frameworks (of readers) and literary and genre conventions. Thus, Nünning's cognitive account of unreliability at this point was an interpretive and comparative view by which the features of the literary work as related to readers' presuppositions and frameworks can explain textual inconsistencies by the hypothesis that the narrator is unreliable.

About a decade later Nünning broadened the study of unreliable narration by synthesizing cognitive and rhetorical approaches. In brief, he suggested that the study of unreliable narration should "take into consideration both the unacknowledged standards and frames of reference according to which readers and critics think they recognize an unreliable narrator when they see one, and the author's agency and the textual signals of unreliability" (Nünning 2008: 69). This one sentence summarizing his view has at least two important facets. First, it exchanges Booth's notion of *the implied author* (criticized at length in Nünning 1999, 2008) with "standards and frames of reference" of which lists

---

[6] For other important approaches with more or less comparative views see V. Nünning (2004), Phelan (2005) and McCormick (2009).

are provided. Second, it implies an extensive view of literary communication over its entire spectrum from author to text to reader: authorial agency and textual signals are taken into account, although it is the activity of readers and critics – interpretation – that is crucial in recognizing unreliable narration. This wide-ranging approach together with the historical contextualization of literary unreliability[7] I find a useful point of departure for a more encompassing scrutiny of unreliability in literature, whose basis I now attempt to provide.

3.2 Basic Features of Unreliability and How We Learn Them

What the above notes on the unreliability and deception in life and literature suggest as far as human behaviour is concerned is that in order to deceive you must know what other people do when they are or seem reliable and then imitate such behaviour. Recent infant psychology has proved Aristotle's (1941/ 2001: 1457; 1448b) *Poetics* right: "Imitation is natural to man from childhood, one of his advantages over the lower animals being this, that he is the most imitative creature in the world". The cognitive superiority of man over other mammals includes a multi-layered theory of mind, which also makes possible advanced forms of deception as well as detecting them (see Oatley 2011: 42–45). Since much unreliability is related to the most advanced human form of communication, language, what has not been properly recognized is its relation to representation or mimesis. How is that which is being communicated to you represented – be it somebody's feelings, CV or work of art? And – for this is the corollary, since most people have designs on you – with what intention?

Thus, perhaps the most basic form of reliability could be viewed on a scale of intentionality which is founded on whether the communicator has the knowledge and ability to communicate what he or she intends to communicate. A naive narrator such as Huck Finn in Mark Twain's (1884/1988) *Adventures of Huckleberry Finn* is a young boy who, however streetwise in some senses, clearly lacks all sorts of knowledge and ability. Thus, as a narrator he is largely *fallible* (even though as a character he can also at times be deceptive). Throughout his life the butler Stevens in Kazuo Ishiguro's (1989/1996) *The Remains of the Day* does his utmost to live up to the dignity that he considers to be the finest trait of his trade. Most readers find that he not only ruins his private life but also that of Miss Kenton in doing so. He is simply *deluded* in thinking that dignity is the end-all of a butler's life. Finally, however cunningly Humbert Humbert

---

7 For important advances see e.g. Zerweck (2001), V. Nünning (2004) and A. Nünning (2008).

in Vladimir Nabokov's (1955/1962) *Lolita* tries to explain away and defend his conduct, most readers find him a petty paedophile, whose subterfuges are *deceptive*.

I would suggest that on the spectrum from unintentional to intentional unreliability, *fallible* and *deceptive* could be placed at either ends, with *deluded* – in a variety of forms – in the middle. Indeed, as we shall see, *fallible* and *deceptive* also come in all sorts of guises and need not be absolute or consistent. What is more, all three can be combined: Stevens can be deceptive too, since at times he tries to pass himself off as an aristocrat, but mostly he is deluded, and as I have noted Huck is both fallible as a narrator and often deceptive as a character. Let me add, since this has not been adequately recognized, that narrators or characters are almost never unreliable through and through, but mainly in particular, often crucial moral respects in their actions towards and pronouncements about some other characters. They can be considered reliable in their depictions or views of setting, action and minor characters to the extent that such accounts are not related to their rendition or interpretation of matters in which they are fallible, deluded or deceptive. Also, as Shakespeare's *King Lear* amply shows, all sorts of unreliability can occur in a single work in drama too: Goneril, Regan and Edmund are deceptive, Lear and Gloucester deluded by them as well as fallible in that they do not at first recognize which of their children are reliable. As for comedy, some of Molière's (1982) finest plays, such as *The Misanthrope*, *The Miser* and *The Hypochondriac*, focus on deluded protagonists with particular fixations, and they are also able to arouse feelings of pity in the audience (thus enriching the comedies with a tragic undertone) in part owing to their respective delusion.

But are Booth (1961/1983: 492) and many scholars after him right in claiming that literary unreliability, most centrally that of character narration in fiction, is a "kind of irony"? Of course, this depends on your definition of irony. In the definitions that *Webster's* (1989: 752–753) gives for *irony*, we find both the classic narrow meaning ("a figure of speech in which the literal meaning of a locution is the opposite of that intended") as well as a broader one (a meaning "different from, and often the direct opposite of, the literal meaning"). Yet where do you draw the line? The "opposite" meaning is much too restrictive for understanding the often rather complex playfulness of irony, whereas "different from" opens the field altogether too wide. This is due to the richness of indirect language use that Raymond Gibbs (1999: 148) has discussed in relation to figures: "The most typical way for people to express their communicative intentions indirectly is to employ figurative language". If so, why should all sorts of indirect and unreliable usages – Gibbs (1999: 153–171) also discusses deception, equivocation, evasion and speaking off-record – be termed ironic? Is it not rather the case that, as

Gibbs (1999: 150) puts it, "understanding metaphor, metonymy, irony, and indirect speech acts requires the same kind of contextual information as understanding comparable literal expressions"? This means that we do not necessarily first understand the literal meaning and then the figurative meaning but use all sorts of contextual information to get at the meaning or meanings of an utterance, so that if the usage is not too novel, we may even get the figurative meaning first.[8] In terms of deciding whether a speech act or a work of fiction is unreliable or not, we look for textual and contextual clues, implicitly comparing it to other similar or related acts or texts that we have encountered.

The contextual information that is crucial is whether there are any markers of what Gregory Bateson (1955/2000: 179) calls "this is play" among mammals or what has been termed *pretend play* in humans.[9] As Paul L. Harris (2000: 28 quote, 194–195) puts it, pretend play in children is "the first indication of a lifelong mental capacity to consider alternatives to reality" and it develops in them roughly in tandem with language. For the Canadian psychologist Keith Oatley (2011: 48), drawing on Harris (2000), irony and other figurative language, such as metaphor, is "a mode of play in which something is both itself and something else". This is how all kinds of fiction work and it is learned by infants at a very early age. What they also discover is the fact that the contextual information suggesting "something else" may come in different forms, including non-verbal ones.

All socialization – in the sense of understanding what it is to be human in a human society – relates to learning whom to trust (see Möllering 2009). And we learn about trust so early, because it is crucial for survival. This may be why we seldom think about its mechanisms and conventions. At about the age of nine months infants learn about communicative intentions and at about the age of two about empathy, which is central for developing a theory of mind, that is, for understanding the reasons behind people's actions (see Tomasello 1999b and Gopnik et al. 1999).[10] More importantly in terms of literature, it is a developed sense of empathy that helps readers understand the contents and causality in what they read, thus understanding literature better (see Bourg 1996 and Miall 2011).

---

8 For neuroscientific evidence of this see Sanford and Emmott (2012: 62–65).
9 See Oatley (2011: 28–49) and the volume edited by Gibbs and Colston (2007), especially Clark and Gerrig (1984/2007).
10 Mark Haddon (2003/2004) dramatizes the lack of such understanding in his seemingly semi-autistic character narrator Christopher Boone in *The Curious Incident of the Dog in the Night-time*.

Perhaps the early workings of trust and unreliability and their relation to literature can best be elucidated by a nursery rhyme. Consider the first stanza of a popular children's song in English, commonly known as "Row, Row, Row Your Boat" or "(Mary) Row Your Boat":[11]

> Row, row, row your boat
> Gently down the stream.
> Merrily, merrily, merrily, merrily,
> Life is but a dream.[12]

What infants learn when they first hear the song is how enjoyable music, rhythm and sounds are in combination with the proximity to the one who is singing it to or with them. Thus, they learn – in accordance with Aristotle – by imitation, in this case also about music, rhythm and the makings of poetry. As Ellen Dissanayake (2000: 29–40) has shown, it is no coincidence that the length of verses in poetry and song lyrics across cultures is three to six stressed syllables, taking 3.5 to 5 seconds to read or sing, the very length of the utterances spoken to infants, often in motherese (or fatherese). Such verses and utterances are simply easy to understand and remember. Infants may at first observe that the song sounds happy (is in a major chord) and that the third line has four playfully descending notes situated on the first syllable of the four occurrences of "merrily". Even more important is the company of the parents, grandparents, older siblings, peers or nannies who first sing it to them. In such a situation infants can usually feel secure, not least since one or more of such familiar people want to do something as fun as sing to or with them, and perhaps even teach them the playful rocking bodily movement – simulating rowing – that may accompany the song, which often is sung as a round (with voices entering at different times). In other words, the togetherness in a safe environment, the joyful rhythmical singing (and rocking), is fundamental.

Later on, infants may learn what the words mean and may reflect on the fact that it is strange that the lyrics suggest that you should just row merrily down the stream (apparently without giving a thought to how to get back up) and that everything you have learned to consider real may be an illusion. Furthermore, the rather strange literary world portrayed and the second-person admonition – seemingly to the girl ("Mary") in some versions of the title or to the infants lis-

---

11 The next two paragraphs draw on Pettersson (2012: 79–80).
12 This is the most common punctuation of the song, although one might argue that the third line continues the description of how to go down the stream and thus that the full stop should come after, not before, it.

tening to the ditty – to stray far away in a boat and the questioning of the real world as they know it are most likely communicated by some of the most trusted people they know. Thus, even before having learned to read, children are likely to have encountered impossible literary worlds and strange acts of narration, which may be deemed by children as fictional or unreliable. In other words, even without reflecting on it, they may understand "merrily" as undercutting what the lyrics seem to suggest (that is, surely adults cannot actually mean that you should not give a thought how to get back home or that life is a mere dream). But such considerations – if indeed infants at all reflect on the import of the words – are likely to be viewed in relation to the primary context of the togetherness of singing (and rocking). In fact, "Row, Row, Row Your Boat" can be read as a kind of proto-narrative based on hypothetical action (see 6.2). That is, it has no event sequencing as such, even if its first verse suggests an action, the manner of which is portrayed in the second verse ("gently") and the continuity of which is implied by the falling notes in the third and fourth lines.

This brief interpretation of "Row, Row, Row Your Boat" adds to the critique of the so-called Exceptionality Thesis, according to which our access to fictional minds is different from our access to actual human or everyday minds (since readers can seemingly get direct access to fictional but not actual minds). David Herman (2011: 1–18) has recently provided a fine summary of the ontogenetic, phylogenetic and folk-psychological arguments against this thesis, which in literary studies builds on the works of Käte Hamburger (1957/1993) and Dorrit Cohn (1999/2000) and whose most recent trend is "unnatural" narratology.[13] But he also turns the critique into two positive arguments: by observing body language and other behaviour, infants, like adults, get access to other minds ("the Accessibility argument") and fictional minds are mediated by the same heuristics as everyday minds ("the Mediation argument") (Herman 2011: 18). Thus, by checking how adults or siblings react when listening to or singing "Row, Row, Row Your Boat", infants can downgrade or relativize any possible implicit illocutionary or perlocutionary meaning of the words mediated by the song.[14]

---

[13] For a critique of the notions of "unnatural" narrative and narratology see Pettersson (2012a).

[14] As Herman (2011: 12) notes, this does not mean that there are no differences between fictional and non-fictional representation, but that recognizing similarities in such representation can on the contrary form the foundation for studying the actual differences in how everyday and fictional minds are represented.

What this surprisingly complex little ditty shows is the importance of context to the interpretation of any (more or less) literary text. The questionable admonition to row your boat down the stream and the view of life as a dream, which might suggest that the person singing the song for or with them is unreliable, are overridden in many ways: by the proximity to trusted people (a trust based on previous time spent together), by the music in a major key and its soothing rhythm and perhaps by the fact – if at all noticed – that it merely presents hypothetical action. As children grow and learn to distinguish between trustworthy and untrustworthy people, between fact and fiction in real life and in literature, they continue to make use of such holistic assessment of unreliability. As long as they are in a safe environment or feel they can trust a narrator, they do so, but only – and this is crucial to note – because the conventions of reliability are in place.

By such mental and linguistic operations in early childhood humans learn to distinguish between real life and fiction as well between reliable and unreliable language uses and behaviour. What they are learning at the same time is that generic conventions – in for instance nursery rhymes and fairytales – are central in judging unreliability in literature.

3.3 Narratorial and Focal Unreliability: A Scale of Intentionality

The reason why literary unreliability can be so hard to pin down is that unreliability comes in so many different forms and is based on a host of aspects. As for such aspects, in an attempt to provide a cognitive narratological account of unreliability I have elsewhere discussed features such as verisimilitude, unreliable narrators and characters, veracity, existential presuppositions, referential familiarity, morality, intentionality and consistency, and exemplified them by Michael Frayn's (2002) novel *Spies* (see Pettersson 2005c: 70 – 83). So far in this chapter I have shown how foundational mimesis or literary representation (cf. verisimilitude) and intentionality are in identifying unreliability on a scale from fallible to deluded to deceptive. Let me now flesh out this scale by considering a host of character narrators and characters in order to show the many ways in which they can be unreliable. In doing so, I hope to illustrate the roles the other aspects mentioned above and some others play and prove that this probing of unreliability is not a feature of realist fiction alone but an age-old phenomenon in literature. Then I go on to demonstrate that the study of narratorial and focal kinds of unreliability should be supplemented by the study of an assortment of expositional and combined kinds of unreliability.

Fallible character narrators and characters are in fact seldom entirely fallible. Huck Finn, I have noted, is in many ways streetwise and can also make use of deception when need be. But most importantly he is not fallible morally: he stands up for his friend Jim, the runaway slave, even if he were to go to hell for it, according to his skewed view of how racism and Christianity are coupled. Still, despite Riggan's (1981) categorization of him as a naif, he is also a kind of moral pícaro, who declines being "sivilized" and lights out for the Territory (see Pettersson 1999e). Often the fallible clowns or pícaros, such as the character narrators in *Tristram Shandy* or *The Golden Ass*, do not learn much, however intelligent or well-read they are.[15] But other fallible narrators go through a development comparable to that of the protagonist in a *Bildungsroman*. The main character in Voltaire's *Candide* may remain as naive as he was at the start but his final decision to tend his garden promises a safe and happy old age for him. Another simple-minded gardener, Chance or Chauncey Gardiner in Jerzy Kosinski's (1970/1996: 103–104) *Being There*, may not develop, but by his simplistic adages he is nevertheless finally about to be asked to run for vice president of the United States. He is a kind of latter-day version of Candide, but his naivety is misinterpreted as great wisdom by leading politicians and the media, who delude themselves into taking his comments about gardening as profound allegorical statements, even if they are not intended as deceptive. Winston Groom's Forrest Gump in the novel by that title may have an IQ of "near 70", yet he has read enough stories of naifs and pícaros – such as *King Lear* (with reference to its Fool), Dostoevsky's *The Idiot*, Faulkner's *The Sound and the Fury*, Lee's *To Kill a Mockingbird* and Steinbeck's *Of Mice and Men* – to know that "idiots [are] always smarter than people give them credit for" (Groom 1986/1995: 9, 10). In fact, he has a formidable career and ends up owning a five-million dollar business. These brief notes on fallible narrators and characters suggest that there is a wide variety of them: intelligent or intellectually challenged, moral or immorally acting naifs and pícaros, who may or may not develop during the course of the story.

But there are also cases in which it is hard to decide whether the character narrator is fallible or deluded. Throughout *The Little Stranger* by Sarah Waters (2009/2010), the Georgian house Hundreds Hall, which the narrator Dr Faraday has known since childhood, is subject to visitations by poltergeist phenomena

---

15 As Riggan (1981: 47) notes, the final conversion of Lucius in *The Golden Ass* seems "merely tacked on to provide a serious counterweight to the general levity of the foregoing portions of the work".

(based on detailed research by the author according to the acknowledgements).[16] Either Dr Faraday – like the governess in Henry James's *The Turn of the Screw* – is a reliable narrator and there are actually supernatural visitations or he is fallible or deluded and *unbeknownst to himself* embodies something like a poltergeist. If so, it is he who is responsible for all the ghastly incidents in Hundreds Hall, as his name may suggest: he – or the poltergeist he embodies – is in a kind of paranormal Faraday cage. The very last sentences of the novel seem to suggest as much: "If Hundred's Hall is haunted, however, its ghost doesn't show itself to me. For I'll turn, and am disappointed – realising that what I am looking at is only a cracked window-pane, and that the face gazing distortedly from it, baffled and longing, is my own" (Waters 2009/2010: 499). Thus, to the very end, he appears unaware of what he may have done and is thus either fallible or, if indeed in some way he is aware of it but does not face up to it, deluded or self-deceptive.

Deluded narrators and characters are a motley crew. We have seen that Stevens in *The Remains of the Day* is self-deluded in the sense that the butler's work ethic he inherits from his father makes it impossible for him to woo Miss Kenton (later Mrs Benn), who once was his potential fiancée and wife. He finally does not abandon his delusion as much as decides to make the best of the rest of his life, as the title implies. The constellation between John Marcher and May Bartram in Henry James's (1903/2001: 460) story "The Beast in the Jungle" is rather similar: the (main) character focaliser Marcher is deluded in thinking that a beast awaits him and gets Bartram to wait for it with him, until Marcher at her grave finally realizes that the beast had been "the chill of his egotism", including his not having understood the love they could have shared.

Riggan (1981: 109–143, 110 quote) discusses an assortment of "self-deluding" fictional madmen, such as those of Gogol and Dostoevsky, but two other mad diarists may show the broader spectrum of delusion. The diary of Guy de Maupassant's (1885/1997) judge in "The Diary of Madman" is only found after his death: it turns out that during his seemingly impeccable life he has both killed and knowingly sent innocent people to death and never been caught. He has deceived everyone, but seems neither fallible nor deluded as such – he has simply acted on an instinct he cannot comprehend, hence giving his diary the heading "Why?" (Maupassant 1885/1997: 113). In some sense his murderous cravings are instinctual (unintentional), in some sense planned (intentional), but as a confession his diary seems completely reliable, even if its contents and the

---

[16] The rest of this paragraph discloses the end of the novel, so if you are going to read *The Little Stranger* you may want to pass over it.

frame story of how the diary was found show that throughout his life he has deceived everybody into thinking he is highly moral man.

Lu Xun, one of the founders of modern Chinese literature, seems to take his cue from Gogol – and possibly Maupassant – in his "Diary of a Madman". The frame story notes that the madman has "long since made a complete recovery" and claims that his diary shows that he suffered from a "persecution complex" in that it depicts his growing fear of cannibalism (Lu Xun 1918/2009: 21). Thus, when writing it, the madman seems to be deluded in claiming that cannibalism was widespread in China. However, as Lu Xun was openly critical of the political mismanagement in China after the toppling of the Qing dynasty in 1911, the fear of cannibalism was with good reason understood as both real and allegorical.[17] The story mentions famine leading to cannibalism, of which there were reported cases when the story was penned, and ends with the oft-quoted words "Save the children..." (Lu Xun 1918/2009: 31). This may seem deluded in terms of the diarist's exaggerated fear of cannibalism, but was understood as pointing to a new generation taking over in China, especially to the unrest leading to the May Fourth demonstrations in the year after its publication.[18] What seems deluded in the diary, and is corroborated as such by the frame story, has both real and allegorical socio-critical meanings intended by Lu Xun. In other words, the diarist may be deluded, but nevertheless acts as a soothsayer.

In Philip K. Dick's (2002: 384) science-fiction story "The Electric Ant" the protagonist Garson Poole, owner of Tri-Plan Electronics, has taken for granted that he is human but learns that he is an electric ant, that is, a robot: "I must never really have run the company; it was a delusion implanted in me when I was made ... along with the delusion that I am human and alive". In other words, he has been deluded that he is human, but now that he knows that he is a robot, he admits that his "posing" as human is "intentional" (Dick 2002: 385). As Poole expires, his secretary notices that she herself and the world she lives in start to disintegrate, apparently because the world she inhabits – including herself – has merely been a "reality tape" implanted in Poole (Dick 2002: 399). She too has been deluded but on a lower level than Poole, since her existence has been implanted in Poole's reality tape. Thus, delusions in "The Electric Ant" are embedded on multiple levels, and ironically the ones controlling them

---

17 For instance, according to Knight (2012: 104), the story "cries out against exploitation in a hallucinatory modernist mode".

18 See Howard Goldblatt's (2000: 479) view that "Lu Xun [in the story] turns the May Fourth slogan *lijao chiren* – established rituals and moral tenets have cannibalized the Chinese people – into an extended metaphor for the Chinese". For a reading of Lu Xun's importance for the nationalist ideology in China see 7.4.

are merely mentioned in passing: "Marvis Bey and her husband, Ernan, on Prox 4 [apparently another planet], control fifty-one percent of the voting stock" of Tri-Plan Electronics (Dick 2002: 390).

However, the outcome of delusions is not always tragic. In Alice Munro's (2001/2002) short story "Hateship, Friendship, Courtship, Loveship, Marriage" Johanna Parry, a rather plain maid living in a small town in Ontario is tricked by some girls into believing that a man in a small town in Saskatchewan loves her and she leaves her job to find him. Thus, readers are bound to expect her fate to be tragic. But since Johanna finds her supposed lover feverish with bronchitis and nurses him back to health, they in fact finally get married and start a family. Like the finger game based on the various outcomes of relationships alluded to in the title of the story, the girls' evil scheme against Johanna misfires: it does not lead to "hateship" but to "marriage", one of many twists of fate in Munro's stories.

Deception too comes in many guises in fiction. According to Robin Trivers (2011), deception and delusion are closely connected, as is suggested by the subtitle of his major survey *Deceit and Self-Deception. Fooling Yourself the Better to Fool Others*. That is, in his view (which is still debated, at least in its strong form), you delude yourself in order to deceive others. In literary studies James Phelan (2008) has intriguingly analysed one of the central techniques by which Nabokov makes Humbert Humbert so ambiguous: he is not only an estranging unreliable narrator (that is, comes across as a paedophile), but he is also a "bonding" one (that is, seeks sympathy by rhetorical persuasion). Phelan goes on to show how there are different kinds of bonding unreliability, just as he has earlier shown how in *Lolita* there is a process in Humbert's narration from self-absorption to a more defensive position with – on the face of it – some concern for Lolita's well-being (Phelan 2005: 98–131).

In other novels with unreliable character narrators, the deception lies less in the narrative than in the strangely motivated actions they depict they have performed. John Banville's (2002/2003) character narrator in the novel *Shroud* is a case in point. He may start out apparently deceiving his readers: "The name, my name, is Axel Vander, on that much I insist", but his entire narrative is for the most part a reliable confession-like account of how as a young man he took on the name and identity of his deceased friend Axel Vander (Banville 2002/2003: 7). The novel is full of different kinds of ironic turns, as when, unwittingly, by turning into Axel Vander the protagonist takes on a Jewish personality in Belgium during the Nazi occupation. He is clearly a rather despicable character, who compares himself at times to Christ during his sojourn in Turin, the home town of the title's Turin Shroud, most likely the ultimate artefactual hoax in the history of Christianity. In *The Book of Evidence*, another Banville novel, the character narrator and murderer Frederick Montgomery may at times – perhaps even throughout – be an unreliable narrator, but he confesses that he has committed numerous nasty deeds and even decides to plead guilty to murder in the first degree, even if he could get away with a more lenient sentence if pleading otherwise. He repeatedly points out that he does not try to exonerate himself (in fact, he shows in great detail what a callous man he is), but focuses on his double identity, which makes his bourgeois self feel liberated by having set free the beast. Thus, these two Banville characters are less unreliable as narrators than as characters: they mainly portray how deceptive and despicable they are as well as the motivations to their deceptions and so do something that has seldom been discussed in terms of unreliability, namely – in part, at least – their frankness about their misdemeanour overrides their unreliability as characters. That is, they gain some sympathy in rather candidly confessing their horrid deeds.

In short, fallibility, delusion and deception figure in narration and characterization; they come in different shapes and degrees; and their nature and meaning can change in the course of the story. But the different kinds of unreliability can also be combined in intriguing ways. To take a recent instance: In Amity Gaige's (2013) novel *Schroder* the protagonist Erik Schroder as a young man changes his identity to Eric Kennedy in Dorchester, Massachusetts, where he as an East German immigrant is taken – and intends to be taken – to be related to *the* Kennedys. Later, when having been divorced for a year, he fails to return his six-year-old daughter Meadow to his ex-wife and goes on a trip that by lengthening the weekend into almost a week becomes a case of abduction. During the trip he lies and deceives a number of people, including Meadow, and in his life story and in the action portrayed during the trip, he is multiply deceptive. But he is also repeatedly deluded in thinking that he is a good father to Meadow: he neglects and endangers her repeatedly, feeds her mainly doughnuts and caffeinated lemonade, and finally his neglect causes her to have a life-threatening asthmatic attack. What is more, the novel is composed of a story of the trip written as a confession in jail by Schroder to his ex-wife in order to explain the motives, both for his false identity and his abduction of their daughter. Since his detailed story shows how narcissistic he has been not only towards his wife and child but also to his father (whom he has not seen for years, so as not to disclose his new identity), as a narrator he is mainly fallible: he thinks he is not such a bad man and does not seem to be aware that he himself discloses a wealth of evidence showing his true nature. Finally, the author points to his true identity by calling the novel by the real name he has never been able to discard, despite living for decades as Eric Kennedy: willy-nilly, he is the East German immigrant he has always been, Schroder. As narrator and character he is fallible, deluded as well as deceptive. Still, just as in the case of Banville's narrators, by Gaige's skilful narration readers understand the motivation behind his unreliable behaviour and may feel some sympathy for him (not least as a father who really does love his daughter deeply), despite his immoral actions.

In poetry, too, intentional deception of different kinds is age-old. In the ancient Indian collection of poetry called *Sattasaī* we find a poem that in a sense spans all modes of literature: it is poetry (has a lyrical form, the musical *āryā* metre), it is dramatic (has a dramatic speaker) and it suggests a narrative (by implicit event sequencing) – all in four lines. What is more, the narrator means the opposite of what she says:

> Mother-in-law sleeps here, I there:
> look, traveler, while it's light.
> For at night when you cannot see
> you must not fall into my bed.
> (Quoted in Ānandavardhana and Abhinavagupta 1990: 98)[19]

I quote the poem from Rājānaka Ānandavardhana's classic poetics *Dhvanyāloka*, whose major contribution lies mainly in that it analyses different kinds of *dhvani* (aesthetic suggestion) that cover a wide field of meaning, including denotation, connotation and allusion as well as the kind of indirection by which what seems a prohibition in fact is an invitation (that is, come to my bed).[20] In contrast to much of *Sattasaī*, in the oldest Japanese collection of folk and court poetry, the *Manyōshū* (1940/2005: 288) from the eighth century, the overall tone of its poems of longing and loss is one of sincerity, but although the speakers seldom are unreliable or ironic towards interlocutors, they can occasionally lie to others: "Come to me, my dearest, / Come in through the bamboo blinds! / Should my mother ask me, / I'll say, 'Twas but a gust of wind".

A more recent, and more well-known, example of unreliability in poetry is Robert Browning's "My Last Duchess" from 1842, in which the Duke as a speaker

---

19 For another translation (from Prakrit, a kind of vernacular Sanskrit) see the *Sattasaī* collection *Poems on Life and Love in Ancient India* (2009: 154). The collection includes a host of poems with ironic or unreliable speakers, many of whom are women.

20 As Thomas Furniss (2012: 298) has noted, (Western) literary theory and criticism did not centrally discuss connotation and denotation until the mid-twentieth century. In Indian poetics different facets of *dhvani* have been studied since *Dhvanyāloka* (see Ānandavardhana and Abhinavagupta 1990). See Hogan (2003/2009: 45–75) for a presentation and contemporary application of *Dhvanyāloka* and Abhinavagupta's commentary on it in cognitive literary studies. Oatley (2002, 2011: 107–132) too makes use of the basis of Indian poetics in *rasas* (literary flavours) in his psychology of reading fiction and viewing films. See also 8.2.

of the dramatic monologue is deluded to say the least: He is in the process of negotiating a new marriage and dismisses his previous wife, the portrait of whom he is showing to a matchmaker, as seemingly unfaithful, because she used to smile at all sort of people: "This grew; I gave commands; / Then all smiles stopped together. There she stands / As if alive" (Browning 1989/2004: 26; ll. 45–47). Browning implies that the Duchess, apparently killed by the Duke's command, was innocent and the Duke a jealous murderer. Thus, the Duke has been deluded by his jealousy and in his monologue he is trying to deceive the match-maker that he had the right to sentence her to death. However, readers have not been taken in by the Duke, but have rather delighted in Browning's deft use of irony.[21] In the twentieth century there is a long line of ironic and unreliable speakers in poetry, not least in English – just think of Dorothy Parker, John Betjeman, Ogden Nash and D. J. Enright.

Thus, a central way of viewing literary narrators, characters and speakers is on a scale of intentional agency, which is dependent on the knowledge and skills they have. For instance, as Schroder simply does not have the makings of the good father he would very much like to be, his intention is undercut by his deficient parenting. In a sense, the scale of intentionality has in many ways been what the literature on unreliable narration has focused on, usually without employing the notion of intentionality. Perhaps a context-sensitive use of such a scale of intentionality in terms of both narration and characterization could be combined with Phelan's six types of unreliability (2005: 49–53) concerning reporting, regarding and reading in terms of *mis-* and *under-*, and I would add *over-* (see Pettersson 2005c: 85–86n11). An instance of, say, *over-reporting* (that is, of the narrator telling more than he knows) is to be found in Banville's *The Book of Evidence* in which the narrator gives names to characters, such as Reck, Mrs Reck and Cunningham, whose names he admits he does not know.

But, as I see it, the main shortcoming of the scholarship on literary unreliability is that it has by and large centred on narrators and (later) characters, whereas unreliability in literature in fact often seems to go beyond narrators and characters and be lodged in the exposition as such or in combinations of expositional, narratorial and focal unreliability.

---

[21] For more examples of indirection and hypothetical action see 6.1 and 6.2.

3.4 Expositional and Combined: Exposition as Manipulation

To my mind, the most important work on exposition in fiction was produced in Israel in the 1970s. In his major work *Expositional Modes and Temporal Ordering in Fiction* Meir Sternberg (1978: 1) starts out by noting that "the function of exposition [is] to introduce the reader into an unfamiliar world, the fictive world of the story, by providing him [sic] with the general and specific antecedents indispensable to the understanding of what happens in it". He goes on to show that exposition comes in many forms, such as preliminary and delayed, and that the latter includes "expositional gaps" employed "with a view to exciting interest" (Sternberg 1978: 35–55, 50 quotes). Further on, Sternberg (1978: 180, 182) discusses the detective story, in which "the author does his utmost to mystify, misdirect, and baffle" what he terms "the curious reader" through "a retardatory structure that achieves its effects – sustained curiosity and suspense – by distributing the expositional material piecemeal throughout while postponing the concentrated, true exposition – the opening part of the fabula [story] – to the end of the sujet [discourse]" (see also Sternberg 2003a, 2003b). What comes across both explicitly and implicitly is that although text-centred in the best tradition of classical narratology, Sternberg is aware that there is an intentional agent who aims to familiarize his or her readers with the fictional world and who can make use of exposition to trick or manipulate them in order to maintain curiosity or suspense. His reference to the scene in which the exposition is completed in the thirty-third chapter of Charlotte Brontë's (1847/1953: 437) *Jane Eyre* in this connection shows his awareness of the use of such manipulation in other kinds of fiction (see Sternberg 1978: 182).[22]

At about the same time as Sternberg and well aware of his work, Menakhem Perry worked on similar matters or what he termed "Literary Dynamics" in his influential essay from 1979.[23] He shows how the order of a fictional text can create meanings, also so that "the reader may be said to be led into a 'trap,' i.e., is not supposed to identify the organizing principle, merely to be affected by it" (Perry 1979: 40). According to Perry's convincing reading, William Faulkner's (1930/1995) story "A Rose for Emily" includes "a series of factual deceptions with which the story misleads its readers". Since the story does not have a char-

---

[22] Indeed, this is an ancient technique: even the character narrator Lucius on the first page of Apuleius' (1994/2008: 1) *The Golden Ass* places hints of writing his story on "Egyptian paper inscribed with the sharpened point of a reed from the Nile" that are only understood in the last book where the Egyptian goddess Isis restores his human shape.
[23] In fact, Perry (1979: 35) notes that he published a version of this essay in Hebrew as early as 1973.

acter narrator as such (it is narrated by in the first-person plural by the townsfolk as "we", apparently through an unnamed narrator), the deceptions are less due to the deluded narrators than to the organization of the exposition. In the course of his reading of the story Perry makes other theoretical and interpretive points, but let me only single out two of the most important ones. First, there are two kinds of comparisons with Emily in the story: that between the "real" Emily and the thwarted view of her by the expositionally manipulated readers, which is brought to coincide with that of the real Emily at the end, when they learn that she is a murderer. The readers' view is also set in contrast to that of the townsfolk, who in narrating the story as "we" clearly also have a thwarted view of Emily, and they too learn the truth about her at the end (see Perry 1979: 354). Second, when meanings in a fictional text are "consistently constructed or rejected", "the reader maintains the rejected meanings as a system of 'hovering' meanings", which are part of the text's "intentions" (Perry 1979: 356). Thus, Perry is able to discuss what I would term *expositional manipulation* on the levels of narration, characterization and interpretation and show that even discarded meanings are part and parcel of the meaning of a fictional narrative.

As I see it, the study of unreliability in fiction should take into account the expositional manipulation of readers. By structural or rhetorical means such manipulation suggests a view of a character or the action that is later shown to be untenable. Again, let me note that calling such indirection *irony* would in my opinion stretch that term beyond its scope. There is play with multiple, corrected and thwarted meaning of all kinds, but it is not necessarily ironic as such. Rather, as Sternberg notes, it aims to create suspense and curiosity in readers – as well as, I would add, a deepened interest in the plot and the motivations of its characters and a broader understanding of the complexity in human behaviour and morals. Also, despite the diffident ways Sternberg and Perry mostly speak of actual intentional agents, all such manipulation is of course brought about by the author in the first place, even though it may be channelled by narrators or speakers (thereby adding to the complexity, as in the case of the narrator speaking in the first-person plural in "A Rose for Emily"). That is, the scale of intentionality in narrators and characters discussed above is not necessarily separate from expositional manipulation, since narratorial, focal and expositional kinds of unreliability are intentional in one way or another and can occur simultaneously. What Sternberg and Perry also demonstrate is the complex and processual nature of what I have termed expositional manipulation, which can give us more detailed tools to deal with unreliability in fiction. More recently, Phelan (2007: 15–22) has been one of the very few who have analysed the ways exposition is used throughout narratives, but what we still lack is a broader understanding of the various ways in which exposition is used to convey unreliability in fiction.

On the basis of the groundwork provided by Sternberg and Perry let me now present a preliminary survey of some techniques and features of fictional unreliability by expositional manipulation, often in combination with narratorial and focal features. Some of them are more or less work-specific, but many are also informed by particular genres or subgenres.

Suggested by title. In Adam Johnson's (2012/2013) Pulitzer Prize-winning novel *The Orphan Master's Son* the protagonist is deluded into thinking that he is not one of the orphans in the North Korean orphanage he grew up in but actually the orphan master's son. This is important to him, since orphans are considered pariahs. However, finally he understands that he has been deluded. By the title of his novel Johnson points not only to the delusion of one of the protagonists but also to the deception that is symbolical of the totalitarian North Korean regime, from the lowest social class to the highest.

Speculative (narratorial). One of Nathaniel Hawthorne's (1835/1987: 75) most widely anthologised stories, "Wakefield", starts out like this: "In some old magazine or newspaper, I recollect a story, told as truth, of a man – let us call him Wakefield – who absented himself for a long time from his wife". Even in Hawthorne's day, showing that the basis of a story is speculative was an old narrative trick, but Hawthorne puts it to multiple use: the unnamed narrator does not remember where he read about a man, whose name he apparently does not recall, and notes that the story is "told as truth", as is so much gossip and legend. The story is full of such hedging and speculation, as for instance when the narrator suggests: "Let us now imagine Wakefield bidding adieu to his wife" (1835/1987: 75). He continuously hedges in his narration (not least by "perhaps"), apostrophizes Wakefield, poses questions and answers them by more speculation, such as "What sort of a man was Wakefield? We are free to shape out our own idea, and call it by his name" (Hawthorne 1835/1987: 76). In this speculative form, Hawthorne's readers finally learn the entire story of Wakefield's absence including a moral drawn from it, but excluding his motivation or his reception when returning home. We could call this an instance of what Brian McHale (1982: 223) has termed "*epistemological* hesitation" in fantastic and modern fiction.

The narratorial speculative technique was taken up by Hawthorne's friend Herman Melville (1851/2002: 18) in his famous opening line of *Moby-Dick*, "Call me Ishmael", in the first chapter subtitled "*Loomings*", and was even more prevalently employed in the fiction of Henry James in terms of what is known about the characters, their actions and morals. The point I am making is that such speculation is not only narratorial but shows that the very exposition too is manipulated, sometimes intentionally by narrators and their use of exposition (*Daisy Miller* by James; see below), sometimes by inadequate, speculative or wrong information ("Wakefield"). Thus, what is presented as the plot or action is simply unreliable. Of course, modernist fiction was to put speculation to an even greater variety of uses.[24]

Speculative (focal). In Adam Haslett's (2002/2003) short story "The Good Doctor" the narrative is focalised by the main character Frank from the East Coast, who having recently graduated as a psychiatrist has landed his first position at a county clinic. He goes on a house call to see the severely traumatized housewife Mrs Buckholdt, who has merely asked for her sedatives to be renewed, but this cannot be done without a doctor seeing the patient. The story is all about how Frank does his best to be the good doctor of the title and how he thinks he knows what is best for Mrs Buckholdt, since he is convinced that "[p]eople like this needed him, needed a person to listen to" (Haslett 2002/2003: 44). Much of the story is about how he speculates as to her condition and tries to form a diagnosis by talking to her. In the course of the story it becomes clear that – in the words of his ex-girl friend – Frank is "a romantic clinging to an old myth about the value of talk" (Haslett 2002/2003: 28), that is, it is he rather than Mrs Buckholdt who has a need to talk. Apparently, Frank has led a fairly comfortable and secure life, so his speculation – his diagnosis – of Mrs Buckholdt seems wrong, which he does not see, but Haslett's readers do. With his naivety and background, he simply has no insight into her life and condition, so to the very end of the story he is deluded about being a good doctor and understanding the needs of Mrs Buckholdt. This is a case of how a character throughout the exposition of the story is unreliable in that he focalises his speculations as to his own identity, his professional identity and that of the other main protagonist. Similarly, to the very end the rather self-satisfied character narrator Don Fenton in James Tiptree, Jr.'s [Alice B. Sheldon] (1972/2014) story "The Women Men Don't See" cannot comprehend why some women might prefer to live with aliens rather than men, but Tiptree's readers get the point.

Biased (by comparison). All unreliable narration and focalisation is about bias in one way or another, but at times bias can be in focus, for instance by the juxtaposition of biased and non-biased stories. Ryonosuke Akutagawa's short story (1922/1959) "In a Grove" is famous not least for providing the basic plot for Akira Kurosawa's film *Rashomon* (1950).[25] In the film there are four ver-

---

24 See e.g. Virginia Woolf's story "The Mark on the Wall" as discussed in 4.4.
25 The title of the film and the setting of its frame story is based on another story by Akutagawa (1915/1959) called "Rashomon".

sions of the same event, but in Akutagawa's rather brief story there are seven accounts relating to the death – apparently a murder by a bandit – of a man in a grove. Most of them seem – at least after the entire story is read – unreliable, since the last version is "THE STORY OF THE MURDERED MAN, AS TOLD THROUGH A MEDIUM" and thus most likely reliable (Akutagawa 1922/1959: 26–28, 26 quote). Despite the title of this final version, which suggests that the man is murdered, it seems to be the definitive version (that is, if indeed a dead man's spirit could speak, it would hardly lie) that throws light on the other six. It discloses that the man committed suicide, since he had been disgraced by having witnessed a bandit raping his wife. In this way, it also shows that most of the other versions are unreliable: the woodcutter lies, because he has stolen the sword by which the man committed suicide; the policeman is fallible, since he too easily jumps to the conclusion that the bandit Tajomaru is the murderer; Tajomaru lies that he killed the man in combat, so as to preserve his bandit's honour; and the man's wife claims Tajomaru killed her husband, since she – according her husband's final version – asked the reluctant bandit to kill him to preserve her honour (the moral code she abides by can only accept that one man alive has known her intimately). The other two versions seem largely reliable: that of a Buddhist monk, who saw the man and his wife on the road before having been assaulted by the thief, and that of the man's mother-in-law, who narrates how the couple started out on their journey. Unlike the film *Rashomon* in which the four stories are left juxtaposed, thus producing what later has been termed *the Rashomon effect* of biased memory, the story does not only show how biased different versions of the same event are but also how there in fact seem to be truthful accounts. Also, it thematizes the different honour codes that override death or jail for the three protagonists. More common than such balancing of bias is, however, that either bias (as in the above example of focal speculation) or ambiguity prevails.

Ambiguous. Perhaps the best-known instance of ambiguity in unreliable narration is Henry James's (1898/1974) novella "The Turn of the Screw". Is the governess a murderer or an innocent young woman? Readers who are not ready to accept the ambiguity will thus make an interpretive decision whether to read the novella as a Gothic thriller or as a tragic realist story. Similarly, if you think that the protagonist in Karen Joy Fowler's (1991/2012) *Sarah Canary* is a strange woman, you read the novel as historical fiction, but if you decide that she is an alien, you read it as science fiction. However, as the last chapter lists newspaper articles on strange occurences in the contemporary world, it seems evident that Fowler (1991/2012: 299–300) here, as in much of her fiction, in fact wants to straddle genres.

But ambiguity in fiction can also be due to delayed exposition and such ambiguity can be even more perplexing. Joanne Harris's novel (2010/2011) *blueeyedboy* is completely composed of texts supposedly posted on the Internet as web journals and comments on them, which makes everything written supremely unreliable. As the main web journal author and protagonist **blueeyedboy** puts it: "On WeJay [web journal] I can vent as I please, confess without fear of censure; be myself – or indeed, someone else – in a world where no one is quite what they seem" (Harris 2010/2011: 25). The characters in the novel take on different personalities, both in their lives and as net characters, as well as steal other people's passwords, so that they can impersonate them or rather their fictitious web personalities. Since the actual persons behind central name tags are unfolded late in the novel, with a central one disclosed close to the end (unless possibly impersonated by someone else, as the protagonist thinks), the novel is expositionally ambiguous. Close to the end **blueeyedboy** may still reflect: "Real life makes so little sense; only fic [net fiction] has meaning", but real life is to have its vengeance – in the fiction authored by Harris (2010/2011: 496–497), of course. Since for much of the novel the identities of the persons are in question before they are finally disclosed, the exposition also makes use of *hypothetical* and *processual* forms of unreliability (see below).

Volatile. A special kind of ambiguity comes across when characters act in highly volatile ways. A prime example of this is Philip K. Dick's posthumously published realist novel *Humpty Dumpty in Oakland*. "The mind is a strange instrument", says one of the characters, and in their actions and pronouncements all protagonists show that this is the case (Dick 1986/2008: 242). Al Miller, a used car salesman, and his landlord Jim Fergessen may think they know each other but their volatile behaviour proves that neither of them knows what he himself or the other thinks. The same is true of their marital relations: husbands and wives simply do not know each other, which leads to tragic outcomes for most of them. This may be an age-old motif, but the characters' impulsive psychological motivation is rather unusual and it is revealed in piecemeal ways. Al in particular is "a humpty dumpty", as his friend Tootie tells him close to the end: "You just stand there, stand around, while it all happen to you. You just perch and watch" (Dick 1986/2008: 247). Al's problem is not that he repeatedly changes his mind or that his acts are ambiguous as such, but that he in fact neither knows himself nor his spouse and friends – and hence acts in rather volatile ways.

Embedded. In discussing Dick's story "The Electric Ant" in 3.3 we saw that the main characters are not only deluded as to their existence, but that the protagonist Poole is a robot and his secretary only a part of his "reality tape", that is, an implanted figment of his imagination. The secretary's delusion is thus embedded in that of Poole, and their respective delusion is controlled by the company stockholders. Similarly, in Johnson's *The Orphan Master's Son* all characters live in a society where the overriding deceptions come from the North Korean regime, so that the deceptions and delusions of the characters, including those of the protagonist Pak Jun Do (cf. John Doe), are largely devised as survival strategies in the totalitarian system.

Contradictory (overt or covert moral versus contents). Daniel Defoe (1722/1972: 1) starts his preface to *Moll Flanders* by complaining that "The world is so taken up of late with novels and romances, that it will be hard for a private history to be taken for genuine" and goes on to note that the rather unreliable ex-prostitute Moll at the end "pretends to be" "penitent and humble" – just as her author pretends that "[all] possible care [...] has been taken to give no lewd ideas". But as so many authors before and after him, Defoe clearly savours the descriptions of immoral behaviour, despite his overt protestations to the contrary. Here the contents of the novel undermine the overt moral stance, but the moral undermined can also be more covert. By his mottos to *American Psycho* Bret Easton Ellis (1991: n.p.) intimates that his point is to show a main character who, though fictional, "represents a generation that is still living out its days among us" (quote from Dostoevsky's *Notes from Underground*) and warns that the moral rules of civilization must be adhered to, otherwise "we'd be killing one another" (quote by Miss Manners [Judith Martin]). However, as the ensuing debate about the novel suggested, many readers felt that Ellis's apparent delight in the gory killings of his protagonist Patrick Bateman in fact implies a fascination with depravity that outweighs his black-humour indictment of callous capitalism.

Contradictory (narratorial). One of the most widely discussed examples of unreliable narration, Ford Madox Ford's *The Good Soldier*, is also a novel of expositional unreliability. Most evidently, in telling his story the character narrator John Dowell leaves a key scene last. This is the one in which he walks out on his friend Edward Ashburnham, well knowing that Edward is about to commit suicide (Ford 1915/1995: 162). A few pages earlier he has professed that Edward is "one of the two persons [he] has ever really loved", the other being his deranged beloved Nancy Rufford, in the same paragraph that he calls Edward and Nancy the "villains" of his story (Ford 1915/1995: 160). Dowell does indeed seem to belong to "the slightly-deceitful" who "flourish", while "the passionate, the headstrong, and the too-truthful are condemned to suicide and madness" (Ford 1915/1995: 161). Many readers may agree with Eugene Goodheart (1986/1995: 377) that Dowell in his feelings and responses is "ambivalent and inconsistent", whereas others, Paul B. Armstrong (1987/1995: 388) among them, would claim that he "struggles, with mixed and increasing success, to give a trustworthy account of his history". For Goodheart, the unreliability in *The Good Soldier* is *ambiguous*; for Armstrong it is at first ambiguous as to reliability but that ambiguity decreases *processually* until Dowell is trustworthy; while for me (in the above reading), Dowell turns out to be among "the slightly-deceitful", that is, he is deluded or possibly deceptive.

Contradictory in thought versus speech or action (focal). One of Virginia Woolf's most recurrent techniques to show the complexity in her characters is the contradiction inherent in what the characters say or do and what they think. A veritable showcase of this is the story "Together and Apart" in which one of the two protagonists, the main focal character Miss Anning, even comments on her mixed feelings when having met Mr Serle: "Of all things, nothing is so strange as human discourse, she thought, because of its changes, its extraordinary irrationality, her dislike being now nothing short of the most intense and rapturous love" (Woolf 1944/1989: 193). Throughout the story both Miss Anning and Mr Serle have long and intricate trains of thought, but what they say are mere platitudes, as when the former, having just met the latter and having thought about the night sky, utters "What a beautiful night!" and straightaway thinks that such an utterance is "Foolish! Idiotically foolish!" (Woolf 1944/1989: 189).

Similarly, the actions and opinions of the characters in Ford's tetralogy *Parade's End* are much like those of Sylvia Tietjens and her husband Christopher, "the products of caprice" or "a matter of contrariety" (Ford 1924–1928/2013: 137). What the characters think and say is largely contradictory throughout the four novels. For instance, Valentine Wannop, Christopher's lover later on, reflects: "She wanted to say: 'I am falling at your feet. My arms are embracing your knees!'", but admits that "[a]ctually she said: 'I suppose it is proper to celebrate together today!'" (Ford 1924–1928/2013: 592). This technique often serves the exposition of Woolf's and Ford's fiction in that the complex disposition of the characters is revealed in delayed ways. This is much like the corrections typical of unreliable narration, yet it is important to note that often it does not throw suspicion on the character, but rather is in line with Ford's (1914/1995: 265) view that literary impressionism attempts to convey "an illusion of reality" and is thus not primarily employed to suggest unreliability.[26]

Misleading. Most Golden Age detective novels à la Agatha Christie or Dorothy L. Sayers knowingly spread red herrings in their narratives so as to keep readers

---

[26] In fact, modernist fiction could be viewed as extending the descriptive impetus of realist and naturalist fiction to the cognition of characters, in which case the use of impressionism, however unreliable it may seem, is at the service of a kind of realism.

guessing who the culprit is. Still, as we have seen when discussing Sternberg's and Perry's views of exposition, much general fiction misleads by expositional manipulation in order to increase the readers' engagement in the fictional world and its characters. Recent psychological thrillers, such as Gillian Flynn's (2012) *Gone Girl* and Paula Hawkins's (2015) *The Girl on the Train*, often make use of fallible, deluded or deceptive character narrators in order to retain the suspense until the final revelation. Since detective novels and thrillers thus finally disclose the fact that readers have been misled in one way or another, they are also processual (see below).

There are different kinds of misleading. As a matter of course, the reader is being misled, but Agatha Christie's characters, especially if they are murderers, of course do their best to deceive both the other characters, especially Hercule Poirot, and the readers as the character narrator Dr Sheppard does in *The Murder of Roger Ackroyd* (1926). Flynn's immensely popular thriller *Gone Girl*[27] has two character narrators, Nick and his wife Amy, who give their respective views on their relationship and especially on how Amy went missing.[28] Amy's narrative, her diary in particular, is directed to dupe *multiple audiences:* first and foremost her husband, but as the novel progresses clearly also the police as well as the media, who in turn may influence the police investigation – and of course ultimately the readers. Later, Nick too in part learns to deceive the police and the media, and most importantly Amy, which makes their cat-and-mouse game particularly enjoyable. Also, there may be *multiple deceivers*, as in Christie's *Murder on the Orient Express* (1934).

Processual / partial. Michael Frayn's (2002) *Spies*, whose unreliability I have analysed elsewhere (Pettersson 2005c), is for most of the novel fallibly focalised by the protagonist Stephen Wheatley as a boy, whereas as an adult narrator, he is deceptive in not letting on what he knows and is thus misleading. That is, the novel is a case of dissonant narration (with the narrating self separated from his experiencing self) until the closing pages, when Wheatley finally discloses the actual meaning of the actions and pronouncements he misunderstood as a

---

27 In January 2016 the number of reviews (not mere thumbs up) on Amazon.com was over 42 000, which may be more than any single book ever has received on that or any other website. For instance, J. K. Rowling's most popular Harry Potter novels barely passed 11 000 reviews, which no books by, for instance, Stephen King, George R. R. Martin or J. R. R. Tolkien reached. However, Hawkins's recent *The Girl on the Train* (2015), had already received over 38 000 reviews and the first novel in the erotic romance series *Fifty Shades of Grey* (2011) by E. L. James [Erika Mitchell] had over 33 000 reviews.
28 Please note that the rest of this paragraph includes some spoilers, so prospective readers of *Gone Girl* may want to read the novel first.

young boy, after which the narration is entirely reliable. In Raymond Carver's story (1988/1989) "Blackbird Pie" the narrator thinks somebody is impersonating his wife's handwriting in a farewell letter to him, until on the last page he gains the insight that he has been deluded in thinking that he really knows his wife and her handwriting and so turns into a reliable narrator. But the shift need not be so absolute. In Tiptree's (1971/2014) story "Love Is the Plan the Plan Is Death", the spider mother finally goes to such lengths in taking care for her offspring that it throws new light on arachnoid evolution. Such shifts from unreliability to reliability in narration often occur in *Bildungsroman*-like stories as the result of a long process (*Spies*) or a sudden insight ("Blackbird Pie") or action ("Love is the Plan the Plan is Death"). They may occur simultaneously in the narration and the exposition, that is, the process or the shift occurs when the narrator discloses or realizes a fact that completes the exposition.

Shifts from unreliability to reliability are quite common, but there can also be shifts from reliability to unreliability. In James's novella *Daisy Miller* a young American man called Winterbourne focalises much of the story and seems quite a reliable focaliser for a while. In his eyes the other protagonist Daisy Miller is an irritating flirt and behaves badly, while after she dies of Roman fever readers understand that, in the words of another of her suitors, "she was the most innocent" young lady (James 1878/1974: 241). Since her death is in part caused by his callousness towards her, Winterbourne and his focalisation finally comes across as unreliable, whereas Daisy is now seen as a moral, if naive young lady victimized by Winterbourne.[29] But the shift to unreliability can come in a supremely ironic last sentence, as in Chinua Achebe's (1958/1984: 191) *Things Fall Apart*, where the tragic fate of the protagonist Okonkwo during the colonisation of Igboland in Nigeria is viewed through the eyes of the British District Commissioner, who aims to write a book called "*The Pacification of the Primitive Tribes of the Lower Niger*".[30]

Local / overridden. Unreliability can occur locally in different ways. As noted above, Stevens in *The Remains of the Day* is mainly deluded, but he occasionally deceives people to believe that he is an aristocrat. However, these few instances of deception do not make him a deceptive narrator; he remains mainly deluded, which is the overriding feature of his character and narration. In Homer's (1967/

---

[29] For more detailed discussions of this inversion in *Daisy Miller* see 6.1 and especially Norrman (1998: 149–216).

[30] Most pointedly, this prospective title most likely satirizes "the International Society for the Suppression of Savage Customs" for which Mr Kurtz is writing his report in *Heart of Darkness* (1902/1976: 71), a novella that Achebe (1977/1990: 19) has critised for being "strangely unaware of the racism on which it [imperial exploitation] sharpened its iron tooth".

2007) *The Odyssey* Odysseus as narrator and character is largely reliable even though he is repeatedly cunning enough to lie and cheat in order to get back to Ithaca alive.[31] In *The Kalevala* (1847/1990: 194) the trickster-like god Väinämöinen's lies are often fortuitous – he simply knows he will not be able to get away with them and finally gives up and confesses, as for instance in canto 16 to the girl of Tuoni: "If I did lie a little / was a fraud the second time / now I'll tell the truth". Such instances of unreliability are local enough not to tarnish the reliability of the trickster-like heroes. Still, one should remember that all kinds of mythological literature include trickster characters who are heroes precisely owing to their unreliability (see Williams 2012). This also goes for Jack Sparrow (played by Johnny Depp), who in the film *Pirates of the Caribbean: The Curse of the Black Pearl* (2003) confesses as much: "Me? I'm dishonest, and a dishonest man you can always trust to be dishonest. Honestly" (my transcription). In such cases, much like sympathetic fallible narrators such as Huck Finn or Forrest Gump, the narratorial unreliability, however encompassing, is overridden by other features, such as heroism, morality and/or sympathy.

Hypothetical. As we saw when considering "Row, Row, Row Your Boat", hypothetical narration may suggest so much that its import, at least on the face of it, is unreliable. T. S. Eliot's (1915/2015) "The Love Song of J. Alfred Prufrock" is a narrative poem that hypothesizes a walk and uses many hypothesizing techniques in order to suggest what could or might have happened (see 6.2). Hypothetical action may also be used in fantastic fiction, which in one way or another includes a what-if premise. But this does not mean that all fantastic fiction is, but rather can be, unreliable.

Fantastic. First I would like to question the oft-repeated claim that "unreliable narration is deeply rooted in the realist novel because it depends on kinds of naturalization based on real-world frames of reference" (Zerweck 2001: 170). It may be true in the sense that even fantastic fiction makes use of realist, pseudo-realist or logical aspects in portraying fictional worlds and characters, but not in the sense that only realist fiction can be unreliable. Even a brief look at literary history shows that different kinds of unreliability are prevalent, which proves that unreliability occurs much before its alleged starting-point in the eighteenth century or so. In fact, Riggan (1981: 39–48) discusses the narrator Lucius in Apuleius's *The Golden Ass* as an unreliable pícaro, but we could go even further back in time. At the very start of *The Epic of Gilgamesh* King Gilgamesh is depicted in no uncertain terms as wise. He is repeatedly referred to as "wise in all matters" and one who "[*learnt*] of everything the sum of wisdom"

---

[31] In a web paper Skalin (n.d.) analyses five scenes in which Odysseus lies.

(*The Epic of Gilgamesh* 1999/2000: 1; 1.2 , 4, 6). How does this square with the fact that even on Tablet 1 his behaviour is anything but wise: he mistreats his people and "[b]y day and by night his tyranny grows harsher" (*The Epic of Gilgamesh* 1999/2000: 3; 1.69)? When finally appeased by having fought Enkidu and becoming his friend, he leaves Úruk, the city state where he is king, and has many adventures before finally returning. In other words, the narrator contradicts himself, that is, seems less than reliable: at first at least, Gilgamesh, however cunning during his adventures, is far from a wise monarch.[32] A more blatant example of unreliability in a fantastic story from about four millennia ago is the Egyptian story *The Tale of the Shipwrecked Sailor*, in which two speakers – one a sailor, the other a giant serpent he meets – tell fantastic stories, but so that their stories nevertheless include a useful moral for the sailor's interlocutor (see chapter 9, point [4]).

In Lucian's (2008: 621, 622) tall-tale novel *A True Story* from the second century CE or so, the narrator starts out tongue-in-cheek by accusing Homer and other authors of "fantastic yarns" consisting of "literary horseplay", that is, "lying", and goes on to claim: "I will say one thing that is true, and that is that I am a liar" – but of course he calls his narrative *A True Story*. Is such play with the status of fiction unreliable? Well yes, at least in the sense that it leaves the narrator's audience, like the Jack Sparrow quote, spinning in the delightfully vicious circle of the liar's paradox. What about the what-if premise in fantastic fiction? Since this premise is usually not presented explicitly and often fantastic fiction on the contrary may purport to be "a true story" (which often gives it away as fiction),[33] fantastic fiction seems closely related to that of unreliable narration. In *The Arabian Nights* there are many unreliable narrators and characters, such as the black slave, who lies that he has cuckolded a man in "The

---

32 One way of trying to hold on to narrative reliability would be to note that since in the beginning the narrator notes that Gilgamesh "brought back a tale of before the Deluge", he is wise only after having returned from his adventures (*The Epic of Gilgamesh* 1999/2000: 1; 1.8). However, the initial presentation of him as wise includes no such modification. For a reading of how the narration in *Gilgamesh* is "a re-enactment of a progressive insight" see Korthals Altes (2007: 192) and for *Gilgamesh* as an early instance of how the human mind is based on a *trickster brain* see Williams (2012: 2).
33 In some narratives, especially orally traded ones, the authority of the narrator is based on the fact that the veracity is in no way undercut. In the Mandingo epic *Sundiata* about the thirteenth-century ruler by that name, the griot Djeli Mamoudou Kouyaté, the authoritative teller of the tale and actual person narrating it, starts out presenting his familial lineage of griots and then asserts his authority in telling the story: "My word is pure and free of all untruth; it is the word of my father; it is the word of my father's father. I will give you my father's words just as I received them; royal griots do not know what lying is" (Niane 2006/2007: 1).

Tale of the Three Apples", which makes the man kills his wife. The father-in-law feels so much pity for his son-in-law grieving for the wife he has murdered that he in turn lies by confessing to the murder. Not only the is actual murderer finally acquitted (owing to the supposedly understandable rage caused by the slave's lie) but also the slave, since his master is able to tell the story so well – the supreme virtue in *The Arabian Nights* – that the Caliph "laughed till he fell on his back and ordered that the story be recorded and be made public amongst the people" (*The Arabian Nights* 2001/2004: 153). Hence, the exposition is delayed, so that the lies, the actual murderer and the fates of all characters are exposed in deferred ways, in keeping with what was to become the structural device of detective fiction, excepting the twist that all culprits are acquitted.

In both Boccaccio's *Decamerone* and Chaucer's *Canterbury Tales* one of the key delights for readers is to try to assess the reliability of the various narrators and characters. In fact, since Chaucer the Pilgrim – that is, the narrator – in his "Prologue" to *The Canterbury Tales* repeatedly emphasizes that his intention is not to tell a "tale untrewe" and compares himself to "Crist [...] in Holy Writ" as well as to Plato, he evidently protests too much and his readers know that his tongue is firmly in his cheek (Chaucer 1964/1979: 34, 36; ll. 737, 741). In a similar way, *Don Quixote* is a kind of fictional treatise on the difference between appearance and reality or, more precisely, on various kinds of deceptions and delusions. It is told by a fictitious Moorish narrator, who knows the thoughts in Don Quixote's mind as well as the adventures where no-one is present except Don Quixote and Sancho Panza, a fact which the latter even comments on, thus questioning the narrator's truthfulness (see Cervantes 2003/2005: 23, 472). Later, when the English novel started out, unreliability was often used. From Defoe's *Moll Flanders* on there are many different kinds of unreliability, not least in (realist) fiction, but of course in poetry and drama too, even though they have so far been shown very little attention in this respect (see however Hühn 2015 and Nünning and Schwanecke 2015).

Finally, let me reiterate that in the history of fiction there is a wide area between realist and fantastic fiction (see 2.2). The premise of Markus Zusak's (2005/2007) *The Book Thief* may be fantastic: the novel is narrated by death personified, but the story is a rather realistic, if somewhat sentimental, story of Nazi Germany. Jenny Diski's novel (1988/1990) *Like Mother* does not just have a fantastic premise but an utterly impossible one: most of the novel is narrated by an anhydranencephalic newborn infant, that is, by a baby girl without a brain, but her description of her and her mother's lives is very realistic. One possible way of reading the novel is that her mother needs to tell the story of her and her baby's symbiotic lives and does so as a separate narrator in dialogue with the infant (who, according to a final twist, may not have existed at all), hence the title which seems drawn from the saying "like mother, like daughter" (see Diski 1988/1990: 187, 189). This shows how closely related imagination (the fantastic narrative perspective), realistic depiction and unreliability can be.

Of course, these notes on unreliability in fantastic fiction only indicate that it appears in various forms throughout literary history and that there is a vast unexplored area that awaits further analysis, not least in terms of specifying the relation between generic and work-specific features in unreliable fiction. What I hope this discussion of expositional and combined forms of unreliable fiction has demonstrated is how central a feature unreliability is in constructing literary worlds and that the study of it must be broadened to include expositional forms that alone or together with narratorial and focal means add to the plethora of unreliable usages in fiction.

In sum, this chapter has attempted to show that (1) life and literature are related in matters of unreliability in that all representation has to do with some sort of imitation; (2) unreliability in literature, especially fiction, can be viewed on a scale of intentionality for narrators and characters; (3) narratorial and focal unreliability should be studied together with the rather neglected forms of expositional manipulation; and (4) fantastic fiction too often is unreliable in different ways.

Now that we have reviewed how literary imagination and mimesis works, how they have been studied, and how they comes across in various unreliable guises, we are ready to consider how literary worlds are shaped by some basic modes and themes.

4 The Shaping of Literary Worlds

So far we have seen that mimesis is basic in understanding literary imagination and provides a ground for assessing the realistic and fantastic features of literary works, whose narrators, characters and exposition may be unreliable. Now let us consider how literary worlds are shaped. First I discuss how literature is implicitly and explicitly framed, so that it is understood as part of what is (now regarded as) literature. Then I present the building blocks of literary worlds, their modes and main themes, and give four examples of literary world-making.

4.1 The Imaginative Frame of Literary Imagination

How do you know you are reading literature? The short answer is, by a number of cues and conventions. They might be explicit: somebody tells you of "a great novel", you find it in the library under fiction or the back cover labels it "fiction" or perhaps even more genre-specifically "fantasy" or "thriller". You may first encounter what Gérard Genette (1987/1997: xviii *et passim*) has called *paratextual* devices and conventions: they may be within the book and include titles, forewords, epigraphs or afterwords (*peritext*), or outside it, either public, such as a review or an advertisement, or private, a letter from the author or a recommendation by a friend (*epitext*).

Such cues are of course important for reading a book in the first place. But part of any decision to read it has to do with what David Herman (2009: 17) has called a literary narrative's *situatedness*, by which he means that "interpreters seeking to use textual cues to reconstruct a storyworld must also draw inferences about the communicative goals that have structured the specific occasion of the telling, motivating the use of certain cues in favor of others and shaping the arrangement of the cues selected". Thus, readers must understand the communicative situation the text occasions, by for instance going on to decide what genre or genres it draws on, using their knowledge of any cues and conventions with which they are familiar. Perhaps the broadest of such conventions is to decide whether what they are reading is literature rather than a factual or instructive text. Even when fact and fiction are blended, as in the non-fiction novel, there are often clues as to its generic status, such as actual dates and locations on the one hand and viewpoints lodged in narrators or characters on the other.

It may be useful to have a general frame for literary communication that is able to encompass the different kinds of imagination that literary works entail. The frame Samuel Levin (1977: 116) proposed some four decades ago for poetry, *I imagine (myself in) and invite you to conceive a world in which* ..., could be just as useful when analysing fiction and drama (which usually takes the form of a dramatized narrative) as it is for poetry. This is in line with Mieke Bal (1985: 121–126), who, as I noted in the introduction, has pointed out that all fiction has the implicit first-person frame (*I say:*). Thus, Levin's phrase focuses in a compact way on the fact that poetry – in fact, all of literature, I would claim – is the result of a double act of imagining (*imagine, conceive*): that of the author (who invites the reader to imagine) and that of the reader (who, by continuing the act of reading, conceives the world imagined), each of which is a complex affair. In terms of literary analysis, of course, Levin's frame does not take us very far, but in providing a framework for all kinds of literature and in recognizing the double act of imagining, it may be helpful in developing a basis for the scrutiny of literary communication. In other words, when perceived, all literary worlds, however realist or fantastic, are the result of complex double acts of imagining.

Peter Lamarque and Stein Haugom Olsen (1994/1996: 39–40, 40 quote) discuss Levin's proposal and other similar ones and worry that such views may not take what they find is central – "the act of story-telling [in prose fiction] and the attitudes appropriate to it" – as the starting-point. True enough, so let us analyse how we learn about such clues. After surveying a host of empirical tests, the developmental psychologist Paul L. Harris (1998: 341–342) summarizes his findings: "young children [ages four to six] are not confused about the ontological status of imaginary creatures", that is, they know such creatures are not real. More recent research, based on two tests with storybook reading for three- to five-year-old children, shows that a majority of all children understand that fantastic, religious as well as realist stories are not real, that is, that they are "just stories" (Woolley and Cox 2007). The percentage goes up considerably when children are five years old, but is already in place for many three-year-olds. This is earlier than previous research has found and has two interesting corollaries: five-year-olds have a better grasp of realist fiction (that is, understand that it too is mere fiction) than three-year-olds and are more likely to claim that occurrences in religious as well as realist texts could really happen (the former most likely owing to having grown up in religious surroundings) (see Woolley and Cox 2007: 689–691). What such empirical tests suggest is that humans learn how to make use of the double act of imagining in particular situations and with particular kinds of language by interacting in real life (e.g. through play) and exposure to literature (if such there is), so that it is quite firmly in place by the age of six.

By accepting literature's invitation to imagine, readers, viewers or listeners older than six years of age thus "willingly" suspend their disbelief. The fact that it is done "willingly" is often taken as a matter of course in discussions of the suspension of disbelief, but it is particularly important to know when and when not to suspend disbelief. In a similar vein, Christopher Collins (1991: xxiii *et passim*) combines Gregory Bateson's (1955/2000) theory of play with fantasy and Coleridge's suspension of disbelief in an attempt to bring psychology and literature together: for him, play, including poetic play, is "initiated as an 'as if' activity, a game of 'pretend,' surrounded by a 'play frame'". This tallies with Harris's view (1998: 342) that both children and adults can "enter into a state of 'fictional absorption'" and thus "temporarily adopt a point-of-view situated inside the make-believe world rather than the real world". Another leading developmental psychologist, Stein Bråten (1998b, 1998c) calls this *altercentric participation*, thus pinpointing that you take another perspective in imagining a fictional world. Harris (2000: 194) has shown that making such use of imagination is so important for humans even at such an early age, because it trains them to understand all kinds of discourse "displaced from the here and now", thus considerably enlarging their knowledge and frame of reference.

Such accounts give a firm ontogenetic grounding for Levin's frame. Parents, nannies, siblings and peers first issue the invitation to imagine, as in singing or playing "Row, Row, Row Your Boat", and this is an important act of socializing children into a culturally and emotionally joint sphere. And as children accept this invitation and conceive a world in which they are going merrily down the stream, they surely disregard the dangers of floating down the stream and any thoughts that life is just a dream in a frightening sense. But from my mimetic viewpoint I would have a major question mark for the conclusion that Harris (1998: 343) draws: "the process of fictional absorption suspends any epistemic reflection on the status of the fictive world". If this were so, mimesis and thus the imaginative act it is based on would not work at all: in fact, children have an "epistemic reflection" on – that is, use their knowledge of – the real world by imagining somebody or herself rowing a boat and going merrily down the river. As I see it, literary imagination is not – or at least not entirely – a question of the duck-rabbit: either you see one (the real world) or the other (the imaginative world). Disbelief may be suspended, but it is suspended by adults and children well aware that there is a world beyond the literary one and that literature may help them navigate in it. In fact, it is this very suspension that makes literary *immersion* (Gerrig 1993) or *absorption* (Vermeule 2010) possible in the first place.

Harris (1998: 343) goes on to maintain that in entering "the make-believe frame" humans engage the appraisal system for emotions, so that "[e]vents that befall the make-believe protagonists will be evaluated just as if they were really happening". He goes on to claim that people so engaged actually "feel emotions themselves, either directly in response to events that befall those characters, or in response to the emotions attributed to those characters", even though such emotions can be "modulated" in different ways (Harris 1998: 344). In drawing such conclusions on the basis of his tests, Harris gives, perhaps without knowing it, a new developmental psychological answer to the age-old paradox of fiction – why we care about fictional characters – that has plagued philosophical aesthetics (see e.g. Yanal 1999). A rather popular answer has been that readers or theatre-goers "simulate" emotions according to various versions of "pretense theory".[1] What Harris claims, then, is that emotions felt when reading (or read to) are real, even though readers (and listeners) are well aware that they are in a make-believe frame. To be sure, Harris writes "as if" in the quote at the start of this paragraph, but the gist of his argument is rather strongly for a complete division between the fictive world and the real one. I would agree with his stance as far as it corresponds to Coleridge's view that readers "willingly" suspend their disbelief and know they are doing so, while feeling with or for the characters. Indeed, if they were not able to do so, literature would not matter much and would not have been so popular for millennia. It is the emotional engagement (or immersion or absorption) that gives a payoff in both delight and benefit (of different kinds), not just *from* another perspective but from *within* another perspective.[2] Still, there is a considerable span between, say, autobiography and fiction or in autobiographically inspired poetry, which shows that suspending disbelief is not an on/off function.

What is more, although Harris (1998, 2000) does not develop his notion that emotions can be modified, I would like to note that this is one of the most important effects of imaginative absorption or immersion. Authors see to it that we feel for the protagonists so that we care about them and the story, at times in order to trick us. At first, as readers we may identify with Winterbourne in James's *Daisy Miller*, only to realize that he is rather an egotistic character and that it is Daisy, who at first seems rather morally dubious, we should feel for (see 6.1). In a similar way, genres can make us modify our expectations: in popular genres or war novels we often have "bad guys" who can rightfully be killed by the "good guys", since it is clear that they are not worth caring for.[3] In realist,

---

[1] For instance, see the papers by Kendall Walton, Susan L. Feagin and Gregory Currie in Hjort and Laver (1997).
[2] Similarly, Polichak and Gerrig (2002: 92) argue that "readers generally adopt the role of side-participants with respect to their experiences of narrative", and Alan Richardson (2011: 685 – 686) terms the reading process of fiction *mental time travel*.
[3] This has seldom been commented on in literary studies before the late twentieth century, even though this black-and-white constellation leads to all sorts of immoral acts. See for instance Vermeule (2010: 248), who at the end of her study of the emotions characters may elicit in readers summarizes her integrated view: "The feelings of absorption and suspension are each so integral to the core experience of fiction that the contest between them will never be unwound".

naturalist and modernist fiction we often are supposed to care at least for (one of) the protagonists, whereas in postmodern fiction or comic science fiction the protagonists' status of human-like characters is often undercut (see Fokkema 1991). Of course, ever since modernism at least, much of Western literature has questioned such moral dichotomies. In short, various kinds of modification are elemental in selecting the depth and breadth of emotional immersion and setting the scene for imagining the literary world.

In his encompassing critical overview of various solutions to the paradox of fiction Jerrold Levinson (1997: 23) faults the suspension-of-disbelief solution Harris (1998) implicitly espouses for its depiction of "consumers of fiction as having both a rather tenuous grip on reality and an amazing ability to manipulate their beliefs at will". I should think that the above presentation of Harris's (1998) empirically based related account of the make-believe frame together with my mimetic argumentation can provide answers to both charges. Since literature is based on imitation and imagination, readers have a grip on reality, on the basis of which they can in varied and pliable ways construct imaginary worlds in terms of their view of what literature is and what the work they are reading. They are not just manipulating their beliefs *ex nihilo* (which would indeed be amazing), but have some sort of pre-understanding of literature and its genres as well as different kinds of paratextual and modifying cues and conventions by which they do so. What developmental psychology can offer to philosophical aesthetics of the kind Hjort and Laver (1997) represents is an ontogenetic view that shows how children have the makings of creative imitation and usually receive training in it, so that the beginnings of literary understanding are in place at a very early age. No grip on reality is lost, no manipulation is entirely novel or implausible but firmly grounded in conventions and experiences. Children, like adults, just use their imagination, but it is cued so that they can answer different kinds of invitations to imagine in appropriate, pleasurable and advantageous ways.

What the psychologists Harris and Gerrig, like anthropologists and literary scholars such as Dissanayake and Miall (2003), have to my mind convincingly shown is that emotions have an intersubjective basis that is crucial for understanding and enjoying literature. Levin (1977) does not ground his view of the frame for poetry in emotions as such, but his frame is explicitly an *invitation* to communicate by co-constructing an imaginary world. Recent research in cognitive cultural and literary studies, whether informed by historicism, narratology or ideology (Zunshine 2010, 2015, Jaén and Simon 2012) or by how the human mind is represented in literary narratives (Herman 2011), can be read as explorations of the different parameters of the imaginative frame of literature.

Now let us examine some of the building blocks of which literary worlds are made.

4.2 Literary World-Making: The Basics

Broadly speaking, world-making is at least as old as *homo sapiens* – in fact, most likely older, since even other primates, apparently even some other mammals and birds, have vestiges of culture. When creatures are able to think about and fashion the kind of world they inhabit, devise myths about the genesis of the world and its cosmology or create a culture, some of whose salient features they are able to pass on to the next generation, they are engaged in different kinds of world-making. Some forms of culture can, then, be considered kinds of world-making.

Poiesîs, I have noted, means 'making'. It is this notion that what could be called the very first fully worked out scrutiny of the human imagination, Giambattista Vico's (1744/1984: 116–297) *New Science*, takes as its starting-point: it is by *poetic wisdom* – learning based on making – that humans have advanced. What makes it possible is the fact that men have "the principal property [...] of being social" (Vico 1744/1984: 3). Not only do humans create a thoroughly human lifeworld by making "man [...] the measure of all things" (thus quoting the pre-Socratic philosopher Protagoras),[4] but "when they can form no idea of distant and unknown things, they judge them by what is familiar and at hand" (Vico 1744/1984: 60). This, it should be noted, is not unlike Aristotle's *imitation* in his *Poetics* (see 2.1). Poetic wisdom, Vico (1744/1984: 116) speculates, "must have begun with a metaphysics, not rational and abstract [...], but felt and imagined". This "corporeal imagination" was produced in the minds of "persons who by imagining did the creating", and they were called "'poets,' which is Greek for 'creators'", who among other things invented "sublime fables suited to the popular understanding" (Vico 1744/1984: 117).

For Vico, poetic logic is how poetic wisdom comes across in signification or language, which centrally consists of tropes (or figures) and fables (or narratives). By apposite metaphors, "the most necessary and frequent" of tropes, the first poets drew on the natural world "with capacities measured by their own, namely sense and passion, and in this way made fables of them. Thus every metaphor formed is a fable in brief" (Vico 1744/1984: 129). Vico (1744/194: 127, 128 quote) also claims that as a notion *fable* draws on both *logos* (word, thought, law) and *mythos* (myth, narrative) and that "mythologies must have been the allegories corresponding to them". Even this brief presentation of some salient features in the *New Science* suggests a number of features related to literary world-making: the corporeal, social and mimetic basis of *poiesîs*, the crafting done by poets and the workings of the

---

4 For a reading of the history of philosophy on the basis of Protagoras see Abel (1976).

imagination. What is more, it suggests the close relations between figures and narratives on the one hand, and larger structures – such as mythology and allegory – on the other, which can build on each other (see chapter 5). Yet Vico has seldom been seen as the precursor he evidently is for, say, cognitive metaphor theory[5] and literary world-making.

In the study of literary worlds prose fiction has been favoured. At first the models centred on characterization, from the British anthropologist Edward Tylor's study of hero myths in 1871 to formalist and early structuralist scholarship (see Segal 1990: esp. vii–viii). Two lines are discernible. One centres on hero myths, as represented by Otto Rank's (1909/1990) Freudian, Lord Raglan's (1936/1990) Frazerian and Joseph Campbell's (1949/1988) Jungian accounts. The other studies the hero in relation to the plot, as when Vladimir Propp (1928/2009: 25–65) detected thirty-one functions in Russian folktales and A. J. Greimas (1966/1983) abstracted a triple "actantial" model of the central characters. Based on "the hero's power of action", Northrop Frye's (1957/1973: 33–35, 33 quote) cyclical theory of modes – mythical, romantic, high mimetic, low mimetic and ironic – combines a categorical scheme with a focus on the hero.

Later, the structuralist theorists Todorov (1969), Genette (1972/1980) and Greimas (1977) worked out more explicit narrative "grammars". Then Thomas Pavel (1986) and Lubomír Doležel (1998)[6] went beyond structuralism by including referential and possible-world theory in their accounts of fictional worlds. In the last decade or so narrative and literary worlds have been combined in various ways. Meir Sternberg (2003a, 2003b) discusses universals of narrative in terms of formal *event structures* that entice readers by *surprise, suspense* or *curiosity*, that is, he analyses both features in fictional narratives and their presumed effects in readers. In James Phelan's (2007) view, if you have a clear sense of the interpretive, ethical and aesthetic features in your *judgement* and combine it with a detailed study of narrative *progression* (cf. event sequencing), you will be able to lessen interpretive divergence and thus form a better understanding of how narrative works.

Patrick Colm Hogan (2003/2009: 98–100, 98 quote), on the other hand, finds across cultures "two prominent structures of literary narrative, romantic and heroic tragi-comedy, derived respectively from the personal and social prototypes for happiness". Thus, he views narrative modes in relation to emotions, but confesses that his dual emphasis cannot account for some texts, such as Beckett's *Waiting for*

---

5 See however Nuessel (1995, 1998).
6 Let me note that Doležel (1998: x) is fiercely anti-mimetic owing to his endorsement of the narrowly imitative understanding of mimesis: for him, mimetic reading is "one of the most reductive operations of which the human mind is capable".

Godot.⁷ Recently, Pavel (2013) too has viewed the history of the novel in terms of an opposition: novels either idealise human behaviour or ridicule/condemn it, which also seems rather problematic. For instance, one of Pavel's (2013: 28) examples of idealised behaviour is *An Ethiopian Story* by Heliodorus, where the characters allegedly "act according to a higher, hidden plan". Still, as we saw in 2.2, its first pages give a naturalist description of the aftermath of a massacre, which is the very backdrop against which the idealised behaviour of the protagonists is set. Two other works categorize narratives by combining modes, much like those of Frye or Hogan, with themes and plot formations. Margaret Anne Doody (1996/1998: 301–464, 305 quote) finds a number of central tropes of narrative or "narrative symbols that move us through a novel's story", the most important ones of which are a rather mixed bag: breaking and entering; marshes, shores and muddy margins; tomb, cave and labyrinth; eros; ekphrasis (of two kinds); and the goddess. Christopher Booker (2004/2012: esp. 6) distinguishes between seven basic (in part overlapping) plots in another motley crew of formal, generic and thematic categories: overcoming the monster; rags to riches; the quest; voyage and return; comedy; tragedy; and rebirth (all of which, he notes, are to be found in Tolkien's *The Lord of the Rings*).

Brian Boyd (2009, 2012), on the other hand, combines his interest in human cognition with evolutionary literary studies in viewing literature as cognitive play that makes use of open-ended patterning. Eric Hayot's (2012: esp. 7) interest lies in literary worlds from the modern age (for him, after 1500) and in broadening our notion of those worlds by including non-Western literature. However, his six "aspects of worldedness" – amplitude, completeness, metadiegetic structure, connectedness, character-system and dynamism – are rather abstract, and the modes with which they are combined (realism, romanticism and modernism) seem to go against his avowed non-Eurocentric intention (see Hayot 2012: 54–88, 119–143).⁸

The view of literary world-making I present below draws on many of these major names and their approaches, but my attempt entails going from the most basic modes to the most universal main themes and then to the inflections such themes are given in literature from different ages and cultures. In other

---

7 Later Hogan (2011: 125–184) has added a third aspect, sacrificial tragi-comedy, apparently to explain the prevalence of Christian themes. Although broader in scope, Thomas Pavel's (2006: 3) historical morphology of the novel has much the same focus: "*the novel tells of the relationships between human beings and the surrounding world*" and it "*has traditionally focused on love and the formation of couples*".

8 Furthermore, Hayot's (2012: 7, 103–117) point about how the shift in cosmology shaped the modern world view seems rather Eurocentric. At least the chronology of how it shaped the world view is completely different in (various cultures in) the East.

words, in this study literary world-making is not centrally about the setting in space and time of the literary world in terms of M. M. Bakhtin's (1937–1938, 1973/2001) *chronotope,* Yuri Lotman's (1990/2000) *semiosphere,* David Herman's (2009: 105–136) *what, where* and *when* or Mark J. P. Wolf's (2012) transmedial *subcreation* with Christian connotations. Nor is it about linguistic and stylistic devices (see Semino 1997/2014, Werth 1999, Stockwell 2002, Gavins 2007) or truth-claims (Valdés 1992), but about basic modes and themes and their variations by an array of techniques. First, however, let me present my view of it in contrast to one of the leading authorities on world-making, Nelson Goodman.

When Goodman (1978: 6) by his *Ways of Worldmaking* popularized the term *world-making* in philosophy (and later in literary and cultural studies), few seemed to realize that his basis could be termed firmly mimetic, since he in fact maintained that "[w]orldmaking as we know it always starts from worlds already on hand; the making is a remaking". He takes his cue from Ernst Cassirer's symbol studies that did so much to further the understanding of the interrelation between language and myth, in stating that there are no worlds – in his sense of man-made worlds – "without words or other symbols", which reveals his radical constructivist stance (Goodman 1978: 1–6, 6 quote). His interest lies in *ways,* or as he also puts it *processes,* of world-making, of which he presents five that can be combined in a listing that does not claim to be comprehensive:

> *composition and decomposition* ("taking apart and putting together"),
> *weighting,*
> *ordering,*
> *deletion* and
> *supplementation and deformation* ("corrections or distortions").
> (Goodman 1978: 7–17, 7, 16 quotes)

As a philosopher with interests ranging from the philosophy of science to aesthetics, Goodman sets out to pinpoint the processes man makes use of in creating science and art. As he admits at the outset, however, he wants to put his "radical realism under rigorous restraints, that eventuates in something akin to irrealism" (Goodman 1978: x). There is no world that the other worlds can view as original or final, hence apparently irrealism. But what is more, "Don Quixote" "applies to no one", because as Goodman puts it elsewhere, a fictional (or fictitious) character, like Pickwick, the character in Dickens's novel *The Posthumous Papers of the Pickwick Club,* or a unicorn "do not represent anything; they are representations with null denotation" (Goodman 1978: 103; cf. 1976: 21). Thus, the rigour in his constructivism leads him to claim that fictional or fantastic characters have no denotation, simply because they are fictitious, so that when we speak about literary characters or unicorns we speak of entities with no meaning. Goodman (1978: 105) tries to find a way out of this paradox by claiming that "what does not denote may still *refer*", but I for one do not understand how this would be possible: even reference should carry some meaning. This sort of rigor about fictional characters has never existed in the myths and stories humans have created and enjoyed for millennia – or we would have no gods, demons or heroes with supernatural capabilities and much less literature.

As I noted above, Pavel (1986) and Doležel (1998) brought reference into the discussion of literary worlds, and this work has been continued. In 2.1 I evoked Jean-Marie Schaeffer's (1999/2010) important work on fiction when laying foundations for a mimetic view of literary imagination. In general, Schaeffer does not so much focus on fictional worlds as provide an encompassing cognitive and mimetic view of literature, building on Aristotle, psychology and literary studies, in particular cognitive literary studies. In his chapter on what he terms *fictional modelization* he discusses world-making and fictional worlds, and although he accepts Goodman's defence of reference, he feels that Goodman's model of world-making rests on "an abusive extrapolation starting from the linguistic model reduced to its logical framework" and thus leaves "no place for facts of a mimetic order" (Schaeffer 1999/2010: 183 quotes; 177–78). And from here on he gives the reasoning behind his mimetic model and shows how "every fictional universe is a 'perspective' universe", that is perceived through *aspectuality* unique to it (Schaeffer 1999/2010: 202). As my brief account of Goodman's view suggests, I think that Goodman clearly has at least an implicit basis in mimesis, although Schaeffer's account of mimesis is more useful for my purposes. Furthermore, despite its drawbacks, Goodman (1978) has lately served as a useful starting-point for studying world-making in narrative fiction and culture. For instance, David Herman (2009: 105–136) develops the *what*, *where* and *when* of story worlds on the basis of Goodman's listing and Vera Nünning (2010) adds nine features inspired by Jerome Bruner's (1991) narrative construction of reality.[9] In my view, such more detailed schemes of literary world-making could be combined with or built on the basic modes and themes I set out study further on in this chapter.

With Goodman's grounding in symbol studies it is somewhat surprising that he seems unaware of the fact that his five ways of world-making are much the

---

9 Later Bruner (2002: esp. 63–87) developed his notion of narrative construction to the self. Vera Nünning's (2010: 229–236) notions of reflexivity (including self-reflexivity), valuation, genre conventions and perspectivization (focalisation or, for Schaeffer, aspectuality) add important aspects to how fictional worlds function. See also 5.1.

same as the four fundamental rhetorical operations, already mentioned in *Rhetorica ad Herennium* and Quintilian in his *Institutio Oratoria* (Book 1, ch. 5, § 6):[10]

> addition (*adiectio*),
> omission (*detractio*),
> permutation (*immutatio*; for instance allegory, chiasmus and enallage [exchange]) and
> transposition (*transmutatio*; for instance, metonymy).[11]

What in effect both the rhetorical operations and Goodman's ways of world-making outline are variations of two kinds of operation: *changes to* (addition and deletion) and *changes in* the existing material, either by rearranging the elements (ordering), transforming them (supplementation and deformation) or modifying their relative importance (weighting).[12] As Goodman (1978: 16–17, 104) points out, such operations can be combined, as when a metaphor is "moonlighting" (that is, used in other contexts)[13] or extended into allegory, in which case material is added and at least the weighting of the material is changed. The building blocks for both rhetoric and world-making are here put in the simplest possible terms in order to show that the transformative moves are rather straightforward. Thus, it is understandable that they have in various ways been used for millennia in science, art as well as language use. In literature, as a matter of course, authors make changes to and changes in any possible existing material (say, familiar stories, such as Cinderella or Faust) or genres. Recent developments in narrative studies, such as Hernadi's (2001, 2002) view of imaginative world-making as a co-creation by author and reader/audience and Nünning et al.'s (2010) specifications, are important additions in that they show the plethora of variations such operations can have. An important addition to the research on narrative comprehension (even if not on literary worlds as such) is Sanford and Emmott's (2012) *Rhetorical Processing Framework*, consisting of scenario-building, rhetorical focusing (cf. foregrounding, defamiliarisation) and experience (or immersion).

---

10 In fact, Quintilian (2001: I, 124) makes his point in passing, so even at this stage the four rhetorical operations may have been taken as a matter of course.

11 For the latter two see Lanham (1991: 114, 154). Goodman's *weighting* could perhaps be seen as part of *permutation* in the classic scheme of rhetorical operations. In *Rhetorica ad Herennium* (1954: 275–409) the operations are interspersed in the discussion of figures of diction and thought in Book IV.

12 *Changes to* and *changes in* in part resemble Brian McHale's (2010: 21) *modeling for* and *modeling of*, a distinction based on Clifford Geertz (1973/1993: 93), even if in Geertz's original view at least only *modeling of* is concerned with "the manipulation of symbol structures".

13 For metaphor as moonlighting see Goodman (1984: 71–77).

To understand how changes to and changes in often work in tandem in literature, we can consider the Greek myth of the tragic lovers Pyramus and Thisbe. Shakespeare read Ovid's version of it in *Metamorphoses* and wrote a comic version of the myth as a play-in-the-play in *A Midsummer Night's Dream*. At about the same time – in the early 1590s – Shakespeare also used the myth for his tragedy *Romeo and Juliet*. In both he preserved much of the plot – a young couple's love is thwarted by the fact that they are members of rival families – but the one is a comic version, the other a tragedy.[14] In terms of the adaption theory presented by Linda Hutcheon and Siobhan O'Flynn (2013: 8), adaptation involves "*a process of creation*", in which "the act of adaptation always involves both (re-)interpretation and then (re-)creation". Both uses in Shakespeare turn a mythical narrative into drama and in *A Midsummer Nights Dream* the tragic import of Ovid's version is changed into comic. Also, in both plays Shakespeare employs only some, mainly plot-related features, and adds characters, action and dialogue. Thus, he makes both changes to and in the material. In doing so, he only makes more evident use of extant material than what most authors do when writing, since as Hutcheon and O'Flynn (2013: 177) so pithily put it, "[i]n the workings of the human imagination, adaptation is the norm, not the exception". Other instances of theme and variation are considered in the next section in relation to the main literary themes.

Now let us consider the modes and themes that form the building blocks of literary worlds.

4.3 Modes and Themes

The basics of literary world-making, we have seen, involve having some material at hand, say, a story (any version of Cinderella) or a theme (selling one's soul to the devil) and making changes in and/or to it so as to produce a new literary world on a scale from the fantastic to the real. In this view, then, even the most radical new departure draws on existing themes and forms.

So what are the most basic building blocks of a literary world? As I see it, there are three main *modes* that literature takes – oral, visual and written – and a host of *themes* that can be grouped in three main strands that are often combined: *challenge* to understand or to perform a task; *perception* (of what

---

14 For further discussion on the motif of star-crossed lovers as exemplifying literary world-making see chapter 9.

and *how*); and *relation* (from cordial to hostile) – all centring on human or human-like agents and their experiences.

Let us start with the modes.

Mode (1): *The Oral.* The oral mode of what we today call literature most likely started with music, dance and chant (see Dissanayake 2000, Gu 2012). This seems true at least of the early literature of China, Mesopotamia and Greece (see Gu 2012: 11). As the Assyriologist Thorkild Jacobsen (1987: xi, xiv quote) has noted, Sumerian literature from southern Mesopotamia may be the oldest literary culture: its first extant literature from about the middle of the third millennium BCE was based on "an extensive and varied oral literature", eventually including genres such as "myths, epics, hymns to temples, gods, or kings, laments for temples, gods, or human beings, wisdom literature, including proverbs, fables, Edubba [school] texts, and copies of then-ancient royal inscriptions".[15] Apparently all or most of it was sung, and it was in metre and rhyme, even though little is known about exactly how it was performed. Together with the fact that the rhapsodes impersonated voices of different personae, this list suggests that Sumerian literature already included the three received literary modes of prose fiction (including the epic), poetry and drama and was mostly concerned with praising temples, deities or kings or lamenting their demise. Similarly, the most ancient Sanskrit literature from about 1500–1000 BCE, the Vedic hymns consists of sung or recited hymns and formulas that praise the gods or pray to them and include creation stories, such as *The Rig Veda*. In China, the oldest literature from roughly 1000 to 700 BCE is to be found in the polished folk songs, mostly in four-character metre, of *The Book of Songs* (*Shijing*), first allegedly collected by Confucius. The oldest songs are ritual hymns of creation and the evolution of the Chinese people as well as songs of praise offered to the rulers and the more recent are folk songs on for instance nature, love, longing and (agricultural) work (see Hinton 2008: 5–35).

Here, then, we have ancient literature in three languages, from three different language families,[16] all of which have started with variations of an oral mode. My brief comments above aim to show the rich variety of forms of the different oral traditions and the importance of the poetic form (metre and rhyme at

---

15 Cf. the numerous genres in ancient Mesoamerican literature (see Léon-Portilla and Shorris 2001). The wealth of oral literary genres should not be surprising in the light of the fact that human languages are estimated to have existed for roughly 200 000 years. Since writing has a history of little more than 5 000 years, written literature only spans about one fortieth of the history of language.
16 Sumerian is a language isolate, Sanskrit an Indo-European language and Chinese belongs to the Sino-Tibetan languages.

times used in conjunction with prose). Much of the oral literature also makes use of formulas, both as an effect and as an aid for memory.[17] But after oral literature was written down and written literature in some sense took over, orality featured as an important component in literature (see Ong 1982/1984) and, conversely, literate features influenced oral modes (see Olson 1994/1996). But it is important to note that even today oral literature is alive and well all over the world by lyrics set to music, which in a great variety of classical, popular, folk and mass forms delight millions of people every day. Moreover, drama still centres on spoken dialogue and monologue. Prose fiction too often includes stylized dialogue and monologue (as in stream of consciousness) as well as hybrid forms, such as free indirect discourse. Finally, poetry can also consist of more or less stylized dramatized speakers using oral features, including apostrophe and colloquialism, especially in poetry inspired by folk songs or in romantic, modern and postmodern poetry. In a broad sense, then, it is the human voice (as well as human action) that is central, both for narrators, characters and speakers.

Mode (2): *The Visual*. The visual mode is of course most evident in drama, which takes place in a theatre, from the Greek *théātron*, 'seeing place'. But there is also a dual emphasis in drama, since the action on stage (the Greek *drâma* in fact meaning 'action' in a play) is played to an *audience*, a term emphasizing hearing. This is understandable, since much of the most dramatic action even in Greek tragedy is not shown on stage but reported (often by messengers). A recent commentator on visuality in the theatre in fact makes the point that "the tactic of hiding and revealing has been central to theatrical representation at least since classical Greek drama" (Johnson 2012: 7). Of course, this varies from culture to culture, as for instance classic Chinese Yüan plays can even show an execution on stage (as in *The Injustice Done to Tou Ngo*). But since much of the drama on stage often has to do with past action and it may be unclear who knows what actually has happened and who tells the truth – all of which Jean Racine's (1677/1987) *Phaedra* so skilfully plays with –, the visual is intricately interwoven with the words uttered on (or at times off) stage.

As for literature primarily written to be read (or read aloud), the earliest literary or semi-literary usages could be said to be different writing systems. The earliest Chinese writing that has been ascertained is oracle bone script on tortoise shells and sheep scapulae from the Shang dynasty, that is, 1600–1046 BCE. It consisted of brief riddle-like texts, used for divination "seeking either the meaning of past events or the course of future events", the answers to which ancestral spirits provided by

---

[17] For a comparative view of how oral literature works in a variety of cultures see Foley (2002) and for memorizing in different oral literatures see Rubin (1995).

the cracks when heated (see Minford and Lau 2000: 10–17). At first, the pictograms (graphic representations) were central in Chinese writing, but by 100 BCE they only consisted of about 4 percent of the characters, having mainly been replaced by more pliable phono-semantic and ideogrammic compounds (see Gu 2012: 33–52). The earliest forms of Sumerian cuneiform writing on clay or stone tablets from the fourth millennium BCE were also in pictograms,[18] which later were replaced by more abstract glyphs and finally by phonetic signs. Still, the origins of writing in the pictogrammic forms suggests at least two key features that affect written literature, most evident in Chinese: the representational aspect is strong, but at the same time so general that the double nature of the specific as made more general by analogy is part and parcel of it (see Hinton 2008: xx–xxi). Furthermore, David Hinton (2008: xxiii) maintains that "[a]s it reflects [a self-generating and sacred] cosmology in its empty grammar and pictographic nature, the poetic language [of Chinese] is nothing less than a sacred medium", as is evident in that the word for poetry, *shih*, combines the meanings of 'spoken word' and 'temple'. As we can see, in combining oral and visual features, the early modes of writing evince literary qualities in their hymns and songs of praise, prayer and (later) more down-to-earth motifs.

The tradition of openness and ambiguity lives on in Chinese and Japanese literature, which makes translations into, say, Germanic or Romance languages more precise than they should ideally be. But it is important to note that writing in pictogrammic or ideogrammic form reached such heights as the fourth-century Chinese female poet Su Hui's *Star Gauge* (*Hsüan-chi Tu*), a collage of metaphysical, scientific and love poems in five colours which can be read in different directions, thus producing over 3 000 poems on a single sheet (!) – most likely, still the most complex collection of poetry in existence.[19] In the early twentieth century Ezra Pound, by rather wilfully editing Ernest Fenollosa's posthumous work *The Chinese Written Character as a Medium for Poetry* (1918),[20] started, or at least centrally contributed to, the boom of imagist and concrete poetry which has lasted to this day in various guises of materially and visually focused concrete, modern, postmodern and Language poetry.

More familiar aspects of visual components in literature are illustrations of literary texts by drawings, photographs and paintings. First, illustrations can accompany the text, on the cover or interspersed, as in Twain's *Adventures of*

---

[18] Sumerian writing most likely influenced the development of Egyptian hieroglyphs, another pictogrammic form of writing. For a comparatively brief overview of the history of writing see Fischer (2003).
[19] See Hinton (2008: 105–109) and his website (fsgbooks.com/classicalchinesepoetry) that includes a colour reproduction and a select translation of *Star Gauge*.
[20] See the critical edition of Fenollosa and Pound (2008/2010).

Huckleberry Finn and many children's books; they can be part of the work as a whole, as in graphic fiction or Blake's Illuminated book of SONGS Of *INNOCENCE and Of EXPERIENCE* (see Blake 2000/2009: 43–96); or they can comprise the entire narrative (with no accompanying text, except the title), as in Shaun Tan's (2006/2007) immigrant story *The Arrival*. Second, drama of all sorts, excepting radio drama, is visual as well as oral. Third, another technique, if not visual in kind but in effect, is the use of description by which readers or listeners get a notion of what characters or settings look like. By this latter form we are already moving to the next mode.

Mode (3): *The Written*. The written mode in phonetic script is increasingly central in most literature of any culture ever since the inception of writing. Much of it is narrative, as is evident in all forms of prose fiction and drama. Even radical experimental forms usually still have vestiges of narrative or what Brian McHale (2001) has termed *weak narrativity*. In fact, as noted in the Introduction and elaborated in 5.2, even lyrical poetry often has narrative elements, a fact that has seldom been noted. Also, literature of all kinds makes use of literary figures (or tropes) such as metaphor, simile, metonymy or irony. Since narratives and figures are so prevalent in literature, their interrelation is one of the most salient aspects of literature and is discussed in chapter 5. The written mode has of course been combined in various ways with the visual (Blake's illuminated books, illustrated books for children and adults, comic books, graphic fiction, novelizations of films) and the oral (drama as performed, readings, performances, poetry slams, audiobooks).

What all modes have in common is that they focus on representing humans or human-like characters, as speakers and agents. Most literature on characterization, such as Hochman (1985), Fokkema (1991) and Vermeule (2010), notes the fact that characters can be seen in two ways: as real people and as artefacts made up of semiotic or descriptive markers (see also 2.2). There is the old humanist tradition stressing the former and the more recent structuralist-semiotic view pinpointing the latter, but perhaps most scholars – and general readers – would agree that literary narrators, characters and speakers (even postmodern ones) are in some sense modelled on humans, but have traits that show that they are "mere" fictions of language.

Thus, communicatively speaking, literature includes not only what Bakhtin (1986/2006: 99) has called *addressivity*, "a constitutive feature of the utterance", which means that a sender is communicating to a receiver, but also a message in which human or human-like characters are acting and/or speaking. Moreover, as literary worlds are formed in the three modes, with narrators, characters and/or speakers, they are done so on the basis of genres. In its strong form the theory of *genre worlds* claims that "textual meaning is carried by formal structures more powerfully than by explicit thematic content" (Frow 2005: 129). But such a strong claim does not work for most literature, in which genres can change or even be invented by new content, as when Mary Shelley in *Frankenstein* (1818) started science fiction *per se* by adding science to the Gothic novel.[21] A more modified stance of genre as a deductive interpretive tool, such as that of Peter Seitel (2003), works quite well for, say, anthropologists learning about indigenous genres, as they do so from the outside. Even for a scholar or reader well versed in a genre such as science fiction, deduction on the basis of their pre-understanding of the genre does not suffice as such, but must be complemented by induction when reading, that is, by understanding how familiar generic features are varied and what possible novel features there are in a new work of science fiction. In Seitel's (2003: 277) felicitous phrase, genres are *frameworks of expectation* – in fact, for authors, publishers as well as readers –, but do not form genre worlds as such but rather frameworks or scaffolding for constructing literary worlds. In other words, Bakhtin's (1986/2006: 60) three aspects of speech genres, "thematic content, style and compositional structure" must be taken into account and studied in inductive as well as deductive ways when dealing with literary worlds. In what follows I will reduce Bakhtin's tripartite scheme of generic features into the classic dichotomy between theme and form (consisting of structure and style).

Put simply, I think that literary world-making can be viewed as being *about* something and that aspects of its contents can profitably be discussed under thematic universals or *main themes*. In fact, they complement the three formal modes by focusing on the most salient literary themes across cultures and ages. In short, I propose that all literary themes can be grouped under three headings, even though they are often combined: *challenge, perception* and *relation*, all of which concern human or human-like agents and their experiences.

Theme (1): *Challenge* is an age-old theme in literature. There are two kinds: challenges for human or human-like characters to *understand* or to *perform a task*. In fact, they are often combined, even if it often is the readers who are supposed to understand and the protagonist(s) who should perform a task. But Hamlet must first understand that his father has been murdered by his uncle in order to perform the task of revenging his father's death. Harry Potter gradually understands what Voldemort has done and what he stands for in order to confront him. Similarly, Lyra in Philip Pullman's trilogy *His Dark Materials* final-

---

[21] Lucian's (1989/2008: esp. 623–630) *A True Story* is at times considered the first science-fiction novel, since it includes motifs such as space travel, extra-terrestrial life and inter-planetary war. But it is actually a tall-tale satire of travelogues that includes motifs anticipating science fiction, none of which is based on science.

ly learns why her parents have acted as they have and can thus better tackle evil forces. In such complex challenges the motivation to act is often instigated by forces beyond the protagonists (the nation or other groups of moral stature) or by the protagonists themselves (who take on the challenge as representatives of the moral group or "the good guys"). Also, understanding need not precede action: only as he is already pursuing the ring does Frodo in *The Lord of the Rings* begin to understand its true meaning and his own relation to it.

In more realistically motivated action the challenges can be evident or the understanding is never reached by the protagonists but only by the readers. In most Jane Austen novels the young women are trying to find a husband owing to considerable social pressure. In Gustave Flaubert's *Madame Bovary* or Kate Chopin's *The Awakening* the protagonists commit or are about to commit suicide and only their readers can understand the challenges they face and the motivation to their actions.[22] In novels, stories and plays by Henry James, Edith Wharton and Anton Chekhov the main characters seldom understand that at crucial moments in their lives they face or have faced major decisions that colour their subsequent lives – and if they do, it is usually too late to do anything but accept the fact.

Much poetry is based on perception of how things are or what people or the world are like, but what has been perceived – the nature of love, death, nature or quotidian life – makes the speaker of the poem accept, rebel against or simply portray his or her reaction to the challenge of understanding such basic aspects of life. Modern and postmodern poetry often adds an acute self-consciousness of such challenges, especially by questioning language as a tool for understanding.

In fact, challenges to *understand* is a central feature in some of the oldest literature. The earliest Chinese literature, we have noted, consisted of riddle-like texts used for divination. In Sanskrit epics and poetry, say, *The Mahābhārata*, Śivadāsa's *Five-and-Twenty Tales of the Genie* and *The Rig Veda*, there are riddles which are crucial for the protagonist to solve and they involve "intelligence, lateral thinking and expertise in metaphor" and consist of cryptic statements rather than questions (West 2007/2010: 363–370). But riddles were staple in much other Indo-European literature and, in M. L. West's (2007/2010: 369) words, they are "deeply rooted in Indo-European thought and expression". Mark L. Bryant (1983: 25–82, 82 quote) has written a history of the riddle in literature and noted that throughout history "interest in riddles seems to coincide with seasons of intellectual awakening". In fact, many poems we today call nursery rhymes – owing to the latter-day setting of their use – are ancient rid-

---

[22] For an analysis of the ambiguous ending of *The Awakening* see Pettersson (2009a).

dles, whose riddle-like quality may have faded. Take "Humpty Dumpty", a rhyme spread in a great number of versions and languages in Europe.

> Humpty Dumpty sat on a wall,
> Humpty Dumpty had a great fall.
> All the king's horses,
> And all the king's men,
> Couldn't put Humpty together again.
> (Opie and Opie 1997: 252)

"Humpty Dumpty" was originally a riddle about what cannot be fixed, but owing to illustrations, especially Sir John Tenniel's drawings to Lewis Carroll's *Through the Looking-Glass*, most adults familiar with it since the late nineteenth century know the answer: Humpty Dumpty is an egg (see Opie and Opie 1997: 252–257).

Riddle-like qualities can be part of the plot through punning, as when Odysseus in Song 9 of *The Odyssey* in outwitting the giant Polyphemus calls himself *outis*, another way of saying "no one", a synonym of *me tis*, and thus a pun on *metis*, 'resourceful', *polymetis* being the most central epithet associated with Odysseus. In a sense, then, Odysseus is not lying, rather he is punning in a riddle-like way that Polyphemus cannot decipher. Such uses of riddles or riddle-like tasks often occur in fairytales and adventure stories. But riddles or seemingly impossible tasks also appear elsewhere. Just think of the prophecy of the three witches in *Macbeth:* if Macbeth could have figured it out, he might not have done what he did – but then we would not have *Macbeth*. Or think of Angela Carter's postmodern fairytales or John Grisham's thrillers, whose plots often depend on the protagonists solving seemingly impossible tasks.

This would suggest that there is continuity in the literary challenges to understanding, and that seems to be the case. Still, perhaps there was something of a shift in the Modern Age when a rational worldview became more widespread. Gothic fiction (Ann Radcliffe's *The Mysteries of Udolpho*), science fiction (Mary Shelley's *Frankenstein*) and detective fiction (Poe's Dupin stories) from the late eighteenth century to the early nineteenth would not have been possible unless there were rational explanations of the supernatural, scientific advances and highly developed "ratiocination" or deduction to solve the various challenges to understanding. However, not all literary enigmas are intended to be solved, as we can see in nonsense and Dada poetry, in Stanislaw Lem's science-fiction novel *Solaris*, where the enigmatic planet does not reveal its intelligence that seems to surpass human understanding, or in postmodern detective fiction, such as Paul Auster's *The New York Trilogy*. And Oedipus may have been able to answer the riddle of the Sphinx, but his intelligence does not suffice to save him from his tragic fate (see 4.4). Perhaps Marcel Danesi (2002: 36) is right in claiming that humans have a *puzzle instinct*, not least in that "puzzles provide a means of 'comic relief,' so to speak, from the angst caused by the unanswerable larger questions".

The challenge to *perform a task* is predominant in most narrative literature, whether fiction or drama. Characters set out to kill the dragon (later an antagonist), get married or perform other kinds of task. Such tasks can simply entail trying to get home (*The Odyssey*), building a city in the sky (Aristophanes' *The Birds*), enjoying the ride itself (Jack Kerouac's *On the Road*) or trying to escape and enjoy the ride (*Adventures of Huckleberry Finn*). It can have major consequences for humanity, such as saving – or at least standing up for – the "good guys", such as a family, town, nation or all of humankind, as for instance in Westerns, detective fiction, thrillers, horror fiction and science fiction. Even characters in romance fiction and comedies have a major implicit ultimate mission: to advance humankind by falling in love and having children. The tasks performed in realistically motivated literature are seldom as goal-oriented as more popular genres, which as we have seen include realistic motivation (see 2.2). There are seldom single overriding tasks to be performed in, say, realist fiction, or if there are, the motivation rather than the action is in focus. The characters may set out to catch the impostor (Molière's *Tartuffe*), kill somebody (Dostoevsky's *Crime and Punishment*), find true love (*The Awakening*) or fight a war (Remarque's *All Quiet on the Western Front*), but what is highlighted is why and how they do so. In poetry too if a speaker, like the one in T. S. Eliot's "The Love Song of J. Alfred Prufrock", is preoccupied with "some overwhelming question", that question looms large as a challenge for readers to comprehend, but what they must concentrate on in order to do so are the twists and turns of this narrative poem portraying his hypothetical moves (see 6.2).

Theme (2): *Perception*. In literature human or human-like perception has to do both with *what* and *how* something is perceived and elaborations and conclusions on that basis. This is an instance of how content and form go together: the theme of perception is closely informed by how things are perceived.

The *what* of perception is central in lyrical poetry, which often both portrays what is perceived and the reaction it causes in the perceiver. In traditional haikus the perceiver may not be mentioned, but the effect on the perceiver makes small movements in nature major experiences for the implied speaker and the reader alike. Here is the perhaps most famous haiku ever by the seventeenth-century haiku master Matsuo Bashō (in Edward G. Seidensticker's translation):

> The quiet pond
>   A frog leaps in,

> The sound of water
> (Bowers 1996: 15)[23]

It has the classic three-stage format of a haiku – which, as here, often also is narrative – and seemingly only portrays a frog jumping into water, with no figurative language (unless you consider "quiet" a metaphorical modifier). But what makes a good haiku so effective comes across here: a minor event in nature makes a great splash on the consciousness, if as readers we learn to delight in perceiving nature and understand our place in it. The ripples of perception go on, if we let them. More complex are Blake's "The Sick Rose" and Eliot's "The Love Song of J. Alfred Prufrock" in that they portray a rose as perceived infested by a worm and a man apparently observing different kinds of setting and people (see 5.2 and 6.2). Apart from nature and other settings, humans and other creatures, human perception can be about things, such as those perceived by the protagonist in Nicholson Baker's novel *The Mezzanine* (see 6.3). Finally, what can be centrally perceived is also the narrator's, speaker's or character's own self, as in "Prufrock" and *The Mezzanine*, and a host of semi-autobiographical genres, from more or less veiled autobiographical fiction (such as Richard Brautigan's *Trout Fishing in America*) to what is termed the non-fiction novel (e.g. Norman Mailer's *The Armies of the Night*).[24] Introspection and self-reflexivity, also as concerns the writing (meta-levels in epics, prose fiction, poetry and drama), is usually based on human perception. And that perception is mainly human-like, as millennia of myths, epics and prose fictions, even animal fables from *The Pañćatantra* to David Sedaris (2010/2012), attest (see 2.2 and 9).

Of course, the *how* is no theme at all, but since what is perceived is closely related to how (and by whom) something is perceived, it should be discussed here as well. The *how* includes the perspective – whether omniscient, limited or unreliable – through which narrators, speakers and characters perceive what they narrate or experience. In fact, all of chapter 3 dealt with how perception through various kinds of unreliability comes across in fiction. That is, perceiving *how* is so important that it influences *what* is perceived to the extent that I felt it had to be discussed before this scrutiny of main themes. Also, how narrators, speakers and characters perceive the world affords elemental features of characters on stage as well as dramatic personae or voices in poetry and popular songs. This is how we get to know Prince Genji, Hamlet, Prufrock and

---

[23] For three other translations see Bowers (1996: 15).
[24] For a reading of Brautigan's autobiographical fiction see Pettersson (2004a) and for an analysis of the non-fiction novel in relation to Norman Mailer's works see Lehtimäki (2005).

Eleanor Rigby (in the song by Lennon/McCartney). The novel, play, poem and song in which they appear are in a sense about portraying the characters' view of the world, and thus their respective *how* revolves around what the characters perceive and how they react to it. In drama the thematizing of perception can make use of many features: the audience may see or hear something, but (some of) the characters do not (thus giving rise to dramatic irony) or the characters may watch a play in the play in a tragedy (*Hamlet*) or a comedy (Pierre Corneille's *The Theatrical Illusion*). But even in drama most often it is a question of who knows what – on the basis of the character's or somebody else's perception – and how reliable they are about telling what they know. What is more, as we have seen, Shakespeare is adept at letting characters in dialogue portray the setting that was not staged in the Elizabethan or Jacobean theatre. Epics and prose fiction can do much the same as drama but has the additional advantage that they can move more easily in space and time by commentary or the memory afforded by narrators or characters.

Theme (3): *Relation.* Most literature is in one way or another about human or human-like *relations*. In fact, as noted above, Hogan (2003/2009) views all of literature as being about tragic-comic relations. Such relations are portrayed by commentary, either in narrative (epics, prose fiction and most poetry) or in dialogue (often in drama, epics and prose fiction). They are mainly about characters engaging in close relations with strong emotions, mainly varieties of love and hate.

Often relations are *cordial*, that is, concern reverence, love or friendship. The centrality of hymns of praise to gods or kings show early versions of such relations, even if they are hierarchical, since by praise and prayers the gods and kings are to be persuaded to meet the wishes of the ones praying and their congregation. Many fairytales and adventure stories have protagonists with friends, relatives, helpers or sidekicks: Gilgamesh has his Enkidu, Tripitaka his Monkey (in the classic Chinese novel *Journey to the West*), Hansel his Gretel, Don Quixote his Sancho Panza, Macbeth his Lady Macbeth, Elizabeth Bennet her mother and sisters, Huck Finn his Jim (and Tom Sawyer), Sherlock Holmes his Watson, Frodo, Harry Potter and Lyra Belacqua their friends. The cordial relations are not only those of worship or friendship but also those of love. The earliest secular literature, whether folk songs or epics with mythical elements, includes (mainly heterosexual) human love relations as an important and often central element. Chinese folk songs, Sumerian poetry, *Gilgamesh*, *The Mahābhārata*, *The Iliad* and *The Odyssey* all have love elements. Also, love poetry has had particular forms, such as ghazals, Provençal love songs and sonnets.

However, since human relations are volatile, cordial relations can turn *hostile*. In fact, all cordial relations mentioned above have that implicit: you worship, since you think the object of your worship may not be or remain friendly;

friends can turn into foes; lovers fall out of love. In fact, literature has always thrived in exploring the thin line between love and friendship on the one hand and antagonism and warfare on the other. Helen is abducted or leaves her husband King Menelaus and thus causes the Trojan War; warring families have children who fall in love (Pyramus and Thisbe, Romeo and Juliet); and *The Mahābhārata*'s complex relations between humans, gods and their families is a veritable classic soap opera of love, hate and war. Moreover, friendships are not just formed on the basis of reciprocated feelings but often formed against others. The feelings can also develop in the opposite direction: at first Gilgamesh fights Enkidu and then Enkidu becomes his dear friend, just as D'Artagnan is about to fight duels with Athos, Porthos and Aramis, only to become their close ally in Alexandre Dumas's, père, *The Three Musketeers*. In Western stories or thrillers the protagonist fights his or her nemesis, while the focus in epics, tragedies and novels, like *The Iliad*, the *Oresteia* trilogy by Aeschylus or Tolstoy's *War and Peace*, is on characters, families and nations in times of strife or war. The war can be between nation states (*The Iliad*), a power struggle between clans within a state (*The Mahābhārata*) or a combination of the two (the fourteenth-century Chinese novel *Outlaws of the Marsh* aka *Water Margin*). Comedies or romance fiction, on the other hand, have a strong antagonistic element in the plot, but it is finally surpassed and the plot usually ends happily. *Lysistrata* by Aristophanes combines hostile and cordial relations in that Athenian women deny their men sex as long as they continue fighting their war. Animal fables or narratives feature non-human creatures, such as Aristophanes' *Wasps*, *Birds* and *Frogs* with insect, avian and amphibian choruses commenting on human action; Mo Yan's *Life and Death Are Wearing Me Out* tells the story of a man reincarnated as various mammals; and Orwell's *Animal Farm* is a political allegory with farm animals. Such plays and novels show that animals may take on human features, even though the relations may be between god, man and animal or between different animal species, all of which usually allegorize human relations.[25]

Presenting literature in this simplified way will, I hope, contribute to our understanding of how literature works. First, it shows how literature's basic modes and themes are few and rather straightforward: the modes are oral, visual and written; the themes deal with challenge, perception and relation. Second, the main themes point to how human-centred all literature is. And third, for this very reason, literature is good training for real life and has evident functional value, both for individuals, groups and the species as a whole.

---

[25] Fables are also used to exemplify literary world-making in 5.3 and 9.

Just as in alphabets, the beauty of the few elements lies in their combination and variation. Fairytales, fantasy and adventure stories often include difficult missions as well as love interests. Science fiction, whether of the "hard" or space-opera variety, can make use of mind-boggling technological advances, battles between the protagonists and hostile forces as well as love. Realist fiction is mostly about human relations, but the narrative perspective can be as enigmatic or unreliable as the actions and personalities of the characters, as in much of Henry James's fiction. Psychological thrillers, such as the those by Stephen King, Barbara Vine [Ruth Rendell], Gillian Flynn and Paula Hawkins, are most likely so popular because they depict familial or other affectionate relations in a realist manner, and the challenge is for the protagonists (and readers) to understand the ins and outs of them by closely perceiving the past and/or present behaviour of their (allegedly) near and dear ones. Thus, all three main themes are put to good use.

Since Life Is A Journey is the most prevalent cognitive metaphor that apparently occurs in all known cultures, it may be that the journey metaphor aptly suits the course of (human) life, not least because that journey often includes human or human-like relations and fascinating perception (and action) along the way, including difficult challenges (tasks to be carried out or problems to be solved). Shakespeare's plays too mostly centre on human relations, but both tragic and comic protagonists also struggle to understand the cordial and hostile motives of other characters. Moreover, some of the suspense and enjoyment for readers or viewers stem from the use of dramatic irony: having recourse to the dialogues and actions of other characters, they know more than the protagonists in *Othello* and *Twelfth Night*.[26] In absurd drama, human relations may also be central, but for instance Beckett's *Waiting for Godot* revolves around the enigma of Godot, which is preserved throughout. Narrative poetry may have features of both prose fiction and drama and focus on human relations, but also, as in "Prufrock", entail introspection and observation of settings and objects. Much lyrical poetry highlights what is perceived, such as the inner depths of the speaker, other characters, settings or objects, all of which arouse the readers' interest in and feelings for the speaker.

Human relations may often be central in literature, but human perception and challenges to understand can be main themes on their own or together, at times with some cordial or hostile human relations. Riddles are perhaps the best examples of such challenges and they occur in a great many cultures and are still

---

26 For a discussion of recent empirical work on suspense see Sanford and Emmott (2012: 229–231).

very popular, although few of them, except so-called nursery rhymes perhaps, usually qualify as literature.[27] As noted above, many genres, especially fantastic ones, include solving riddles or performing tasks, whether by force or lateral thinking. But there is, for instance, also philosophically or scientifically inspired fiction that does not rely much on the theme of human relations. G. K. Chesterton's and Jorge Luis Borges' fiction centres on philosophical issues through conundrums and paradoxes. Similarly, many science-fiction authors would agree with Kurt Vonnegut's (1977/1982: 109) reasoning: "I try to keep love out of my stories because, once that particular subject comes up, it is almost impossible to talk about anything else. Readers don't want to hear about anything else". In much of the best hard, new wave, comic, metafictional and weird science fiction, the novel ideas or what Darko Suvin (1982/1988: 76) has termed *cognitive novum* is what matters, even though there may be marginal love interests and much mysterious or absurd antagonism, as in the works of Arthur C. Clarke, Stanisław Lem, Octavia E. Butler, Fredric Brown, James Tiptree, Jr. [Alice B. Sheldon], Philip K. Dick, Karen Joy Fowler and Neil Gaiman. In such imaginative authors, the focus is not only on strange events and creatures, but on the difficulties the narrators and characters – and readers – have in fathoming what is going on, much like what Brian McHale (1982, 1987) has called *ontological hesitation* or *the ontological dominant* in postmodern fiction and science fiction.

Thus, three overall modes and three themes seem to cover most, perhaps even all, of literature and appear in a range of genres and variations that have come and gone in various cultures throughout millennia. They show how rather simple means can prevail owing to their pointed human interest and the enjoyment and benefit they have been able to afford people. To drive home this point let us briefly consider a rather basic formula that is spread over almost the entire Indo-European language family, the most prevalent in the world. In *How to Kill a Dragon. Aspects of Indo-European Poetics* the Harvard professor Calvert Watkins (1995/2001: 297) claims that the formula *hero slays serpent* is found "in a vast number of cultures around the world; it may be quasi-universal". He goes on to show how it comes across in different versions in a number of languages and cultures and their literatures, such as Vedic, Avestan, Hittite, Luwian, Iranian, Greek, Germanic and Irish (Watkins 1995/2001: 297–544).[28] The symbolical

---

[27] Perhaps the most encompassing collection of nursery rhymes in English, Opie and Opie's (1997) *Oxford Dictionary of Nursery Rhymes* includes some five hundred, with comments on their history and spread in other languages. On the Internet there are many sites on riddles, the most inclusive of which may be riddles.com with about 11 000 unedited riddles to date.
[28] Vedic refers to the four Vedas, the oldest Sanskrit literature; Avestan, Hittite and Luwian are extinct languages.

import shows why the formula has had such popularity and longevity: "[t]he dragon symbolizes Chaos [...] and killing the dragon represents the ultimate victory of Cosmic Truth and Order over Chaos" and in more down-to-earth, cyclical terms, "it is a symbolic victory of growth over stagnation [...] and ultimately [...] of rebirth over death" (Watkins 1995/2001: 299). All this in one fell swoop, as it were.

Perhaps another reason the formula is so widespread lies in the fact that it brings into play all three main themes of literary world-making. The task of slaying the dragon is something of a mission impossible (*challenge*), and the hero usually sets out to do so in order to save a kingdom or community that is endangered by the beast, at times in order to receive a reward, such as, in later versions, marry the ruler's daughter (*relation*). The (usually male) hero faces challenges to understanding by taking on the well-nigh impossible task and facing the enigmatic dragon (or serpent or snake). In doing so, he attains honour for himself, but more importantly safeguards the community, and may even be integrated into that community by the honour bestowed on him for having slain the dragon. In this way, there are cordial and hostile relations, even if the latter in the oldest myths is between man (or god with human-like features) and beast. Still, the bare essentials of the myth would not be enjoyable and suspenseful without the aspects that human *perception* affords: description of the situation, the hero and his hardships and, if not the dragon itself, at least its actions and the result of its ravages.

As time went on, this basic formula turned into one with stronger human – or, if you like, less overtly allegorical – interest, since, as Watkins (1995/2001: 471) notes, "[t]he serpent adversary of myth can easily become the human adversary of epic 'reality'". Hence, there are two "themes" with variations of the basic formula: (1) *hero slays hero* and (2) *hero slays anti-hero*. Also, there is a popular variant of revenge or what Watkins (1995/2001: 482) calls "the reciprocal formula 'the slayer slain'". As he goes on to show, this is what *The Iliad* is all about: revenge for the insult of the (supposed) abduction of a woman, revenge for slain brothers in arms (Hector kills Patroclus, so Achilles kills Hector). The various versions of the thwarted love motif – from Pyramus and Thisbe to Liang Zhanbo and Zhu Yingtai (in the medieval Chinese ballad "The Butterfly Lovers") to Romeo and Juliet and many other versions – combine the revenge formula of rival families with the love between two of their members (see chapter 9). But the impetus need not be love, it can be friendship, loyalty, kinship or simply a job to be done for an appropriate pay. Ancient and contemporary myths, epics, fairytales, adventure stories, fantasy fiction, Western fiction, science fiction, thrillers, horror fiction and detective stories, whether on paper or on screen, all have heroes facing impossible tasks for such reasons: they all have their dragons to slay. Not a bad little formula, whose stages Joseph Campbell (1949/ 1988) was the first to trace in *The Hero with a Thousand Faces*.

A final point: In classic Indian poetics the emotional effect of literature is given in eight rasas (the *erotic, comic, tragic, furious/cruel, heroic, fearsome/timorous, gruesome/loathsome, wondrous*),[29] to which Ānandavardhana, a Kashmiri scholar in the ninth century, added a ninth, the *peaceful*.[30] These emotions can occur in all three major themes of literary world-making. However, in the early twentieth century the nonsense author Sukumar Ray, based on Radindranath Tagore's view of the unique characteristics of children's rhymes, suggested that, as the comic rasa mainly stood for happiness, *whimsy* should be added as a tenth rasa (Heyman 2007: xlii–xliii). This is an interesting, if somewhat questionable,[31] point, since humour and nonsense, especially in verse form, often only make use of various themes as vehicles rather than ends in themselves. Riddles, Dada and nonsense are often about the fun in solving or understanding them. Or the point can be satirical: Dorothy Parker's (1999) poetry mostly mocks adult relations; Ogden Nash's (1994/2001) poems are about relations between humans or humans and animals (by way of human perspective); and John Betjeman's (1970/ 1972) and D. J. Enright's (1987) poems afford all sorts of insight into the human condition. Even Dave Eggers's (2005: 201–206) "There Are Some Things He Should Keep to Himself" in the short-story collection *How We Are Hungry*, which consists of a mere heading followed by six blank pages, gives an imaginative pointer for readers to think about what those things are, thus imagining the life of the male character mentioned in the title of the "story".

Nonsense in its more pure forms is in many ways even more radical. In Anushka Ravishankar's (2010: lii) perceptive terms, "the quintessential nature of nonsense" is "the ability to be nothing and something at the same time", hence its affinity with mysticism, as in the Zen riddles called *koans*.[32] Of course, some Dada (Tzara 1977/1992), classic nonsense rhymes in English and German (Rhys 1927/1961) and in Indian languages (Heyman et al. 2007) as well as modern nonsense short stories (Lennon 1997) make some sort of sense: at the very least,

---

29 For a brief but insightful introduction on rasas see Ingalls (1990: 15–20).
30 For the motivation of adding the peaceful (*śānta*) as a rasa see Ānandavardhana and Abhinagupta (1990: 520–525).
31 In fact, the oldest extant poetics of dramaturgy, *The Nātyaśāstra* (2010: 66), equates the rasa of the comic with the bhava (everyday emotion) of laughter, and so does modern scholarship (see Ingalls 1990: 16). This would suggest that the comic covers a wide range of responses, not just happiness-related ones. By terming nonsense the tenth rasa, Heyman's (2007) point is evidently to underline its specific characteristics as against the comic in general.
32 For a classic collection of koans in English see Reid (1957/1991).

they are quirky attempts to communicate various perceptions by playing on themes and language. But their point is rather that they do not make sense in any received way and that they probe the relation between language and meaning, between *this* and *that* of metaphorical and other meaning-making.

4.4 Examples of Literary World-Making

Literary worlds, we have seen, are made up of rather basic building blocks: three main modes (oral, visual and written) and three main themes: challenge, perception and relation. They are given a great number of variations and combinations so as to make up the rich and varied literary forms in different eras and cultures. Let us now examine four particularly intricate instances in which the main modes and themes blend so as to produce multifaceted kinds of literature. They are classics, if in rather different genres: a Greek tragedy, a complex narrative poem from the late fourteenth century, a modernist short story and a particularly probing science-fiction novel.

Perceiving and Knowing in Sophocles' Oedipus the King

One reason why Sophocles' *Oedipus the King* (henceforth *Oedipus*) is perhaps the most well-known and most widely discussed Greek tragedy, even in Aristotle's *Poetics*, is that it is so rich in its use of all three main themes. The fact that it centres on perception is evident in the very name of the protagonist, whose complex meaning draws on the Greek *oida*, 'I know', and is related to *eido*, 'I see', as the translator Paul Roche has noted (see Sophocles 2001/2010: 212).[33] As the play begins, Oedipus says: "I come to see it [the commotion in the city of Thebes, owing to the plague] with my own eyes, no messenger's. / Yes, I who men call Oedipus the Great". This implies much, especially to most of the original audience who was sure to be familiar with the story of King Oedipus. Since he is "the Great", it is clear that he has already answered the riddle of the Sphinx, thus ridding Thebes of the horrid Sphinx and becoming its king (this is corroborated in the words of the Priest in his reply to Oedipus). That is, Oedipus has successfully met one challenge, by his insight. The challenge that now confronts

---

[33] Roche goes on to discuss the multiple meanings of the name Oedipus, including its reference to the character's lameness, and notes that its meaning is something like "Know-all-see-all-swollen-foot" (Sophocles 2001/2010: 212). From here on, the references to *Oedipus the King* are given by page number in brackets to Roche's translation (Sophocles 2001/2010: 209–263).

him is to purge Thebes of the plague that troubles it, owing to the fact that the murderer of Oedipus' predecessor Laius has not been found.

At the same time, in his first lines Oedipus shows his reliance on perception, or more precisely his sight, which is reiterated throughout the play: he must *see* what is going on in the city of which he is king. Despite his denigration of seeing by proxy, this is precisely what he (and the audience) gets in the Priest's answer to him: a description of the afflicted city, in keeping with the tradition in Greek tragedy that most of the action is reported, thus focusing on the effect of the news on the main characters. Throughout, seeing is used metonymically for knowing in that Oedipus as a kind of precursor of the detective in detective fiction must catch the murderer. As an unyielding detective, he uses all his senses, especially his eyesight, in pursuit of the murderer, also by making use of the blind seer Tiresias, according to the play's prevalent paradox of blinded seeing and insightful blindness. When Oedipus finally realizes that he is the culprit and metes out punishment by blinding himself, he also anticipates postmodern detective fiction in which the detective can turn out to be the culprit. But it is his relentless quest to know, to discover the truth by his very own eyes, that makes him meet his two challenges: he seeks to understand who he himself is (and who his real parents are) and to perform the task of catching King Laius' murderer, and so save his city from the plague.

When he is able to meet both challenges, Oedipus at the same time wins and loses, that is, his victory is a Pyrrhic one: he learns his true identity as a patricide who has wedded his mother, but he has also solved the murder and thus rids his city state from the plague. Aristotle (1941/2001: 1465; 1452a) was among the first to laud *Oedipus* as a paradigmatic tragedy in his *Poetics*, not least for its deft use of plot: "The finest form of Discovery [in tragedy] is one attended by Peripeties [reversals], like that which goes with the Discovery in *Oedipus*". Both challenges are met at the same time and the very act of meeting them leads to Oedipus' downfall. And his insight is portrayed in terms of sight: "At last it's blazing clear. / Light of my days, go dark. I want to gaze no more" (253). What this means in terms of the Indo-European formula of the hero slaying or vanquishing the dragon (or antagonist) that threatens the state is one of the most important psychological insights in any literature: the enemy can be within.[34] Early on, the blind Tiresias warns Oedipus for his pursuit of knowledge ("The rotting canker in the State is you"; 226), but Oedipus must learn the truth and catch the murderer.

---

[34] The enemy within is an abiding motif in myth and religion. For instance, in some versions of Islam, the notion of "the greater jihad" signifies this inner struggle (as against "the lesser jihad" of the holy war).

Thus, the third major theme, that of human relations, is also central in the play. To know about one's family and family history is a crucial fact in learning about who you are. All the major facts Oedipus learns about himself have to do with his immediate family: that he was given away as an infant, that he has, unknowingly, murdered his father Laius and wedded his mother Iocasta. Having blinded himself, Oedipus main concern is the well-being of his daughters (and half-sisters) Antigone and Ismene. In other words, this nuclear family displays the most dramatic cordial and hostile relations: parents' love and fear of children and children's filial and sexual love of parents; in short, patricide and incest, love and hate. But on a higher social level it is about the survival of the state, by the very familial relations in Oedipus' family, on which the prosperity of the state is dependent. Hence, it is understandable that a relation of the family continues to reign after Oedipus, as Creon, Iocasta's brother who wrongfully has been accused by Oedipus of having murdered Laius, becomes king in accordance with a kind of poetic justice.

This should suffice for one play, but Sophocles still deepens the emotional impact. A Palace Official comes on stage and tells of the simultaneous ravings of Iocasta and Oedipus he has seen, since he "was there" and what he saw is "stamped upon [his] memory" (255). As I have noted, in Greek tragedy such dramatic action is not shown, most likely since the effect of telling it is stronger (and easier to stage), as the grief of the teller and the listener can give it greater impact by their reactions to Iocasta's having hanged herself and Oedipus' having rammed the pins of her dress through his eyes. What is shown is Oedipus in the company of his daughters, who witness their father's affliction, just as their father thinks of their future and has no thought of his own suffering. Here Sophocles points not only to Antigone and her fate (in, among others, his play *Antigone*) but also to an outside view of Oedipus, who has dominated the stage for the entire play. The choral dialogue strengthens this view by its comment (once again pinpointing sight): "Oh, the pity and the horror! / I cannot look – and yet so much to ask, / so much to know, so much to understand" (256–257).

Here we have one of the many pointers to the audience to take heed of what has occurred on stage. But Sophocles gives the theme of understanding a final twist as Creon answers Oedipus' plea to keep his children by his side: "Stop this striving to be master of all. / The mastery in your life has been your fall" (263). Although the audience, spurred by the chorus, of course have tried to make sense of, that is, *understand*, what they have *seen* and heard on stage, they must learn humility – a point that is driven home by the final, even then familiar moral in the envoi of counting no humans blessed before they are dead.

As even this brief reading of *Oedipus* may suggest, Sophocles is able to offer touching variations on literature's main themes of challenge, perception and relation in a supremely tightly-knit dramatic form.

Learning about Love in Chaucer's "The Parliament of Fowls"

A fable of human relations, or more precisely love, "The Parliament of Fowls"[35] (c. 1382) is one of Geoffrey Chaucer's most accomplished early works. In terms of genre, it is usually counted among Chaucer's dream visions, which number "The Book of Duchess", "The House of Fame", The Parliament of Fowls" and "The Legend of Good Women", most likely written in this order.

"The Parliament of Fowls" is a dream vision in that most of its 699 lines (that is, lines 95–694) describe the dream of the narrator.[36] Preceding his dream, the narrator reads the sixth book of Cicero's *De re publica* (*On the Commonwealth*), known as "Scipio's Dream", which is summarized in lines 36–84 and whose moral is that "man [...] / That loveth comun profit [...] / He shal unto a blisful place wende, / Ther as joye is that last withouten ende" (ll. 46–49). It is his adopted grandfather Scipio Africanus who shows Scipio Aemilianus Heaven, by way of "the galaxye" [the Milky Way] and its music of the spheres, "where rightful folk shal go after they dye" (ll. 56, 55). This is in keeping with Cicero, who has Scipio Africanus chide his grandson twice for having his "thoughts continue to dwell upon the earth" rather than on "Virtue", which would secure safe passage to Heaven (Cicero 2007: 261, 263, cf. 262). Chaucer renews the genre of dream vision in at least two ways: (1) as the guide for Chaucer's narrator, Scipio Africanus shows him the natural world with Dame Nature presiding over the birds, and (2) after the dream the narrator does not seem to have learned anything but only goes on to study. Thus, in both thwarting an absolute moral and in focusing on love and its different forms in nature by introducing a naive narrator (much like what was to become Chaucer the Pilgrim in *The Canterbury Tales*), Chaucer gives the dream vision a new shape: earthly and ironical.

---

35 The title of the poem varies in different versions, but today the title is often normalized, even if the text is in Middle English, usually according to one of the fifteen extant manuscripts. The text employed here is "chiefly based" on the Fairfax manuscript in the Bodleian Library and is edited by Kathryn L. Lynch (Chaucer 2007: 97–116, 96 quote). References are given by line number.
36 I prefer to call the poem's speaker "the narrator", since to my mind the convention of calling him "Chaucer" does not necessarily take into account the ironic perspective the distance between Chaucer and his narrator affords.

However, Chaucer more or less retains Cicero's (2007: 264) emphasis that the "noblest efforts" of the virtuous soul "are in behalf of your native country". In "The Parliament of Fowls", both in the dream and preceding it, "comun profit" is highlighted. This profit is largely, but not absolutely, built on hierarchy. Nature is "the vicaire of th'almighty Lorde" and her "rightful ordenaunce" is to retain the hierarchy among all of her creatures, here the quarrelling birds (ll. 379, 390). The main issue is the dispute among the highest birds, the male tercels (eagles), for the love of the one female tercel. But Nature, representing love, refrains from ordaining who should love whom, but only *advises* the female eagle to choose the worthiest, that is, the royal tercel (ll. 630–637). Hence, the female eagle can ask to postpone her decision by a year, possibly because she is too young to be sexually active (natural motive) but in any case to delay parliamentary decision-making (political motive).

What makes "The Parliament of Fowls" so rich is that it seamlessly draws on so many traditions, literary and other. Most likely, the dispute between the male eagles is a poem *à clef*: in 1380–1382 Anne of Bohemia had three royal suitors, the foremost of which was King Richard II (whom she was to marry in 1382) (see Lynch 2007: 93). Thus, by Nature's open-minded view of love, Chaucer interweaves the natural world with the political world, in a way that is "at once novel, realistic, and sensible in a fourteenth-century context" (Boitani 2003: 71). Moreover, by the various views propounded by the over thirty different birds in the dream, the entire spectrum of social classes in Chaucer's England is exposed in a humorous bird parable, from birds of prey to waterfowl. Typically for Chaucer, the dream is also richly allusive: not just Cicero and his commentator Macrobius are mentioned, but a great number of allegorical personifications (Pleasure, Beauty, Desire and about a dozen others) and mythical characters (Cupid, Venus, Tristram and again about a dozen others) appear as different kinds of love are debated. Also, there are more or less evident references to Hippocrates, Boethius, Dante, Boccaccio, the *Romance of the Rose* and Alain de Lille. Thus, Chaucer's dream vision of the birds debating is, mostly in passing, suffused with allegorical and allusive layers.

The frame story of the narrator studying love by reading books gives the impetus to the dream: "The lyf so short, the craft so long to lerne", he complains, not about art (as Hippocrates did), but about love, about which he laments, "I knowe nat Love in dede" (ll. 1, 8). Even though the dream gives an exposé of different views of love, when waking up the narrator is none the wiser and simply goes on to read about love, so "That I shal mete som thing for to fare / The bet; and thus to rede I nil nat spare" (ll. 698–699). Chaucer gently pokes fun at the scholarly narrator, either by the fact that he still understands nothing about love or that love simply cannot be learned from books (but should be experienced "in dede") or both. If the narrator misses the moral about the real nature of love, generations of readers have got it: not least since it may be the first to mention and take place on Saint Valentine's Day, "The Parliament of Fowls" is often considered to have started the tradition of celebrating love on that day.

But within the dream there are also different levels of meaning. Entering the garden of nature, the narrator reads on the golden inscription of the gate that it is a "blissful place / Of hertes hele", while on the other side there is a black inscription to the effect that it leads to "mortal strokes of the spere, / Of which Disdayn and Daunger is the gyde [guide]" (ll. 127–128, 135–136). This is usually understood to suggest the two sides of love, but since the second inscription is on the *inner* side for those exiting (not entering) the garden, it could also be a warning of how real life and the love it may harbour may be the opposite of life and love in the dream. Before the dream, the narrator notes that what he aims to learn about when reading about love is about its fleeting "dredful joy" (l. 3), and thus the ambiguity of love comes across both in the dream and outside it, even if the narrator remains confounded when having woken up.

As for generic features, drawing centrally on the long narrative poem *Romance of the Rose* by Guillame de Lorris and Jean de Meun (1994/2008: esp. 3–42; chs. 1 and 2), Chaucer makes use of the topos of *locus amoenus* (ll. 183–294).[37] Especially the descriptive section of the garden (ll. 183–210) is crucial, since it underscores the strength and beauty of nature. It is at the service of the plot in the sense that it gives Dame Nature, who in turn serves God, the right to reign supreme over all creatures. The cyclical quality of nature is repeatedly emphasized (ll. 23, 236, 321, 661), as the birds choose their mates on every Valentine's Day, which marks the beginning of spring, but at the same time the meeting of the birds is unique to the birds at each parliamentary meeting. Yet it is Nature, who firmly but tenderly guides the choices made, so that there is "comun profit" or, as Piero Boitani (2003: 68) has it, so that love is not just sensual but "directed towards the *bonum commune*".

In terms of literary world-making "The Parliament of Fowls" mainly displays the theme of human relations: the narrator wants to learn about love and the birds in the fable-like dream quarrel about its true nature. Moreover, throughout the dream the narrator is the perceiver and thus human perception is implicitly highlighted, just as when Nature has to decide among the varieties of love, she is faced with a challenge to understanding, which she solves by letting the birds themselves choose. Thus, all major themes are employed. As for inflections, the hierarchy between the frame story of the narrator reading and the enclosed

---

[37] For a classic discussion of *locus amoenus* see Curtius (1948/1990: 183–202).

dream vision is kept intact, even though in the very dream Scipio Africanus seems aware of the frame, since he aims to show the narrator "mater of to wryte" (l. 168). The divine pantheist hierarchy also remains intact, whereas in matters of love Nature by giving love free rein implies that in natural, including human matters, social hierarchy is not absolute. As for aspirations, that of the narrator to learn about love is thwarted (which affords much of the irony in the poem), but most birds are happy with Nature's Solomonic decision, and of course readers – if not the "dulle" scholarly narrator (l. 162)[38] – learn much about how differently love can be viewed. Even when employing allusive and allegorical meta-usages, Chaucer shows his distance to them, especially to Cicero's straightforward moral of praising virtue, and thus points the way to a more relative, proto-modern view of human hierarchy, morals and of course love.

Interpreting Interpreting in Woolf's "The Mark on the Wall"

Virginia Woolf's "The Mark on the Wall" from 1917 is one of the most enigmatic modernist short stories. It makes use of all main themes, but focuses on perception. This has to do with a key trait of modernist fiction that has often gone without notice: modernism represents the true endpoint of realism in fiction. If naturalism took the realist tendency to its *social* (and often sordid) extreme, modernism took it to its farthest *cognitive* reach by portraying the inner workings of the mind, including the relation between imagination and perception. Woolf's early short stories are among the first to probe the cognitive limits of fiction, and often do it with the exuberance of exploring new and exciting territory. "The Mark on the Wall" is a case in point. Its plot is rather simple: the first-person narrator – apparently a young or middle-aged woman, since she admits that she is not "a very vigilant housekeeper" – spots a mark on the living-room wall, does not inspect it carefully and has some hypotheses as to its cause, until finally a man, most likely her husband, announces that it is a snail (Woolf 1944b/1989: 84).[39] Almost the entire story centres on the narrator ruminating on the mark on the wall and thus, in terms of literary world-making, on the theme of human perception.

Two kinds of realism are highlighted in the story: the narrator watching the mark at a distance (hence her different hypotheses of what may cause it) as well

---

38 However, Chaucer is not uniformly critical of scholars, as shown in "The Miller's Tale", where the young scholar Nicholas is smart enough to outwit and cuckold the old miller.
39 Subsequent references to "The Mark on the Wall" (Woolf 1944b/1989: 83–89) are given by page number in brackets.

as what was to become the hallmark of modernist fiction, the narrator's stream of consciousness as she is watching the mark. Her act of perception and rather vague description of the mark help her reach what she terms "a satisfying sense of reality" (88), while the inner description of her thoughts is much more detailed. Much of the tension in the story in fact stems from the interaction between the two: perception triggers trains of thoughts, which tend to wander haphazardly until the narrator once again concentrates on the mark.

In portraying the narrator's thoughts, Woolf makes use of an array of ways of hypothesizing the action. To merely mention some longer ones: she entertains "that old fancy" of "the cavalcade of red knights riding up the side of the black rock [of a castle tower]" (83); in an extended simile she likens life to "being blown through the Tube at fifty miles an hour" (84); she imagines what happens after life (84), and how Shakespeare is about to write (85); she comes to think of "a pleasant track of thought" she wishes she could think, but then "the image disappears" and a disturbing future vision takes over (85–86, 85 quotes); and finally she remembers the time when there was "a rule for everything" and hopes that the patriarchal standard "will be laughed into the dustbin" (86). At this point, she presents a new hypothesis of the mark casting "a perceptible shadow" looking like a tumulus, which prompts a fantasy of men excavating the tombs or camps on the South Downs in Sussex and Hampshire (86–87, 86 quote); then she dismisses knowledge, which leads her to "imagine a very pleasant world" that soon becomes a submarine one (87–88, 87 quote); and finally she voices her belief in something steadfast, such as wood, which leads her to a fantasy of trees growing until they are made into sundry wooden objects (88–89).

Even these few notes show how rich the narrator's imagination is and how she simply cannot concentrate on the mark itself. Moreover, they indicate that what she imagines is often based on actual people, places and phenomena – Shakespeare, the South Downs, trees growing and used as material – and her imagination works in the past (memories, historical persons), in the present (fantasies based on perceptions) and the future (the disintegration of patriarchy). Hence, the common juxtaposition of the real and the imagined is far from definite: her fantasies are based on perceptions and her perception of the real digresses into similes and fantasies.

Still, what the narrator aspires to do is simply to interpret the mark on the wall. Her hypotheses range from a nail (83), a hole or a small rose leaf (84), something that casts a shadow (86), "the head of a gigantic old nail" (87), a summary of hypotheses: "a nail, a rose-leaf, a crack in the wood" (88), often presented hypothetically, as queries. Her hypotheses go in circles and none of them is strengthened, let alone proven right. Even more disquieting is the fact that she has little faith in proof any kind and even doubts reaching any kind of knowledge: "What are our learned men save descendants of witches and hermits who crouched in caves and in woods brewing herbs, interrogating shrew-mice and writing down the language of the stars?" (87) She repeatedly refers to the Table of Precedency of Whitaker's *Almanack*, in which the entire British social hierarchy is given their proper order (86, 88, 89), but it is juxtaposed with a future in which it is cast aside, "leaving us with an intoxicating sense of illegitimate freedom".[40] Still, even this clash between social order and freedom may be illusory, since she adds "– if freedom exists..." (86). Nothing is defined, nothing is conclusive for the narrator, whose mind seems disturbed, since for her "[e]verything's moving, falling, slipping, vanishing" (89).

The emphasis on the narrator's stream of consciousness makes the Woolf critic Olga Vorobyova (2005: 210) assert that the entire story is about the megametaphor "LIFE IS A FANCY / A FLEETING ILLUSION". To be sure, the inconclusive hypothesizing and fantasizing throughout the story seem to point that way. But such a reading overlooks Alex Zwerdling's (1986: 6) well-motivated view that Woolf was "as interested in the forces of 'the real world' as in the responses of people whose lives were deeply affected by those forces" and, even more to the point, Jane Goldman's (2006: 90) recent observation that in "The Mark on the Wall" "[t]he very pressing matter of the war, and how it is to represented, looms significantly at the story's margins". That is, at the very end, "[s]omeone", possibly the narrator's husband, ironically complains "Nothing ever happens. Curse this war; God damn this war!" (89), thus corroborating an earlier hint (86) that a war is on. This puts the narrator's anxiety and her frantic and fragmentary trains of thought in a very real perspective: it seems duress caused by, most likely, the First World War. This social kind of realism, much like that of naturalism, is only touched on here, but it demonstrates Woolf's careful structuring in that in the very first paragraph of the story the war is adumbrated by the old fancy of the fairytale-like red knights on horseback.

Thus, it is appropriate that it is "someone", the harbinger of that war (to the reader, if not the narrator), who is able to ascertain what the mark on the wall is – a snail. Just as the war overrides any fantasy, the narrator is left with no hypotheses of the mark but a final and incontrovertible interpretation. In other words, the dramatic monologue of the narrator has been a narrative of the various hypotheses of the mark she perceives, and by her distressed stream of consciousness, the entire narrative has been at the service of describing her character. But the disclosure that a war is going on in turn serves to explain this distress

---

[40] The ironic use made of Whitaker's *Almanack* seems evident and it is corroborated in *A Room of One's Own*, where its alleged "final order of values" is denied (Woolf 1928/2000: 104).

and perhaps even suggest an argument (or moral, if you like) of what war can do to a human psyche. Hence, Woolf's story shows the riches of human perception, how it can encompass both the real and the fantastic. It even forms a kind of allegory of interpretation (or of reading the very story itself), but does not leave it that. The aspiration of the narrator to identify what causes the mark on the wall is continuously thwarted, but at the very end her aspiration is fulfilled, as someone casually notes that the war is going on and that there is a snail on the wall. The narrator's hypothesizing and fantasizing have been as real as the attempts at interpreting her perceptions of the mark on the wall, but they are seen in the perspective of duress during wartime.

Thus, in "The Mark on the Wall" Woolf combines all three main themes: it may focus on perception (of the snail and the narrator's trains of thought), but it also includes a challenge (to understand what causes the mark) and a relation (apparently that of husband and wife during a war).

Understanding Oneself and Loving the Alien in Lem's Solaris

If "The Parliament of Fowls" mainly thematizes human relations (by way of the parable of birds) and "The Mark on the Wall" human perception, its fallibility and imaginative reaches, Stanisław Lem's science-fiction novel *Solaris* (1961) focuses on the third major theme of literary world-making, that of being faced with the double challenge to perform a task (exploring Solaris) and to understand the utterly indefinable alien the planet turns out to be. In fact, the perplexity is still there in the last sentence: "I knew nothing, and I persisted in the faith that the time of cruel miracles was not past" (Lem 1961/1991: 204).[41]

The first-person narrator is a psychologist called Kelvin, whose Christian name readers later learn is Kris. In trying to analyse the planet Solaris he arrives on in the novel's first chapter, he is both very much a scientist, like Lord Kelvin, but also has increasingly the religious and mythical connotations of his first name drawing on Christ. His aspiration as a scientist is to know what Solaris is and how it functions, but that aspiration is not only thwarted but inverted. Solaris, which seems to be an ocean-like live entity, does not only enter his conscious mind, but his unconscious as well: it learns more about Kelvin than he knows about himself. In fact, Kelvin and his fellow scientists on Station Solaris learn that human intelligence is simply too primitive to be able to comprehend Solaris.

---

41 Subsequent references to *Solaris* are given by page number in brackets.

Hence, in the science-fiction theorist Darko Suvin's (1982/1988: 76) view, Solaris is "a fictional yet cognitive novum", a term Suvin draws from Ernst Bloch's social theorizing of "a totalizing phenomenon or relationship deviating from the author's and implied addressee's norm of reality". But even though Lem in 2002 proclaimed that his aim in *Solaris* was "to create a vision of a human encounter with something that certainly exists, in a mighty manner perhaps, but cannot be reduced to human concepts, ideas or images",[42] he could not do so in a science-fiction novel without a "variant of the epic adventure or voyage-of-discovery plot" (Suvin 1982/1988: 77). Similarly, elsewhere Lem (1981/1984: 183) discusses the possibilities of science fiction and asserts: "The writer must arrange his ostensibly realistic material, drawn from the fund of common experiences, in such a way that its resemblances to the structure of some venerable myth (Faust, Odysseus, Oedipus) is evident to the reader". This blend of the real and the literary-mythical is what makes *Solaris* such a powerful novel, as its allusions imply: Kelvin arrives on the *Prometheus* and is expecting that spaceship or the *Ulysses* to come to Station Solaris at the end; from the start he thinks the station is "shaped like a whale" (cf. Moby Dick);[43] and when Sartorius, one of Kelvin's fellow scientists, is frustrated with the quest for knowledge and seeks mortality rather than immortality, he is called "Faust in reverse" (184).[44]

The science-fiction novum of *Solaris*, explored for pages on end by the hypotheses of the scientists on Station Solaris and the paraphrased advances in Solaristics, must be seen against this literary-mythical backdrop. More importantly and rather typically for fantasy and science fiction, the actions, thoughts and feelings of the protagonist are explored in detail, so that readers can empathize with his plight. As Kelvin suffers from the traumatic memory of his wife Rheya (in Polish, Harey) having committed suicide owing to his callousness and Solaris can delve into his unconscious, the planet creates a simulacrum of his deceased wife. Her first incarnation he sends off into space and the second has another scientist help her to commit suicide, when she realizes that she is a simulacrum. Still, at the end of the novel Kelvin seems to settle for the possibility that Rheya, even though she is a mere simulation of his dead wife, might come back, which would indeed be a cruel miracle. Despite himself, Kelvin may not have learned much about Solaris, but he has learned about himself and realized the fact that he loves Rheya so much that a simulacrum of her will do.

---

42 See Lem, "The Solaris Station" on *Stanisław Lem – The Official Site* (http://english.lem.pl/arround-lem/adaptations/soderbergh/147-the-solaris-station?start=1), accessed 13 December 2012.
43 In fact, in "The Solaris Station" Lem compares *Solaris* to *Moby-Dick*.
44 Thus, Sartorius seems much like the Mephistophelian Professor Diogenes Teufelsdröckh in Thomas Carlyle's novel *Sartor Resartus* (1836).

But just as in "The Parliament of Fowls", the irony is that as readers we learn more than the narrator. In the planet Solaris we are presented with one of the most enigmatic creatures in all of world literature, and our minds, like that of Kelvin, may not suffice to entirely comprehend her or him or perhaps it in its multiple guises. But it does have "mimoid" features that generate creatures to all scientists on Station Solaris based on their memories and feelings. Thus, it is "clear that the ocean was not aggressive" (116). It also has the amorphous and mirror-like qualities of complex literature in which readers interpret and co-create beings and their actions on the basis of their own experience.

In a final twist Lem intimates that the narrator could have learned even more from his dreams at the end of the novel. Kelvin dreams that he becomes "alien matter": "The conviction of its substantial, tangible reality is now so overwhelming that later, when I wake up, I have the impression that I have just left a state of true perception, and everything I see after opening my eyes seems hazy and unreal. / That is how the dream begins" (179). Then he goes on to dream of being born into a new kind of being and feeling "invaded through and through, I crumbled, disintegrated, and only emptiness remained" (180), but dismisses it all as a dream.[45] But perhaps in fact he has here made contact with Solaris, become part of it in a way that he cannot fathom and more deeply than the tentative touch of the wave on its surface later on (203). In fact, what he describes is the Chinese third-century BCE philosopher Zhuangzi's famous enigma whether he dreams of being a butterfly or a butterfly dreams him. Now Zhuangzi's (2009: 21, 76n11) point with his parable is not the impossibility to know what is a dream and what is real, but what he calls "the transformation of one thing into another" or *dai*,[46] to be able to understand that Daoist "oneness depends on the multiplicity of distinct identities and viewpoints, not on collapsing them into literal unity".[47] Just as Guildenstern in Tom Stoppard's *Rosencrantz*

---

[45] Not knowing what is real – the dream or the reality in which the dreamer awakens – is of course an age-old motif in literature, as it figures even in the nursery rhyme "Row, Row, Row Your Boat" (see 3.2). As we have seen, Chaucer's narrator in "The Parliament of Fowls" does not seem to learn anything from his dream, nor does Jeppe in Ludvig Holberg's classic play *Jeppe of the Hill* (1722), whereas Pedro Calderón de la Barca's's Segismundo in *Life Is a Dream* (c. 1635/2002: 167) realizes in the final act: "let us learn how to make good use / of this brief time allotted to us, / because all we enjoy in real life / is what we enjoy in dreams!"
[46] For a definition of *dai* see Zhuangzhi (2009: 213–214).
[47] Thus I think Raymond Tallis's (2012a) recent contextual reading of Zhuangzi's parable as lacking radical doubt owing to the fact that it is the philosopher, not the butterfly, who tells it in fact is not contextual enough: the Daoist context and the stated moral override the immediate context of the philosopher as narrator. In *Sarah Canary* Karen Joy Fowler (1991/2012: 296–297) makes oblique use of the parable, which by its Daoist emphasis on retaining multiple

and Guildenstern Are Dead refers to this parable (with no mention of Zhuangzi) by saying that he envies the Chinese philosopher "in his two-fold security" (Stoppard 1967/1974: 43),[48] Lem seems to suggest that as Kelvin has made contact with Solaris, he has in a sense become part of Solaris, but his conscious self is too undeveloped to get it. By his decision to stay on Solaris, with the mere possibility of once more encountering Rheya, however simulated, he shows that in his being he has in some sense merged the multiple identities of a human and Solaris. In *Solaris*, then, the main theme may be the challenge of learning what Solaris is by perceiving it in detail, but the love Kelvin feels for Rheya, even though she now is a mere simulacrum, is what makes him stay on Solaris and continue his mission to understand it.

In the next two chapters we explore some of the key inflections of literary worlds. In this way I attempt to begin to answer Ansgar and Vera Nünning's (2010: 22) call for a particular kind of research into world-making: "it is through a careful examination of the key concepts, metaphors, narratives, and other symbolic forms that we can gain an insight into the mechanisms of construction that are involved in our cultural ways of world-making". Figures and narratives are combined in nearly all kinds of literature, so let us now consider how their relation has been viewed in cognitive literary studies.

---

viewpoints strengthens the central ambiguity in the novel (which concerns whether the protagonist is an alien or not).

48 For a discussion of meta-usages in *Rosencrantz and Guildenstern Are Dead* see 6.1.

5 Key Combinations: Figures and Narratives

5.1 Figures versus Narratives, Figures into Narratives

Figures and narratives inform or inflect each other in any number of ways. Similes and metaphors can be extended and even form allegories, in parts of a literary work or the entire span of it. In narratives (and descriptions) figures are central ways of making the literary world come alive. The very prevalence of both in literature and language use in general may seem to suggest that there is no use asking which came first, figures or narratives. In a survey of cognitive narratology, Manfred Jahn (2005: 68) maintains that "all [...] story arcs of explanation – to use a narrative metaphor – boil down to the formula 'seeing X as Y'", that is, one of the classic definitions of metaphor. In this way, he is attempting to illustrate the constructivist basis of cognitive research by drawing on the American linguist Ray Jackendoff's computational view. But I take my cue from him in order to show that narrative and figure, especially metaphor and its extensions, are closely related: there are both narrative metaphors and metaphorical narratives. In fact, the relation between figures and narratives is so central in literature that the scholarship on it is extensive. Let me review some of it in order to clarify where I stand.

As far as I know, the most radical questioning of metaphor in general and metaphor theory in particular has been presented by G. E. R. Lloyd, the Cambridge Emeritus Professor of Ancient Philosophy and Science. He simply asks whether Aristotle in taking "the fateful step" of proposing a literal/metaphorical dichotomy was not discovering but in fact inventing that dichotomy (Lloyd 2003: 101). Now the easy answer would be that Aristotle simply put his finger on a central way language works, in his case, Greek. But by comparing ancient Greek with ancient Chinese, which does not on the face of it have such a distinction, Lloyd points to a serious theoretical dilemma: once a distinction is made, it is not only used rather readily but also extended to other material (in other languages). The solution he has propounded in order to get away from unclear cases and Eurocentric figurative thinking is the notion of *semantic stretch* by which literal and figurative usages form a kind of scale (Lloyd 2003: 112–113, 2012: 84–92). To be sure, such a pliable notion may be insightful, at times even useful, but I for one would be loath to dismiss a few millennia of scholarship on the manifold uses of rhetorical figures in a great number of languages. It is by such uses that for instance metaphors are extended into narratives and allegories.

In 1.2 we noted that for Aristotle imagination has the double role of *mediating* between sense perception and the intellect and *reproducing* phenomena in the world. Hence, it is understandable that Aristotle's view of mimesis has an imaginative aspect to it. But we also saw that in *De Anima* Artistotle (1986: 186–201, §§ 427a–429a) was the first to present a positive view of *phantasia*, with two rather separate meanings: an interpretive act as well as a faculty to produce something approaching (though not explicitly described as) a mental image (*phantasma*). When in his *Poetics* Aristotle (1941/2001a: 1477, § 1457b) notes that metaphors can combine two spheres – as in "As old age (D) is to life (C), so is evening (B) to day (A)" –, he also paved the ground for an extended view of metaphor. This was developed in particular by Quintilian (2001: 433; Book 8.6), since for him metaphor in "its continuous application ends up as Allegory and Enigma [the obscure form of allegory]". Here and in his ensuing discussion, Quintilian (2001: 451–459) apparently was the first to discuss *allegory* in ways that show how figures can be extended into narratives,[1] which Giambattista Vico, over one and a half millennium later, was to discuss in terms of how metaphors can be extended into fables (see 5.2).

Vico's notion of bridging figures (or tropes) and narratives was finally taken up by Hayden White (1973) in *Metahistory. The Historical Imagination in Nineteenth Century Europe*, where he showed how four central tropes – metaphor, metonymy, synecdoche and irony – inform narrative fiction as well as historiography. Later, he strengthened his thesis into a starkly put and often repeated phrase: "All stories are fictions", which are "true only in a metaphorical sense" (White 1999/2000: 9). But however eloquently White has tried to defend this thesis, which in effect means that every narrative historiographical account is a fiction, its strong form simply overextends the reach and use of figures. If I tell you, face to face or in writing, a narrative of what I did this morning: I got up, washed, had breakfast and started writing, it is a true (if shortened) account of what I did (as a video camera may have proved), even if I were to use more metaphorical language, such as "having jumped out of bed, I sprinkled my face with water and then, after having savoured my coffee, let my fingers dance on the keyboard". Such an account of a morning – if it had a bit more verve, perhaps – might have literary qualities, but this does not mean that it becomes literary fiction as such. Still, in its weaker form White's version of Vico's proto-constructivist approach has made important connections between figurative and narrative uses and has spawned much interesting research.

White's (1973) four tropes are also based on the "four master tropes" outlined in Kenneth Burke's (1945/1969: 503–516) *A Grammar of Motives*, where

---

[1] Less than two centuries before Quintilian, Book IV of *Rhetorica ad Herennium* (1954: 345–347) briefly discusses allegory as comparison, argument and contrast, but not how it can be extended into allegory.

Burke shows how they "shade into one another". Some years later, Roman Jakobson (1956/1987: 111), with no reference to Burke, went on to see language in terms of a twofold character, combination based on metaphor and selection based on metonymy, and claimed that in romanticism and symbolism metaphor was primary, whereas realism was based on metonymy and "synecdochic details". Thus, like so many before him, he finds metonymy (exchange of one name for another) and synecdoche (part for whole) closely related. But in viewing language through this dual grid, he leaves out one of the master tropes, irony. In chapter 3 we saw that unreliability in literature comes in many guises, some of which even go beyond irony. Any account of language and literature must be able to deal with it. Also, Burke's point that all master tropes – or figures – are combined and blended is especially evident in literature. A particularly rich example is Markus Zusak's (2005/2007) novel *The Book Thief*. As noted at the end of 3.4, it blends the real and the fantastic: Death is personified and can be viewed as metonymically representing the Nazis and their obliteration of Jews or as metaphorically (and paradoxically) representing a live creature personifying the termination of life.[2] As the narrator of the novel, this affords much irony, dramatic and other. What is more, in its language the novel makes much use of actual rhetorical figures, especially metonymy ("Their uniforms walked upright..."), metaphor ("the moon was sown into the sky that night") and personification ("The words trotted out, involuntarily"), and combines various figures ("the words were on their way, and when they arrived, Liesel would hold them in her hands like clouds, and she would wring them out, like the rain") (Zusak 2005/2007: 56, 63, 93, 86). Such pervasive use of figurative language seems to suggest that human agency is neither intentional nor in charge and that forces beyond their control make people act and speak despite themselves. Thus, the rhetorical figures underscore the narrative and make the portrayal of Germans suffering under the Nazi regime even more touching.

In recent years the most stimulating discussions of figures and narratives (often with no reference to Vico, let alone his predecessors)[3] have been conducted in cognitive studies, cognitive linguistics and cognitive literary studies. However, a further specification is needed: there is a basic, if not always recognized, divide between cognitive studies in the life sciences and in the human sciences.

---

[2] In medieval plays, like *Everyman* (1956/2000) and other allegories of Christian life, Death is often personified. In more recent literature in English perhaps T. F. Powys's (1931/2011) libertine John Death in his novel *Unclay* is the most memorable personification of death before the satirical figures of Death in Terry Pratchett's *Discworld* series (e.g. Pratchett 1994/1995 and 1996/1997) and Zusak's novel.

[3] Christoph G. Leidl (2003: 32 *et passim*) makes this point in relation to Aristotle and Quintilian.

Final rapprochement between the two can only be attained if neurophysiology ever reaches the point when what happens in the brain when a person is reading or writing can be identified in some detail, and then related to literary creation and interpretation, respectively. By brain scanning we can now see that particular areas are activated when performing such activities, which is a start. Empirical studies of narrative have on their part aimed to close the gap by reader-response experiments.[4] Still, despite some building material, we are still rather far from being able to see what the bridge between cognition and literary interpretation might look like.

To move on to more particular issues, in cognitive studies in the human sciences a dichotomy runs deep. Perhaps it was most strikingly voiced three decades ago by Jerome Bruner (1986: 11–43, 11 quote) in his view that there are "two modes of thought" – the paradigmatic or logico-scientific mode and the narrative mode – and that they are "irreducible", "(though complementary)". His view draws on Roman Jakobson's (1960/1987: 71) classic division of language into paradigmatic and syntagmatic structures, by the functions he termed "*selection* and *combination*" (which was based on the metaphor–metonymy distinction in Jakobson 1956/1987). But in fact some years later Bruner announced that his division into two modes of thought was misguided: cognition is so complex that no such divisions hold, since *narrare* (telling) and *gnarus* (knowing) are "tangled beyond sorting" (Bruner 2002/2003: 27 quote; 115–116n19).[5] But, as we shall see, the dichotomous view he reinforced in 1986 is symptomatic of much of the development of cognitive studies from the early 1980s to the first decade of this century.

Perhaps the central trend in cognitive studies in the human sciences has been the study of *figures and tropes* (cf. Bruner's paradigmatic mode of thought). The often explicitly advanced view is some version of what Raymond W. Gibbs, Jr. (1994) has termed *the cognitive wager*, according to which language is based on fundamental cognitive categories, especially figures or tropes (which can be blended). The universalist claim of the cognitive wager was an important trend in the 1980s and 1990s and has been elaborated ever since.[6] The emphasis on blending and con-

---

[4] For a survey of work on brain scanning and empirical studies related to narrative comprehension see Sanford and Emmott (2012).
[5] This is no surprise, since *narrare* etymologically stems from Proto-Indo-European *gno-, the same root as that of *gnarus*, that is, you must *know* something in order to have something to *narrate*.
[6] See Lakoff and Johnson (1980, 1999), Lakoff (1987), Johnson (1987), Turner (1987, 1991, 1996), Lakoff and Turner (1989), much of Ortony (1993/1998), Gibbs (1994, 2008a), Fauconnier (1997/1999), Katz et al. (1998), Fauconnier and Turner (2002/2003), and some of Jaén and Simon (2012) and Zunshine (2015). Even though this list is in no way exhaustive, it may suggest that few central new studies in this approach have been published in the last decade.

textualization in some recent works entails a greater understanding of the complexity in the use of figures. Still, rather little has been done to develop what was touched on in Lakoff and Johnson (1980), namely, socioculturally situating the use of figures, let alone dealing with ideological usages of them.[7]

The other important branch in cognitive studies from neurophysiology to psychology to philosophy has been the focus on *narrative* as fundamental in human cognition, in various guises: narrative as cognition in Damasio (1999/2000), the narrative construal of life story and reality in Bruner (1990/1994, 1996), and narrative psychodynamics in Lloyd (1989) (cf. Bruner's narrative mode of thought). Probably most influentially, Antonio Damasio (1999/2000: 184–185) has maintained that in their core consciousness humans are "telling a narrative or story in the sense of creating a nonlanguaged map of logically related events". If there is any truth in this claim, then the narrative properties of human cognition must be studied in much greater detail. Yet Damasio's view also begs the question of how narrative as a "nonlanguaged map" may ultimately be couched in language in human brains. Perhaps cooperation between cognitive studies and life-story studies in psychology and folkloristics might be enlightening in this respect.

Most importantly, as far as the figurative and the narrative branches of cognitive studies are concerned, what is needed is rapprochement between the two. A modest attempt in this direction is my study of one of the culturally speaking most universal figures, Life Is a Journey, in which I make the case that it should be studied both in its figurative and narrative senses, their extensions and interrelations (see Pettersson 2001a and its references). In one of the oldest extant narratives, the funerary autobiography *The Tale of Sinuhe* (1998/2009: 27–43, 43 quote; B 311) from about 1800 BCE, Sinuhe's (most likely fictional) life story, which largely concerns his exile outside Egypt, is rendered so that in the last line (before the colophon) he speaks of living his old age favoured by the king "until the day of landing came". Even at this point, "landing" was a widespread metaphor for dying in Egyptian (see *The Tale of Sinuhe* 1998/2009: 53n84), but it is especially suited to ending Sinuhe's autobiography, since his life has consisted of a journey to and sojourn in a foreign country (Retjenu or Canaan). And this journey is also an allegory of human life and of free will as

---

[7] See however Fernandez (1991) and Kövecses (2005) and some of Lakoff's later political works, such as *The Political Mind. Why You Can't Understand 21st-Century American Politics with an 18th-Century Brain* (2008).

against the divine destiny, that is, an extended metaphor and a narrative of Life Is a Journey, all in one.[8]

Another instance of how figures and narrative blend, but this time more implicitly, is found in one of the shortest and most famous poems in English, Ezra Pound's "In a Station of the Metro". Here is the original version of it (with its original spacing and punctuation):

IN A STATION OF THE METRO

The apparition   of these faces   in the crowd :
Petals   on a wet, black   bough .
(Pound 1913)

The colon – or semicolon in later versions[9] – can be read as a kind of copula standing for *is* (suggesting metaphor) or *is like* (simile). The noun *apparition* seems to imply a perceiver (to whom, in a station of the metro, faces seem petals), as does the deictic marker *these*, even if no perceiver is expressly present. Mieke Bal (1985), as I have noted, has maintained that all literature has the first-person frame (*I say:*). Hence, Pound's brief poem could be seen as an abridged narrative, based on the frame "When entering a station of the metro, it struck me that ... is (like) ...". In fact, Pound has noted that its "*hokku*-like sentence" (hence, apparently, the original triple groupings of the words in the lines) is in fact condensed from a thirty-line poem (quoted in Ellmann and O'Clair 1988: 381n).[10] In this way, even a brief poem that has no verb, and is thus composed of a mere truncated figure, whether metaphor or simile, can have implicit narrative features (see also 5.2).

Japanese literature also provides examples of how not just figures but poems too are combined with narratives. In the oldest collection of Japanese poetry, the *Manyōshū* (2005: 18, 288), the poems are often given short contextualising heading-like preambles, such as "After the death of the Emperor Temmu" or simply

---

8 Here we find an intriguing use of narrative stance: Sinuhe is narrating in the first person (after starting out in the third person), thus he is describing his death from the otherworld. This may seem an unreliable or fantastic position to modern readers, but for Egyptians for whom humans could live on in afterlife it may not have been.
9 In later versions the words are the same, but the triple grouping of the words in each line is deleted as are the spaces before the punctuation marks. Also, the colon is changed into a semicolon. See e.g. Pound (1916/1988: 381).
10 Since Pound recalled in 1958 that he first was contacted by Mrs Fenollosa "in or about 19[13]", it is possible that he already at this point was also aware of Chinese poetry through Ernesto Fenollosa's famous essay "The Chinese Written Character as a Medium for Poetry" that he was to edit and publish in 1919 (see Fenollosa and Pound 2008/2010: 2 quote).

"On the cuckoo". Compiled by imperial decree, the second major collection of Japanese poems, the *Kokinshū* from the early tenth century, has in part a more pronounced courtly character. Some poems attributed to Ariwara no Narihira in that collection (*Kokinshū* 1984/2012: 165–169) also occur in *The Ise Stories* (aka *The Tales of Ise*), which in part were written about the same time. Here poems are embedded as illustrations of 125 amorous narrative episodes in the (fictionalized) life of Narihira, from a shy young man meeting a woman to his moment of death in the last episode (*The Ise Stories* 2010: 14–15, 247–248). In this way, the court poetry helped to spawn the literary court romance tradition known as *monogatari*, whose greatest achievement except *The Ise Stories* is Murasaki Shikibu's (Lady Murasaki's) *The Tale of Genji*, the thousand-page novel from the year 1008 that includes a few hundred poems, many of which were classic by then. Thus, the brief annotations and preambles to poems led to brief narrative sketches and finally to the classic Japanese novel and a tradition of generic blending of travelogue and poetry that lives on in Matsuo Bashō's (1966: 97–143) seventeenth-century travel sketches, which especially in "The Narrow Road to the Deep North" seamlessly combine narrative and poetry.

Much as in cognitive studies in the humanities in general, in cognitive literary studies there is a dichotomy between cognitive poetics or stylistics drawing on the figurative approach on the one hand and cognitive narratology on the other. Some of the figurative theoreticians are also literary-critical practitioners, which entails that they attempt to show that their theoretical views can be applied to literature (see Lakoff and Turner 1989, Turner 1987, 1991, 1996). Many of the papers in the 2002–2003 special issues on cognitive literary studies in *Poetics Today* discuss only this branch.[11] This is also true of most of Elena Semino and Jonathan Culpeper's (2002) volume on cognitive stylistics, and much of Peter Stockwell's (2002) introductory study of cognitive poetics. In fact, in many cases it seems that the cognitive angle has meant that older disciplines (such as stylistics and poetics) have been able to renew themselves by going cognitive (see Pettersson 2005b).

Understandably, cognitive narratology too draws on earlier narrative theory, especially the study of point of view, focalisation and figuration (such as the work of Cohn 1978/1983, 1999) and representation (Ricœur 1983/1990, 1984/1985, 1985/1988). Above all, Monika Fludernik's (1993 and especially 1996) work has been of paramount importance in combining the study of both focalisation and representation in a cognitive-narratological synthesis. Scholars with a background in stylistics and narratology have also discussed specific nar-

---

[11] See *Poetics Today* 23:1 (Spring 2002) and 24: 2 (Summer 2003).

ratological issues from a cognitive point of view (see much of Nünning 1998, van Peer and Chatman 2001), and David Herman's (2002/2004, 2003, 2013) work suggests that narratology, rejuvenated by cognitive aspects, may enter a new era. Also, Herman's (2011) important edition on the representation of consciousness in fiction for over a millennium may be symptomatic in the sense that cognitive or post-classical narratology has focused on developing the study of narrative perspective. Still, cognitive literary studies should heed Bernaerts et al.'s (2013a: 10–13, 10–11 quote) warnings of the threats posed by a "blindness to tradition, the potential backfire of eclecticism, a new essentialism based on naive positivistic optimism, and a reductionist teleological thinking".

What is more, scholars with a primarily figurative background have also touched on narrative issues. Mark Johnson's (1987: 171) theory of imagination combines four trope-related dimensions (categorization, schemata, metaphorical projections and metonymy) with a narrative one (narrative structure), and later he has discussed narrative identity (Johnson 1993). Perhaps most intriguingly, Mark Turner (1996) examines parable and narrative imagining in a study that also discusses blending, but is not able to account for how the figurative and the narrative are combined (see below). Nevertheless, I would envisage that some such bridges are going to be built in the near future. In fact, Turner (2002) seems to view blending in a way that encompasses the narrative and the figurative, despite his rather unwarranted dismissal of Arthur Koestler's (1964/1989) view of blending (termed *bisociation*) in *The Act of Creation* as "exceptional" and untheorized (see Turner 2002: 15–16n2). On the contrary, as Turner mentions in the footnote quoted, Koestler's discussion of blending as a basic mental operation is rather extensive, but he overlooks the fact that the first part of Koestler's (1964/1989: 27–97) study provides a theoretical background to bisociation as a central activity, not only in humour but all creative acts. My own disagreement with Koestler (1964/1989) concerns his view of bisociation as a transitory state, whereas for instance much comic poetry would suggest that unresolved incongruity (just as much cognitive blending in general) works by the very fusion of seemingly incompatible qualities (see Pettersson 2004b: 160, 162–163). In any case, novel readings of Koestler's (1964/1989) rather overlooked seminal work could be fruitful for cognitive literary studies, not least in indicating ways of combining its figurative and narrative branches.

To move on to language and literature, even a cursory view would suggest that figures and narratives are closely related. Compare for instance:

(a) Mary is a lion (metaphor)
(b) *Mary is a lion* (heading of narrative, i.e. crypto-narrative)
(c) Mary is a "lion" (metaphor with irony)

(d) [Mary fights courageously.] JOHN: Mary is a lion! (drama; narrative implicit)
(e) He thought that Mary was a lion (free indirect discourse)

Such examples show the close interrelation between figures, such as metaphor and irony, and narrative, even when dramatized or embedded in free indirect discourse. A text type such as description can, in Chatman's (1990: 6–37) sense, be used *at the service of* another, such as narrative (see 6.3). But an example in Christina Alm-Arvius's (2003: 122) study on figures of speech implies that what can be read as description as well as narrative (more specifically, parable) may be done so by an extended metaphor, perhaps "intended as a figurative outline with a moral point": "First you must sow the seeds, then water and look after the crop as it is growing. Then, after all this work, you can reap the harvest". It is somewhat surprising that such rather evident affinities have not attracted more attention. Still, some important intimations of a rapprochement between cognitive studies and literary studies have existed for a long time, at least ever since Aristotle. A greater awareness of the affinities between narratives and figures might help us to build bridges between and within cognitive studies and literary studies.

Moreover, as Frank Nuessel (1995, 1998) has shown, Giambattista Vico made a kind of cognitive wager centuries ago, even if Lakoff and his collaborators never have acknowledged it. Similarly, symbol studies in diverse guises from Ernst Cassirer and Susanne K. Langer to Norbert Elias and Victor Turner to latter-day practitioners, such as Ellen Dissanayake and Terrence Deacon, have had an abiding interest in the interrelation of myth and narrative (see 1.3). Another line to explore is the research on intersubjective attunement in infancy: in evolutionary terms by Michael Tomasello (2008), in developmental terms by Stein Bråten (1998), in aesthetic terms by Ellen Dissanayake (2000) and in narrative and mnemonic terms by Susan Engel (1999). There have also been interesting results in the study of iconicity in fiction (see e.g. Ljungberg 2005). Perhaps the most intriguing is Ralf Norrman's (1998) study of how a variety of figures (such as paradox, oxymoron, antithesis, ambiguity and irony) make use of structural symmetry and thus can be shaping forces in fiction.

As far as narrative is concerned, it is rather astonishing that similarities in the processual structure of learning and narrative (equilibrium → disequilibrium → new equilibrium) in, say, Jean Piaget and Tzvetan Todorov have gone unnoticed. Furthermore, as we shall see, decades ago, Paul Ricœur (1983/1990: ix–xi, ix quote) noted that both metaphor and narrative make use of the function of *predicative assimilation*, based on "the productive imagination". In cognitive narrative studies some of the most promising seems to be Herman's (2002/2004, 2003, 2009, 2011, 2013) work, which indicates that there is a growing interdisciplinary interest in cognitive literary studies (see also Zunshine 2015). Lately, we have also seen even more encompassing versions of cognitive literary studies in which "perceiving, knowing and being become intricately intertwined, collapsing category boundaries that may forever shift the terms of academic analysis", so that developmental, evolutionary, cultural and interdisciplinary paths are taken in conjunction with cognitive studies (Hart 2012: vii).[12]

Hence, despite such promising advances, the relation between (extended) metaphor and narrative in literary studies has not received as much attention as it deserves. Indeed, there is even a recent study that rephrases Bruner's (1986) argument that "story and metaphor are two distinct sense-making processes", even if much of it goes on to analyse how narrative, metaphor and allegory are interrelated in fiction (see Popova 2015: 2). Elsewhere I have called for a rapprochement of the figurative and narrative trends in cognitive literary studies and proposed possible ways of achieving this end in theory (Pettersson 2001a, 2005b). By considering some poetry and fiction below, I aim to explore what literary-critical practice might suggest about the relation between extended metaphor and narrative as one of the key combinations in literary world-making. To be sure, literary texts have been analysed in cognitive metaphor studies, but most practitioners have concentrated on a top-down search for cognitive metaphors, despite the emphasis on the corporeal basis of meaning. As we shall see, some conclusions to be derived from a bottom-up literary-critical practice are rather far-ranging. I will suggest that broad hermeneutic-generic circles with attention to the specifics of each literary work are best suited to producing lasting literary-critical contributions. Thus, my claim is that literary-critical practice and its recognition of the richness of sense and sensa (sensuous qualities) in literature should inform not just cognitive literary theory but also the study of literary worlds.

Before going on, however, I think we should note that some applications of cognitive metaphor theory have entailed a number of shortcomings. First, applying cognitive metaphor theory is often not even understood as an interpretive move in the first place, which it evidently is (see Johansen 2005 for a critique of Lakoff and Turner 1989). Second, such applications often reduce much of the literary work to surface manifestations of cognitive metaphors, at times questionably interpreted as such. Third, cognitive readings do not seem to be able to deal with the complexity and specificity of literature or with how it is read (see Pettersson 2005b). Fourth (as we shall see), cognitive literary criticism at times displays a disregard of other literary theory and criticism, which may lead to thwarted results or unsustainable claims of theoretical or critical novelty.

---

[12] Jaén and Simon (2012), the edition in which Hart (2012) is the foreword, is a case in point.

One of the most important recent contributions to metaphor theory is Raymond Gibbs's *The Cambridge Handbook of Metaphor and Thought* (2008a). In his introduction, Gibbs (2008b: 3, 4) notes that "[t]here is now much greater attention to the ways that context shapes metaphor use and understanding" as well as "greater recognition of the complex ways that metaphor arises from the interaction of brains, bodies, languages, and culture". That is, metaphor is now studied in relation to other figures, text types, languages and cultures, which helps understanding the many shapes metaphor takes. Important foundations for this work were laid by Paul Werth (1999: 317–329), who showed how literary works can make use of sustained metaphor or mega-metaphor in ways that are cumulative. Let me now attempt to contribute to this development by analysing how lyrical poetry may include narrative features and, in turn, how prose fiction, even novels, may be based on extended metaphor, thus shaping literary worlds. The chosen test cases suggest that cognitive literary studies could well be a useful starting-point for literary analysis, if pursued by bottom-up literary-critical analysis that takes into account various figures, text types and contextual features.

5.2 From Metaphor to Narrative to Allegory

First let us briefly consider a few central theorists who have pointed the way towards broadening our understanding of the relation between metaphor and narrative.

Some of the most important recent advances stressing the affinity between metaphor and narrative come from three scholars: Mark Turner, Jørgen Dines Johansen and particularly Paul Ricœur. In *The Literary Mind* Turner (1996: v, cf. 7) discusses conceptual blending, including the kind of narrative blending he terms parable, defined as "[t]he projection of one story onto another". But he does not study the interrelation of analogy (such as metaphor) and narrative at any length, except, for instance, when noting that proverbs often consist of "a condensed, implicit story to be interpreted through projection" (Turner 1996: 5–6). Yet such points are merely touched on in Fauconnier and Turner's (2002/2003: 287–288) *The Way We Think* a few years later. Similarly, in the context of presenting his semiotic-pragmatic model of literature, Johansen (2002: 203) argues that "poems are truncated narratives", representing "the peak moment, as it were, of a narrative made autonomous – or rather relatively autonomous". Thus, the reader supposedly contextualizes the poem by inscribing it "in a minimal narrative". When discussing how a literary text acquires an iconic dimension, Johansen (2002: 334) defines the notion of allegorization as a "metaphoric reading", which entails going from *sensus litteralis* to *sensus plenior* (from a literal to a fuller meaning) and which attunes the text to "important aesthetic, moral, or epistemological issues". Thus, both Turner and Johansen imply that narrative plays a key role in all kinds of literature, not just prose fiction.

Ricœur (1983/1990: ix) is even more explicit about seeing a connection between metaphor and narrative. In fact, he stresses that his trilogy *Time and Narrative* and *The Rule of Metaphor* "form a pair" and "were conceived together". According to Ricœur (1983/1990: ix–xi), both metaphor and narrative make use of productive imagination, since they generate *predicative assimilation*, a view familiar from Coleridge.[13] Extending his theorizing on the basis of Aristotle, Ricœur (1977/2003: 46) asks "whether the secret of metaphor, as a displacement of meaning at the level of words, does not rest in the elevation of meaning at the level of *muthos* [plot, story]". On this view, he goes on, "metaphor would not only be a deviation in relation to ordinary usage, but also, by means of this deviation, the privileged instrument in that upward motion of meaning promoted by *mimêsis*" (Ricœur 1977/2003: 46). Thus, in literature at least, metaphor can be viewed as a mechanism akin to the second, configurating sense of Ricœur's (1977/2003: 64) mimesis, which "opens the kingdom of the *as if*". It is important to note that Ricœur's (1977/2003: 79–80, 283) view of mimesis is referential in the broader sense of combining imitation and imagination, which is why in his view metaphorical discourse, like narrative, can both discover and invent new ideas.

In short, Ricœur, Turner and Johansen view metaphor from their respective theoretical background – hermeneutics, cognitive literary studies and semiotics – and point to various kinds of interrelation between metaphor and narrative. However, they provide few examples of such affinity in literary-critical practice, although Turner (1996) offers some literary instances of cognitive blending.

Perhaps the most fruitful approach for analysing extended metaphors in relation to narrative is Ricœur's hermeneutic account, since it draws in part on the tradition that views metaphor not primarily as a figure of speech but as symbolic activity (see Schön 1993/1998: 137).[14] Symbolic activity refers to an elaboration of one central meaning of the term *symbol:* "a word, phrase, image, or the like, having a complex of associated meanings" (definition 3 in *Webster's* 1989). In this tradition of symbol studies the main representatives are Ernst Cassirer and his foremost student Susanne K. Langer, who both focus on the proximity of metaphor and narrative (primarily in the form of myth). Cassirer (1944/1974: 109) emphasizes that "[l]anguage and myth are near of kin" and that the former is "by its

---

13 In 1.5 we saw that for Coleridge (1817/2000: 307) narrative, like metaphor, "grasps together".
14 At roughly the same time, Kenneth Burke (1941/1961: 8) employed the term *symbolic action* even more broadly for "poetry, or any verbal act".

very nature and essence, metaphorical". Langer (1988: 40, 47) goes on to develop this view in relation to the work of art, which she considers "a single symbol" and, more precisely, "a metaphorical symbol". Although Ricœur's oeuvre includes only passing references to this tradition (notably to Cassirer), I think a note by Richard Kearney on "the common project" of Ricœur's entire oeuvre hits the mark, since he characterizes this project as "the retrieval of thought in symbolic mediation and the extension of symbolic mediation into thought" (Kearney 2004: 15).[15] In other words, symbolic and cognitive aspects are interlinked throughout Ricœur's work, which is a useful starting-point for studying the relation between extended metaphor and narrative in literary worlds.

What is more, viewing metaphor as a kind of conceptual representation as well as a figure of speech may make us more apt to recognize the dynamism inherent in the uses of metaphor, especially its extensions. Even before Ricœur, Northrop Frye (1957/1973: 82–84, 89 quote) regarded the symbol as an image (as against a sign, an archetype or a monad), and famously went on to claim that "all [literary-critical] commentary is allegorical interpretation, an attaching of ideas to the structure of poetic imagery". Frye's (1957/1973: 90) definition of allegory is general but still specific enough to be helpful: "A writer is being allegorical whenever it is clear that he is saying 'by this I also (*allos*) mean that.' If this seems to be done continuously, we may say, cautiously, that what he is writing 'is' an allegory". This definition tallies with the etymology of *allegory* as the combination of the Greek *allos* (other) and *agoreuein* ('to speak openly, as in the assembly or market') (see Fletcher 1964: 2n1). What is more, Frye's view of allegory as constructed on a continuous or sustained use of symbol is also in line with Madeleine Kasten's definition of allegory in the *Routledge Encyclopedia of Narrative Theory*. She claims that allegory achieves its "effect [of multiple meaning] through the use of sustained [...] metaphor" (Kasten 2005: 10). Such definitions show an affinity with Werth's (1999: 318) "double-vision" account of sustained metaphor, which could well be regarded as related to allegory.

Some promising work on similar lines has been done more recently, for instance in the tracing of various kinds of affinities between metaphor and narrative. Gibbs and Matlock (2008) study how readers can simulate the bodily actions suggested by both metaphorical language and extended narratives in order to understand what they are reading. Semino and Steen (2008: 238–41) present recent research on the relation between metaphor and narrative and show what uses various genres have made of metaphor. Charles Forceville (2008: 478)

---

15 It is worth noting that Ricœur (1983/1990: 57) develops his term *symbolic mediation* expressly on the basis of Cassirer's *The Philosophy of Symbolic Forms*.

broadens the perspective by considering metaphor in relation to various multimodal representations and suggests that metaphor should be defined in relation to the mode in which it is represented. In Fludernik (2011), a number of scholars also discuss the relation between metaphor and narrative.[16]

Let me now present some instances of the affinity between extended metaphor and narrative, since it is one of the key ways in which literary worlds are shaped. I do so by analysing two lyrical poems, where imagery usually is considered central, as well as Magnus Mills's novels, which may represent the most extensive genre of prose fiction. By discussing some instances of the diverse relations between extended metaphor and narrative in William Blake's lyrical poetry and the contemporary British author Magnus Mills's fiction, I try to show what is distinctive in the way that metaphor and narrative combine to form literary worlds in different kinds of literature. The two case studies seem to suggest that there is a wide variety of ways in which metaphor and narrative can be combined by fleshing out the symbolical dimension through various kinds of allegory.

Lyrical poems, which are often simply metaphorical or descriptive, may make use of multiple text types. Take William Blake's famous short poem "*The SICK ROSE*".[17]

The SICK ROSE

O Rose thou art sick.
The invisible worm.
That flies in the night
In the howling storm:

Has found out thy bed
Of crimson joy:
And his dark secret love
Does thy life destroy.
(Blake 2000/2009: 81)

---

[16] See the papers by Benjamin Biebuyck and Gunther Martens, Michael Kimmel, Michael Sinding and Tamar Yacobi in Fludernik (2011). This chapter is based on my paper for that volume.
[17] In my view, it is important to read Blake's lyrical poetry multimodally, which includes recognizing his use of typography and punctuation, but space does not permit me to develop this argument here. I only leave out the full stop after the titles of poems, since this was a widespread convention at the time and has no significance in Blake's poetry. In quoting Blake's poems I follow the typography of his writing on the plates in *William Blake. The Illuminated Books* (Blake 2000/2009).

The first sentence simply states that the rose is ill, by apostrophizing it. The second sentence (that is, the rest of the poem) gives a longer description of how this came to be. But as the fact that the tense moves from the present to the present perfect to the present suggests, the second sentence is a brief narrative of how a flying "worm" has found the rose and is killing it with his "love". From the subtitle of the collection in which it is included, SONGS Of *INNOCENCE and of EXPERIENCE*, we know that the collection aims to show *"the Two Contrary States of the Human Soul"* (Blake 2000/ 2009: 43), and we can thus gather that the sick rose is a symbol for the plight, or one kind of plight, of humankind. By depicting the rose's bed as one of "crimson joy" and calling the worm's action "dark secret love", Blake strengthens the anthropomorphic dimension implied in the title and suggests that a symbolic reading is plausible. In terms of Seymour Chatman's view of text types *at each other's service* (1990: 8–12), we can see that the second sentence of *"The SICK ROSE"* is a brief narrative, which forms a more detailed elaboration on the short descriptive first sentence, that is, it explains why the rose is ailing. At the same time, the two sentences of the poem expand its title by depicting an actual rose that is languishing because of a worm, and its descriptive and narrative features supply a deeper symbolic sense that has a bearing on human life.

So far I have only explicitly considered the classic aspect of narrative in *"The SICK ROSE"*, the event sequencing as suggested by the perfective aspect of the present perfect tense. But further features of narrative can be observed in the poem. In his useful textbook of narrative studies, *Basic Elements of Narrative*, David Herman (2009: 9 *et passim*) singles out four elements typical of narrative: (1) *situatedness*, (2) *event sequencing*, (3) *worldmaking / world disruption* and (4) *what it's like*. *"The SICK ROSE"* fulfils all these requirements. Besides displaying event sequencing (2), the poem features generic situating (1) in terms of displaying communicative discourse in the form of a poem (in a book of poems, an anthology, or, as here, in a literary study) and within that poem the apostrophizing of a rose. *"The SICK ROSE"* also represents an imaginative story world, in which roses can be sick and worms can be invisible, fly and love roses (3). In this world, an apparently previously healthy rose has fallen ill, having been contaminated by a worm's love. And this sequence of events would not be of any particular interest without the symbolical anthropomorphizing import (that Herman terms *what it's like*): flowers are not usually "sick" (but are infested or wilt) and worms cannot feel love (4). In other words, much of what, according to Herman (2009), prototypically characterizes narrative can be applied to a typical lyrical poem. The vague and apparently symbolic metaphor of the ailing rose appears in a poem that has many features in common with narrative. In terms of Chatman's hierarchical view of text types, what we have in *"The SICK ROSE"* is an apostrophe followed by a narrative at the service of a description (of how the rose has been infested and is dying). It would, however, not be a classic poem were the description not at the service of some sort of symbolic level, which in terms of text types could be termed an argument.

What about the poem's symbolic features? Blake criticism often indulges in sweeping statements such as: "The symbolism of the red rose for corporeal love and of the worm (or flesh) for the source of the sickness is plain. [- - -] The 'howling storm' in which the worm comes is a symbol of materialism" (Keynes in Blake 1967/1982: 147). Apart from the questionable reading of the poem (the bed is of "crimson joy", not the rose, which is only red in the illustration), such specific interpretations are dubious. To be sure, reading the symbolic import of the poem as that of heterosexual love or corrupting materialism is a rather common strategy, but the hundreds of hits in Google Scholar show that there is a plethora of other readings. One of the most interesting ones in recent years is by Jon Mee (1998), who in a political interpretation claims that the rose referred to George Rose, a rather corrupt statesman and journalist. According to Mee, George Rose personified corruption in contaminating the English Rose, that is, England. Again, the double meaning of the rose in this reading is rather dubious: if this had been Blake's (however veiled) point, should not the worm in some sense be identified with George Rose (whereas, on the contrary, as a statesman, George Rose stands for the English Rose)? If the illustration is taken into account when interpreting the poem, the caterpillar in it in fact traditionally symbolizes destruction and Blake often equates it with the clergy (see Keynes in Blake 1982: 147) – another aspect that should be considered in a political reading of the poem. Apparently Blake meant to leave *"The SICK ROSE"* open for multiple possible readings, not least by his use of a suggestive illustration, including two human figures prostrate on the branches of the rose, apparently a man and a woman. Even Blake's (1977: 149) drafts of the poem imply that no easy equation of the rose with woman and of the worm with man is possible, since Blake wavered about the gender of the worm. The illustration too is ambiguous: the worm may be the woman (or man or worm) coming triumphantly out from between its petals or the woman may be trying to escape from the rose with a worm or serpent around her waist.[18] Thus, in *"The SICK ROSE"* the symbolic meaning brought about in part by narrative or narrative-like progression seems evocative and intentionally vague.

Now we are now ready to discuss a somewhat more elaborate poem by Blake, "A POISON TREE", and a cognitive reading of it, which focuses on meta-

---

18 May these few notes on *"The SICK ROSE"* suffice, since my point here is merely to show the affinity between metaphor, description and narrative in the text. Like all poems in SONGS Of INNOCENCE and of EXPERIENCE, its evocative symbolical character gains additional depth by forming ironies, both within itself and with other songs of innocence and experience.

phor and allegory (Crisp 2008). Here is Blake's (2000/2009: 91) final version (or, to be exact, one of them):[19]

A POISON TREE

I was angry with my friend;	[1]
I told my wrath, my wrath did end.	[2]
I was angry with my foe:	[3]
I told it not, my wrath did grow.	[4]
And I waterd it in fears,	[5]
Night & morning with my tears:	[6]
And I sunned it with smiles,	[7]
And with soft deceitful wiles.	[8]
And it grew both day and night,	[9]
Till it bore an apple bright.	[10]
And my foe beheld it shine,	[11]
And he knew that it was mine.	[12]
And into my garden stole.	[13]
When the night had veild the pole:	[14]
In the morning glad I see:	[15]
My foe outstretchd beneath the tree.	[16]

As against a rather tenacious line in literary criticism of viewing allegory as a continued or extended metaphor,[20] Peter Crisp (2008: 293) in his analysis attempts a firm separation between metaphor and allegory: "Extended metaphors create a conscious, and rather strange, experience of metaphorical blended spaces, while allegories refer to and characterize fictional situations functioning as their metaphorical sources". He argues that there must be a particular point at which this change from extended metaphor to allegory occurs (although it may differ from reader to reader), and locates it in line 10 between "Till it" and "bore an apple bright" (Crisp 2008: 302). However, since what Crisp terms a *fictional situation* remains rather vague, it is difficult to draw such lines. I think Crisp (2008: 300) is right in suggesting that "grow" in line 5 is still a conventional,

---

19 "A POISON TREE" as rendered here is based on my reading of the plate, which slightly differs from the punctuation as given in David Bindman's transcription (see Blake 2000/2009: 410). Unfortunately, there is no space here for a wholesale interpretation of "A POISON TREE" (or indeed "*The SICK ROSE*"), which of course should discuss Blake's illustration in some detail. For a cognitive reading of "A POISON TREE" see Herman (2010).
20 See e.g. Quintilian (2001: 451–459), Fletcher (1964: 3), Murrin (1969: 205), Johansen (2002: 334) and Kasten (2008: 10).

if metaphorical, verb indicating increasing anger, and only "waterd" and "sunned" in the rest of the second stanza (not "verse" as Crisp has it throughout) signal an innovative metaphor by extending and developing the cognitive metaphor Emotions Are Plants. But I cannot see that there is a particular cut-off point at which this extended metaphor becomes an allegory nor that in reading the poem's third stanza "the conscious awareness of a blended space" gives over "to conscious awareness of a *fictional situation*" (Crisp 2008: 303).

On the contrary, in my view, Angus Fletcher (1964: 81–82), one of the leading traditional allegory theorists, may be right in portraying the move from metaphor to allegory: "Surprise [which for Fletcher is typical of metaphor][21] diminishes as the analogy is extended, because we see more and more clearly the meaning of the hidden tenor. In most cases allegories proceed toward clarity, away from obscurity, even though they maintain a pose of enigma up to the very end". In the case of "A POISON TREE", however, there is little surprise, since, as Crisp (2008: 299) notes, it starts with the conventional metaphor of anger growing. I would say that the last two lines drive home the allegorical import by describing the speaker's reaction to seeing his enemy dead (ll. 15–16). But throughout, the fictional situation is constructed in tandem with the extended metaphor, and even at the end of the final stanza, there is no radical change from metaphor to allegory: the allegory builds on an extended metaphor based on Emotions Are Plants. What is more, it should be noted that the polysyndeton (And ... And ... And ...) used from the second to the fourth stanza is a traditional way of signalling event sequencing. Thus, the speaker's relation to his foe is developed as a narrative culminating in the foe's death: the metaphor of increasing wrath viewed as growing a poison tree is extended by narrative, which, by implying that the foe when stealing into the garden has devoured the poisoned apple, finally becomes an allegory.

As for the ending of the poem, it drives home the allegory but seems to ironize both the speaker and his foe: the former since he has acted rather immorally by poisoning his enemy, the latter since he was rather easily fooled. The title of the poem does not guide the reader's interpretation, whereas the original title "Christian Forbearance", the original capitalizing of "Glad" and the later omitted line "And I gave it [the apple] to my foe" in the second stanza (all of which Crisp fails to mention), suggest that by the allegory's irony, Blake, at least originally, primarily targeted the speaker and his allegedly Christian virtue.[22] What is rarely noted is that even

---

[21] Cf. Ricœur's (1991/2008: 168) view that the metaphorical utterance is based on "predicative impertinence" that produces "a shock between semantic fields".
[22] For an informed discussion of Blake's double-edged view of allegory see Frye (1949: 9–11).

though "A POISON TREE" may be read as an allegory, its form is primarily that of a parable, which Gerard Steen (2005: 418) defines as an "anecdote that is meant to be understood as a [...] metaphor for a moral or spiritual aspect of life, in particular good behaviour". In "A POISON TREE" Blake simply turns the parable on its head by suggesting that foregoing overt aggression is not Christian behaviour. What is more, as in the case of *"The SICK ROSE"*, Blake took great care not to make his moral too explicit or simplistic. Painting the tree in his illustration as rather barren and leafless and the foe lying in a cruciform position was apparently Blake's way of pointing to an ironic condemnation of the poem's speaker.[23]

Crisp's (2008) reading has its merits, but exposes some of the dangers of literary criticism based on cognitive metaphor theory, if the theoretical and critical basis is not as secure as in, say, Margaret Freeman (2005). As I have noted, a cognitive reading of Blake's poem can stand on firmer ground, if the extant drafts are compared to the established final version; if allegory theory is taken into account; if the allegorical, narrative, parable-like and ironic features are recognized in the poem, which shows no clear-cut move from extended metaphor to allegory; and if literary-critical and text-critical practice is more firmly wedded to both cognitive metaphor theory and cognitive narratology. It is the fact that "A POISON TREE" by its use of various literary techniques retains its allegorical "pose of enigma" that makes it so intriguing.

5.3 Extended Metaphors in Novels

Novels too can be based on extended metaphors, which at times are signalled by their titles. Before I move on to discuss Magnus Mills's fiction, let me briefly consider how titles are employed in literature. Nils Enkvist (1994: 55) views the use of titles in literary works as "the semantic equivalent of priming the pump: it is one of the most economical devices of starting the contextualization and scenario-building".[24] However, in literature this scenario-building, or rather world-making, is most likely done in more multifarious ways than elsewhere. Titles can metaphorically epitomize the entire narrative in all sorts of ways. *The Odyssey* stands for the protagonist's adventurous and fantastic journey, and by allusion to it Joyce's *Ulysses* invites readers to interpret a rather realistic portrayal of some Dubliners metaphorically in terms of that epic. An intertextual allu-

---

23 See e.g. the comment by Keynes in Blake (1967/1982: 49).
24 Enkvist (1994: 55–56) also includes an illuminating analysis of taxonomies of literary titles on the basis of work done by Harry Levin and Laurence Lerner.

sion in the title can also suggest how to read a novel, as in Jay McInerney's *Bright Lights, Big City*, which, by evoking the title of Jimmy Reed's blues song that thematizes the dangers of the city, implies that the portrayal of cocaine-addled yuppies in New York City should be understood as having a moral undercurrent. But there are rather different kinds of symbolic novel title. A title may refer to the name of the protagonist (Flaubert's *Madame Bovary*), the theme (Chopin's *The Awakening*) or it may form an ekphrastic pointer to the main character and hint at how she is depicted (James's *Portrait of a Lady*). In less realistic literature it may be more usual to have ironic titles (Beckett's *Happy Days*) and titles achieving greater symbolic breadth by remaining enigmatic (Kafka's *The Castle*). It is well-known that some novels, especially modern and postmodern ones, summarize the plot in the first paragraph, so that the rest of the novel forms an elaboration of it.[25] In *The Castle* the symbolic plight of the protagonist is similarly presented in the first lines, as there is not "even a glimmer of light to show that the castle was there" and K. stands "for a long time gazing into the illusory emptiness above him" (Kafka 2005: 9). The subsequent narrative can be read as an extended description of this plight, whose symbolic dimension grows as K.'s attempts at entering the castle are thwarted.

Magnus Mills is one of the most prominent contemporary British authors of allegorical fables, if *fable* is understood in the general sense of "a brief narrative told in order to provide moral instruction" (Tate 2005: 157).[26] However strange the society is in most of his novels – *The Restraint of Beasts* (1998), *All Quiet on the Orient Express* (1999), *The Scheme for Full Employment* (2003), *The Maintenance of Headway* (2009), *A Cruel Bird Came to the Nest and Looked In* (2011) and *The Field of the Cloth of Gold* (2015), it is recognizably British, even though in *The Restraint of Beasts* and *The Scheme for Full Employment* there are speculative features that suggest these may be future versions of Britain.[27] In *Three to See the King* (2003) and *Explorers of the New Century* (2005), desolate areas are inhabited and explored, respectively, by a handful of people. In all his novels, except *Explorers of the New Century*, an unnamed first-person male narrator tries to deal with characters whose motivations he struggles to understand. Like the narrator,

---

25 A famous instance is the opening of Vladimir Nabokov's novel *Laughter in the Dark* (see 8.2). Elsewhere I have termed this *metafictional determinism* (see Pettersson 1994: 138–142).
26 For a discussion of fables in different kinds of literature see chapter 9.
27 In contrast, *A Cruel Bird Came to the Nest and Looked In* (Mills 2011/2012) portrays an allegorical fairytale version of Britain, where the cabinet ministers, including the narrator, are totally incompetent. As the title's allusion to the Anglo-French negotiations in 1520 to outlaw war suggests, *The Field of the Cloth of Gold* (Mills 2015) presents an allegorical fable of political strife in the history and present state of Britain as well as Europe.

these characters are rather tight-lipped and their simple words and actions seldom betray the strange and at times sinister intentions they harbour. The phrases in the titles of the novels serve as central symbols for the action by which the allegorical fables are constructed.[28] How the fables form allegories can perhaps best be understood through Deborah L. Madsen's (1996: 144) view of twentieth-century forms of allegory: "Modern allegories, such as Kafka's, treat interpretation as valid only in terms of subjective individual perception. Postmodern allegories, however, question the authenticity of this personal identity in relation to the invisible cultural systems of value which may be projected through the individual consciousness and into the world".

Those of Mills's novels that are set in Britain focus on the character narrators and their experiences, but these narrators are in fact lost in a cultural system that they should be familiar with. The vagueness of the allegory of Mills's latter-day moral fables could thus be viewed as a postmodern feature. In fact, in an early short story, "Only When the Sun Shines Brightly", Mills (1999/2004) explicitly rewrites Aesop's (2002/2008: 94) well-known fable about the wager between the north wind and the sun that compete regarding which of them can make a man take off his coat (with the sun finally prevailing). In this story the first-person character narrator is disturbed by a plastic sheet fastening itself onto a neighbouring building, and even though the wind blows like a fury, only when three men tug at it does it finally come off. Mills's point seems to be that age-old morals, such as those of Aesop, do not hold anymore. In order to drive home his point of the lack of a clear-cut moral to his story, Mills (1999/2004: 34) retells Aesop's original story of the wind and the sun and leaves his Kafkaesque protagonist just as disturbed by the silence after the sheet has been removed as he was by the noise it made.

In *The Restraint of Beasts* the full import of the metaphor of the title – that which turns the novel into an allegory – is gradually revealed. First it is noted that fences are being built for "the restraint of beasts" (the non-metaphorical sense of herding cattle), but on the following pages the fencers Tam and Richie are compared to "wild men, head-bangers with long Viking hair", who by "a prolonged stare" from their boss are rendered "meek and mild" (Mills 1998/1999: 10,

---

[28] The most complex title is *All Quiet on the Orient Express* in that it is a portmanteau phrase referring to the narrator's (ultimately defeated) dream of taking the Orient Express to Turkey (see Mills 1999/2004: 3), to the antagonistic social interaction in the village in which he is an outsider by alluding to the Erich Maria Remarque's famous First World War novel *All Quiet on the Western Front* (originally *Im Westen nichts Neues*), and possibly to Agatha Christie's novel *Murder on the Orient Express*.

11–2).²⁹ Thus, men are early on compared to beasts that are to be restrained (in the metaphorical sense). The beastly quality of men emerges in various ways during the course of the novel, by arguments, such as those between the Scots and the English (27, 51, 68, 80), fights between men (26–27, 82), between men and women (105), between father and son (161–162, 175, 184), and the clash between personal identity and company identity (employees complain when the company uniform is to be worn day and night) (172). These disputes finally lead the contracting company to segregate genders (202), not to pay wages to employees (208) and to incarcerate them (214). Similarly, the metaphorical sense is strengthened towards the end of the novel, as the fencers' employer calls the electric fence "[t]he final solution to the problem of the restraint of beasts" (159) and makes the connection between man and beast explicit by "forever talking about 'rounding us up' and 'shipping us off' as though we were being transported to some sort of penal colony or corrective camp" (183).

In this way, Mills gradually extends the metaphor of Man Is A Beast, in two senses: (1) man is a beast that needs to be restrained for what he does to other humans, and (2) in restraining and incarcerating other humans, man acts in beastly ways. For about three fourths of the novel, the former sense is prevalent. Men must indeed be restrained because of their violent disposition and carelessness (for instance, Tam, Richie and the narrator each accidentally kills a man). The institutionalized violence of (2) is in focus at the end of the novel as the fencers' contractor makes them build the electric fence of their own jail, or rather pen, since they will most likely end up as meat for the contractor's factory. At the end of the novel, Mills has established both senses (1) and (2) as well as their allegorical moral that man must be restrained and that such restraint (especially when enforced by incarceration) can become institutionalized violence. Thus, the allegorical import of the novel proceeds in Fletcher's (1964: 82) sense towards an evident allegorical meaning, which still retains "the pose of enigma". Here, the word *pose* is apposite, since Mills seems to be suggesting that there is some truth in both (1) and (2): men can act beastly, but the restraint of such action can become even more beastly. This is corroborated by the Nazi phrase "the final solution" (159).

For Mills, then, Ricœur's (1974/2004: 28) view of myth (equated with plot) as "subordinated to the symbol" is apt. The titles of his novels are phrases that are allegorized by "metaphoric reading", as Johansen has it (2002: 334). In fact, Mills's allegorical visions cover most aspects of society: politics (blue-collar workers in *The Scheme for Full Employment* and *The Maintenance of Headway*,

---

29 Subsequent references to *The Restraint of Beasts* are given by page number in this edition.

the ruling class in *A Cruel Bird Came to the Nest and Looked In*, territorial warfare in *The Field of the Cloth of Gold*), religion (*Three to See the King*), and (social) philosophy (*Explorers of the New Century*). Mills may eschew simplistic moral teachings, such as those in Aesop's fables, but despite his black-humour plots and strange, even deranged protagonists, he makes serious moral points. For instance, *The Scheme for Full Employment* shows that, despite the lack of viability in the instituted full employment scheme, the hierarchical strife within it, and the envy it may cause, humans have a deep-seated need to be of use and to belong to social groups.

In short, Mills's novels display that long narratives can have symbolic titles as starting-points and then go on to develop them into extended metaphors by way of plots and morals, thus adding mimetic dimensions to the allegories. In Ricœur's (1977/2003: 46) terms, metaphor thus extended is indeed "the privileged instrument in that upward motion of meaning promoted by *mimêsis*". By means of their morals, Mills's novels, although at times displaying features of alternative history or science fiction in imaginative worlds discontinuous with the one readers know, clearly comment on that world by the moral views they advocate. These mimetic qualities are corroborated by the characters' disposition and colloquial dialogue. That is, however strange the plots, settings or characters in these novels, the way in which the characters react and speak makes them recognizable, even possible to empathize with. In this manner, Mills's allegorical fables go beyond the literary worlds portrayed and question the values in contemporary British society and elsewhere, perhaps even more so than much realist fiction (see Pettersson 2007).

Before considering the implications of such literary-critical readings for literary world-making, I would like to draw some conclusions as concerns the interpretation of Blake's poetry and Mills's fiction. "*The SICK ROSE*" exemplifies how metaphor and narrative, description and argument, even in a brief poem can go together, be used at each other's service and display a kind of metaphorical and narrative-like progression that serves to extend the symbolic import. The relationship between the rose and the worm is so evocative, because it is not straightforwardly portrayed but given vague allegorical meanings. In "A POISON TREE" the inhumanity of the speaker is evident (his foe has apparently not done anything to deserve being poisoned) and Christian hypocrisy is implied – at least for readers familiar with the original illustrated poem, the drafts of the poem or with Blake's other poems which ironically expose Christianity, from "The Marriage of Heaven and Hell" to "The Everlasting Gospel". Mills's fiction, on the other hand, develops the metaphors suggested by the symbolical phrases of their titles into narratives that turn into allegories displaying an interpretive openness similar to that in Blake, with some moral import. Both authors tend to use irony, even multiple irony, which makes their moral hard to pinpoint, and both are careful not to spell out their moral.

In sum, the two case studies have shown that both extended metaphor and narrative must be taken into account when interpreting poetry as well as prose fiction. Blake's poems and Mills's novels suggest that titles can be symbolic and develop their central metaphor by means of narrative into various kinds of allegory. Of course, you can discuss extended metaphor without discussing narrative and the other way round, but total neglect of either may lead to a thwarted view of the poem or novel studied. I would suggest that this is also true of other figures and text types that are centrally employed in literary texts. Thus, the contextual study of metaphor that Gibbs (2008b: 3) considers prevalent in contemporary cognitive studies should still be pursued. What my test cases indicate is that such work should be interpretively and text-critically attuned and that it should ask questions such as: What edition is being used? What is the work's manuscript and/or editing history? What light can other works by the author throw on the one studied? What theory and methodology are the most useful ones in interpreting the work? How does the literary form and genre influence the reading of the theme and motifs of the work? What figures and text types are used and how are they combined? In other words, literary theory should not be applied in a top-down manner that disregards how crucial formal and thematic features are combined in literary works.

Of course, this is no revolutionary insight in literary studies. In an idealistic presentation of the Russian formalist method, Boris Eichenbaum (1965: 102, 103) makes the point quite succinctly: "We [Russian formalists] speak and may speak only about theoretical principles suggested to us not by this or that ready-made methodology, but by the examination of specific material in its specific context. [---] We posit specific principles and adhere to them insofar as the material justifies them. If the material demands their refinement or change, we change or refine them". What the above readings suggest is precisely that no simple or ready-made theoretical frameworks suffice and that each literary work must be understood in relation to its contexts. As James Phelan (2007: 23–24) has put it when arguing for the study of hybrid forms of fiction, "there is no theoretical or practical reason why, in any specific text, the relationships among events, character, attitude/thought/belief, change, and audience activity need to stay within the boundaries of narrativity, lyricality, and portraiture". Such a view could inform both literary theory and critical practice.

So let us see in what ways research on extended metaphor and narrative can profitably be combined. Above I mentioned that the configurating sense of Ricœur's mimesis "opens the kingdom of the *as if*" and is thus closely related to metaphor. In fact, in his treatise on metaphor, Ricœur (2003: 253) also states:

"'Seeing X as Y' encompasses 'X is not Y'; seeing time as a beggar is, precisely, to know also that time is not a beggar. The borders of meaning are transgressed but not abolished". Thus, by drawing on Wittgenstein's notion of *seeing-as* by way of Marcus Hester's (1967) literary application of it, Ricœur is able to come to a cognitively-informed view of metaphor that need not do away with traditional metaphor theory. In fact, Hester (1967: 188) stresses that "metaphor is a *fusion* of sense and sensa [sense data]" and that in poetic metaphor "thought and sensation are inseparable because the object of reading is a *sensuous object interpreted*". In terms of cognitive literary studies and literary world-making, this means that both the thematic and formal qualities of literary works must be taken into account.

In other words, this chapter, like the volume *Cognition and Literary Interpretation in Practice* (Veivo et al. 2005), points to the fact that cognitive literary theory, like all literary theory, if it is to be of use in literary-critical practice, must have a firm grounding in the practice it is supposed to theorize. In fact, Michael Silk (2003: 146) faults some of the leading authors on metaphor – Aristotle, Jakobson and Ricœur – precisely for this: "they treat poetic usages as if they were merely the scaffolding behind which and through which they can mount their own constructions. But poetic usages are not their scaffolding: they are their bricks". What I hope this chapter has shown is that figures and narratives are important bricks shaping literary worlds.

Now we have surveyed the combinations of two of the most central bricks, let us see how other kinds of inflection are employed so that readers understand how to interpret the literary worlds they enter.

6 Other Imaginative Inflections

In the two previous chapters we have considered how literary worlds are shaped, including their imaginative frame, basic modes and themes, and the way they combine figures and narratives. We have seen how they function in examining how the real and the fantastic on the one hand and mimesis and genre on the other are combined (chapter 2), how unreliability colours literary worlds (chapter 3) and how metaphors are extended into narratives and allegories (chapter 5). Such are some of the central ways in which literary imagination comes across. But there are other ways in which literary imagination is inflected.

In order to understand the import of such inflections, we must consider what the rhetoric of Western literature may look like in a comparative perspective. In a number of works the French sinologist François Jullien has compared and contrasted ancient China and Greece. One of his main theses is evident in the title of his study *Detour and Access. Strategies of Meaning in China and Greece*. He maintains that in all kinds of ways – military tactics, political rhetoric and literature – Chinese culture traditionally makes use of indirection and distance, in short *detour*, while Greek (and all of Western) culture and literature is characterized by a head-on approach, that of straight *access* to the subject at hand (Jullien 1995/2000). Jullien is by no means the first to have made this or related observations, but when he states that "Westerners find it natural and normal to meet the world head-on", I for one raise an eyebrow. Is this supposed to be true of *all* Westerners at all times? Is there not a world of difference between how, say, a Frenchman and a Finn communicate in speech and writing? And even if we would believe that the Chinese indeed make use of different kinds of detour in their culture, is this not true of Westerners as well? When Jullien (1995/2000: 57 quote, 355– 369) claims that Greek allegory refers to meaning on *another level* and the Chinese make use of detour by what he terms *allusive distance*, are we not speaking of different kinds of indirection rather than an absolute distinction? Perhaps another scholar comparing the cultures of ancient China and Greece, G. E. R. Lloyd (1990: 142), is right in claiming that we should not speak of different kinds of mentality as much as of their "context of communication" and "styles of reasoning".

To be sure, detour may well characterize much of the Chinese culture, especially in ancient times, but the aim of this chapter is to consider some significant inflections to be found in all main forms of literature across the world. Unreliability is such a widespread inflection that I have chosen to discuss it earlier on in this study, in 3.2. There we saw that unreliability and irony have much in common and are widely used in all kinds of literature, ancient to contemporary.

Now let us focus on other imaginative inflections or styles of reasoning, such as *indirection* and *hypothetical action*, which show that Western literature also makes use of different kinds of detour. By *indirection* I mean that plots, characters and (at times) settings are represented in less than chronological, causal or other straightforward ways and by *hypothetical action* that what is stated in literature is hypothesized, questioned, negated or that its meaning in other ways remains ambiguous or vague.

6.1 Indirection in Fiction and Drama

Without indirection, there would be little interest in the plots, narrators and characters that make up the narratives in prose fiction and drama. All plots would be chronologically and causally narrated and no characters would change drastically by sudden revelations or expositional manipulation (see 3.4). Since plots together with narrators and characters, including their actions and pronouncements, in effect stand for most of the thematic interest in prose fiction and plays, it is understandable that literary studies have largely concentrated on the ways they are represented. Narrative theory has studied how emplotment (Ricœur) or narrative order (Genette) is presented as a discourse (*sjuzet*) on the basis of the chronological story (*fabula*); how complex literary characters can be; and how plot and character interact with each other and with the setting. As a character, Tess in Thomas Hardy's (1891/1983) *Tess of the d'Urbervilles* changes as she is acted upon by other characters and by fate, and her life story forms the plot of the novel, which is in continuous interaction with the portrayal of the setting, including changes in season and weather. But what makes it come alive are formative changes in action, coincidence (a letter from Tess not reaching her fiancé Angel at a crucial point) and the late revelation that Angel does not have a character to suit his name. There is little anachrony in the way the plot is depicted, but enough delayed exposition to retain the suspense in this novelistic tragedy of Tess as "A Pure Woman", as Hardy (1891/1983: 3) labels her in the subtitle. More evidently perhaps, detective stories and thrillers are largely read precisely for the suspense afforded by their surprising plot twists, which nevertheless should be plausible.

Similarly, drama theory has discussed the structure of plays, with Aristotle's *Poetics* and Gustav Freytag's five-part "pyramid" structure of ancient and Shakespearean drama in *Freytag's Theory of the Drama* (*Die Technik des Dramas*, 1863) as perhaps the most classic instances. But in drama, too, indirection gives life to the action: not only is there a subgenre called "comedy of errors", but all sorts of mistaken identities and misjudgements are just as important in tragedies. If

Othello knew Iago's true character or if Oedipus knew who his parents are, there would be no tragedy. But as Western drama developed, the structure became less evident, especially in absurd or experimental drama. The Irish critic Vivian Mercier famously reviewed Beckett's *Waiting for Godot* in *The Irish Times* in 1956 and claimed that it is "a play in which nothing happens, twice". Here, instead of action, it is the very waiting for Godot that sustains the suspense, and gives depth to the absurd plight of the protagonists Vladimir and Estragon. In Japan the nō play has for centuries had a clearly codified structure, with little variation and rather little indirection, but its interest lies not in the unfolding of the plot as much as in ritualistic pattern it takes the audience through. In a modern realist play, such as Yasmina Reza's (1994/2005) *"Art"*, the focus is ostensibly on how (abstract) art is perceived – as suggested by the quotation marks in the title – and what its worth is, but on reflection it in fact thematizes friendship, since how you evaluate art is part and parcel of who you are and how you relate to your friends. Thus, indirection is essential in much prose fiction and drama.

Here are a few different kinds of indirection in prose fiction.

Substitution and Inversion

Like event sequencing, formal indirection takes as many shapes. Metaphor, we have seen, can be extended in different ways and is related to other figurative usages such as simile and catachresis (misapplied word or mixed metaphor). Metonymy, like metaphor, involves substitution (even if it is contiguous rather than analogous) and is related to synecdoche (part for whole), enallage (grammatical substitution), hyperbole (overstatement) and irony (meaning – at least in part – something else than what is allegedly intended). Thus, in a broad sense, many figurative uses have to do with the *substitution* of meaning.

One of the most interesting and far-ranging kinds of such substitution, if rather disregarded, is what could be termed *structural inversion*. As far as I know, the Finland-Swedish literary theorist and critic Ralf Norrman is the only one to have analysed it at length in literature. In his study *Wholeness Restored* Norrman (1998) argues that symmetry is a shaping force in human thinking and shows how it is used in indigenous cultures and literature. By what rhetoricians call chiasmus (A – B → B – A) one half is repeated and inverted and that very inversion creates the symmetrical shape (Norrman 1998: 11). Norrman (1998: 22) invites us to think of *Macbeth*'s first line: "Fair is foul, and foul is fair", which signals that chaos and cosmos have changed places, that social and moral order is inverted (and as such suggests the topic of the play).[1] He goes on to claim that such symmetry is so prevalent that this use of inversion amounts to what he terms "*a unified, comprehensive theory of paradox, oxymoron, antithesis, ambiguity and irony*" (Norrman 1998: 24).

If this sounds rather sweeping, Norrman spent much of his career working towards this conclusion by studying ambiguity in Henry James and chiastic patterns in Samuel Butler (Norrman 1977, 1982, 1986). What is more, in the analytical chapters in *Wholeness Restored* he exemplifies his thesis of inverted patterns in Butler's non-fiction, Kurt Vonnegut's fiction, Raymond Chandler's *The Long Goodbye* and James's *Daisy Miller*. In fact, Norrman (1998: 27) maintains that the basis for this symmetry is "a belief in *the similarity of dissimilars*". He does not draw an even more far-ranging conclusion, since he does not seem to notice that this phrase is almost verbatim Aristotle's (1941/2001a: 1479, § 1459a) definition of metaphor in his *Poetics:* "metaphor implies an intuitive perception of similarity in dissimilars". In this light, Norrman's patterns of structural inversion of the latter part inverting the former can be seen as a form of substitution that is related to how metaphor works.

For instance, in 3.4 we saw that Winterbourne as the main focaliser in *Daisy Miller* turns out to be unreliable, hence exemplifying the processual move from reliability to unreliability. In other words, the main pattern of the novel is one of inversion. Norrman is able to show that a kind of inversion is also used in dialogue, as when Daisy asks her hostess Mrs Walker as she enters her party, "Is there any one I know?" and receives the answer "I think everyone knows you!" (quoted in Norrman 1998: 179). Even this one instance makes amply clear that what Norrman (1998: 149 *et passim*), following René Girard, calls *the scapegoat mechanism* is at work to Daisy's disadvantage. Inversion features on the level of motifs in various crossings between the social and moral values of Europe and the United States, but it is most evidently lodged in the two main characters, Winterbourne and Daisy. At first Winterbourne, who focalises much of the action, seems a likeable man and Daisy comes across as a rather morally questionable character, but as the plot unfolds it is evident that Daisy is a naive American girl not accustomed to European norms and Winterbourne a callous man whose words and actions contribute to her downfall (Norrman 1998: 149 – 216). This inversion in characterization, I would add, is all the more disturbing owing to James's narrative technique: readers usually empathize with the sus-

---

[1] Even if never explicitly mentioned in Mills's (2011/2012) novel *A Cruel Bird Came to the Nest and Looked In*, *Macbeth* (and quotes from it, and to a lesser extent, *Hamlet*) forms a subtext to the turmoil concerning the rulers of Greater Fallowfields (cf. Great Britain), thus underlining the allegory of the novel.

tained focalising consciousness (here most often that of Winterbourne), unless it has evident signs of unreliability. Winterbourne has some such signs, but not enough to make him unreliable at first, and his cruel nature, like Daisy's innocence, is only gradually revealed.

Hence, a whole range of figurative usages, from particular phrases to structural plot devices, such as expositional manipulation, are based on substitution between two meanings or larger elements, at times by inversion. This may be the most prevalent form indirection takes. It may occur as changes in characterization, as in *Daisy Miller*, but thematic usages based on the thwarted aspirations of characters are also common. However, at least overtly, inversions need not be based on opposition or result in symmetry. In chapter 3, for example, we discussed how different kinds of unreliability – deceptive, deluded or fallible – can be expressed in partial, processual or ambiguous ways that may invert or colour what is narrated.

Thwarted Aspirations

Thwarted aspirations are another instance where form and content often go together. The plot may be about a thwarted quest, which affects the character of the protagonist, and may or may not lead to an insight into the futility of the very quest. When analysing North American folktales Alan Dundes (1964: 62) makes a point about their basic patterns: "*Folk tales can consist simply of relating how abundance was lost or how a lack was liquidated*". The latter seems widespread in literature as well as myth: a lack must be liquidated or, to put it another way, aspirations must be fulfilled. This is what Sumerian and other Indo-European rituals and myths are about: the function of prayer or of sending a hero to slay a dragon is done in order to liquidate a lack (of, say, rain) or fulfil an aspiration (such as to restore order). In popular fiction and comic plays the heroes must experience adventures and mistaken identities before their aspirations are fulfilled by the happy end. Thus, aspirations can be thwarted for some time (in order to afford the plot with suspense), but they may also be thwarted throughout. In naturalist novels and tragedies the aspirations of the protagonists are continuously thwarted and remain unfulfilled and they end up defeated or dead. Such genres are thematically rather straightforward, however much anachrony they may use. More intriguing in this sense, are realist fiction, postmodern fiction and experimental drama. The two latter are seldom paired with realist fiction, but in this respect they are related: the aspirations of the characters are thwarted in a number of ways.

In her "Prelude" to *Middlemarch. A Study of Provincial Life* (serialized 1871–1872; 1874) George Eliot announces the theme of her realist novel. Many latter-day women may have "the passionate, ideal nature" of Saint Theresa and in them "loving heart-beats and sobs after an unattained goodness tremble off and are dispersed among hindrances, instead of centring in some long-recognizable deed" (Eliot 1874/2000: 3, 4).[2] This puts the protagonist Dorothea Brooke's life in a nutshell. She has high ideals that will remain "unattained", since there are "hindrances" on the way. The motto of chapter 2 – from *Don Quixote* – announces her main hindrance (12): like Don Quixote (as compared to Sancho Panza's down-to-earth realism), she is all too idealistic in her view of reality, in her case Mr Casaubon, the scholar whom she will marry, since she shares his passion for science. In a sense, the rest of the novel, after Dorothea's first infatuation with the rather egotistical Casaubon is about her coming to her senses. This theme of idealism, as inspired by books (romantic or scientific) is a prevalent theme in much fiction and drama. In *Don Quixote* and *Adventures of Huckleberry Finn* characters like Don Quixote and Tom Sawyer finally fare reasonably well, despite their uncritical love of romances, but the ending is much grimmer for Flaubert's naively romantic protagonist in *Madame Bovary* as well as for the single-minded scholar in Patrick White's *Voss*.

In *Middlemarch* the other main character Dr Tertius Lydgate also has rather grand aspirations, concerning "above all to contribute towards enlarging the scientific rational basis of his profession" (122). In this sense, he comes much closer to the intellectual hubris evident in Goethe's Faust and White's Voss. In the end, Lydgate has set up "an excellent practice", "but he always regarded himself as a failure: he had not done what he once meant to do" (685). Both Dorothea and Lydgate also direct their passions to the opposite sex and much of the novel is about their love troubles, in and out of marriage. And Eliot might have left it at that: they both have considerable social aspirations which tally with the objectives of many well-to-do intellectuals at the time of the Reform Bill in the Britain of the 1830s, an era on which Eliot did much research so as to give life to the provincial fictional town of Middlemarch.

But Eliot raises the theme of thwarted aspirations to another level, when she on the last page of the epilogue discloses her humane moral: "there is no creature whose inward being is so strong that it is not greatly determined by what lies outside it" (688). She goes on to speak of "[a] new Theresa" and of how "we insignificant people with our daily words and acts are preparing the lives of many Dorotheas" and of how the fact that "things are not so ill with you

---

[2] Subsequent references to this edition are given by page number in brackets.

and me as they might have been, is half owing to the number who lived faithfully a hidden life, and rest in unvisited tombs" (688). The cynic might say that Eliot's narrator here reverts to telling rather than showing, but in fact she has been telling all along and commented rather (if not entirely) omnisciently on the action. What Eliot does by these final comments is to turn the thwarted aspirations around: what people consider they have or have not accomplished may not be what they think. The ripples of human actions and words are, as Eliot puts it, so "incalculably diffusive" that "the growing good of the world is partly dependent on unhistoric acts" (688), such as those of Dorothea and Lydgate. By her emphasis on how people are determined by society (here, as the title of the novel announces, by Middlemarch), Eliot may point to naturalist fiction, but by her detailed study of the unfathomable consequences of human action, she also produced one of the richest variations of thwarted aspiration in the English language.

In a sense, were it not for the conciliatory epilogue, the continuously thwarted aspirations of Dorothea and Lydgate would point to the central plot formula in Western mainstream fiction and drama after the late nineteenth century: characters seldom get what they want, and if they do, they might not be satisfied. This is true of most non-musical drama and prose fiction. Just think of the novelists and playwrights who have received the Nobel Prize for literature in the last century. Who has not centrally written about thwarted aspirations? Even writers whose literary fame is in decline, as for instance John Galsworthy and Pearl S. Buck, made some use of them. Indeed, perhaps the fall in literary reputation for some twentieth-century authors is due to an even stronger emphasis on thwarted aspirations as the true plight of modern and postmodern humankind.

In postmodern American fiction, such as Joseph Heller's (1961/1978) *Catch-22* and Thomas Pynchon's (1966/1974) *The Crying of Lot 49*, the protagonist's quest for meaning is continuously foiled by larger systems and remains so to the end. The individual versus society may have been a key motif in realist American fiction from Twain's *Adventures of Huckleberry Finn* to Sinclair Lewis's *Babbitt* to J. D. Salinger's *The Catcher in the Rye*, but in postmodern fiction the system is more amorphous, enigmatic and inhumane. Yossarian in *Catch-22* may be able to escape, but the system prevails, and Oedipa Maas in *The Crying of Lot 49* will never understand the forces behind the mysterious mail distribution company Trystero (or Tristero). They are, like most postmodern characters, children and grandchildren of Kafka's K. and Joseph K. Their aspirations are thwarted since they do not understand the inscrutable system they are up against. But this was in the heyday of postmodern fiction, which I would claim had its flowering from about 1960 to 1990. Even though the editors of *Postmodern American Fic-*

tion. An Anthology straightforwardly claim that "[i]n the history of postmodern American fiction, the publication of Toni Morrison's *Beloved* (1987) is a crucial moment", it actually just about marks the end of postmodern fiction proper (Geyh et al. 1998: 291). This is due to the fact that Morrison employs postmodern techniques, such as radical shifts in narrative perspective and order as well as ambiguous Gothic elements (Beloved as a ghost), and claims that the story of Sethe's traumatic life as an ex-slave "is not a story to pass on", while at the same time displaying a pointedly realist, even socio-critical tendency (Morrison 1987/1988: 275). Of course, Morrison does pass on the story of slavery, and she does it with such skill and passion that it became one of the most widely read and taught novels of the late twentieth century. In doing so, she helped to set a salient trend for the mainstream fiction in the last few decades: realism as blended with other (often fantastic) genres and with postmodern techniques. Furthermore, in her novel she dares to go against the penchant for thwarted aspirations in both realist and postmodern twentieth-century fiction as two of the protagonists, Sethe and Paul D, finally set out to heal each other's scars of slavery (Morrison 1987/1988: 273).

Meta-Usages

By *meta-usages* I denote the various ways literature can show self-consciousness about itself. Literature that centres on such an awareness is often termed *metafiction*, *metadrama* or *metapoetry*, according to its references to the very main mode it represents. A common view of the self-conscious use of literary technique is that it is largely a modern and especially postmodern phenomenon with some forerunners, such as Laurence Sterne's *Tristram Shandy*. But is it really? Before literacy all literature was oral, in other words, was not based on any one received account. To be sure, rituals and conventions of different kinds most likely had strong demands on phrasings to remain much the same, but stories and popular songs were prone to change with each performer and performance. This must have meant that the second time listeners heard excerpts of what was to become *The Mahābhārata* or *The Iliad*, they could compare them with a previous version, depending on their memory of it. When Aeschylus, Sophocles and Euripides wrote their tragedies, they – and their audiences – were well aware of the mythologies they made use of. In poetry too we find poems commenting on poetry, from Tecayehuatzin of Huexotzinco's (c. 1490/2001) pre-Columbian dramatized poem presenting an Aztec poetics (briefly discussed in 1.5) to contemporary Language poetry, often spelled L=A=N=G=U=A=G=E poetry to make a point. Such awareness of theme and variations and of the requirements of and changes in genre may not be elaborate meta-usages, but it certainly reveals considerable self-consciousness in producing and interpreting literature.

One of the richest instances of meta-usages in literature is found in Shakespeare's *Hamlet* (c. 1601) and its latter-day version Tom Stoppard's *Rosencrantz and Guildenstern Are Dead* (1967). For his play, Shakespeare drew on previous versions on Hamlet, possibly by Saxo Grammaticus, and/or the so-called *Ur-Hamlet*. But more importantly, he stages a metadrama or play-in-the-play, "The Murder of Gonzago", which mirrors the current feelings, memories and fears of the royal spectators, especially King Claudius, and at the same time exposes that he has killed his brother (Hamlet's father), a deed that prompts the action of the play he is in. As if this were not complex enough, in his play Stoppard adds many different twists to the story that are all meta-usages of sorts. The most evident twist is the *inversion* of the roles of the characters: however aware that they are minor characters in a play, Rosencrantz and Guildenstern are now the protagonists and the major characters in *Hamlet* have minor roles. In Stoppard's play there are thwarted aspirations among both groups. Guildenstern tries to understand what ails Hamlet and states early in Act Two: "Thwarted ambition – a sense of grievance, that's my diagnosis" (Stoppard 1967/1974: 40).³ But throughout the play, the aim of Rosencrantz and especially the sharper Guildenstern is to figure out their deterministic plight as characters. Guildenstern asks The Player – the head of the Tragedians, an acting troupe that later reports to have performed "The Murder of Gonzago" for King Claudius – "Who decides?", apparently meaning the way they act. "*Decides?* It is *written*", the Player answers, "We follow directions – there is no *choice* involved" (58). And this is the plight of all actors on stage: they must, at least more or less, do and express what is written.

Thus, in Stoppard's play there are three groups of actors: Hamlet and the other protagonists from *Hamlet*, more or less acting out their roles and acts in Shakespeare's play; the Tragedians performing a dress-rehearsal mime version of "The Murder of Gonzago" and other deaths, their forte as actors; and finally Rosencrantz and Guildenstern between the other two groups, increasingly aware of how determined they are. All three groups and their respective niche in the play intermingle, but most importantly the missing fourth wall illusion of drama is shattered by Rosencrantz shouting "Fire!" in order to demonstrate that free speech exists and, according to the stage directions "*regards the audience [...] with contempt*" when they do not react to his alarm and tells Guildenstern: "They should burn to death in their shoes" (43). In another scene close to

---

3 Subsequent references to this edition are given by page number in brackets.

the end, in which Rosencrantz and Guildenstern decide that they have some free will, if "within limits", Hamlet enters, "*clears his throat noisily and spits into the audience*" (84). Hence, what Genette (1972/1980: 234–237) has termed *metalepsis* in narrative, the crossing of narrative levels, occurs within the play and between the play and the audience.

As far as the aspirations of Rosencrantz and Guildenstern go, most of them are thwarted: they know no more of their past than before, they have little free will and they must die, as they were ordained to do in *Hamlet*. But whatever awareness the play may show of meta-usages, the two protagonists do not notice that one of their aspirations has in fact been fulfilled. They have actually become major characters and even if Hamlet, the audience and they themselves may have a hard time telling them apart, it is clear that they have different personalities – Guildenstern is the brainy one with Rosencrantz as his sidekick – and they have their spell in the limelight. The only aspect of meta-usages that Stoppard's play bypasses is one that Western literature has employed for centuries starting with Dante in *The Divine Comedy* and Chaucer in *The Canterbury Tales:* the author as character.[4] In fact, in postmodern fiction the author – usually the author of the very work itself – has become such a ubiquitous device that Aleid Fokkema (1999: 41) has called it "postmodernism's stock character".

Finally, Stoppard also addresses the very basis of literary imagination, the willing suspension of disbelief that also sustains the dramatic illusion. What is real and what is not – that is, actual life or playacting – is continuously probed in the play. The Player claims that people do not die in a believable way, but actors do on stage. Once an actor was actually hanged on stage, but "he just *wasn't* convincing! It was impossible to suspend one's disbelief", he complains (61). Later, Guildenstern even inverts the suspension of disbelief that the spectators, not the actors, are to uphold: "I've lost all capacity for disbelief" (72). The tables are turned even in this most basic way as far as sustaining the belief in the literary world the characters inhabit.

Such are, then, some fundamental inflections that affect the modes and themes in fiction and drama: substitution, thwarted aspirations and meta-usages. Poetry too makes use of such inflections, but it can also focus on various ways to hypothesize what happens or may have happened.

---

4 For a variety of analyses of the author as character see Franssen and Hoenselaars (1999).

6.2 Hypothetical Action in Poetry

So far we have seen that what is stated in literature, as heard or read with a willing suspension of disbelief, can be modified in various ways, such as by blending realist and fantastic elements, unreliability and irony, narrative and figures and, in the section above, indirection. But sometimes listeners or readers are only invited to entertain the idea that something may have happened or may happen, in which case the action portrayed is hypothetical. This of course colours the way what is said or written is understood. In other words, if the suspension of disbelief makes everything that takes place in literature hypothesized or fictional, then in a sense this kind of *hypothetical action* is doubly so. In fact, since I noted in 4.3 that the oldest Chinese writing consisted of divination by oracle bones, hypothetical action could be viewed as an ancient literary technique.

On the whole, in prose fiction, actions are portrayed in a more straightforward manner than in poetry, since emplotment of action is often at the centre of attention. Still, it is evident that there is always what Wolfgang Iser (1978/ 1984: 165–172) decades ago termed *gaps* in narration. Some years later, the narrative theorist Gerald Prince (1992) discussed different kinds of deletion in narratives. There is the *unnarratable* or *nonnarratable*, which can be due to the narrative perspective chosen, adherence to norms of decorum or simply deletion of tedious or repetitive action (Prince 1992: 28–29). Less evident and less discussed is what Prince calls the *disnarrated* in fiction, which means that "events that *do not* happen though they could have and are nonetheless referred to (in a negative or hypothetical mode) by the narrative text" (Prince 1992: 30). Prince shows that the disnarrated has been touched on by a number of scholars in different traditions: Viktor Shklovsky in Russian formalism, Claude Bremond in structuralist narratology, William Labov in sociolinguistics and Marie-Laure Ryan in narrative theory, and briefly exemplifies how variously it is employed in prose fiction (in contrast to some non-literary genres) (Prince 1992: 31–38).

Related and age-old ways of suggesting a non-narratable view is by blends of the real and the fantastic and by unreliable narration or focalisation and expositional manipulation (see 2.2 and 3.4). In prose fiction such techniques can occur either locally or as part of a work's entire structure, and once readers understand their use in, for instance, *Don Quixote* by Cervantes, *Daisy Miller* by Henry James or *The Good Soldier* by Ford Madox Ford, they learn to go beyond what the text "actually says". Such uses of indirection, ambiguity and irony are by now widely discussed in literary studies and taught to students as a matter of course. But more in the vein of Prince's *disnarrated* in prose fiction is the science-fiction author Samuel R. Delany's (1971: 141) point that "[f]antasy takes the subjunctivity of naturalistic fiction [*could have happened*] and throws it in reverse [*could not have happened*]". In this way, Delany implies that all prose fiction could be viewed in a hypothetical way: naturalist fiction (like realist fiction, I suppose) entails hypothetical action, whereas fantasy displays a kind of negated hypothetical action. In other words, much prose fiction, by being based on a what-if premise, includes various kinds of hypothetical action. For instance, David Herman (2002/2004: 303–330, 303 quote) has explored *hypothetical focalization* in prose fiction, defined as "hypotheses, framed by the narrator or a character, about what might be or might have been seen or perceived" and Laura Karttunen (2015) has studied how hypotheticals in narratives are part and parcel of emplotment, especially through displaying intense emotion. A fine example of a novel full of such largely unreliable focalisation is Paula Hawkins's (2015) recent domestic noir thriller *The Girl on the Train*, which turns on what the protagonists think they "know" about the people closest to them.

Prince (1992: 38) sums up the function of the disnarrated as follows: "The disnarrated guides reading by constituting a model that allows texts better to define themselves, to specify and emphasize the meanings they wish to communicate, and to designate the values they develop or aspire to". Since, as far as I know, related techniques of what I term *hypothetical action* in poetry have not been studied, they merit scrutiny. Also, such techniques seem to suggest that the hypothetical in poetry is employed in even more radical ways. Hypothetical action may not underline what is communicated or present a moral stance in the way Prince suggests that the disnarrated does in prose fiction, but it can be the key inflection through which entire poems are to be understood.

By analysing how some poetry in various ways hypothesizes meaning, I hope to show how poetical meaning can simultaneously be thwarted and enriched. In what follows I aim to show how three significant poets in the Anglo-American canon use various kinds of hypothetical action to suggest that some meanings are being questioned, negated or merely implied, and remain present in this ambiguous or vague state. In focusing on various formal and thematic means by which these poets hypothesize meaning, I hope to pinpoint some central ways in which poetry communicates by what is merely suggested and thus help scholars as well as students to better comprehend its workings.

There are, of course, a number of literary features by the density of whose use poetry differs from prose fiction: metre, rhyme, complex or convoluted syntax, unusual words or usages, figures of various kinds, diluted or seemingly minimal cohesion and coherence, and the portrayal of strange poetical worlds or viewpoints. All of them may pose problems for unaccustomed readers and most of them have been studied in some detail.

Let us now consider some linguistic, thematic, rhetorical and metrical techniques that question or negate a poem's ostensible contents. If it seems strange that I discuss poetry in terms of action, let me reiterate that much poetry, even lyrical poetry, is in fact narrative. As we shall see, hypothetical action comes in various local and recurrent guises, but what they all have in common is that they question the import of the poem, just as unreliability and irony does. My examples from different kinds of Anglo-American poetry from three centuries may suggest just how widespread and different such techniques are, how central both occasional and more sustained hypothesizing techniques can be for the understanding of a particular poem and just how much they contribute in the final analysis to the way some poetry communicates.

Blake's "The Tyger": The Act of Creation Questioned

Perhaps the best-known instance of hypothetical action – even though the term has not as far as I know been used in literary criticism – is William Blake's "*The Tyger*" (see Appendix 1). The poem seems to offer an imaginative account of how the tiger (or a kind of tiger) was created or might have been created. In the first stanza we learn that an "immortal hand or eye" could have framed the tiger explicitly addressed in the first line. Stanzas 2 to 4 portray an act of imagined creation: the tiger's fire burns and a hand grasps the fire, twists the sinews of its heart and the heart begins to beat. Apparently, the act of creation is viewed in metaphorical terms as the work of a blacksmith, since the furnace implies the means, the hammer and the anvil the tools, and the chain the blacksmith's material in close relation to the actual materiality of the tiger for which the brain apparently stands. In the fifth stanza the creator seems to contemplate the finished creation (the tiger), and in the final stanza the first stanza's astonishment at the finished creation is repeated but with a twist: now the creature created is so awe-inspiring that it fills the speaker with a sense of terror.

This brief paraphrase of the poem may give some insights into its contents, which can be corroborated by reference to Blake's use of the blacksmith as creator elsewhere in his works. Perhaps most notably, in Chapter IV of "The Book of Los" the blacksmith god in his human form Los (standing for Imagination) beats on an anvil with his hammer, forms Urizen (embodying Reason or Law) by holding his spine and moulding his brain, and finally smiles when seeing his work finished (Blake 1977: 271–272).[5]

---

[5] For a suggestive reading of "*The* Tyger" in the light of possible sources see Ackroyd (1995/1996: 147–149).

However, such straightforward reading and comparison cannot capture what is crucial in interpreting "*The* Tyger". In fact, this poem states nothing at all, since everything, as Blake criticism has recognized, is hypothesized by the central overall technique of apostrophized questioning. For instance, in his annotated edition of SONGS Of *INNOCENCE and Of EXPERIENCE* Geoffrey Keynes notes this fact, but then offers what may seem a more questionable reading of its effect: "The poem is deliberately composed of a series of questions, none of which is answered. It contains the riddle of the universe, how to reconcile good with evil" (Blake 1967/1982: 148–149).[6] In the final version of the six-stanza poem there are as many as fourteen question marks. Each stanza ends with one, and the second stanza has three question marks (at the end of lines 2, 3 and 4).[7] The third and the fourth stanzas also have question marks at the end of the second line and the fifth stanza at the end of the third line. What is more, in the fourth line of the third stanza as well as the first and third lines of the fourth stanza, question marks are employed as a medial caesura, and the question marks in the fourth stanza are thereby a formal way of emphasizing the climax of the creation.[8] But what should be specially noted here is that this incessant questioning is juxtaposed with the poem's fairly even and stately, primarily trochaic tetrameter (despite shifting stresses), which somehow seems to corroborate the fact that the creation has taken place (perhaps even that the tiger is pacing on its four paws).

The apostrophized questioning seems to be a premeditated technique, since in the first notebook version Blake included a stanza which is not as clearly interrogative as the ones in the final version.[9] What is more, in the notebook versions there are no question marks, which is a valid point, even if this lack of punctuation is typical of the notebook versions of Blake's "SONGS *of* EXPERIENCE". Still, the very progression of the questions suggests the various stages

---

6 Cf. Jerome McGann's (1973: 12) view: "As with so many of Blake's lyrics, part of the poem's strategy is to resist attempts to imprint meaning upon it".
7 In some versions of the plate of "*The* Tyger" the question mark at the end of the second line is rather straight and has at times wrongly been interpreted as an exclamation mark, as for instance in *William Blake. The Complete Poems*, edited by Alicia Ostriker (Blake 1977: 125).
8 If "*The* Tyger" seems overly interrogative, it is far from the most extended poem composed entirely of questions that I know, Ron Silliman's (2007) forty-page prose poem "Sunset Debris".
9 "*Could fetch it from the furnace deep / And in (the) thy horrid ribs dare steep / In the well of sanguine woe / In what clay & in what mould / Were thy eyes of fury rolld*" (Blake 1977: 145). Here as elsewhere in his first notebook version of the poem, it is evident that Blake still had exaggeratedly pointed phrases – "*thy horrid ribs*", "*the well of sanguine woe*" – that he was to discard in the second notebook version (Blake 1977: 146–147).

of the act of creating the tiger, in part viewed in terms of a birth, from an emphasis on the cosmic location of the creation (cf. the creation of the heavens and the earth in *Genesis*) to the human act of welding iron in a forge:[10] "distant deeps or skies" – "the hand, dare sieze the fire" – "twist the sinews of thy heart" – "thy heart began to beat" – "the hammer" – "the chain" – "In what furnace was thy brain" – "the anvil" – "what dread grasp, / Dare its deadly terrors clasp".

In short, generations of critics and teachers have been right in detecting a kind of act of creation in Blake's "*The* Tyger", but in doing so have seldom acknowledged the fact that almost everything in the poem is hypothesized, with the exception of the apostrophizing of the tiger, which implies that the act of creation has indeed been completed. Recognizing the hypothetical form of the poem – the fact that nothing is stated with certainty – is also a way of explaining why some readers have so much trouble comprehending it. This would also help readers appreciate one of the many techniques by which Blake keeps the meaning of his lyrical poems vague and ambiguous. Related techniques are juxtaposition between the text and the engraved illustration, between the contrary poems "The Lamb" and "*The* Tyger", between "*The* Tyger" and the surrounding songs "*The Angel*", "*My Pretty ROSE TREE*", "*AH! SUN-FLOWER*" and "*THE LILLY*", as well as the differences in the various plates of "*The* Tyger". Thus, as so often in literature, form and meaning go together in the poem – or, to be more precise, are juxtaposed to bring about complex ambiguous meanings. As for the poem's language, the act of creation suggested by the semantic import of the words as taken in succession is undercut by the overall questioning, which seems to suggest that the meaning of the poem is hypothesized. This tallies with Blake's frequent emphasis on "Imagination" in many senses.[11] Not only does he imagine the act of creation but he also invites his readers to question his imaginative portrayal in ways that make it so utterly memorable.

---

[10] For a discussion of the complex notion of the "Hand" in Blake's poetry, variously representing "the aggregate form of the Sons of Albion" and "a figure of terrible beauty" see Mitchell (1978: 201–203, 201, 203 quotes).

[11] For instance, Blake's early and late letters show how central "Imagination" is for him. In letters dated 23 August 1799 and 12 April 1827 Blake (1956/1968: 30, 162) notes that "To Me This World is all One continued Vision of Fancy or Imagination" and that his "Spirit & Life" constitute "The Real Man The Imagination which Liveth for Ever".

Meeting Apart in Emily Dickinson's "I cannot live with You"

Emily Dickinson is a veritable master of hypothetical action. In a single poem, such as "I cannot live with You" (No 640, c. 1862), she uses many different means to undermine anything stated (Dickinson 1960: 317–318; see Appendix 2). The poem consists of eleven characteristically brief four-line stanzas and a final one of six lines. The theme of the poem is announced in its first line – "I cannot live with You" – and the rest of the poem consists largely of variations on the theme of separation or rather, perhaps, of explanations as to why the separation will come about.

The separation between "I" and "You" is evident in the poem's tripartite structure. The first three stanzas present an extended metaphor of the "Life" of "I" and "You" as porcelain, apparently "Quaint – or Broke", discarded "of the Housewife" and locked up by "the Sexton" behind a shelf. Dickinson's characteristic use of fragmenting dashes and enjambment gives the lines multiple meanings, which the definite articles (the Shelf, the Sexton, the Key, the Housewife) do little to pinpoint, since the nouns they precede seem symbolic aspects of the separation between "I" and "You". The major section of the poem, stanzas 4 to 11, develops the Christian motif (suggested in the character of the sexton) by separating "I" and "You": "You" is associated with Christ (stanza 6), a shining face contrasted with that of Christ (stanzas 6 and 7) and Heaven (stanza 8), whereas the separation from "You" would be "Hell" to the "I" (stanza 11). As against the putative "Life" in the initial extended metaphor, this central sequence of the poem thematizes death, from the statement that "I could not die" and the suggested possibility of the Other (apparently "You") having died (since "the Other's gaze" is to be shut in stanza 4) to death-related freezing (stanza 5) and some kind of climactic resurrection of "You" that would grieve "I", because of the separation it would entail (stanzas 6 to 11). Despite the focus on separation between "I" and "You", the former is a keen observer whose eyes, gaze and observations are repeatedly mentioned (stanzas 4, 5, 7 and 9). Dickinson's careful uses of ambiguity, contrast and vagueness in depicting the separation and tension between "I" and "You" is finally corroborated by the oxymorons in the final stanza – "We must meet apart" and "Despair" as "White Sustenance". Other motifs too are reiterated: the homely "Door" harks back to the sphere of Shelf and Housewife in the first stanza and "Prayer" to the sustained use of Christian motifs. But the poem's ending continues the stress on paradoxical usages, in that the separation is both represented by "the Door" and "Oceans", and in that "Prayer" does not seem to provide "White Sustenance", whereas "Despair" does.

The metre, however, would suggest a somewhat different structure. The first six stanzas are rather even: four iambic lines consisting of 3, 2, 3 and 2 stresses, which also could be read as consisting of two lines of iambic pentameter, with stresses 3 + 2 and 3 + 2. In fact, if read two lines at a time, most of the poem could be seen as variations of iambic metre, mostly pentameter, but also tetrameter (the last two lines in stanza 8), hexameter (the two middle lines in stanza 12) and even heptameter (the two first lines in stanza 9). Yet considering each line separately, the even rhythm is broken with the seventh stanza, which scans as having 2, 3, 3 and 2 stresses, the eighth stanza, with 2, 3, 2 and 2 stresses, and the ninth stanza, with 4, 3, 3 and 2 stresses. In other words, in their first two lines these three stanzas disturb the pattern of 3 + 2 stresses, which still occur in the last two lines of each stanza. Finally, in stanzas 10 and 12 the two first lines are regular (3 + 2), but the end of them are the most irregular in the poem: here the stresses seem to be 1 and 3 and 3, 3, 4 and 1, respectively. Thus, the most evident shifts to more varied metre occurs right in the middle of the poem, between stanzas 6 and 7, and in the final lengthy stanza.

Apart from Dickinson's shifting metre and syntactically fragmenting dashes and enjambment, the most central overall strategy used is the subjunctive (or conjunctive) mood of the verbs. If the first line of the poem is a straightforward statement (though a negated one), the next line juxtaposes its "live" with "Life", notably by using the subjunctive mood (with an evident hypothetical future sense): "It would be Life". In the first lines of the fourth, fifth and sixth stanzas "I" addresses "You" but uses *could* in different ways, two of which again include negation: "I could not die", "Could I stand by" and "Nor could I rise". As a question, the second instance ("Could I stand by") is clearly in the subjunctive mood, but the two other uses of *could* are ambiguous by polysemy: they could be read as past-tense usages (cf. I *was* not *able to* die; Nor *was* I *able to* rise) or as subjunctives (cf. I *would* not *be able to* die; Nor *would* I *be able to* rise). The phrase "I could not" in the eighth stanza is likely to be in the past tense, since it is contrasted with "You [...] sought to" in the previous lines. In the eighth stanza "I" and "You" merge as "Us" and are for the first and only time in the poem perceived by the third-person plural, but also in the subjunctive mood: "They'd judge Us". In the ninth and tenth stanzas the use of the subjunctive mood reaches a kind of climax: "were you lost, I would be"; "were You – saved"; "Where You were not"; "were hell to me". This is also a kind of climax of the reasoning as to why "I" and "You" cannot live together, and the final stanza draws the inevitable oxymoronic conclusion: "So We must meet apart". Hence, the most sustained use of the subjunctive mood occurs in stanzas 4, 5 and 6, but when, in stanzas 7, 8 and 9, the metre turns out to be less regular, there is only one use of the subjunctive mood. This means that irregular metre and the subjunctive mood occur largely separately, most likely so as not to make the reading too hard.

The hypothetical action signalled by the use of the subjunctive mood and its future sense of what might occur is strengthened by other means. In the first stanza Life is personified and resides "Behind the Shelf", to which a sexton holds a key, joining "I" and "You" in "Our Life", metaphorically fragile from the start ("His Porcelain"). In the fourth stanza the relation between "I" and "You" is made more comprehensive by the contrast between "One" and "the Other", in which the former must wait (again with a reference to the future) to shut the latter's gaze, apparently after the Other's demise. This seems to anticipate the death motif in stanza 5 and the implicit resurrection motif – suggested by (the negation of) "I" and "You" rising and the reference to Christ – in stanza 6. Then follow referential links from Christ to sight (apparently by "my homesick Eye" viewing the glowing of Christ's "New Grace") in stanzas 7 and 9, and from dying and Christ to Heaven, Paradise and Hell in stanzas 8, 9 and 10. But such a progression of motifs and action in stanzas 1 to 11 – from Life to Death to resurrection to Heaven, Paradise and Hell – is continuously hypothesized by the use of the subjunctive mood with a future sense (at times ambiguously related to the past tense) as well as by negations, a question (in the fifth stanza), metaphorical links, personifications, metonymies ("my homesick Eye", "Sight") in the middle of the climactic rise from "freeze" to "Frost" to "Death" in stanza 5.

An even more detailed analysis would suggest that the dashes, whose variations in length, height and angle in Dickinson's manuscripts Paul Crumbley (1996) has studied in detail, make many lines and relations between lines even more ambiguous. Detailed scrutiny of Dickinson's multiple formal and thematic means of hypothesizing any meanings in her poem can help critics to avoid the pitfalls of mis- or overinterpretation.[12] In short, just as "*The Tyger*", Dickinson's poem intimates a progression of motifs and figures (the tension between "I" and "You" as developed throughout from Life to Death to meeting apart), a progression that is hypothesized by a number of linguistic, thematic, rhetorical and metrical means. Such multiple formal and thematic juxtapositions and contrasts are key features in her poetry.

---

[12] For instance, in her reading of "I cannot live with you" Barbara H. Milech misquotes the poem (two lines are left out), misinterprets many passages and overinterprets its import it in a biographist manner: the poem supposedly suggests that Dickinson chose "passion [...] and poetry [...] over wifedom and motherhood" (Milech 1991: 133–138, esp. 137).

Prufrock's Imaginary Walk: Recurrent and Local Techniques

T. S. Eliot's "The Love Song of J. Alfred Prufrock" is a classic of early Anglo-American modernist poetry.[13] It has intrigued readers for about a century by now, not least because Prufrock's nebulous dilemma is couched in a first-person narrative poem whose actions are largely hypothetical. Eliot makes recurrent use of two techniques to imply that a walk may or may not have taken place: shifts in space and shifts in time (especially tense shifts).

The spatial locations of the poem suggest both progression and cyclical action. In the first verse paragraph Prufrock as speaker invites "you" to take a walk with him in what seems a seedy harbour setting of "half-deserted streets", "one-night cheap hotels" and "sawdust restaurants with oyster-shells".[14] But the walk seems merely proposed, at least not explicitly taken, although the description of the setting implies detailed knowledge of it. The third verse paragraph continues the urban description by way of the fog in a feline personification, thus leaving out the narrator, except as an implied observer making this metaphorical connection.[15] The urban street setting recurs in verse paragraph 4, at the end of which Prufrock considers "the taking of a toast and tea", thus suggesting that "you" and "me" may move into a house and its bourgeois setting, but at no point is it stated that they enter it. The drawing-room location is already suggested in the second verse paragraph ("In the room the women come and go / Talking of Michelangelo"), which is repeated verbatim in the fifth. From the sixth to the fourteenth verse paragraphs, the drawing room remains the central location, even though the tenth verse paragraph seems to revert to the seedy urban scene and the eleventh starts to depict an imagined underwater scene. The drawing-room objects and phenomena – such as necktie, music playing in an adjacent room, perfume, dress, table, shawl, tea, cakes, ices, cups, marmalade and pillow – indicate the speaker's familiarity with the setting. The twelfth and fifteenth verse paragraphs continue the suggested or negated role play of the eleventh (in which Prufrock claims he "should have been a pair of ragged claws"), as he maintains that he is *neither* a prophet *nor* Prince Hamlet. Verse paragraph 16 seems to revert to the sea, but the suggestion of rolled trousers implies what is corroborated in verse paragraph 17: now the location is a beach, not

---

[13] The poem is too long to include as an appendix, but it is readily available on the Internet and in Eliot's selected and collected poems and various anthologies. My quotes are from Eliot (2015: 5–9).
[14] That is, I gather the sawdust restaurants with oyster shells may suggest a harbour setting.
[15] The narrator's status as an observer is in keeping with the title of Eliot's first collection *Prufrock and Other Observations* (1917), in which the poem was included.

the seedy harbour implied at the start. The view of the sea is continued in the eighteenth and nineteenth verse paragraphs until the underwater scenery takes over in the final one.

In other words, there is spatial progression from an urban setting (at first seemingly harbour-like then more generally urban: windowpanes, chimneys, houses) to a detailed portrayal of a drawing room, to a beach, to an underwater scene (mentioned even in the eleventh verse paragraph), and finally to a possible future death by drowning. There is, then, also a cyclical quality in the apparent marine setting of the first and last verse paragraphs as well as the first-person plural employed in them. Needless to say, these are only some of the parallelisms between the different verse paragraphs that further contribute to the cohesion of the poem. It should be noted that the narrating "I" and "you" are never portrayed as in fact moving in the settings, even if the descriptions of the settings, and at times the actions and observations of the characters, including those of the narrator (such as the taking of toast and tea or wearing the bottoms of trousers rolled), imply that they move from one setting to another. However, at one point the deictic marker *here* suggests the actual presence of "I" and "you" in the drawing room ("here beside you and me" in the twelfth verse paragraph) and the narrator as observer is mentioned repeatedly throughout. Finally, at the end the first person plural recurs, apparently merging "I" and "you" ("We have lingered"), just as in the first line of the poem. Yet the actions in the final verse paragraphs are undercut, because what is perceived seems to be a fantasy of mermaids and a sojourn with sea-girls under the sea.

The other recurrent technique that keeps all the action in the poem hypothetical has not to my knowledge been given proper recognition, although it has been touched on in Eliot criticism.[16] I am referring to the poem's repeated tense shifts, whose predominant features I shall now try to outline. The first verse paragraph merely presents an imperative in the present tense to "you", as if the walk suggested has been agreed on ("Let us go *then*, you and I"; emphasis added). The present tense is also used about the women walking in the drawing room in verse paragraphs 2 and 5 – apparently in a generic sense: they always walk back and forth there. The fog in the third verse paragraph is portrayed in the past, the received tense of narrative, even if the present tense still occurs in the relative clauses. In the drawing room scenery the central tense is the future ("there will be time" is repeated in verse paragraphs 4 and

---

[16] For instance, in one of the most detailed readings of "Prufrock" Rudolf Germer (1966: 74) notes the third stanza's shift from the present to the past tense (ignoring the present tense in the relative clauses), but considers it unimportant.

6). Uttering the question seems possible even in verse paragraph 7, 8 and 9, which all start in the perfect tense implying Prufrock's familiarity with the drawing-room world ("I have known"), but end with a future question in the subjunctive mood, thus showing Prufrock's insecurity. What he proposes to utter (in the future tense) in verse paragraph 10 is an observation in the perfect tense apparently pertaining to the location in the first.[17] The past hypothetical ("I should have been a pair of ragged claws") in the following verse paragraph intimates Prufrock's defeatist mood. In the twelfth verse paragraph the present tense continuing the portrayal of the drawing room leads to a question in the subjunctive mood ("Should I ... Have the strength").

The shift from Prufrock having the chance to utter his question to having lost that opportunity is not so evident, since the future perfect in the past hypothetical has already been introduced in verse paragraph 11. Even so, the past-hypothetical impersonal constructions in verse paragraphs thirteen and fourteen ("would it have been worth it") announce that Prufrock has missed his chance to say his piece. From now on, the present tense recurs, but does not concern any action of consequence: Prufrock is not Hamlet but "an attendant lord"; he admits that he grows old; the wind stirs the water; and finally he seems to merge with "you" as "we drown". The future tense occurs repeatedly in verse paragraphs 16, 17 and 18 but concern trivial activities or a negated imaginary activity ("I do not think that they [the mermaids] will sing to me"). As all the action at the end of the poem seems to pertain to Prufrock's imagination, he does not perform any actions of consequence: the role play and the imaginary seascape recur and so do the perfect tense and the past participle in verse paragraphs 13, 17, 19 and 20, together with either the present or the perfect tense ("I am Lazarus, come from the dead"; "I have heard"; "I have seen"; "We have lingered"). Thus, when the perfect tense in the indicative mood is used to emphasize the observing "I" and the movements of "we", the subject matter is fantastic, which keeps the actions portrayed imaginary or hypothetical.

What is more, "Prufrock" includes a large number of local techniques for hypothesizing the action: questioning (verse paragraphs 1, 6 [three times], 7, 8, 9 [three times], 10, 12, 13 [with no question mark], 14, 17 [twice]); negation (1, 12 [twice], 13 [twice in quotation], 14 [twice in quotation], 15 [four times], 18); per-

---

[17] Elsewhere I have proposed a "social" reading of the poem based on the fact that the only instance in which Prufrock tries to utter his question before it is too late (in the tenth verse paragraph) seems to pertain to his aim to shock his drawing-room acquaintances by telling them about the seedier world he is also familiar with (the first and tenth verse paragraphs). That is, "some overwhelming question" is a question in the sense of 'issue' or 'matter' rather than 'query' or 'proposition' (see Pettersson 1993).

sonification of the fog as a feline creature (verse paragraph 3); parenthesis (6 [twice], 9, 12); hypothetical utterance ("They will say..." in verse paragraph 6, "Shall I say..." in 10); role play ("a pair of ragged claws" in verse paragraph 11, Lazarus in 13, "an attendant lord", possibly "the Fool" in 15); and sea fantasy (verse paragraphs 11, 17–20). Other techniques are intermittent allusions to art and literature, of which the mention of names like Michelangelo, Lazarus and Hamlet are the most evident, the use of iambic metre (although in no way regular) and other repetitions, parallels and juxtapositions in motifs, metre, rhyme and language – all of which make "Prufrock" a much richer poem than these few comments may suggest.[18] However, my aim has not been to offer yet another interpretation of the poem but rather to demonstrate how the poem makes use of two recurrent techniques for hypothesizing the action – the imaginary progression in space is complemented by a progression in tense shifts – as well as a number of local ones.

Techniques of Hypothetical Action

By analysing these classic poems by Blake, Dickinson and Eliot I have tried to show that the techniques by which anything stated in the poems is hypothesized are rather evident, since they are largely based on linguistic, thematic, rhetorical or metrical means. Thus, they can be examined by literary scholars and taught to students who may have difficulties in reading poetry. My claim is simply that hypothesized action is a rather prevalent way in which literary worlds are inflected and that it thus deserves the attention of scholars. Such attention recognizes that "*The* Tyger" addresses the creature created at the same time as its very creation is continually in question; that the tension between "I" and "You" in "I cannot live with You" is undermined by the use of negation, the subjunctive mood, fragmented syntax, changes in metre and various figures, such as extended metaphor and oxymoron; and that the meaning of "Prufrock" is kept so ambiguous and vague by a plethora of fragmenting and cohesive means, such as shifts in space and time, especially tense shifts.[19] Each of these poems coheres due to fea-

---

18 In his detailed analysis of "Prufrock" Thomas R. Rees (1974: 43–45) has noted that 85 percent of the lines are iambic and that of these lines 40 percent are in pentameter (half of which are irregular) and 30 percent in hexameter, even though there are also trimeter, tetrameter, heptameter and short staccato lines.

19 Note that fragmentation and cohesion are not always juxtaposed, since consistent use of what seems like a fragmenting device, such as shifts in tense, syntax or metre, can in fact effect cohesion.

tures of dramatic monologue and a progression of sorts in the form of undercut action: the tiger apostrophised throughout the poem is explicitly addressed in the first and last stanzas, and the intervening stanzas portray and question the creation of the tiger; Dickinson's "I" addresses "You", and moving from Life to Death, they finally come together oxymoronically when meeting apart, sustained by despair; and Prufrock addresses "you" in the first line and, after an imaginary walk in space and time, "you and I" seem to merge as "us" when about to drown in the last verse paragraph.

As such, the above analyses do not provide novel readings of the poems, but may help readers understand their complexity. Still, just as Peter Verdonk (1990: 108) focuses on "the meaning generated by [the] structuring elements" in Philip Larkin's poem "Talking in Bed" and the "deeply human experience" that the reading of it conveys, the techniques of hypothetical action contribute to the multifaceted delight of reading poems by Blake, Dickinson, Eliot and countless others. Hence, the analyses offered here could help to fortify the bridges between the study of language and literature, which scholars in stylistics, poetics, literary semantics and literary pragmatics have been building for decades, and the new ones that are being constructed today, not least in cognitive literary studies.

But most importantly for this study, if Stephen Halliwell (2002: 16) is right in claiming that mimesis signifies and communicates "hypothesized realities" consisting of imitative and creative elements, then to examine how techniques of hypothetical action probe the limits of those realities will help us make better maps of how representation shapes literary worlds. And if Roger D. Sell (2002: 20) is right in asserting that fictional discourse (in a broad sense) is "no less communicative than non-fictional", then surely analysing features that question and undermine the overt meaning communicated is an important facet of literary studies.

In fact, the above discussion can provide a brief checklist of features that hypothesize meaning in poetry – and, *mutatis mutandis*, in other kinds of literature:

- negation: *no*, *not*, negative prefixes and suffixes, double negation, contradiction
- questioning, with or without question mark
- tense shifts
- the subjunctive mood
- the passive voice
- fragmented syntax: e.g. incomplete phrases, omitted verbs
- polysemy
- metre: e.g. variations, enjambment
- shifts in space, theme, person, etc.

- hypothetical utterance: e.g. "Shall I say..."
- parenthesis: e.g. when used as comments, thoughts or asides
- role play
- fantasy: depiction of actions apparently impossible or fantastic
- rhetorical figures: e.g. (extended) metaphor, metonymy, oxymoron, irony
- clashes in and between the above techniques and progression in action or depiction
- clashes between form (e.g. tense, metre) and contents (theme, motif)
- other means of creating ambiguity, contrast or vagueness

By analysing these – and related – formal and thematic features and their interaction, critics and teachers can pinpoint how an action in a poem may be hypothesized, and so understand and teach how meaning in poetry may come across in many different ways. Such features may be especially useful in helping students see how form and content may strengthen or undermine each other in ways that thwart and enrich meaning.

Finally, I should perhaps register a caveat. The above analyses seem to suggest that techniques for hypothesizing meaning, especially recurrent or structural techniques, are more likely to be used when there is some reliance on particular subject matter or some kind of progression (narrative, metaphorical, spatial, thematic or other). In other words, despite the kinds of erasure which McHale (2005) detects in postmodern poetry, it may, comparatively speaking, in fact make less use of hypothetical action than the above poems. For instance, in keeping with the title of one of his collections, *Chinese Whispers*, John Ashbery's (2002) poetry moves serendipitously between various kinds of subject matter and register and thus the various hypothesizing features are only some of the means used.

Still, as my three examples suggest, pre-postmodern poetry sometimes does hypothesize the action by various means, both recurrent and local. In attuning themselves to poetry's ways of making and undermining meaning, readers will come to understand and appreciate some of the essential linguistic, thematic, rhetorical and metrical means by which hypothetical action contributes to shape literary worlds.

6.3 Genres and Text Types, Their Hierarchies and Blends

Other central ways of inflecting literary worlds is by blending genres and text types, which are mainly narrative, description and argument. Despite the common prioritizing of narrative, there is in fact no particular hierarchy between text types, in that each story or novel forms its own pattern. Now let us consider how the main forms of literature are informed by blends of genres, subgenres and text types.

How Genres and Subgenres Are Formed

In 2.3 we discussed a key form in literature, *genre*, and in particular how two genres, realist fiction and science fiction, can merge and how mimesis and genre often are co-determined. Using Erving Goffman's notion of *keying* in *Frame Analysis* (1974), which draws on Gregory Bateson's (1955/2000) seminal analysis of how play is initiated by a ludic sign, John Frow (2006: 46) has defined aesthetic practices in generic contexts by maintaining that they are "keyings of the real: representations of real acts or thoughts or feelings which are not themselves, in the same sense, real".[20] I would add that genre makes us aware that the willing suspension of disbelief works in different ways for different genres, and indeed differently for works within a genre. Generally speaking, genres in literature are forms of literary imagination authors and publishers, readers and audiences, are aware of to the extent that they know the requirements of their respective form of willing suspension of disbelief. Printed books, especially prose fiction paperbacks, often have the genre denomination printed on the back cover in order to make it easier for bookshops and readers to know what sort of writing each book entails.

In 5.2 I noted that even a lyrical poem like Blake's "*The SICK ROSE*" has evident narrative features. Since prose fiction and drama too usually have marked narrative features, most literary genres are narrative. But one could also argue that most of literature is dramatic, as the history of Western literature shows. In poetry there is often a speaker and indeed *lyrical* poetry derives its name from that it was first performed to the accompaniment of a lyre (or other instrument) as a kind of performed, sung monologue. Also, bards performing what were to become *The Iliad* and *The Odyssey* apparently dramatized the various voices. Dramatic art in the West has been developed on the basis of rituals and Greek tragedy, from a speaker and a chorus to multiple speakers and actors. Prose fiction has had a wealth of different genres in Western fiction, but most of them have narrators presenting the action in the first, second or third person and dramatizing it by motion and dialogue.

---

20 This notion seems related to Bateson's (1955/2000) famous notion of "this is play" as against "this is real"; see 2.1.

Perhaps the basic ways genres change can be divided into three aspects: genre formation, *changes to* genre by exterior means and *changes in* genre by the development of the genre itself. Often the three aspects are so interrelated that it can be hard to discern how and what caused the change of genre or created a new subgenre.

Thus, genres are formed in many different ways. One is by introducing new elements. In *Frankenstein* Mary Shelley created the first science-fiction novel by adding science as a key feature propelling the plot to what otherwise might have been a Gothic novel. To take a more recent example: if the postmodern novel indeed can be termed a genre, flourishing between about 1960 and 1990, it seems to have started to change in the late 1980s in many different ways. At roughly this point, more genre blending and realist features were introduced (as in Thomas Pynchon's *Vineland* and Toni Morrison's *Beloved*, both published in the late 1980s), and metafictional self-consciousness had reached something of a saturation point and started to wane.[21] As for genre blending, Julian Barnes' (2005/2006) novel *Arthur & George* combines the detective story, biographical fiction, the (post)colonial novel, realist fiction and the postmodern novel so effortlessly that it does not seem a postmodern novel but rather a successful generic fusion. When there is more evident hierarchical use of genres within a literary work, as when a novel includes a letter by one of the characters, Frow (2006: 46) makes a useful point: the "generic *force*" of the inserted genre is suspended, but not its "generic *structure*". For instance, a letter in Jane Austen's *Mansfield Park* is not a real letter, but in the context of the novel it functions as one (Frow 2006: 46–48). This goes for any genre incorporated, if it evidently is lower hierarchically than the main genre represented; if not, the work becomes a hybrid, like *Arthur & George*.

Genres may also develop by thematic or formal changes, which can in turn be propelled by changes in society. The thematic change is evident in vampire fiction: apparently modelled on John Polidori's novella *The Vampyre* (1819), Bram Stoker's *Dracula* (1897) depicted a heteronormative Gothic vampire. Later, Anne Rice introduced the gay vampire in *The Vampire Chronicles* (1976–2003) and then Jewelle Gomez the lesbian vampire in *The Gilda Stories: A Novel* (1991). Finally, Stephenie Meyer with her *Twilight* series (2005–2008) initiated the moral and romantic heterosexual teenage vampire – and perhaps each of them has contributed to form a vampire subgenre of its own. Evidently, such changes were not only occasioned by literary means but also by changes in the view of sexual norms. The development of haiku, on the other hand, shows for-

---

21 For a discussion of realist features in postmodern fiction see Pettersson (2007).

mal changes at work in genre formation: as we have seen, *hokku* was the first stanza in a longer collaborative poem (*renga*), but developed into the separate three-line poem known as haiku.

Thus, in order to spot different subgenres you must be familiar with the genre. Take fantasy. If readers happen to pass over the foreword as well as the prologue of *The Lord of the Rings*, they will nevertheless know they are encountering fantasy from the word go: by the cover or the maps of a non-existent shire and the fact that Bilbo Baggins is "a hobbit", who is turning "eleventy-one" or 111 years old (Tolkien 1954–1955/1976: 34). In *Harry Potter and the Philosopher's Stone* J. K. Rowling (1997: 7) starts from the opposite end by emphasizing the realist backdrop of her series: "Mr and Mrs Dursley, of number four, Privet Drive, were proud to say that they were perfectly normal, thank you very much". Even the final self-satisfied colloquial phrase – "thank you very much" – implies that the point of view is that of the Dursleys. But in the second sentence Rowling (1997: 7, 8) supplies the first of her many anticipations of fantasy: the Dursleys are "the last people you'd expect to be involved in anything strange or mysterious" and on the following page such a mysterious incident does indeed occur, when Mr Dursley sees "a cat reading a map". Here we see how different subgenres in fantasy work: Tolkien creates an imaginative world with little or no relation to the real world, whereas Rowling presents her magical features against the backdrop of a late twentieth-century Britain recognizable in many details. In this sense, Philip Pullman's (1995/2007: 3) trilogy *His Dark Materials* is something of a blend: it starts out by presenting Lyra Belacqua and her animal dæmon who speaks, but she inhabits Oxford in Great Britain, even if it soon proves rather different from any Oxford that has ever existed.

This goes for any genre: the more general the features, the more inclusive the genre seems; the more specific, the more exclusive. Hence, genres are usually more open than subgenres, despite the fact that all genres and subgenres can be blended. Understandably, then, Alastair Fowler (1982) prefers to define genres by family resemblances, which means that genres are seen as an amalgam of traits. When defining the genre of any literary work, then, the question is on the basis of what traits to draw the line.

Text Types at Each Other's Service

Text types too blend and form hierarchies in literary works. As I have noted, in *Coming to Terms* Chatman (1990: 10) makes an important observation when he states that narrative, description and argument "routinely operate *at each other's service*" in prose fiction. This is a significant point, since description and argument are rather under-theorized in the study of prose fiction. In one of the few volumes devoted to description in fiction, Werner Wolf summarizes the most prevalent view of it: "In narrative fiction at any rate, description usually constitutes a subordinate frame that operates under the auspices of the dominant frame 'narrative' and usually helps prepare the ground on which the characters act" (50). In so doing, Wolf (2007: 50) builds on and refers to Gérard Genette's claim in *Figures II* (1969) that description is a mere aid to narration (*ancilla narrationis*), a point which was turned on its head as Michael Riffaterre in 1986 called it *mater narrationis*. Perhaps a more tenable position was taken by Seymour Chatman (1990: 24), who, as an answer to Genette, titled a chapter "Description Is No Textual Handmaiden" and stressed that "Description has a [metonymic] logic of its own, and it is unreasonable to belittle it because it does not resemble the chrono-logic of Narration". Later on, Ansgar Nünning (2007: 95–96 *et passim*) has highlighted and studied description and David Herman (2009: 92 quote, 90–97, 105–136), in part relying on Chatman (1990), has analysed "the (fuzzy) boundary between description and narrative" and shown that text types reinforce each other in contributing to the what, where and when of storyworlds.

Argument is perhaps even more seldom than description studied as a literary text type as such. If literature has an argument, it is usually thought of as its moral or allegorical import. The use of allegory was widespread well before *Rhetorica ad Herennium* and Quintilian's *Institutio Oratoria*, which, we have noted, were among the first to discuss it, at least in extant writing. Plato's famous parable of the cave in *The Republic* is often called an allegory, even though few may remember that its very point is the educational and political moral that "the last thing to be seen […] in the realm of knowledge is goodness" and thus that "political power should be in the hands of people who aren't enamoured of it" (Plato 1994/2008: 244, § 517bc; 249, § 521b). This shows that the moral of an allegory can be misunderstood or neglected. In 5.3 we saw that *The Restraint of Beasts* by Magnus Mills is a kind of latter-day fable in that it develops a double, somewhat paradoxical moral of how restraining violence can be more condemnable than the violence it seeks to keep in check.

Now let us consider changes in text type hierarchy in three realist, or postrealist if you like, minimal plot novels by the contemporary American author Nicholson Baker: narrative is used at the service of description, description at the service of narrative, and ultimately both narrative and description are at the service of a kind of argument.

First, however, let me note that minimal plot sequencing is not a feature of post-realist fiction alone. Some of the classics in the genre are Xavier de Maistre's (2006) *A Journey around My Room* and *A Nocturnal Expedition around My Room*

(1794 and 1825 in French) and their fictional explorations of the indoors landscape of a single room. As de Maistre's translator Andrew Brown (2006: xi) notes in his introduction of a recent reprint of the two books, de Maistre's isolated narrator is forced "to supplement the paucity of events in the room by resorting to memory, imagination, daydream and storytelling – which sometimes seem to merge into one another". Baker's techniques in vitalizing his novels are in fact much like those of de Maistre, which suggests that even narratives that on the face of it seem rather plotless are kept alive by a variety of techniques. In a word, as Alain de Botton (2006: viii) has noted as regards de Maistre's fiction, what is needed is a kind of openness to new impressions or, in short, "Receptivity". It is this receptivity in the character narrators in Baker's three novels that has made Arthur Saltzman (1999: 1) dub their author "A Columbus of the Near-at-Hand". When plot is relinquished or marginalized, the subsequent attention to detail can lead to significant discoveries.

In *The Mezzanine* a young man called Howie returns from his lunch hour to take the escalator to his office on the mezzanine floor of a corporate building: hence, the main plot focuses on his roughly ten-second escalator ride (Baker 1988/1989). In *Room Temperature* a man called Mike is feeding his infant daughter, affectionately called "the Bug", a bottle of milk during about twenty minutes (Baker 1990/1991). In a later novel, *A Box of Matches*, Baker (2003/2004) returns to the minimal plot novel by describing the middle-aged family man Emmett's routine of getting up while still dark to start a fire and make coffee in thirty-three chapters, each depicting his morning ritual.[22] In other words, all three novels have minimal plots, so Baker must use other means to secure the readers' interest. Elsewhere I have shown that some of the main techniques are analepses, prolepses, extended similes and metaphors, digressions and imaginings (Pettersson 2012c: 45–50). But what Baker's three novels also demonstrate is that various narrative techniques and text types blend: narrative serves description, description serves narrative, and the description of objects, their use and history, is central.

Even more importantly for keeping readers reading, all techniques in the novels serve character description – and thus, as we shall see, the argument of the novels. The three semi-autobiographical first-person narrators are in many senses Everymen as well as have many features that link them to their creator.[23] They are Everymen also in the sense that their names are only men-

---

[22] Subsequent references to Baker's three novels is from here on given by page number in the text, which should make clear which novel is being discussed.
[23] For instance, Mike in *Room Temperature* is born on January 5, 1957, two days before Baker (41).

tioned in passing (and quite late in *The Mezzanine* and *Room Temperature*) and that they lead quotidian lives that resemble those of many American men. But Howie, Mike and Emmett are also given distinguishing features, especially by the vivid depiction of their current life situations (with exposition of their pasts) as a single man, the father of an infant and a middle-aged family man, respectively. What is more, in their inner lives and thoughts, they resemble their creator, as is evident in the related meticulous attention to details in Baker's (1996/1997) collection of essays, *The Size of Thoughts*.

Some literary allusions and narratorial statements seem to give clues as to how these narrators are to be understood. The paperback Howie in *The Mezzanine* reads during his lunch hour is Marcus Aurelius's *Meditations*, the classic guide to self-improvement. Since Howie is some sort of minor official in a somewhat Kafkaesque corporate world, the allusion seems to be rather ironic. He quotes *Meditations* briefly: "Observe, in short, how transient and trivial is all mortal life ...", but immediately counters it by thinking "Wrong, wrong, wrong!" (120). He may be impressed by *Meditations*, but is "tired of Aurelius's unrelenting and morbid self-denial" (124), and sings the praises of the footnote and his own digressive frame of mind by, among other things, lauding digression as "sometimes the only way to be thorough" (122).

In *Room Temperature* Mike defends his view of life when feeding his infant daughter by stating a motto for the miniaturist frame of mind he cherishes as much as Howie and Emmett: "I certainly believed, rocking my daughter on this Wednesday afternoon, that with a little concentration one's whole life could be reconstructed from any single twenty-minute period randomly or almost randomly selected" (41). The quotidian lives that Howie, Mike and Emmett are leading are significant as such, and the seemingly most insignificant action can epitomize all of a man's life, just as memory and thought can illustrate the riches of what may seem an uneventful life. In *A Box of Matches* Emmett repeatedly refers to his favourite poet Robert Service (1874–1958), but only mentions the title of one of his poems, "The Men That Don't Fit In" (27). In that poem we can read (even though Baker does not quote it): "It's the steady, quiet, plodding ones / Who win the lifelong race" (Service 1940: 42; ll. 19–20).

This, I think, is the key to interpreting the character narrators of *The Mezzanine*, *Room Service* and *A Box of Matches*. They may seem to be versions of James Thurber's Little Man: obsessed with detail, prone to inactivity, rather laughable, even losers of sorts. Yet in their lives and minds, they have disregarded, unfathomable riches, as suggested in an undercut way by Thurber's (1942/1954) most famous short story "The Secret Life of Walter Mitty". Also, they all have redeeming social features: as a single man Howie keenly observes his co-workers and has had some loving relationships (mother, father, girlfriend); Mike is a very happy father and loves his wife dearly; and Emmett finally decides to give up his ritual to get up in the morning, so that he can creep back into bed with his loving wife. The three novels can be read as eulogies of the riches in the quotidian lives of men.

Thus, the narrative techniques are Baker's way of showing how original the minds and lives of all humans are. By literary allusions and narratorial statements, readers are led to understand that the narration together with the descriptions in the novels and their wealth of digressions serve to reveal the hidden cognitive treasures of the Little Men. Moreover, as the quotes from Baker's fiction may have suggested, apart from the digressive play, much of the enjoyment in reading Baker lies in his style, not least his long and winding syntax and his precise and abundant vocabulary that draws on various areas of expertise. All such formal features serve to describe the rather related characters of Howie, Mike and Emmett not only as Baker's alter egos but also as unsung heroes of the quotidian, and narrative technique forms a central part in that description.

As far as what McHale (2001: 165) terms *weak narrativity* is concerned, I have tried to show that only on the surface does Baker narrate "poorly" or "distractedly" (McHale's terms), that there is much narrative coherence in the very way his narrators tell their digressive stories. That is, they do not make use of what Marie-Laure Ryan (2009: 56) has called "aesthetically deficient plot twists", such as *cheap plot tricks* or *plot holes*, but present a wealth of additions and twists to their almost non-existent main plots. Indeed, how they tell their stories in many ways portrays them as characters and substantiates the argument for the significance of the inner lives of the Little Men.

What Baker's three novels reveal is that fiction that seems more or less plotless and thus exemplifies weak narrativity may include a wealth of brief narratives in the form of analepses, digressions and imaginings, which then can be used at the service of description. In turn, the descriptions of objects can include narratives, especially analepses, so that narrative and description can be used at the service of each other. Finally, since both narrative and description serve character description, which in my reading takes a stand for "the steady, quiet, plodding ones", they are at the service of the text type of argument, at least for readers who recognize Baker's hints to that effect. But the hierarchy could also be viewed in quite a different way: character description (or its implicit argument for holding the Little Men in high regard) can also be seen as serving the life narrative of the three character narrators.

In other words, it is not a question of the chicken or the egg: you simply cannot have one without the other. Baker's miniaturist fiction is so enjoyable, because description, narrative and argument go seamlessly together to present the digressive logic of the diffident and learned narrators. What Baker achieves, then, by slowing down the action and all-but obliterating plot is a kind of defamiliarization. In his classic argument for why defamiliarization is needed, Viktor Shklovsky (1917/1998: 5) points out: "Automatization eats away at things, at clothes, at furniture, at our wives, and at our fear of war". Bypassing the patriarchal stance of the time ("our wives"), we can focus on the very important last point, "our fear of war", which suggests how serious an effort defamiliarization can be. For Shklovsky (1917/1998: 12) and thousands of literary scholars after him, defamiliarization in literature is "the very hallmark of the artistic", but it is so much more, since it can revolutionize not only individual perception and literary appreciation but also social life. In Baker's novels, this logic amounts to digressions and detailed descriptions that slow down and renew perception so that the quotidian comes alive. Thus, description is blended with detailed perception, historical precision with flights of the imagination, so that everyday life gains in significance, for the narrators and their readers alike.

To sum up, in this chapter we have seen that literary worlds are made richer and more complex by imaginative inflections. Indirection of various sorts (substitution, inversion, thwarted aspirations and meta-usages), hypothetical action, hierarchies and blends in genre and text type were identified as some of the key ways in which the basic literary modes and themes create the infinite variety of literary worlds. Such hierarchies and blends can also occur in ways discussed in previous chapters, as in combinations of the real and the fantastic (chapter 2), in unreliable usages (chapter 3), in the co-occurence of the main themes (chapter 4) or in the intricate combinations of rhetorical figures and narratives (chapter 5).

Throughout chapters 2 to 6, my aim has been to show that such themes and techniques are prevalent in different cultures and at different times. As a conclusion to this discussion, let me single out a particularly rich instance of how the themes and techniques of literary world-making are combined in a classic novel. Henry Fielding's *The History of Tom Jones. A Foundling* clearly both draws on and satirizes the romance-novel. It is a moral allegory of how the everyman Tom Jones looks for and finally finds his true love Sophia (Greek for 'wisdom'), which simultaneously delights in describing Tom's lewd adventures during his picaresque quest. This is in accordance with the intrusive authorial narrator's aspiration to serve his readers "HUMAN NATURE" on his "BILL OF FARE TO THE FEAST" of which the novel is composed (Fielding 1749/1963: 28, 27). In short, Fielding knows how to appeal to both the genteel and visceral interests of his audience as well as to construct a particularly vivid literary world by blending the real and the fantastic; genres, text types and rhetorical figures; and the themes of challenge, perception and relation, which are combined in Tom's actual and metaphysical quest for Sophia. May this suffice to suggest how literary modes, themes and techniques constitute the workings of literary imagination.

Now let us change the perspective from what literary worlds are and how they are shaped to what effects they have on readers, that is, how they can change the world.

7 How Literary Worlds Shape Us

7.1 Imagined Selves and Communities in Fiction and Beyond

This chapter continues the discussion of how imagination by way of literary worlds can create a shared frame of mind (see 1.3), that is, how they may come alive in popular imagination to such an extent that they shape the worldview and actions of large populations.

Humans would not bother about literary worlds unless they contained valuable experiences, either pleasurable, beneficial or both. The very fact that the basis of literature is mimetic and blends the imitative and the creative suggests that however imaginative its worlds are and however distant in space or time, they are always in some sense about the world listeners, audiences or readers are familiar with. Artefacts considered literary are authored by one or more persons and co-created or *conducted* with interpreters, to use Wayne C. Booth's (1988: 72–73 *et passim*) term.[1] In philosophical aesthetics there is a persistent debate whether tenable literary interpretations of any one literary work are *monist* or *multiplist* in nature, that is, whether they are variations of one view or radically different (see Krausz 2002). Still, what is evident is that there is often a considerable interpretive discrepancy, so that individual readers of even a three-line poem, such as a haiku, differ in their readings. Elsewhere I have tried to show that interpretive discrepancy in scholarship can be decreased by taking into account biographical, contextual and other ancillary evidence, that is, by what I have termed *contextual intention inference* (Pettersson 2009a). But in doing so, I certainly do not mean to police the very different readings in and beyond academia, which are one of the hallmarks of the richness of literature. Readers and audiences have always freely made use of their lives and opinions when imagining literary selves and their actions and assertions, and hopefully always will.

Yet despite interpretive divergence, it is evident that literary or semi-literary books have had a vast impact on human history. Ancient myths have become part of world religions – *The Old Testament* or *The Hebrew Bible* is a case in point – and have thus influenced the worldview of generations of people all over the world. Utopias have traits that at times are meant as moral teachings, at times as undercut thought experiments, and have inspired social reform. Just think of the pointers on education in Plato's (1994/2008) *Republic* and the

---

[1] Cf. Hernadi's (2001: 67) view of literature as "the co-creative play of imaginative world-making".

most likely tongue-in-cheek dismissal of private property in Thomas More's (1999/2008) *Utopia*.² On the other hand, it is often difficult to see where to draw the line between a utopia and a dystopia, since they often have traits of both. For instance, both Plato and More include slaves in their utopias, which means that their societies are utopias only for some people. Similarly, Jonathan Swift's *Gulliver's Travels* (1726) and Samuel Butler's *Erewhon* (1872) have both utopian and dystopian traits, depending on what their readers consider to be good models for society. The saying "one man's meat is another man's poison" is just as true for the effects of literature on society.

Still, it has been evident for millennia that literature indeed affects people, both individually and en masse. In a recent study of storytelling Jonathan Gottschall (2012: 139–155) titles a chapter "Ink People Change the World" and notes how the imperialist dreams of Alexander the Great were fuelled by *The Iliad* and how Goethe's *The Sorrows of Young Werther* (1774) led over a hundred young men to commit suicide allegedly owing to unrequited love, like the hero of that novel; how Harriet Beecher Stowe's *Uncle Tom's Cabin* (1851–1852 serialized; 1852 as novel) had a major effect on the Civil War in the United States and its outcome; how anti-totalitarian novels, like Arthur Koestler's *Darkness at Noon* (1940) and George Orwell's *Nineteen Eighty-Four* (1949), warned a generation of the dangers of totalitarianism, and how other novels, like *To Kill a Mockingbird* (1960) by Harper Lee and *Roots* (1976) by Alex Haley, changed people's attitudes to race, not just in the United States but more globally (also by way of their film and television adaptations, one might add). Such a list can easily be extended, both as concerns the effect of literature on particular individuals as well as nations and beyond. But in fact Gottschall (2012: 141–142) is rather uncritical of August Kubizek's memoir *The Young Hitler I Knew* (1953 in German), since he thinks that the oft-quoted anecdote of how Adolf Hitler at the age of sixteen was first inspired to become a great leader having seen Richard Wagner's early opera *Rienzi, the Last of the Tribunes*³ "seems to be authentic". However, as Jonas Karlsson (2012) has recently convincingly shown, Kubicek's memory is not to be trusted and thus the story of Hitler's early Wagnerian inspiration in this form is most likely spurious, although of course Hitler's later fascination with Wagner, including *Rienzi*, is well-documented. This shows how carefully one must tread when claiming causal connections between art and life.

---

2 Both Plato's and More's utopias consist of speakers and characters that may be unreliable in one way or another, so the import of their narratives is in many ways ambivalent.
3 The libretto is based on the novel by the British author Edward Bulwer-Lytton.

In almost all of its forms – even monologue – drama centres on human relationships and portrays human formations and hierarchies, such as cordial or hostile relations in terms of clashes between individuals, families or classes. Early ritualistically or mythically informed drama, such as Sumerian and Greek, portrayed and gave voice to aspirations and feelings that were fundamental in the audience's worldview at the time. The British drama theorist Martin Esslin (1987/1996: 171) even claims that "all drama, without exception, by its very nature, must carry powerful political implications and meanings". But he hastens to qualify his statement by pointing out that political or ideological drama seldom has lasting effects, even though there are examples to the contrary.[4] The real impact of drama is more subtle: it "tends to exercise its most powerful and lasting impact by reflecting the attitudes of the more advanced groups among the population, exposing them to public outrage and discussion and thus gradually penetrating the consciousness of society" (Esslin 1987/1996: 172–173). This is what Chinese Yüan plays and *commedia dell'arte* did in criticizing the powers that be, what Henrik Ibsen and Bertolt Brecht did about gender and ideology, and what Wole Soyinka's *Death and the King's Horseman* (1975), Caryl Churchill's *Top Girls* (1982), Tony Kushner's *Angels in America* (published 1992) and David Mamet's *Race* (published 2010) more recently have done about raising the consciousness of (post)colonial questions, women's rights, gay rights and race issues, respectively.[5] The world on stage not only mimics and fictionalizes the real world but also informs it.[6]

A key notion that has informed human behaviour in the last few centuries is *nation*. In one of the most influential studies of that notion Benedict Anderson (1983/2006: 6) defines it as "an imagined political community – and imagined as both inherently limited and sovereign". As in any act of imagination, the notion of nation must be entertained by individuals, but what makes it a community is that these individuals conceive it as "a deep, horizontal comradeship" in a particular limited space, which is sovereign and has something of a joint history

---

4 Esslin (1987/1996: 172) mentions the well-known instance of how the performance of Pierre Beaumarchais' *The Marriage of Figaro* in 1784 apparently gave a spark to the French Revolution (and thus also to the American Revolution).
5 As significant plays in the postwar period, they are of course thematically richer than such single themes suggest. *Angels in America* is particularly multifaceted in that it combines gay rights with topics like AIDS, race and right-wing politics.
6 For informed chapters on drama's complex relations to reality see Esslin (1976/1996: 23–32, 95–105).

(Anderson 1983/2006: 7).[7] Nations draw on what Anderson (1986/2003: 12) calls "the *religious community* and the *dynastic realm*", that is, on inherently hierarchical and communal notions already in existence. More specifically, as nationalism as a notion got a foothold in the Americas and Europe in the eighteenth and nineteenth centuries, it did so by two new print-modes: the newspaper and the novel, that is, by both (alleged) fact and fiction (Anderson 1986/2003: 24–25, 61–65).

Anderson's broad exposé of the rise of nationalism in various parts of the world is impressive and it is based on a wealth of narratives, including a reflection on the "biography of nations" (Anderson 1983/2003: 204–206), but understandably perhaps it only touches on how narrative *per se* is fundamental in forming nations. Only recently has there been some theoretical and empirical research on the impact narratives have (see e.g. Green, Strange and Brock 2002/2013). Especially interesting for the present purposes is the research on the power of fiction to mould people's views. As Green, Garst and Brock (2004: 174) put it, "fiction can be a powerful tool for shaping attitudes and opinions", especially when "we become drawn into them [stories] – when our cognitive resources, our emotions, and our mental imagery faculties are engaged" (cf. Strange 2002/2013). In other words, the better literary worlds are constructed and the more prone we as readers (or listeners) are to enter and delight in them, the more they can apparently affect us.

Perhaps the most evident community-making form may be national anthems and other texts used at the service of national unity.[8] Some of the most topical lyrics in the Balkans in recent decades are the poems collected by the great Serbian man of letters Vuk Karadžić beginning in the 1810s. The resurgence of Serbian nationalism since the late 1980s was not least due to the fact that 1989 marked the six-hundredth anniversary of The Battle of Kosovo, a major combat in which the Christian Serbs were defeated by the Islamic Turks. This lost war is the topic of many of the narrative poems Karadžić (1997: 131–158) collected, not least "Tsar Lazar and Tsaritsa Milica", in which the hero Miloš Obelić [Obilić] is slain, but not before (allegedly) having killed the Turkish leader, Sultan Murad.

---

7 I would put the point about sovereignty somewhat more loosely: limited spaces can be sovereign or have hopes that they ultimately are recognized as sovereign, as in the case of Kurdistan. That is, the idea of a sovereign nation can be entertained before the nation exists.
8 For an encompassing collection of national anthems in the original language and English translation see Bristow (2006).

> Duke Miloš slew   the Turkish tsar, Murad,
> all together   twelve thousand Turkish men.
> May the good Lord   bless the one who bore him!
> For he remains   in memory for the Serbs,
> to be told now   and again, forever,
> as long as man   and Kosovo exist.
> (Karadžic 1997: 146; ll. 193–198)

Such lines were, and still are, behind the Serbian nationalism that maintains that Kosovo should be under Serbian rule. In Finland a young poet called Johan Ludvig Runeberg was so impressed by the lyrical and narrative poems collected by Karadžić (which he read in German translation) that he translated a selection of them into Swedish in 1830.[9] Later, he seems to have been so taken by the notion of uniting a nation by a lost war that he – when Finland was still under Russian rule – wrote two collections *The Tales of Ensign Stål* (1848/1860), the first of which starts with what is still the Finnish national anthem "Our Land" (literally "Our Country") (see Runeberg 1952).[10] As in the narrative poems of The Battle of Kosovo, Runeberg sang the praises of bravery in a lost war, the War of 1808–1809, the result of which was that Sweden lost Finland to Russia – and thus became the Finnish national poet. To take a better-known instance, a few decades before Runeberg, Francis Scott Key wrote "The Star-Spangled Banner" in order to spur nationalist feelings on the basis of a battle won – in fact, the battle *defending* Fort McHenry in Baltimore against the assault of the British navy.[11] So whether battles or wars are lost or won, they can serve nationalist sentiments. Of course, nationalism can also inspire a people through a vision of the future, as in Book VI of Virgil's (1968: 170) *Aeneid*, where Anchises in the underworld tells his son Aeneas of his future as the leader of the expanding Roman empire (in Dryden's classic translation): "Rome, 't is thine alone, with awful sway, / To rule mankind, and make the world obey, / Disposing peace and war by thy own majestic way".

In order to show how we are affected by literary worlds more implicitly but not less effectively, let us now study texts from three different continents – North America, Europe and Asia – that have contributed to nationalist thought and thus done much to shape the twentieth and twenty-first centuries. I have chosen

---

[9] For centuries the language of the Finnish ruling class was Swedish, which is still one of the two official languages in Finland, spoken by a minority of about five percent of the population.
[10] The use of myths in Runeberg's poetry and various translations of the Finnish national anthem are discussed in Pettersson (1999f) and (2001b).
[11] For a detailed account of "The Star-Spangled Banner" and its checkered history see Ferris (2014).

texts that are rather unknown for the reading public in order to show how the impact of literary worlds can be considerable, even if the original author or work is less well-known than the ones mentioned above. Nor were all the texts to be discussed regarded as distinctly literary when first published, although I would argue that they shaped history in part owing to their literary qualities and in part to the way they were able to fuel and channel widespread sentiments.

7.2 Origins of the Modern Hero

According to a commonly accepted view in historiography, the late eighteenth and the early nineteenth centuries was the time of the rise of nationalism in the Americas and Europe. Let us now see how a Kentucky schoolteacher's short biography of a hunter and soldier was both seminal in creating a new genre of fiction and in transforming the view of individualism and nationalism in the twentieth century, first in the Western world and then worldwide.

Pennsylvania-born John Filson was about thirty-five years old when he moved to Kentucky to work as a schoolteacher and land surveyor. A year or two later he had seen enough of the state to write a brief history of how it was settled called *The Discovery, Settlement and Present State of Kentucke* (1784). Less than half of its 118 pages was the actual account of the settlement and thus the bulk of the history was made up of its four appendices, the first and longest of which is "The ADVENTURES of Col. DANIEL BOON [sic]; containing a NARRATIVE of the WARS of Kentucke" (Filson 1784/2007: 49–82).[12] This thirty-page narrative was to have a major impact on politics and literature in the United States and beyond. How could that be? It certainly seems rather non-descript: a mere appendix to an idealized account of the Kentucky settlement history, whose goal was rather evidently to attract people to emigrate to Kentucky. Also, as it was signed "DANIEL BOON" (82), that is, in misspelling the name of the object (BOON for BOONE), its supposed first-person autobiographical narrative seems rather questionable. Yet it had the makings of such a mythical eyewitness narration of somebody who had been in the frontline when settling the West and fighting the Indians[13] that Filson's little book – or

---

[12] Subsequent quotations from Filson (1784/2007) are rendered in normalized typography and their references given by page number in brackets.
[13] I here use the term *Indian* for 'Native American', since it is used in Filson's text and other sources on Boone and is still widely in use, even though most people consider *Native American* more politically correct.

rather its appendix – became immensely popular, not only in the United States but also in Britain. What is more, it was immediately translated into French (1785) and later into German (1790), thus making Daniel Boone into the epitome of the romantic American back-to-nature hero. Also, as the book was published in Boone's fiftieth year and he lived for over three more decades, the hero was still alive when the fame of Filson's appendix grew.

So what made the narrative in the appendix so alluring? Clearly it was published at the right time, as Rousseauvian sentiments were spreading on both sides of the Atlantic. It also provided an inside view of the Indian Wars, which were exotic and alluring for East-Coast Americans and Europeans, supposedly by a man who seemed to be a noble savage and who apparently had successfully fought and defeated the Indians on their own terms. It mattered little that the author Filson turned Boone into its first-person narrator – having supposedly heard it *"from his own mouth"* (6) – or that Boone's biographers were to show that it was far from true, since even the classic study by John Bakeless (1939/1989: 395) notes that "there are a good many lies in it". Nor did it matter that Filson's account of the defeat of the Indians was patently premature, as attested by the fact that he himself was killed by the Shawnees in Ohio four years after its publication. Thus, the story of how Boone was made into a myth that not only invaded the American consciousness but Western culture and history in general is an instructive one in that it shows how literature, myth-making, publishing, historiography and politics go together.

When Boone, well-knowing the questionable status of Filson's claims about him in "The Adventures", in his old age often liked to hear it read aloud, exclaiming "All true! Every word true" and "Not a lie in it!" (quoted in Faragher 1992/1993: 7), he most likely had a relativist view of truth. As Bakeless (1939/1989: 395) puts it, for him it was "literature, real book language, nearly as good as *Gulliver's Travels*, which he had carried in the wilderness". Perhaps Boone was influenced not just by frontier tall tales but also by the fictional stance in Swift's fake travelogue, which in fact is called *Travels into Several Remote Nations of the World / By Captain Lemuel Gulliver*. In its preface the fictitious editor Richard Sympson vouches for Mr Gulliver, who is "distinguished for his veracity", just as Gulliver himself in the last chapter tells his gentle reader that he has "given thee a faithful history of my travels" (Swift 1726/1960: ix, 313). Still, the untruths in the pseudo-autobiographical account of "The Adventures" seem to originate in Filson's rather than Boone's imagination. As a relative put it, an account by Boone himself would have been "plain and intillagible [sic]. Boone did not pen the errors himself" (quoted in Faragher 1992/1993: 7). In fact, Boone often corrected other accounts, such as Daniel Bryan's book-length epic poem *The Mountain Muse* (1813), which depicted him as an avid Indian killer: "I never killed but three", he is quoted to have said (Faragher 1992/1993: 320).

Bakeless (1939/1989: 394) puts the difference between Filson and Boone in a nutshell: "Comparison of Filson's orotund, pseudo-Johnsonian style with the blunt, simple, and vigorous language of Dan'l's illiterate but salty letters and official reports reveals the pious fraud at once". Boone's enthusiasm with Filson's account may have been due to the fact that its noble-savage depiction of him was in line with the sort of person he would have wanted to be, and that however idealistic in other respects, it was not as overly romanticised as those of Bryan and his ilk. But there were other features in the account that made it so endearing to Boone and so popular on both sides of the Atlantic. It was simply able to fuel a number of the central ideas and emotions related to the persistently advancing frontier not just as an American phenomenon but also as a sign of pan-European Western expansion. And it did so in two versions: Filson's more detailed account, which was translated into the main European languages, but even more persuasively in the printer John Trumbull's shortened, more action-focused North American version, starting with the first edition published in 1785, a year after Filson's original account (see Faragher 1992/1993: 6).

In fact, the charms of Filson's account of Boone are many. Perhaps rhetorically most importantly, it starts out with pious Christian pointers that contributes to the subsequently widespread notion of Manifest Destiny, often in the sense of a God-given right to expand the American territory (and later, the American view of democracy). In the first paragraph of "The Adventures" Boone – that is, Filson's Boone – refers to "Providence" and how "the mysterious will of Heaven is unfolded", so that Kentucky has become "the habitation of civilization" (49). This shows both the right of the settlers to turn "the habitation of savages and beasts" into "a fruitful field" and at the same time anticipates the end of the narrative, Kentucky as settled (49). Similarly, at the end Boone offers thanks to "that all-superintending Providence which has turned a cruel war into peace, brought order out of confusion, made the fierce savages placid, and turned away their hostile weapons from our country!" (81) Such a frame to Boone's alleged autobiographical account was important in many respects: the makings of Boone's life is seen as a duty performed, ultimately derived from Heaven but with national right (the account was published within a decade after the Declaration of Independence) and a cultural mission (spreading Western civilization to the "savages" and cultivating the land). God, nation ("our country") and civilization are one – and they motivate and sanction Boone's actions, which thus are to be read as both real and symbolical.

The detailed account of the settling of Kentucky can be viewed as an illustration of the toil of making the land ready for settlers, since the ultimate intention of Filson's *Kentucke* was to lure new settlers to the state now supposedly rendered safe by scouts and pioneers such as Boone. Battles against Indians are described in great detail in "The Adventures", and even if the cruelty of the Indians often are in focus, Boone does not shirk from showing in a rather matter-of-fact way the retributions of the armed forces in which he fights. For instance, he notes that "the savage treatment" by Indian men of even their own women and children "is shocking to humanity, and too barbarous to relate" but also that General George Rogers Clark in a raid "took seventeen scalps, and burnt the town to ashes, with the loss of seventeen men" (72). The many details often add to the realism of the autobiography, and only occasionally are there what seem touches of tall tale, as when Boone escapes from Indian captivity and travels 160 miles – whether on foot or by horseback is not disclosed – on only one meal (66). The hardships of the army, the scouts and the pioneering settlers are depicted in some detail. The constant threat for them is that Indians attack, which gives the right for the army to retaliate, as their God-given mission is to settle the land (which of course already was settled, if by "savages").

Boone's adventures are thus viewed throughout as furthering and epitomizing this mission. The bare facts of his employment are not very dramatic: He leaves his family in 1769 as a kind of scout for businessmen and pioneers; is in charge of three garrisons during a campaign against Shawnee Indians in 1774; then continues to fight various tribes of Indians under different command, mostly in the army, and becomes a colonel, finally rejoicing in the peace that ensues as Kentucky has been settled. But this was not what its allegedly autobiographical account was read for as much as for the adventures Boone encounters during the approximately fifteen years depicted. In that time – from Boone's early thirties to his late forties – he fights and kills bears, bucks and Indians; is captivated and befriended by Indians, who clearly hold him and his honour code in high regard; saves ladies from Indian captivity; and is even adopted by the Shawnee. In the midst of such an action-packed life Boone is also a natural philosopher, who marvels on "how little nature requires to be satisfied" and when "disposed [...] to melancholy", dispels it by contemplating "the diversities and beauties of nature" (53, 54). In short, he personifies the noble savage, even if his rhetoric, courtesy of Filson, is hardly credible, as ragged cliffs to him look like "the ruins, not of Persepolis or Palmyra, but of the world!" or as he states that "Peace crowns the sylvan shade" (58, 81). Most importantly, however, this story is the first to contain the Western formula of fiction, film and television that John G. Cawelti (1999: 25) has studied in great detail, starting with James Fenimore Cooper's fiction: "the tripartite division of townsmen [here pioneers and settlers], savages and intermediate hero with a vision of the landscape".

Of course, Filson was not entirely original, since he drew on Indian war narratives, captivity narratives and colonial Puritan writings, but in the words of Richard Slotkin (1973/2000: 21), the most eminent scholar of the American myth of the frontier by his trilogy on the subject, "it was the figure of Daniel Boone, the solitary, Indian-like hunter of the deep woods, that became the most significant, most emotionally compelling myth-hero of the early republic". Filson's role in this myth-making is indisputable, not least since like the Indian war narratives, it was applicable to "the universal problem of the colonial period: the problem of acculturation, of adjusting the mores and world view of one's native culture to the requirements of life in an alien environment" (Slotkin 1973/2000: 22). Thus, the account of Boone's life personifies the colonizer's dilemma more generally: Boone is the precursor of – in point of fact, the mould for – Cawelti's "intermediate hero", since he represents the white settlers and their newly-formed "country", but can deal with the indigenous population on their own terms by outwitting and out-shooting them. In other words, he is a catalyst for the Western expansion, but by his very double allegiance Boone and his symbolical offspring are intermediary in that expansion, also in the sense that they are expendable when a territory is settled, and have to "light out for the Territory", as Huck Finn was to do, or simply retire (Twain 1885/1988: 362).

Cawelti is right in this sense: it was Cooper's five novels about Leatherstocking or Natty Bumppo published between 1823 and 1841 that were elemental – if not seminal – in creating the Western hero. Leatherstocking has inherited most of his traits from Filson's Boone, including one that is not very pronounced in Filson's "Adventures", most likely owing to its intention to draw settlers to Kentucky, that is, his final departure from the settlement he has made possible. Cooper's Leatherstocking is the loner who gladly and ably helps his own people, but cannot become part of the society they have created, as he is spurred on to unsettled territories by his solitary disposition and love of nature. As Cooper was penning his Leatherstocking series, the first biography about Boone was published, Timothy Flint's *Biographical Memoir of Daniel Boone, the First Settler of Kentucky* (1833), a very popular account that ran in fourteen editions by 1868. This biography included the folkloric emphasis on Boone's solitary disposition and was even further from truth of Boone's life, which was recognized by historians even then. But Flint answered any criticism by saying that his book "was made not for use, but to sell" (Faragher 1992/1993: 322–326, 323 quote).

After Boone's death in 1820, the legend completely took over, as John Mack Faragher (1992/1993: 320–342) has shown in perhaps the best biography there is of Boone: Bryan's poem was followed by seven stanzas on Boone in Lord Byron's *Don Juan*; Leatherstocking personified Cooper's ambivalence about Western expansion and progress; Chester Harding and many others popularized Boone and the myth of his life by their paintings; Noah Ludlow wrote a song called "The Hunters of Kentucky" that became Andrew Jackson's campaign song when running for presidency twice in the 1820s; Davy Crockett drew on the Boone legend to such an extent that many conflated the two; border romances and dime novels were published with Boone-like heroes; and later films, radio shows, television series and post-Western fiction were based on the legend of Daniel Boone.

The growth of the legend of Boone and the related myth of the frontier was so immense, not just in the United States but the rest of the world, that it is almost impossible to see all the waves it created in various cultures, even globally. Let me just single out a few in terms of the arts, literary studies, historiography and politics.

I mentioned that the Boone legend grew by exposure in different arts and media, but at the same time the intermediate Western hero became a central figure in popular culture. The hero spread by way of Cooper's novels and their emulators, dime novels in the late nineteenth century and, with the advent of new cheap way of making paper, pulp fiction in the next century. But the most momentous work extending and moulding the Western hero was Owen Wister's *The Virginian* (1902), which sold 300 000 copies in its first year and over 2 million copies by 1968, thus making it "perhaps the single most read novel written by an American" (Shulman 1998/2009: vii).[14] The hero was still an outsider (a Southerner in Wyoming), a loner and a natural philosopher, not a hunter, scout and officer, but a cowboy who is well-versed in all the ways Boone supposedly was. However, what makes it different from Filson's "Adventures" and Cooper's Leatherstocking novels is the role given to women, or rather the idealized woman. Filson's Boone may occasionally think of his wife, who had to live for long stretches of time "bereaved of me, her only happiness" (72) and Leatherstocking is infatuated twice during the series, but the Virginian (whose name is never disclosed and is thus even more of a symbolical hero) falls head over heels in love with Molly Wood, an Eastern schoolteacher gone west. As Molly educates the barely literate hero by English literature, the central authors are Shakespeare, Jane Austen and Sir Walter Scott. And it is Scott's *Kenilworth* (1821) that is the novel they most repeatedly discuss. But it is not the romance in Scott's Elizabethan novel that captures the imagination of the Virginian but the character of Queen Elizabeth: he is impressed by her way of wielding power and in his close-lipped way claims that she "would have played a mighty pow'ful game" of

---

[14] This may have been true in the 1960s, but by now for instance Harper Lee's *To Kill a Mockingbird* (1960) has sold over thirty million copies and remains a steadyseller, not least after the publication of *Go Set a Watchman* (2015).

poker and would even have beat him; in short, "She was a lady" (Wister 1902/ 2009: 106, 136).

Scott's Queen Elizabeth is of course intended to mirror Molly's lovable and strong-willed character. In this way, the romantic element is firmly planted in the Western. Yet the idealized woman is not only turned into the hero's love interest, but more clearly than in Filson or Cooper, she stands for the social order that the hero makes it his duty to defend. That order may be represented by pioneers, the settlers or the townsfolk, but according to the Western code it is the physically weaker, if often the mentally and spiritually stronger sex that stands for family and the social order in general. In Cawelti's (1999: 31) words, women are the "central agents" of civilization. By the publication of *The Virginian*, the frontier was in effect gone and the Indians had been defeated.[15] To be sure, the Virginian is attacked by Indians, but it seems to happen mainly so that Molly can nurse him back to health and the romance gets started. More important in the novel is the way the adversary of the Western hero becomes a mystified evil, here personified by the cowboy Trampas. Apart from Indians, the hero is confronted with some sort of evil character or characters, who pester him or the society he stands up for so long that he finally must act. This is what Jane P. Tompkins (1992: 229) calls "the moment of moral ecstasy" in the Western: "The hero is *so right* (that is, so wronged) that he can kill with impunity".

Righteous acts of violence are already part of Filson's "Adventures", but now they are extended from national and colonial concerns to the family and the loved ones and become one of the most widespread patterns in popular culture. Perhaps this simply owes to the dramatic build-up that is inherent in the Western or "the satisfying sense of relief the plot's culmination in violence affords" (Tompkins 1992: 228). This pattern is part of the Western in all formats – fiction, film, radio shows and television series. But its spread is almost impossible to map: through invasion fiction and pulp fiction it was extended to science fiction (especially the space opera variety but other subgenres as well), (hard-boiled) detective fiction and further on to Cold War thrillers and horror fiction, again spreading into other media. Even though Grace Kelly's Amy in *High Noon* (1952) tells Gary Cooper's sheriff that "There has to be some better way for people to live!" (see Tompkins 1992: 227) and Bob Dylan – however ironically – warned us not to hate "With God on Our Side" (1964), the audiences for the arts, as they merged the popular and the elite, have turned a deaf ear and continue to relish

---

[15] Frederick Jackson Turner's (1893/2008: 1) essay "The Significance of the Frontier in American History" starts out quoting "a recent bulletin of the Superintendent of the Census for 1890" stating that "there can hardly be said to be a frontier line" anymore (see below).

"the moment of moral ecstasy". The crooks, the aliens and the politically misguided must be punished, and so the sheriff and his offspring continue to fight their duels – and people love them for it. In the last few decades "the bad guys" in literature and other media have become more and more difficult to distinguish, but in much popular and consumer culture, not least computer games, the good guys continue to fight the bad guys, with God, the audience and (usually)[16] the computer game players on their side.

American literary studies and historiography join forces in furthering the blend of myths of Daniel Boone and the frontier as shaping forces of the American character. It was the historian Frederick Jackson Turner who first focused on it in his famous speech "The Significance of the Frontier in American History" (1893). In his essay based on that speech he does not mention Boone by name but discusses the heritage of the frontiersman, starting with his initial transformation: "The wilderness masters the colonist. [---] It strips off the garments of civilization and arrays him in the hunting shirt and the moccasin" (Turner 1893/2008: 4). Turner traces how the frontier was moved so that in effect it was closed in 1890 and mentions how "[e]ach [region] was won by a series of Indian wars", thus paving the ground for the notion of *how the West was won*, which later was popularised by a film and then a television series by that title. There is no space to discuss Turner's (1893/2008: 38) rich essay here, but it should be noted that it ends with a prediction that "the expansive character of American life" will go on, since "the American energy will continually demand a wider field for its exercise".

In a later essay Turner (1910/2008: 114–115) also rather presciently calls scholars from various fields to cooperate to better understand the social forces in American history. In literary studies this challenge was taken up by Henry Nash Smith, whose important study *Virgin Land. The American West as Symbol and Myth* (1950) begins and ends with a discussion of Turner's groundbreaking essay. But chronologically speaking, it starts its scrutiny of the myth of the American West with the eighteenth century and Daniel Boone in particular. The central question Smith (1950/1973: 49–58) discusses in analysing Filson's "Adventures" and some early biographies of Boone is whether he was an empire builder or a philosopher for primitivism. He does not settle the question, but concludes that "[t]he image of the Wild Western hero could serve either purpose", and goes on to discuss Leatherstocking and his "haunting similarity" with Boone (Smith 1950/1973: 58, 59). Smith's work was influential in many

---

16 In some computer games players can choose to be evil player characters, which is popular among players who are bored with siding with the good guys.

senses. It showed that the myth of the frontier has made use of the wide variety of material Turner had suggested: historiography, social studies, literary studies, art history and political history, thus laying the foundations for what was to become American Studies. More specifically, it brought the myth of the desert-turned-into-garden to literary and cultural studies and showed how central it is to understanding American literature – despite the fact that, as Smith (1950/1973: 250–260) notes, it was only one of several competing views of history, even in Turner's day.

It is the myth of the frontier in American life and thought from the late seventeenth century to the late twentieth century that the historian Richard Slotkin traces in his trilogy *Regeneration through Violence* (1973/2000), *The Fatal Environment* (1985/1986) and *Gunslinger Nation* (1992/1998). As those main titles suggest, violence has been in focus in much of that myth, and he finds that Filson's narrative of Boone "constituted the first nationally viable statement of a myth of the frontier" (Slotkin 1973/2000: 269). On about a hundred pages he painstakingly examines how Boone is made into a myth by Filson and others, a myth rich in the contradictory meanings I have briefly outlined: the Puritan heritage, the primitivist ethos and the colonialist motivation in terms of a mission for nation and civilization (Slotkin 1973/2000: 268–368). More than Smith, Slotkin goes into detail about how Boone and the frontier myth was also used in politics, as when the close friends Owen Wister, President Theodore Roosevelt and the painter Frederic Remington knowingly formed the myth according to their right-wing views, or President Kennedy in 1960 launched his New Frontier programme with more liberal leanings, or President Reagan made use of his film-star cowboy image in his attempt to "revive the 'cowboy economy' under 'post-industrial' conditions" (Slotkin 1992/1998: 645). In foreign politics too, irrespective of political party, presidents could draw on the myth that the American imagination was suffused with: American troops could be sent to Korea, Vietnam, Grenada or Iraq when the American way of life allegedly was in jeopardy, since a large segment of the population could see that retribution was called for and that "the moment of moral ecstasy" would come (even if often it did not).

Of course, Filson's appendix on Daniel Boone in his *Kentucke* travelogue did not cause all of this to happen. But it did incite the imagination not only in United States but all over the world through popularisations of the myth of the Western hero and the frontier myth in especially the arts, including popular culture, to such an extent that more than most books that supposedly have "changed the world", it in fact did.

7.3 The Literary Spark for a World War (or Two)

In the July of 1870 the Franco-Prussian War started. During the autumn the joint Prussian and German forces had made considerable progress, defeating Napoleon III and his army, even though the French continued to fight a few more months under the newly formed Third Republic. A British Lieutenant Colonel by the name of George Tomkyns Chesney was so distressed by the strength of the victorious Prussian-German forces that he felt he had to do something so that his country would be spared the fate of France. He wrote a fictional narrative of how Germany conquered Britain called *The Battle of Dorking* and sent it in outline in January 1871 to be anonymously published in *Blackwood's Magazine*, one of the most popular journals among British intellectuals and politicians. By the time it was printed in May 1871, the German states had formed a German nation state and crushed France. *The Battle of Dorking* raised a stir: the May issue of *Blackwood's* was reprinted six times and the novella was published separately in June, selling 80 000 copies within a month (see Reiss 2005: 106 and Whyte 2006: 53). During the year 1871 it was also published in the United States, Canada and Australia and in translation in Germany, France, Italy and Brazil (see Clarke 1992: 224–225). What is more, it launched the genre of what now is termed *the invasion novel* or *invasion fiction*, with a number of other works published even in 1871. In the next forty years or so, over 400 titles of invasion fiction were published and their scaremongering led to the warmongering resulting in the First World War. How could a short novella by an officer have such an impact that its ripples are still felt in world history?

First of all, the outcome of the Franco-Prussian War and Germany's unification made the timing perfect. Before 1870 there was no Germanophobia to speak of in Britain, but now Britons were shocked by the power the united Germany showed. In contrast to Germany, whose naval power was growing more powerful, Britain's navy was rather dispersed owing to the Commonwealth. Furthermore, as a high-ranking officer with an evident gift for military strategy, Chesney was able to portray the invasion of Britain in a convincing way. *The Battle of Dorking* also displays Chesney's considerable talent as a fiction writer; in fact, he would write three more novels later on. But most importantly perhaps, Chesney was clever enough not to write a straightforward pamphlet but a realist novella that displayed in detail the invasion and its consequences. Apparently, it was this novel combination that struck a chord in the British popular imagination, which was used to Gothic and murder mysteries but not to a finely crafted war narrative that extrapolated what very plausibly seemed the imminent future of Britain.

What Chesney did was this. He gave the story a dramatic rhetorical frame: the war has been over for fifty years as a grandfather tells the story.

> You ask me to tell you, my grandchildren, something about my own share in the great events that happened fifty years ago. 'Tis sad work turning back to that bitter page in our history, but you may perhaps take profit in your new homes from the lesson it teaches. For us in England it came too late. And yet we had plenty of warnings, if we had only made use of them. [– – –] We English have only ourselves to blame for the humiliation which has been brought on the land. (17)[17]

The tone is vernacular and somewhat elegiac as the unnamed grandfather tells the story of the battle as a character narrator. Even the first lines include much anticipation of the war to come. Most importantly, the point that makes the novella into a pamphlet is clearly signalled: "We English" are to blame, since there were plenty of warnings, so that in fact the danger and subsequent "humiliation" could have been averted. As the description of Britain (in fact, London and South East England) goes on, a few pages later it is evident that "fifty years ago", in fact means the very near future, since Napoleon – evidently Napoleon III – has just been "ignominiously beaten" (20), with reference to September 1870. In effect, what Chesney is saying is that this is about to happen any day now, *unless* Britain strengthens its military forces. In other words, *The Battle of Dorking* was intended and understood as a plea for more funding for the defence, especially the navy. Lieutenant Colonel Chesney had just returned from serving in India and was apparently shocked how ineffective the British army at home seemed, especially in comparison with that of the unified Germany.

But this plea may have fallen on deaf ears had Chesney not been able to create such an astute combination of military know-how and literary means. The present situation is first given exposition and then the narrative moves into the future as an army reform falls through, so that although there are a fair amount of soldiers, the army as a whole lacks "organization and forethought" (21). The narrator gives a plausible broader panorama of how Britain is more and more isolated, yet after provocation declares war on Germany and fears an invasion, since it is so badly prepared (22–26). As the invasion is about to start, the narrator focuses on his own (and his family's) experiences: he is a young man working in an office but through his club he knows a man called Travers from the Treasury (29–35). From here on, the narration follows closely how the narrator as a volunteer soldier moves about in a London that is depicted

---

[17] Subsequent references to Chesney's (1871/1914) *The Battle of Dorking* are given by page number in brackets.

in great detail. What makes the portrayal of London under the invasion so compelling is the double perspective that Stephen Crane was to use so powerfully a few decades later in *The Red Badge of Courage* (1895): the narrator is a foot soldier, subject to rumours, the strategic indecision of his superiors, delay, hunger and fatigue. He also witnesses the chaos, confusion and looting in London as the invasion starts, ominously on Friday the 13th of August (30) – apparently the August of 1871, three months after the first publication of *The Battle of Dorking*.

At the same time the narrator gets hold of enough information so that he has a general, if vague view of how the battle is proceeding, and is thus able to provide a broader perspective. After many hardships he is sent to Dorking, which is depicted in great detail and "seemed made for a battle-field" (50–62, 51 quote). The narrator's long and anxious wait for the battle to commence effectively adds to the suspense. Most of the battle action is portrayed in one dramatic ten-page paragraph (65–74), where the double perspective is put to good use: the deaths of the soldiers and the narrator's own wounds are depicted realistically and without sentimentality ("besides the bayonet-wound in my leg, a bullet had gone through my left arm, just below the shoulder, and outside the bone"), just as the progress of the battle at large is portrayed with the British troops finally falling back (74). Thus, the narrator's fate mirrors that of the British army.

This is effective enough as a battle description. But Chesney understood that the stoically depicted battle scenes needed something that would hammer in the outcome of the invasion into his readers' minds. This is done in three ways. First, the wounded narrator struggles to go to the centre of London from its outskirts (again, name-checked and portrayed in detail) and on his way there he perceives the total havoc caused by the war: famine, looting, chaos. Second, the focus is moved to the personal level as the narrator visits the home of Travers, where he finds his friend killed and his friend's wife wounded, and discovers that "a splinter of a shell" has "carried away the back of [their son's] head" (89). Their house has been taken over by German soldiers, who are "rough and boorish, but not uncivil" (88). Third, the last few pages show what has happened in the fifty years after the invasion: Britain is a mere colony of Germany, as "the citizens of the proudest nation on earth" live on sufferance and have to pay "ransom" by exceedingly high taxes (92). The grandchildren of the narrator are now "to seek a new home in a more prosperous land" and he himself is about to "be laid to rest in the soil I have loved so well, and whose happiness and honour I have so long survived" (95). Thus, the moral that all this could have been "easily prevented" by "political courage and foresight" is driven home again and again (94, 95).

I have considered *The Battle of Dorking* in some detail, since it is often simply mentioned as the first piece of invasion fiction with no apparent merits in its own right. As this brief analysis of the novella shows, it is well-crafted and thus its impact is not only due to propitious timing but also to its considerable merits as a persuasive political fable. Its impact on science fiction is most apparent in that H. G. Wells used it as a kind of blueprint for his novel *The War of the Worlds*, which is usually given credit for having launched the subgenre of invasion fiction in science fiction. As the above account of *The Battle of Dorking* suggests, Chesney's novella is the one that started it,[18] since it is manifestly near-future fiction told from a future point of view. As we saw in 2.3, what Wells did in *The War of the Worlds* was to change the Germans into Martians, thus in fact launching the subgenre of *alien invasion* in science fiction. Yet Wells's novel draws on *The Battle of Dorking* in its use of a character narrator participating in the action with a double perspective combining the personal and the strategic in its detailed descriptions of London with surroundings and the hardships during the war and its aftermath. In fact, as Tom Reiss (2005: 106) has noted, by combining entertainment with shock, "Chesney had accidentally invented the thriller". Perhaps *The Battle of Dorking* should also be read as the first *political thriller*, so that the John le Carrés and John Grishams of the last half a century should be grateful to Chesney for having paved the ground for them. In fact, perhaps authors of the modern war novel with its character narrators in the midst of action could also give Chesney some credit. In other words, Chesney should finally receive the recognition so long denied to him in literary as well as political history.

But Chesney's impact on literature is only a sideline in the history of the twentieth century, even if this sideline continuously intertwines with history.[19] I have noted that *Blackwood's Magazine* was read by politicians, who by August 1871 passed a bill in the Houses of Parliament in order to arrange "the first mass peacetime maneuvers of home troops", and the drills started the following month (Reiss 2005: 106). For the next four decades or so, some politicians, two Prime Ministers among them, complained about the exaggerated fear caused by the immensely popular invasion fiction, but that fear was not to be dispelled. A lesser writer called William Le Queux spewed out about 150 novels, mostly of invasion fiction, between 1894 and 1927, and became the favourite author for many, including Queen Victoria. At first, the enemy could also be the French

---

18 In point of fact, as Clarke (1992: 22) has noted, *The Battle of Dorking* was anticipated by "A history of the sudden and terrible invasion of England by the French in the month of May 1852", a story published anonymously in 1851, but it did not have much impact.

19 The following paragraphs draw on the seminal research done on invasion fiction by I. F. Clarke (1992, 1995) as well as Reiss (2005) and some papers in Fred Bridgham's (2006) *The First World War as a Clash of Cultures*, especially Whyte (2006).

or the Russians, but after the Transvaal Crisis in 1896 and Erskine Childers's immensely popular *The Riddle of the Sands* (1903),[20] a spy novel of Germans infiltrating themselves in Britain, Germanophobia was rooted in Britain.

Many of these novels by, among others, Chesney, Le Queux as well as Childers were translated into French and German, but often with the tables turned at the end of the plot. For instance, in German translation Le Queux's[21] perhaps most popular novel, *The Invasion of 1910* (1906), ends in German victory, as "the Kaiser chivalrously offered his hand for peace with honor" (Whyte 2006: 71–72; 72 quote; trans. Whyte). In Germany the Transvaal Crisis had the effect of turning the Germans (who had much capital invested in Transvaal) against Britain, so the invasion fiction that by now was highly popular in Germany was turned even more pointedly against the British.[22] Thus, a war of words, or in broader terms, "a clash of cultures", led to an unprecedented arms race in Europe (see Bridgham 2006). As noted, some politicians tried to allay the heated sentiments spurred by invasion fiction. Other quarters went about it by humour and satire. In fact, *The Battle of Dorking* was ridiculed as early as 1871 and P. G. Wodehouse later published the invasion satire *The Swoop!, or How Clarence Saved England* (1909). Another trend was the mixed-marriage novel that was popular in Britain in the 1900s and early 1910s, with E. M. Forster's *Howards End* (1910) as its finest specimen. It showed the clash between German and English cultures usually ending in mutually augmented understanding of the other culture (see Whyte 2006: 81–92). But such counter-moves had little impact against the onslaught of invasion fiction. The war started in fiction was to be acted out as the First World War.

But one war was not to be enough. Apparently the "ransom" the British had to pay in *The Battle of Dorking* was fresh in the memory, by way of Chesney, Le Queux and others, so that when the Treaty of Versailles was negotiated, the exaggerated reparations meted out on Germany almost seemed to retaliate the wrongs inflicted on Britain in invasion fiction by the Germans. Also, during the war, authors in both Britain and Germany signed petitions for the war and wrote British propaganda. Even H. G. Wells, though a pacifist, wrote two more invasion novels before the war, *The War in Air* (1908) and *The World Set Free* (1914; written in 1913). As noted above, after the war Le Queux kept on publish-

---

20 *The Riddle of the Sands* sold over a million copies in at least twenty-seven languages.
21 In point of fact, the novel was actually a collaborative effort between Le Queux, a naval expert called H. W. Wilson and the former Commander-in-Chief of the British army Lord Roberts, still another instance of how closely literature and politics were interwoven in invasion fiction (see Whyte 2006: 56–57).
22 For a survey of the rise of invasion fiction in Germany see Whyte (2006: 63–80).

ing, and *The Battle of Dorking* was reprinted, not only in Britain, but as the Second World War had started, in Germany under the title "Was England Erwartet!" or "What Awaits England!" (see Reiss 2005: 112).

Perhaps invasion literature had run its course after the Second World War? By no means. Wells's *The World Set Free* had not only "invented" the atom bomb about three decades before physicists did but also inspired one of its godfathers, Leó Szilárd, to create the bomb Wells had extrapolated. Wells's point in *The World Set Free* was that the atom bomb should make people see the impossibility of war when a mass destruction weapon had been invented. This in turn spurred Szilárd, Albert Einstein and Bertrand Russell to work for peace after the war (see Reiss 2005: 114). However, at the same time Chesney's aftermath lived on in a variety of Cold War thrillers with for instance Ian Fleming's James Bond apparently modelled on Le Queux's refined agent Duckworth Drew (see Reiss 2005: 111). Of course, Bond's enemies today are rather different from those in Sean Connery's days as James Bond, but this goes for invasion fiction in general. On a global scale of colonialism, John Rieder (2008: 126) has shown that *The Battle of Dorking* made the colonizer the colonized, which was an intriguing perspective for "a wide variety of science fiction visions of personal, national, and global catastrophe". And Tom Reiss (2005: 108) puts his finger on the reason to the longevity of invasion in fiction and film: "The invasion theme persists because it is eminently adaptable to the fears of the moment – terrorism, pandemics, ecological disasters". I. F. Clarke's (1992: 224–262) checklist of imaginary wars 1763–1990 includes a dozen titles before *The Battle of Dorking* and between five and twenty titles for most years during the twentieth century.

So, just as Filson's Boone did not just become the Western hero but the modern hero *par excellence*, Chesney's invasion fiction has infiltrated the European and later much of the global popular imagination with its invasion by alien nations and planets, crooks and terrorists, from natural to man-made disasters and apocalypses.[23] And this is no coincidence, since Filson's Boone and some invasion fiction protagonists are what Cawelti (1999) calls "intermediate heroes". In fact, although Cawelti did not recognize it, they are all largely based on the age-old hero fighting the dragon for the benefit of the society he in some sense represents (see 4.3). Contemporary readers and film audiences still love to imagine that they are about to be invaded from some quarters – and each time they shiver

---

23 A recent development is to be found in Magnus Mills's (2011/2012) *A Cruel Bird Came to the Nest and Looked In*, an allegory of how Greater Fallowfields (cf. Great Britain) is overtaken by economic invasion by the City of Scoffers (cf. the Soviet Union, owing to its insignia the hammer and the anvil), a city that in turn fears an invasion by a great power from the West (cf. the United States).

with fear and excitement and count on a hero or heroes to save the day. Clarke's (1992: 217) point that invasion fiction has "an almost unbroken record of failing to forecast the true course of future wars" gives little consolation, since except delighting readers, it has also roused animosity and hatred between and within nations and by extension caused much destruction and warfare.

7.4 A Chinese Author at the Service of Ideology

Like Filson and Chesney, Lu Xun (1881–1936), in many ways the founding father of modern Chinese literature, had a mission. If he could be called a radical, his mission was mostly rather general: he was critical of the traditional Chinese society after the toppling of the Qing dynasty in 1911 and became a prominent member of the cultural and political May Fourth (1919) movement, even if he did not become a Marxist until about 1930. He wrote a range of essays and a history of Chinese literature but is mainly remembered as a writer of about thirty realist short stories satirizing Chinese people, their foibles and backwardness.

With this in mind, does it sound likely that the highest Marxist authority in China, Mao Zedong (1940/1967: 62), as early as in 1940 (four years after Lu Xun's death and nine years before the Communist revolution) would extol such an author as "[t]he chief commander of China's revolution" and "the firmest, the most loyal and the most ardent national hero, a hero without parallel in our history"? In fact, the canonization of Lu Xun, "the saint of modern China", was to become second only to that of Mao. Lu Xun was put on reading lists in schools and universities and a veritable "Lu Xun industry" was instituted, consisting of museums, scholarship and paraphernalia by, of and on the author, which even continues in post-Mao China with a theme park centring on the "Lu Xun experience" (Lovell 2009: xxxii, xxxiii). This begs some questions: What did Lu Xun do to deserve such a lofty position in Communist China and how did the Lu Xun cult come about? The answers to such questions are interrelated, but let us first consider what Lu Xun in fact did.

Perhaps most important was what Lu Xun stood for. In the preface to his first collection, the symbolically titled *Outcry* (1923), he introduced the striking metaphor of an iron house with sleepers, who should be awakened by the author crying out, even if they were to die in agony. The interlocutor in the preface, Jin Ying, an editor of the radical journal *New Youth*, answers him: "But even if we succeed in waking only the few – there is still hope, hope that the iron house may one day be destroyed" (Lu Xun 1923/2009: 19). This puts much of Lu Xun's authorial profile in a nutshell: on the face of it, he may write short satirical prose vignettes, but metaphorically they stand for an outcry against the iron house of political and cultural stagnation. Also, when he goes on to voice his realization that "hope is a thing of the future", Lu Xun (1923/2009: 19) seems prescient as to what his writing can ultimately do, at least as viewed from a later perspective. And what his writing did was to make realist fiction central in Chinese literature, not least by portraying a variety of the Chinese: bourgeois tradesmen, peasants, peddlers, madmen, the young and the old, men and women.

In the preface he also declares why he abandoned his promising medical career. If you want to change the Chinese people, "[t]he first task was to change their spirit; and literature and the arts, I decided at the time, were the best means to this end", so he became "a crusader for cultural reform" (Lu Xun 1923/2009: 17). But he did even more, since as he put in his essay "Silent China" a few years later, the new generation could not use the "crabbed, archaic language" of traditional literature describing "outmoded sentiments", but needed a new voice: the vernacular (Lu Xun 1927/1973: 163). Finally, after his conversion to Marxism he could also write essays by the title "The Revolutionary Literature of the Chinese Proletariat" and maintain that "[men] should indeed live – in order to make progress", in accordance with Marxist teachings (Lu Xun 1973: 175, 180).

Evidently, this was to fit the Marxist ideology in a number of senses: the old order was dismissed by the metaphor "iron house", and the prophetic "outcry" fiction was to awaken the Chinese people, as it depicted them realistically in their own language. In all, Lu Xun seemed almost teleologically to point forward to the supposedly righteous emergent power of Communism, and thus to embody energy and hope, manifest in the hopeful tone at the end of many of his stories. It must have seemed to Mao that if there had not been Lu Xun, he – or somebody very much like him – must have had to be invented to serve as cultural icon for his modern China. But as a matter of fact, in order to function as a national hero Lu Xun was in part invented, or perhaps rather re-invented, just as Filson mythologized Boone as a Western hero and Chesney turned Britain into a conquered country so as to inspire a military build-up.

Some facts of the twists and turns of the Lu Xun cult show the varied uses made of a single author at the service of inculcating different kinds of ideology into the minds of over a billion Chinese during more than half a century. David Holm (1985: 160–161) has shown how it started even in the commemorative events at and following Lu Xun's funeral in 1936. There were of three kinds of event: meetings and memorials; speeches and articles; and scholarly research in a number of journals dedicated to the works of Lu Xun. Merle Goldman (1985: 180) goes into even greater detail concerning the various phases of the cult, in which the author's "life and work have been twisted to symbolize values that do not reflect – and that have at times been diametrically opposed to – the ones he truly supported". The development of the cult that Goldman (1985) depicts during about half a century could be described in two circles.

The first circle starts as the cult of Lu Xun is corroborated when Mao in one of his most extensive talks on literature and the arts, given at the Yenan forum meeting in 1942, makes selective use of Lu Xun: Lu Xun was right to be a satirist in his day, but now satire is seldom needed, since now "we can shout at the top of our voices" and writers should rather follow the great author's example and be "'oxen' for the proletariat and the masses" (Mao 1942/1967: 33, 40). But at the Yenan meeting the cosmopolitan aspect of the May Fourth movement – which Lu Xun heartily endorsed, since he was both a cosmopolitan and a nationalist – was also harshly criticized and Lu Xun's disciples purged. In fact, despite his pro-proletarian rhetoric, Lu Xun had in the 1930s vehemently quarrelled with the Party cultural politics, especially with the Shanghai cultural leader Zhou Yang. After Lu Xun's death, for some decades Zhou Yang was given much power in Chinese cultural politics, so that for instance Lu Xun's writings denouncing him were left out of the 1958 collected edition of Lu Xun's works. Also, even Lu Xun himself was indirectly criticized for not having followed Party policies strictly enough. At this point, Lu Xun's role as a cultural symbol for Mao was clearly reduced. However, as Mao during the Cultural revolution in the late 1960s gave more power to his fourth wife Jiang Qing, Zhou Yang fell out of favour (largely because Jiang Qing thought he had bypassed her when she was an actor in Shanghai in the 1930s). So Lu Xun's letters denouncing Zhou Yang were published, mostly to warn people against rotten forces within the Party, thus indirectly criticizing Deng Xiaoping and other leaders who seemed to threaten Mao's sovereign position in the Party. Thus, Lu Xun once again became associated with Mao, in part through Jiang Qing, which closes the first circle of Lu Xun's fate in the ideological strife in the Communist Party.

The second circle begins with the fact that Lu Xun again was endorsed by Mao, who claimed that the author was his close associate and that they struggled together against corrupt Party politicians, which was far from the truth (apparently they did not even meet face to face). In short, Lu Xun was used in at least three ways in the 1970s before Mao's death in 1976: in the Anti-Confucian campaign he was supposedly against Confucian traditionalism and moderation (which was in part true); in the *Water Margin* campaign Mao, like Lu Xun before him, extolled the virtues of some passages in that classic fourteenth-century Chinese novel; and in Mao's (and others') castigating allegedly corrupt leaders and Mao's fellow competitors for power, mainly Zhou Enlai and Deng Xiaoping. But Mao died in 1976 and his fellow leaders, the Gang of Four, headed by Jiang Qing were arrested. Now in terms of culture, the Shanghai group could again assert itself, and Zhou Yang could by a devious move sing the praises of his lifelong enemy, so much so that – irony of ironies – he was made chair of The Lu Xun Society of China. Apparently at this point, Lu Xun was read in less slanted ways, even if the ideological changes continued. In recent years, the May Fourth writers have been regarded as more realistic than much exaggeratedly idealistic Communist literature and Lu Xun's criticism of corrupt Party officials has again been found appropriate for any purging of corruption in the Party and the Chinese society at large. However, in 2007 Lu Xun was starting to be excised out of textbooks in schools in China, especially some of the essays, such as one that touchingly depicts the death of a female demonstrator, which could incite demonstrations in memory of the bloodbath in Tiananmen Square in 1989 (see Lovell 2010: xxxv). Hence, Lu Xun can still be made useful for all sorts of causes, either for or against the Party or some of its factions. Thus, the second circle is left open.

In short, the opinions concerning Lu Xun in China from his death to the contemporary post-Mao China shed some light on the development of modern China. I have drawn a bare outline of a complex web of ideological, political and cultural power struggles related to Lu Xun so as to illustrate how central a single author was in inculcating whatever ideology that some of the powers that be in China stood for over three quarters of a century. For most of that time the main power was of course invested in Mao himself and the people he authorized to write about Lu Xun. So what did Mao himself think? The first point to note is that he was an unusually well-read man, who had studied the Chinese classics as a young man and gone on to become well-versed in Western classics from the ancient Greeks to philosophy to modern ethical, economic and political theory, of course mainly of Marxist persuasion.[24] Hence, his endorsement of Lu Xun is not due to a narrow interest in a contemporary Chinese author, but very much the result of conscious policy-making. In Mao's essays on literature and art Lu Xun figures prominently in the early 1940s, when the Communist leader tried to consolidate and increase his following, which apparently worked. Then – at least in the selection of his cultural essays available in English – Mao does not discuss Lu Xun until a speech in March 1957, just as he is launching the Hundred Flowers Campaign, which led to the infamous purge of intellectuals. "Can the Lu Hsun [old spelling] type of essay be used against mistakes and shortcomings within the ranks of people?", Mao asks, and answers: "I think it can" (1957/1967: 156).

---

24 For a summary of Mao's wide reading see Barnstone (1972/2008: 4–5).

This is typical for not only Mao but all ideological use of Lu Xun after his death: take phrases, sentences or even full essays by the author out of context and you can prove anything. This is easily done with Lu Xun, who especially in his later essays – praised by Mao (1957/1967: 155) as supposedly "penetrating and powerful and yet so free from one-sidedness" – was uncommonly pugnacious and vindictive. Mao and his followers had to turn a blind eye on much of Lu Xun in order to praise some one phrase or opinion – and the rest is literally history.[25] For instance, Mao (1937/1967: 46) was especially critical of myth and fantasy, a venerable age-old tradition in Chinese literature he clearly knew very well, since "myths are not built out of the concrete contradictions existing in given conditions and therefore not a scientific reflection of reality".[26] It was this sort of simplistic Marxist theory of literature reflecting society that made him so enamoured of Lu Xun, the founding father of modern Chinese realist fiction turned Marxist. But what did Lu Xun in fact write before and during the very years that he turned into a Marxist? In his last collection *Old Stories Retold* (1936) he delighted in satirizing mythical Chinese stories in fantastic and humorous fantasies. For instance, in the last story "Bringing Back the Dead", the philosopher Zhuangzi (the one with the famous butterfly story) awakens a man who has been dead for five centuries against the advice of ghosts and with the help of the God of Fate. Yet the irony is that the man resents being alive, a moral that cannot very easily be made to fit any ideological use (see Lu Xun 1936/2009).

Granted that such stories were rather, if not entirely, different from Lu Xun's two other collections of short stories, what was characteristic of his fiction? In the words of Lu Xun's most recent English translator Julia Lovell (2009: xxxvi), "Lu Xun's paradoxical brand of nationalism (a passionate attachment to, yet disgust with, China) still retains a powerful hold over Chinese consciousness". Indeed, as Shelley W. Chan (2011: 5 *et passim*) has shown, the Nobel Prize-winner for Literature of 2012 Mo Yan adopted Lu Xun as "his model". But more importantly, what Lovell puts her finger on may be what has kept the Chinese

---

25 It may be interesting to note that Philip Short (1999) in his major biography *Mao. A Life* entirely bypasses Mao's relation to Lu Xun, possibly since they apparently never met, possibly since his discussion of Mao's literary and cultural interests is rather brief. But it is not surprising that Lu Xun is not mentioned in *Quotations of Chairman Mao Tsetung*, since it is characterized by general guidelines. Hence, its chapter on "Culture and Art" is rather brief, and although over half of it are quotes from the 1942 Yenan talks on literature and art, not one includes any of the many references to Lu Xun in those talks (see Mao Zedong 1966/1976: 299–303).
26 Mao's harsh criticism of myth is rather paradoxical, since in the words of Willis Barnstone (1972/2008: 23), "as a traditional Chinese poet, Mao is servant of Chinese mythology: not a poem is without its mythical allusion". For Mao's poetry see Mao (1972/2008).

reading Lu Xun both for ideological and other purposes: he shows a love-and-hate for China that they may recognize in themselves.

Most patently, however, the ideological usages of Lu Xun largely bypass the complex qualities in his finest short stories. His two perhaps most famous stories, "Diary of a Madman" and "The Real Story of Ah-Q", have double frames of sorts: in the former there is a narrator who passes on a story he has heard, in the latter the protagonist is set in contrast to crowds and people who think he is deluded or laughable. Moreover, they are largely unreliable: the madman thinks all or most people are cannibals and the odd-job man Ah-Q turns all his misfortunes to victories (see Lu Xun 1921/2009). Both are deluded, but have also been considered to voice something very true about the Chinese. As we have seen in chapter 3.3, the madman is right in claiming that during famines cannibalism has occurred in China and he is also right metaphorically speaking, since at that time a stifling tradition seemed devour the people. Ah-Q, on the other hand, is an exaggerated portrayal of a good-for-nothing who can only survive by his "life lie", much like some characters in Henrik Ibsen's plays. In fact, Lu Xun wrote an essay on Ibsen's *A Doll's House* just about when "The Real Story of Ah-Q" was published and ends it by maintaining that "[u]nless some great whip lashes on her back, China will never budge. Such a whip is bound to come, I think" (1923/1973: 154).

In his preface to *Outcry* Lu Xun even shows that he is much aware that the hopeful endings in some stories, such as "Save the children..." in "Diary of a Madman" (Lu Xun 1923/2009: 31), seemed forced: "I often stooped to distortions and untruths", "because my generalissimos did not approve of pessimism". Elsewhere he even claims that *Outcry* "might also be described as 'written to order'", an order he was "glad to obey" (quoted in Anderson 1990: 87). So in fact Lu Xun was the first to ideologically tamper with his own texts. Still, he was such an accomplished author that, in the words of Charles Laughlin (2008: 223), all his stories "contain clues to the ambivalence about their revolutionary significance". But when the whip came down, Lu Xun's stories, much richer than any ideological mythologizing of his works could suggest, were among the first to drive the oxen towards the China of today.

Taken together, Filson's Boone, Chesney's Britain and Mao's Lu Xun are major figments of the imagination that did much to shape history: the Western hero permeated the West and later the rest of the world by his supposedly moral right to retribution; Chesney's story started an entire genre that paved the way for the First World War, whose aftermath of course in many ways caused the Second World War and the world we live in today; and the ideological uses of Lu Xun has pervaded pre-revolutionary, Communist and post-Mao China as a protean cultural idol for the masses. They are blatant examples of how literature knowingly can be used for rhetorical and ideological purposes, by the author or forces other than the author or both, and of how, when set in motion, such forces take unforeseeable shapes.

Of course, many other examples of literature responding to politics in the past century could be mentioned. Wilfred Owen (1920/1973: 542–543) famously underlined in his poem "Dulce et Decorum Est", written during the First World War, that children should no longer believe the "old Lie" that it is sweet and honourable to die for your country (as he in fact eventually did). In *Slaughterhouse-Five* (1969) Kurt Vonnegut questioned the moral right to retribution by thematizing the Allied bombing of Dresden during the Second World War, a bombing he himself as an imprisoned German-American soldier survived. And Lu Xun's paradoxical nationalism lives on in Mo Yan's works which are outspoken about mismanagement and corruption in China in the twentieth and twenty-first centuries. Thus, as almost anything humankind creates, literature can be used in a variety of ways, and such uses are seldom if ever possible to predict.

Above we have considered three lesser known instances of the impact of literature on the popular imagination, and ultimately of how literature in fact can and does change the world and how it then can write back so as to change the world in another way. At least two of them, the Western hero and the theme of invasion, have entered the popular imagination on a more or less global scale. In fact, they have done much to inform not only popular culture but also the mindsets of individuals and entire nations in ways that have had and continue to have considerable political consequences. Real life affects imagination in its many forms, and in turn imagination can change life as we know it through literature and other media. And the wheel keeps spinning.

8 Why Literature Matters

8.1 Benefit through Delight

In a sense, there is no need to discuss whether literature matters. The previous chapter shows that it matters in that it can effect changes in the world we live in. It is also proved by the fact that people in cultures across millennia have told stories, composed poems and acted out imaginative dramatic displays – and, what is more, have usually had an audience for it. But the question *why* this is so has had a number answers, usually combining two features. Let me start with a classic formulation in English, then present a variety of views and finally illustrate my discussion by literary examples.

In 1595 Sir Philip Sidney published "The Defence of Poesy", one of the most thoughtful answers to the question why imaginative literature or *poesy*[1] matters: it simply aims "to teach and delight". That phrase is often quoted but usually without its context: "Poesy [...] is an art of imitation, for so Aristotle termeth it in the word *mimēsis*, that is to say, a representing, a counterfeiting [...] or figuring forth – to speak metaphorically, a speaking picture – with this end: to teach and delight" (Sidney 1595/2004: 10). In this one sentence Sidney – inspired by Aristotle and Horace, among others – puts in a nutshell much of what I have been trying to maintain in this study: literature has a mimetic basis (in the Aristotelian sense) in that it combines imitative and creative aspects (chapter 2) as well as figurative and narrative usages (chapter 5), perhaps also letting its audience understand the possible counterfeit or unreliability involved (chapter 3). Apparently Sidney here draws on the contemporary French scholar Joseph Justus Scaliger, who in his *Poetices* makes the same connection between (evidently Aristotelian) mimesis and delight, and then draws the conclusion: "imitation is only means to the ultimate end, which is to teach with delight" (quoted in Alexander 2004b: 325n35). That is, for Scaliger teaching is primary: delight is only used to sweeten the medicine. In fact, even though Sidney's much-quoted phrase seems to give equal weight to the two aims, in his subsequent discussion teaching is superior, as when he discusses "delightful teaching" (Sidney 1595/2004: 12).

The dual function of literature (and many other arts) lives on today in functionalist and aestheticist views. Literature serves some kind or kinds of function and is thus a means to an end (cf. "to teach"); or it is considered an end in itself, a form of art of little or no use (cf. "to delight"); and of course the functionalist and aestheticist stances have also been combined. In terms of the functionalist

---

[1] For a brief discussion of Sidney's use of *poesy* see Gavin Alexander (2004a: lviii).

means-to-an-end view, literature is mainly regarded in four ways. It can be (1) *simulative*, that is, it can simulate everyday experience, thus helping readers to navigate in the actual world. For instance, Jørgen Dines Johansen (2002: 432) asserts that "[l]iterature matters because it is capable both of simulating everyday experiences (obviously including fateful ones as well) and of transforming/transfiguring them". Especially in philosophical aesthetics the discussion of simulation has been going on for decades.[2] In literary studies in the 1980s there was quite a prominent trend of (2) *ethical* views, so much so that there was something that has been termed *the ethical turn*. Major names from rather different quarters of literary studies represented that turn, including narrative theorists (Wayne C. Booth, James Phelan), philosophers (Martha C. Nussbaum, Cora Diamond) and postmodern theorists (J. Hillis Miller, Charles Altieri).[3] Both simulative and ethical views, then, seem to be about what Sidney had in mind by literature's aim "to teach".

As Suzanne Keen (2007: vii) has shown, the ethical stance often has an emotional basis; indeed, she even speaks of a "widely promulgated 'empathy-altruism' hypothesis". That is, the ethical stance may or may not be grounded in (3) an *empathetic* stance: by empathising with characters in fiction and drama or speakers in poems, readers become versed in various ethical attitudes, which, according to some critics (e.g. Nussbaum 1990), will make them more altruistic or compassionate. As is evident in Keen's (2007: 37–64) useful review of the considerable literature on empathy and the novel, the empathetic view of literary reading has in the last three centuries been both condemned and applauded. In other words, the "empathy-altruism" hypothesis has also been challenged. Indeed, Keen (2007: vii, xxv) finds, rightly I think, "the case for altruism stemming from novel reading inconclusive at best" and argues for "a more nuanced study of the consequences of experiencing aesthetic emotions". Hence, like the simulative stance, some versions of the ethical and empathetic ones explicitly or implicitly claim that literature is functional in the sense of strengthening readers' sociocultural competence.

Finally, a more or less functionalist view has been advanced in the last few decades by literary critics and theorists from an evolutionary perspective (Dissanayake 1988, 1992, 2000, Carroll 1995, 2004, Hernadi 2001, 2002). The point is that art, including literature, is part and parcel of (4) the *evolutionary* (or adaptive) make-up and need of human beings. In fact, the above three func-

---

[2] For various positions on simulation see Hjort and Laver (1997), Currie and Ravenscroft (2002), Nichols (2006) and Zunshine (2006), who advocates a related theory-of-mind view.
[3] All names mentioned are represented in a useful anthology on the ethical turn edited by Davis and Womack (2001).

tional stances could be subsumed under it in the sense that, as we have seen, reading literature may make people socioculturally more competent and thus more desirable as mates. As Joseph Carroll (2004: xxii) puts it,

> We use imaginative [including artistic] models to make sense of the world, not just to "understand" it abstractly but to feel and perceive our own place in it – to see it from the inside out. Making sense of the world in this way, through narrative and through the other arts, is both a primary psychological need and a necessary precondition for organizing our behavior in ways that satisfy all our other adaptive needs.[4]

I have briefly surveyed instances epitomising four functionalist stances – simulative, ethical, empathetic and evolutionary – in order to show that they are different but not altogether unrelated. All four seem to presuppose some kind of imaginative act behind the reading and/or writing of literature and/or literary criticism. By way of imaginary worlds inhabited by fictitious narrators, speakers or characters, literature transforms experiences, opens vistas or helps readers see the past, present or future of the world they live in from the inside out. In other words, they all point towards the combination of imagination and mimesis that this study is based on.

What is more, the four above stances can be related to aestheticist views. Christopher Butler (2005: 14) argues that pleasure is fundamental in dealings with arts, but he does so by a line of reasoning that has a functionalist affinity. The hypothesis he attempts to prove is that "we all have a drive to explore and understand, whose satisfaction gives us much of the pleasure we get from [literature]". But of course, other – and more fully-fledged – aestheticist, end-in-itself or art-for-art's-sake views have been propounded at least ever since Théophile Gautier (and others) in the mid-nineteenth century, though in the last few years most aestheticist critics have tempered their position by functionalist considerations. For instance, in the introduction to their volume *The New Aestheticism* Joughin and Malpas (2003: 3) argue for "equi-primordiality of the aesthetic" in relation to the political, historical and ideological aspects of literature. Similarly, Raymond Tallis (2000: 354, 360) has repeatedly discussed "the uselessness of art", but at the same time pointed out that art's importance lies in providing pleasure, in "rounding off the sense of the world, celebrating the wonderful and beautiful uselessness of human consciousness" (cf. Tallis 1995: 79–208).

---

4 Hernadi (2002: 39) puts the evolutionary benefit in somewhat different terms: literature trains cognition, emotion and volition, especially by integrating them in more fluid ways than workaday mentation.

So there are (at least) four functionalist views and an aestheticist one that often seems to be combined with some kind of functionalist view. So is that "delightful teaching"? Not exactly, since the aim of teaching fits best the ethical stance and must be considerably broadened in order to entail simulative, emotional and evolutionary aspects (that is, literature teaches you about life, in particular how people act, which can have considerable advantages). Thus, teaching as such is simply too narrow; *benefit* may better encompass what literature can effect by ritual or mythical exampla, allegories, moral guidelines and portrayals of advantageous or disadvantageous behaviour. In fact, Sidney (1595/2004: 11) may suggest such a view, since he also maintains that excellent poets may teach by "having no law but wit, bestow that in colours upon you which is fittest for the eye to see". As listeners, audience or readers we are not necessarily taught, but we learn something about how – or how not – to behave. If on the other hand you prioritize a functionalist view, the other aim – "to delight" – is merely what makes the teaching palatable. But does this sort of view really tally with people's views, however different they may be, of why they read literature, see it performed and possibly do so because they think it matters in one way or another?

Perhaps we should go back to Horace's (1929/2005: 479; c. ll. 333–334) "Ars Poetica", on which at least Scaliger and Sidney drew, to see how the relation between the dual aims is stated: "Poets aim either to benefit [*prodesse*], or to amuse [*delectare*],[5] or to utter words at once both pleasing and helpful to life". This is much more broadly put: what Sidney calls "to teach" is more clearly related to all the functionalist modes discussed, that is, what I have termed *benefit*. But what is more, Horace maintains that the central aim in a poem (and most likely poem here stands for literature in general) can *either* be that you learn something useful *or* you are delighted *or* both. A nonsense rhyme does not teach you much about life (if something about language and humour) and a heavily didactic poem gives little pleasure, but you may enjoy and learn something from both of them. Now all the above theorists claim, explicitly or implicitly, that what they hold forth about the aims of literature is based on literature. So let us have a look what the aim of literature seems to be in a few different kinds of literature.

Of the three main themes of literary world-making differentiated in chapter 4, two – *perception* and *relation* – are all about somebody (author, narrator, speaker) knowing by imagining a literary world and communicating (mainly through characters or actors) it to or with (in some kinds of performance)

---

5 *Prodesse* literally means 'to be of use' or 'to be of benefit', *delectare* 'to delight' or 'to charm'.

some people who do not know it or know less about it (listeners, readers, audience). As words, to *narrate* and to *know*, we have noted, have the same etymology. For instance, even if, say, a nature poem is largely descriptive, it also imparts knowledge of the thing or phenomenon depicted as well as the perceiver's reaction to it. The third theme, *challenge*, especially the challenge to understand, questions what the audience (of different kinds) knows or what anybody can know. In other words, it presents a meta-perspective of knowledge, which most importantly sets its readers or audience thinking. In a very general sense, then, all impart knowledge of sorts. But that knowledge and how to use or benefit from it can lead to a range of responses: you can learn about different ways of life, by emulating or rejecting them; understand the workings of unreliability better; entertain the thought of hypothetical action; solve a riddle or meet a challenge in your imagination. And all such forms of benefit can of course be slanted or inverted in the course of reading. So what the audience learns is never clear, not least owing to the fact that people interpret literature in such different ways. As we saw in 2.2, *The Pañćatantra*, the age-old Indian collection of tales allegedly by Visnu Śarma (1993), understood this in that it expressly aims to teach the princes *how* not *what* to think.

So, yes, something is being communicated or "taught", but what the audience actually learns is never certain. For instance, readers of a didactic poem may be put off by its patronizing tone and perhaps "learn" the opposite of what was intended. They benefit in some sense, but this is not necessarily what the poet, according to Horace, intended.

Delight, on the other hand, I would argue, has always been there, in one way or another. As Phillip B. Zarrilli (2010: 29) points out when presenting some of the earliest forms of oral performance: "Masking, costuming, impersonation, dance, music, narrative, and humor are strategically utilized in some rituals, not only to achieve efficacious ends but to please the gods, ancestors, and/or humans gathered to participate or witness". Semi-literary tales of the lives of great teachers (Gautama Buddha, Confucius, Jesus Christ, Muhammad) in religious texts or texts about or based on such texts – say, *The Jātakas* (on Buddha), Zhuangzi's writings (on Confucius, Lao-Tzu and Mencius) and John Milton's *Paradise Lost* (on *The Bible*) and *One Thousand and One Nights* (with its invocation referring to *The Qur'an*) – are usually full of interesting action, characterization and pithy sayings. In short, they contain literary delights. What is more, they are persuasive as religious or semi-religious tracts in part precisely because they contain pleasurable and enticing literary techniques. And of course the influence may go well beyond religious sentiments, as implied by the fact that several stories in *The Old Testament* or *The Hebrew Bible* are much the same as in *Gilgamesh*.

In chapter 2.2 we saw that Sumerian poetry, however much about mythological characters, took its motifs from the human sphere: courtship, wedding, death and mourning. What we now term poetry was in effect originally ritualistic texts performed for audiences, and the allegorical mythological action often had to do with inducing a better crop – this is how they benefit or "teach". Yet by the human motifs on a mythical level, the poems and the narrative dramas they consist of ensure that the audience or congregation is kept enthralled or in suspense – this is how they "delight". The same is largely true of *The Mahābhārata*, *The Iliad* and *The Odyssey:* there are gods, god-like creatures and humans, but all act in ways that are largely recognizable as having human-like strategic or emotional motivations, such as love, anger, revenge and grief.

Moving on to secular literature *per se*, in ancient Chinese (*The Book of Songs* 1937/1996), Prakrit (Hāla's *Sattasaī*; *Poems on Life and Love in Ancient India* 2009), Tamil (Ramanujan 1985) and Japanese poetry (*1000 Poems from the Manyōshū* 2005), the poems mainly focus on love but also on war, which only occurs marginally in *Sattasaī* and the *Manyōshū*. But what makes such literature contain the dual aim of benefit and delight is the fact that it is about the *effects* of love and war on particular speakers or characters: soldiers complain of hardships and nostalgia, lovers pine for or miss their loved ones (whether their love is illicit or not), who are usually absent due to travel, war or death. They offer hundreds of shards in which singers, speakers and audience alike can mirror their own circumstances and feelings, and in some way become wiser, comforted or delighted by the narrative twists.

The same is true of mythical plays, such as Kālidāsa's *Abhijñānaśākuntalam* (discussed below), or fantastic folk tales, as for instance the ones collected and (re)written by Somadeva in India, Pu Songling in China, the brothers Jacob and Wilhelm Grimm in Germany or Charles Perrault in France (see 2.2): they may be fantastic but their characters, whether human or not, act and speak in patently human ways. The allegorical and fable-like aspects are delightful as such and what morals they may seek to instil can, as noted above, be taken with or without a grain of salt. Such combinations of fantastic action with realist human motivation run deep in medieval and Renaissance world literature, often with an allegorical intent, as in religious narratives (William Langland's *Piers Plowman*), political plays (Chinese Yüan music dramas) or plays showing the range of human behaviour (Shakespeare). As more and more realist features enter into, say, European novels in the eighteenth and nineteenth centuries the morals can at times be more outspoken but the thematic or formal delight by which they provide takes on human life is unmistakable. Such takes have been discussed in some detail above when the focus has been on combinations of the real and the fantastic, mimesis and genre (chapter 2), unreliability (chapter 3), the makings of literary worlds (chapter 4), the blend of figures and narratives (chapter 5) and the imaginative inflections given to the central themes (chapter 6). And as the literary techniques and self-consciousness about literature and its genres increased in modern and postmodern literature, authors have gone on to provide all sorts of delights that more and more specialized audiences savour.

Thus, I would say that first and foremost literature delights, and by that very delight – as psychologists have shown[6] – we may learn something from it. Rather than "teach", then, literature often tries to benefit its audience in oblique ways, so that they learn about the received worldview by a ritual or are swayed by a speaker, moved by a poem, won over by a story and its moral – or indeed decide not to be swayed, and in this way learn what designs language and literature as well as people can have. Except for situations where literature is required reading, what literature people decide to read or what theatre to attend is based on free choice, even if there can be considerable social pressure involved. This is why no pedagogical curriculum can keep on resuscitating literature that does not delight. Delight of some sort is simply the main ingredient in all classics, and they matter, as all literature does, since they delight first and benefit – possibly in anti-intentional ways – second.

But if the main response is delight and much of literature and its enjoyment is based on free choice, is it merely a frivolous activity with little or no consequence? The answer, as we have seen, is a resounding no. In the previous chapter we saw that humans not only shape literary worlds but are shaped by them, both on a personal level and in the public domain, which is a major reason why literature matters. The influence of literature is immeasurable, not least since it in such manifold ways is able to combine the individual imagination with popular imagination. In the above we have touched on a number of them: the main themes in literary world-making matter to people and learning about such themes in imaginative ways can better prepare them for life. Knowing about literary techniques is also important, since understanding rhetoric and language use in general, whether unreliable, allegorical or figurative, is useful in order for people to recognize the various persuasive uses they encounter elsewhere. What is more, as far as I can tell, in terms of reviews on Amazon.com, factual books, including self-help books, political memoirs or analyses of contemporary society, cannot compete with the five-digit figures of the most popular novels. People simply seem to *care* more for stories about literary worlds.

---

6 See e.g. Green, Garst and Brock (2004) and its references.

8.2 A Sense of Wonder

So far this chapter has considered the means by which literature benefits and delights. But I have saved a crucial feature last, perhaps the one that is the most fascinating: literature usually provides a sense of wonder and it does so in manifold ways. In *Webster's* (1989; *s.v.* wonder) we find many related meanings to *wonder:* 'something strange and surprising', 'the emotion' stirred by such events or a 'miraculous deed or event'. As we have seen, literary imagination does indeed move on this scale from the surprising to the miraculous, thus giving rise to emotions connected with wonder, even though it is based on imitative and creative forms of mimesis.

Apparently humans have hankered for experiencing a sense of wonder through stories as far back as we know. In one of the of the oldest extant stories from Egypt, *The Tale of King Cheops' Court*, a story from the late Middle Kingdom (c. 1940–1640 BCE) about the rulers from about seven centuries earlier, King Cheops complains of being bored, at which point his princes divert him with stories with fantastic elements beginning with the phrase "I shall let your Majesty hear a wonder". One of the stories is about how Cheops' father Sneferu, just like his son, was bored and then regaled by fantastic stories (*The Tale of King Cheops' Court* 1998/2009: 106–120, esp. 109–110, ll. 4.18–5.1). Thus, even at this point there were embedded stories and stories of adultery and magic that diverted not only kings but wider audiences – and an awareness of literature's sense of wonder.

As so often in literature, then, the sense of wonder in Egyptian storytelling was based on a number features and their combinations. As Brian Boyd (2012: 2) has pointed out, all of literature has "two main strands, narrative and verse", that is, he seems to take for granted that poetry and drama, whether in verse or not, is mainly narrative. He goes on to note that literary narrative and verse often blend and exemplifies it by *The Iliad*, *Paradise Lost*, Alexander Pushkin's novel in verse *Eugene Onegin* and *Hamlet*. And as we saw in 5.2, even lyrical verse is often narrative. Furthermore, there are instances in which the novel – the magpie genre *par excellence* – has narrative and dramatic passages (in the sense of pure dialogue) as well as lyrical poems, as for instance in the classic Finnish novel *Seven Brothers* by Aleksis Kivi (1870/1984). Hence, even the classic literary modes blend in a number of ways. So whether you see narrative and verse as the central modes or the traditional literary-historical ones of prose fiction (including the epic, which may also have lyrical features), drama and poetry, the point is that patterning is involved in all literature. In the work quoted above, Boyd (2012: 11) epitomizes the argument of chapter 6 of his magnum opus *On the Origin of Stories* in one phrase: the "common core" of literature is "*cognitive play with open-ended pattern*". By "*open-ended*" Boyd (2009: 85–90) means that patterns created by humans in art are unpredictable and can be combined. Thus, what he puts his finger on is that humans in their art delight not just in patterning but in *play* with patterning.

Such play is the source of much wonder in literature. Especially in all kinds of narrative, as listeners, readers or audience we want to be surprised. This is so even when we know the outline of the narrative from the start. Vladimir Nabokov's (1933/1961: 5) narrator famously gives away the story in the first paragraph of his novel *Laughter in the Dark*, but goes on to ponder – in a way that seems to draw on Horace's dual aim of literature – why the narrative is still worth his readers' attention: "This is the whole story and we might have left it at that had there not been profit and pleasure in the telling; and although there is plenty of space on a gravestone to contain, bound in moss, the abridged version of a man's life, detail is always welcome". In terms of pattern, the point is that the entire novel is determined at the start, but that there is indeed "profit and pleasure" in the very act of narrating a story, especially as concerns the motivations of the characters, and that this gives a creative leeway to the telling that fascinates readers.[7] Thus, whatever pattern is employed in a literary work (say, a particular genre or subgenre, as such or blended with others), it is open-ended in the sense that some detail may change the reading of the summary or the familiar story.

In fact, as audience for literature, we would not want to have it any other way. We want to know what happens next, and if we do, then how and why it happens, but perhaps most of all, we want to be surprised, especially by the ending, which should be plausible but in some sense unexpected. In classic dramas too we know what to expect: in tragedies most or at least some of the main protagonists die and in traditional comedies there will be a happy ending, usually by a marriage or two. But the way the action and dialogue furthers the plot and brings forth the ending should have enough surprise elements to sustain the audience's attention. In brief descriptive lyrical poetry on the other hand, attention can be maintained by figurative usages, syntax and the evocative vagueness of the meaning implied – just think of famous poems like William Carlos Williams's "The Red Wheelbarrow" or Pound's "In a Station of the Metro" (see 5.1).

These are basic formal ways in which a sense of wonder is instilled in a literary audience. But the notion of play that Boyd in line with host of evolutionary-minded theorists in the last century or so focuses on also corroborates the

---

[7] As I have noted, this is also true of Greek drama, since most of its spectators were familiar with the story but were curious to see each playwright's version.

age-old view that form and contents go together in art and literature.⁸ To be sure, play comes in different shapes in different societies and at various times, even if its import has been variously interpreted. To contrast the two perhaps most influential names in the theory of play: Johan Huizinga (1950/1992) considers play a shaping force in society whereas Roger Callois (1958/2001), although building on Huizinga, views it as an activity separate from ordinary life, both of which stances can easily be substantiated. Children's games, however important for ontogenetic development, may not have widespread social importance as such, but coronation ceremonies can be of major significance in the life of a nation. In literature, play in Boyd's sense of variation of pattern is crucial, since it is what safeguards the unexpected in literature or, to be more precise, literature's sense of wonder, by giving a new twist to what is in some sense conventional. The conventional can consist of formal features, familiar themes or even particular effects on the audience. Formal and thematic features have been discussed throughout this study and many of them or their combinations can induce a sense of wonder by, for instance, how the real and the fantastic are combined, how unreliability comes across, how the main themes of literary world-making are varied and receive figurative uses and other inflections, and how literary worlds have shaped the world as we know it.

As for the effect on the audience, the most advanced treatise is that of *bhāvas* (emotions) giving rise to *rasas* (flavours) in Sanskrit dramas according to the ancient dramaturgical treatise *The Nātyaśāstra* and the development of its notions in the ninth-century Kashmiri scholar Ānandavardhana's *Dhvanyāloka*. Since according to the editor of *The Nātyaśāstra* in English, there is "extreme contiguity" between *rasas* and *bhāvas*, they can largely be "equated", and there are eight major forms of them in *nātya* (drama): love, humour, compassion, horror, the heroic, fear, repulsion and wonder (*The Nātyaśāstra* 2010: 54, 62n1 quote).⁹ These flavours or emotions are to be shared by the poet, possibly by the actors expressing them and by the audience viewing the drama (see Ingalls 1990: 18 and Ānandavardhana and Abhinavagupta 1990: 412). There are other emotions too

---

8 Some of the most notable ones are Yrjö Hirn (1900), Johan Huizinga (1950/1992), Gregory Bateson (1955/2000), Roger Callois (1958/2001), Victor Turner (1982), Kendall Walton (1990), Ellen Dissanayake (1988, 1992, 2000), Joseph Carroll (1995, 2004), Robert Storey (1996), Mark Turner (2006), Denis Dutton (2009), Stephen Davies (2012), Nancy Easterlin (2012) and Christopher Collins (2013). Davies (2012: 121–135) and Easterlin (2012: 27–33) include brief comparisons of the difference in emphasis in evolutionary approaches to literature and art. Unfortunately, the Finland-Swedish aesthetician Yrjö Hirn's (1900) seminal work is often bypassed in more recent advances (it is, however, touched on in Davies 2012: 12–13).
9 As I noted in 4.3, Ānandavardhana adds a ninth rasa, peace, in *Dhvanyāloka* (see Ānandavardhana and Abhinavagupta 1990: 257 *et passim*).

(thirty-three are enumerated in *The Nātyaśāstra* 2010: 54), but the main point is that in each play one of the eight primary emotions reigns supreme, although others may occur. From a Western point of view, what is extraordinary in this Indian literary tradition is that it prioritizes the communication of emotions rather than genres. As a poet, you first choose the emotional modus in which you write, then a genre or form in which you want to express it. In this view, then, the sense of wonder as such is only one of the rasas.

However, above I have suggested a much broader view of the sense of wonder inherent in literature. Let us now look at different classic examples of literature, a Chinese poem, an Indian play and a Greek epic in order to show that the sense of wonder occurs in many guises and can be communicated in subtle ways.

In the Chinese *The Book of Songs* (*Shijing*), the most ancient collection of poetry in the world, there is a seemingly simple poem "In the Wilderness Is a Dead Deer" ("Ye you si jun"):

> In the wilderness is a dead deer
> white grass wraps it up
> There is a girl harbouring spring in her chest
> a fortune-bringing knight leads her
>
> In the woods there are shrubby bushes
> in the wilderness there is a dead doe
> white grass wraps and entangles it
> There is a girl like jade
>
> Slowly! Gently!
> Do not move my girdle kerchief
> Do not make the dog bark!
> (Quoted in Svensson Ekström 2006: 106–107;
> trans. Bernhard Karlsson modified by Svensson Ekström)[10]

There is much to marvel at in this brief poem, in Chinese consisting of four characters per line, which gives it a symmetrical feel. It seems to juxtapose hunting (the dead deer) with love-making (the girl and the knight). There is also repetition in "white grass" enveloping the deer and in the statement "There is a girl", which seems to juxtapose the deer and the girl: both are apparently in the wilderness, but one is dead, the other alive. But once you have read the poem, you

---

10 Arthur Waley's (1996: 20), Ezra Pound's (in Minford and Lau 2000: 108) and David Hinton's (2008: 23) translations of the poem may be more fluent, but as far as I understand, this translation is the most accurate.

start to see that the fates of the deer, which also has been called "a doe", and the girl are not just compared but may be one and the same. As readers, we are turned back to the start, since chronologically the end of the poem seems to be in the first lines. Hence, people who still think that self-consciousness in literature is a modern or even a postmodern phenomenon should read this poem.

Also, there is the relation between the knight and the girl. In Arthur Waley's (1996: 20) translation of the poem the knight does not lead the girl but "seduced her" (notice the past tense), thus changing the ambiguity concerning seduction in this translation into a juxtaposition between the speaker's maintaining that seduction has taken place and the girl's admonition to the knight not to make the dog bark, which suggests she succumbs to him willingly. Still, she seems to resist him in the penultimate line, which keeps the seduction ambiguous (in both translations).[11] Is the girl seriously spurning the knight or does she succumb willingly, as the last line suggests? And what has in fact happened to her: is she seduced, raped or murdered? We cannot know for sure. If this sort of "tension between violence and pleasure, rape and seduction, appearance and actual fact" is not ample cause for a sense of wonder, I do not know what is (Svensson Ekström 2006: 109).

Sinologists have recognized such intriguing uses of metaphor and indirection a long time ago. "The 'Great Preface'" to *The Book of Songs* is considered "the most authoritative statement on the nature and function of poetry in ancient China" and apparently it received its final form in the first century CE (Owen 1992: 37). It displays a broad understanding of irony, indirection and unreliability in literary communication, as when stating: "When an admonition is given that is governed by patterning [in literature] [...], the one who speaks it has no culpability, yet it remains adequate to warn those who hear it" ("The 'Great Preface'" 1992: 46). This shows that literary authors could write with such indirection (of which there were different means) that they could, at least at times, get away with, say, social criticism by referring to the authority of the later much-quoted clause "the one who speaks it has no culpability",[12] but also with letting ambiguity prevail, as in "In the Wilderness Is a Dead Deer".

Based on a story from about a millennium BCE, Kālidāsa's play *Abhijñāna-śākuntalam* (*The Recognition of Śakuntalā*) from about the fifth century CE thematizes how sexual desire can become true love. It dramatizes a short narrative

---

[11] In the translations by Pound and Hinton the girl actually seeks to make love, so there is no ambiguity.
[12] However, as Owen (1992: 46) notes, "the authorities did not always respect the right of literary sanctuary". Of course, we know by the reception of Salman Rushdie's *The Satanic Verses* (1988) that this is still the case.

that starts the "Origins" section in *The Mahābhārata* (2009: 23–25; Book I: 62–69). Here King Duhsanta falls in love with the spiritually descended girl Śakuntalā, who marries him and gives birth to his son, but then he rejects his wife and son until "a heavenly voice" urges him to accept them. He does so and the boy is installed as prince regent and given the name Bharata (Bearer of the earth), thus starting the lineage of Bhārata. Kālidāsa makes this brief but important episode in *The Mahābhārata* into a seven-act play where the water spirit Śakuntalā, in part raised by birds (cf. *śakunta*, bird), stands for Nature and King Duhsanta for the Royal Court. This produces juxtapositions on several more or less allegorical levels: woman and man, wife and husband, nature and humankind, romance/fairytale/myth versus human tragedy (a king taking advantage of a lowly subject), barren royal lineage and newly-formed royal lineage, mother/father and child – and ultimately desire and love, ignorance and knowledge, appearance and reality, chance versus fate.

Some of this is briefly suggested in the story in *The Mahābhārata*. But Kālidāsa's masterstroke is to deepen the action by showing how in the course of the play Duhsanta learns the true nature of love: there is no "heavenly voice" urging him, but it is his own soul-searching that takes him from mere desire for a beautiful girl to his wish to learn the true nature of Śakuntalā and finally love her. The crucial development comes with Duhsanta's recognition (*abhijñānam*) of his love for Śakuntalā, but it forms a dramatic arc: first he receives her signet ring and meets their son (who does not recognize him), then many other turns lead up to the forthcoming recognition (Kālidāsa 1989/2006: 251, 272–274). He is moved by the fact that she has led a strict life owing to his callousness and that her arduous life shows in her face and demeanour. In an aside he speaks (in verse, as is typical of stated morals or climactic scenes):

> Dressed in dusky garments
> her face fined thin from observing strictest vows,
> her hair bound in a single braid; pure, upright,
> she keeps the long vow of cruel separation
> from me who acted so heartless to her.
> (Kālidāsa 1989/2006: 275)

But neither Śakuntalā nor her son recognizes Duhsanta, since in his remorse he does not seem to be the king they know. Thus *he* has to plead to *her* to be recognized and when she finally does identify him, he addresses her "Dear love" and again reverts to verse:

> The light of memory has pierced through
> the sightless night of my delusion;

> by Fortune's grace, you now stand before me,
> O Lady of the most gracious face!
> (Kālidāsa 1989/2006: 275)

These few lines epitomize the recognition of what true love is based on: it requires time (memory); recognition of what is mere appearance (delusion); it calls for the workings of fate (Fortune's grace); and truly knowing the object of one's love (the most gracious face). Thus, Śakuntalā and Duhsanta can be blessed by Mārīca, the Divine Primal Parent and Indra's father, who proclaims that their son will become "a Sovereign of the World" and that "the future will see his name proclaimed *Bharata*. He who bears the world" (Kālidāsa 1989/2006: 280).

The wonder of true love has been restored and affects all the allegorical senses and juxtapositions mentioned above. What is more, Bharata was to become the name of the author of *The Nātyaśāstra*, the world's still most detailed dramaturgical treatise, or at least Bharata Muni is its alleged author. And – wheels within wheels – the epithet for the country itself, Mother India or Bhārata Mātā, draws on this myth, which as we have seen ultimately goes back to *The Mahābhārata*. Thus, the true love between Śakuntalā and Duhsanta has spawned a name that not only lives on in literature, but in literary theory and in the very national symbol of India.

In addition, let me note that it is hardly a coincidence that Shakespeare's *The Winter's Tale* has a similar climax, even if I am not the first to do so and it is not known through what sources Shakespeare may have come across the motif. The sixteen-year separation between the two lovers Leontes and Hermione, King and Queen of Sicilia, in *The Winter's Tale* is occasioned by the latter's jealousy that seemingly shocks his wife to death. In the last scene of the play Paulina, the loyal friend of Hermione awakens her statue to life: "'T is time; descend; be stone no more; approach; / Strike all that look upon with marvel" (Shakespeare 1982/1987: 339; V.iii: 99–100). By pointing out the "marvel", Shakespeare here shows his awareness not just of the wonder occurring on stage but also its effect on the minds of his audience.

The Iliad provides us with another major instance of wonder. It occurs in the very climax of the epic in the last book. Achilles[13] has slain Hector in battle and Hector's father Priam comes to Achilles' tent outside Ilium (Troy) in order to be-

---

[13] Richmond Lattimore's (1951/2011) translation is usually considered the one that most closely follows the original Greek, which is why I use it. However, although he prefers the more Greek sounding versions of the names, such as Achilleus and Hektor, I prefer to abide by the more prevalent usage in English (Achilles, Hector, Patroclus).

seech Achilles to hand over his son's body. This is depicted in one of the most striking extended similes in all of Homer:

> As when dense disaster closes on one who has murdered
> a man of his own land, and he comes to the country of others,
> to a man of substance, and *wonder* seizes on those who behold him,
> so Achilleus *wondered* as he looked at Priam, a godlike
> man, and the rest of them *wondered* also, and looked at each other.
> Homer (1951/2011: 510; 24.480–484; emphases added)

What makes this passage so striking? In fact, a number of things. Homer employs various forms of the word *thambos*, 'wonder' or 'marvel',[14] three times in order to highlight it. By the extended simile, the listeners or readers are reminded of Patroclus, whose death makes Achilles pursue and kill Hector, since Hector has slain Achilles' dear friend Patroclus. It was Patroclus who in his youth killed a man, which led to his exile and thus to his meeting Achilles. But, as the Homer scholar Richard Buxton (2004/2011: 154–155) has recently asked, who is the "man of substance" who "comes to the country of others"? It seems to be Priam, who enters Achilles' tent (part of Greek territory in the sense that it is on the land occupied by the Greek forces), but it could also be Achilles, who has entered into Priam's country. Also, unlike Patroclus, they are both rich but have only slain enemies in battle. What is crucial here and what mainly causes the wonder is that Achilles and Priam realize that, although enemies, they have much in common: they are both grieving for men they love, Achilles for Patroclus and Priam for Hector. Hence, Achilles relents and hands Hector's body to his father for proper burial rites. Even if the war goes on at the end of *The Iliad* this wondrous scene of appeasement points beyond the end of the epic to the peace that will follow.[15] Moreover, the wonder in the above quote refers twice to the audience in the tent watching the meeting between Achilles and Priam. Their being stunned is understandable, since such a meeting is unexpected and extraordinary, but they are also aware of the fact that the outcome of that meeting influences the course of their lives as warriors. Finally, of course Homer, like Shakespeare in *The Winter's Tale*, draws his audience – nowadays, his readers – into the scene by focusing on the wonder the audience in the tent may feel.

---

14 In Robert Fagles's (1990/1991: 604) translation *thambos* is rendered "marvel" and "marveled" in all instances.
15 This appeasement is in fact anticipated during the very battle between Achilles and Hector, since Achilles tells his combatant that the war god Ares will see to it that one of them must be killed and may imply that Ares could then be satisfied (Homer 1951/2011: 464; 22.261–267).

But what neither Buxton (2004/2011) nor any of the central commentators of *The Iliad*[16] mentions in their analyses of the scene is that what sparks the wonder in Achilles is the simile of a man who has murdered his countryman, which makes him think of Patroclus. But Achilles has no way of knowing about this simile and nothing else in the scene explicitly refers to his deceased brother in arms. That is, in this climactic scene Homer makes use of a subtle metalepsis (*sensu* Genette): he moves from narrative level to another – Achilles is apparently aware of what the narrator tells – and by doing so, he induces recognition in Achilles of how his grief is similar to that of Priam, and his fury subsides. Readers who note this blend of narrative, simile and metalepsis in *The Iliad* may have still another reason to marvel at what literature can do.

These three instances may show in quite different ways how a sense of wonder in literature can be communicated to its audience, which indicates that wonder is not only a kind of emotion that some literature communicates. It can occur in very different kinds of works, whose main focus – or *rasa/bhava* – can be quite different. In "In the Wilderness Is a Dead Deer" we marvel at the ambiguous juxtapositions and the way what happens last comes first; in *The Recognition of Śakuntalā* the entire course of the play displays how Duhsanta learns the meaning of true love and thus helps to lay the foundations of India as a nation; and in the last book of *The Iliad* the common humanity of the enemies is stressed in a complex way that points beyond its ending. The versatile ways in which wonder comes across may have to do with what was discussed at the start of chapter 5, G. E. R. Lloyd's notion that the *semantic stretch* of literature can combine the literal, metaphorical and mythical. In comparing especially Greek and Chinese usages, Lloyd (2012: 86) maintains that this stretch is "a pervasive characteristic manifested to a greater or lesser extent throughout all natural languages", even if its use in literature is best recognized. Perhaps his argument can be made use of in another way, so that one might claim that by the complexity of literature we may learn about the uses of behaviour and language we have not been aware of elsewhere and can then make use of in our lives. And such complexity in a literary work, whether formal, thematic or both, can give us a sense of wonder, which makes us remember it. This may turn the work it figures in into a classic, which in turn will ensure that its sense of wonder is not lost.

The examples I have used are a short lyrical poem and the climaxes in a play and an epic. But I would go on to claim that it can be lodged at the very start and

---

[16] Neither the six-volume compilation *The Iliad: A Commentary*, edited by G. S. Kirk (see especially Volume VI by Nicholas Richardson 1993: 323), nor the most thorough narratological study of *The Iliad* by Irene J. F. De Jong (1987) mentions Homer's use of metalepsis in this climactic scene.

carry the entire work. *The Odyssey*, you may remember, starts out like this: "Tell me, Muse, of the man of many ways, who was driven / far journeys, after he had sacked Troy's sacred citadel" (Homer 1951/2011: 27; 1.1–2). The man of many ways – or, in Fagels' translation, "the man of twists and turns" (Homer 1996/2006: 77) – is of course Odysseus. The epithet that is used of him is *polytropos*, 'resourceful', 'clever in many ways', with the latter part, *tropos*, meaning 'turn', 'direction' or 'way', that is, the basis of the English word *trope*, where the 'turn' is a figurative one. Thus, this one word – *polytropos* – signals much: it anticipates the action, which will have many turns; it portrays the protagonist, his life and cognitive disposition (resourceful); and suggests his language use (cunning in the use of tropes or figures), which metonymically stands for the entire epic. So a single word in the first line of *The Odyssey* represents the action, the character and language of what is to come. And what is to come is supposedly given to the narrator (and his many sub-narrators) by the very Muse, who is invoked by the narrator, who of course already is narrating. If a single word, which evidently is only mentioned once more in *The Odyssey* (Homer 1951/2011: 160; 10.330),[17] in an intriguing first line can do so much to create a complex anticipation of what is to be narrated, then it is no wonder that Homer keeps fascinating generation after generation, even in translation.

A final instance: Johann Wolfgang von Goethe (1819?/1969: 272) has the speaker in a brief poem called "Parabase" ("Parabasis") end his life-long study of the unity and complexity of nature by the beautiful line: "Zum Erstaunen bin ich da", which could be translated as "I am here for the wonder of it all" or "I exist in order to be amazed". This is one of the broadest definitions of wonder in human life: we are here to marvel at the wonder of being alive in a rather incomprehensible but utterly fascinating universe. Recently Raymond Tallis (2012b) has written about wonder from a similarly broad perspective. He notes that through what he encounters in his daily life, he, like all of us, "*should* be in a permanent state of wonder" (Tallis 2012b: 1). We have comparatively little definitive knowledge about the how, what and why of, say, the universe and human cognition, so there is much to marvel at.

But when it comes to literature, I would argue that as listeners, readers or audience as well as authors we learn about different themes and techniques to such an extent that we do not wonder at every turn, since we are well aware that literature, like all language, makes use of conventions. The thematic and formal means shaping literary worlds have been the topic of this book, and

---

[17] I make this claim based on the authority of Cunliffe's (1924/1977: 338) *A Lexicon of the Homeric Dialect*.

it is their complex and varied features that afford much wonder. In Margaret Anne Doody's (1996/1998: 479) words, the "truly invariable 'objective'" of the novel through the ages is that it *"makes us feel the sense of being alive"*, which I gather goes for all literature. When we encounter striking literary usages in theme or form, we savour them and pause to wonder at the riches literature can hold. We are here to be amazed not only at the universe but also at what some of its infinitesimal creatures on a blob of mud can create through their imagination.

9 Ten Reasons to Study and Teach Literary Worlds

Now let us consider how this comparative approach to the shaping of literary worlds can benefit scholars and students of literature. I would suggest that there are ten ways in which the import of this book can be useful in studying and teaching literature. In what follows, the points are introduced and exemplified by reference to some of the examples given above as well as to two age-old and much-varied literary features, one thematic, the other formal: the motif of star-crossed lovers and the genre of the fable, especially the animal fable. They can sometimes be combined, as when the lovers are different species of animal, bird or plant or one of the lovers (or his/her helper) is of, or turns into, another species.

A comparative focus on the imaginative makings of literary worlds:

(1) *Offers an overall view of what literature is.* The literature we have today is in part based on oral tradition and ever since literature has been written (for about five millennia), it has been given a wide variety in theme and form. It can be beneficial for scholars and students alike to see how the human imagination has gone about creating literary worlds, what its main themes are and how their variations are due to thematic and formal features. Such a comparative view of how literary worlds in various eras and cultures are shaped can make it easier to see what is truly original in individual literary works. And it covers all kinds of literature, from lowbrow to highbrow, from mythical adventures to postmodern novels, from riddles to poems to plays to epics.

When you see the musical *West Side Story* for the first time, you may have no idea that it is based on Shakespeare's *Romeo and Juliet* or you may be content with spotting that tragedy as its subtext: two young lovers finally die owing to the strife between their clans. But if you look more closely at the motif of "star-cross'd lovers" (the very notion of which derives from the Prologue of *Romeo and Juliet*; Shakespeare 1982/1987: 701; l. 6), you may find that Shakespeare used the even then traditional motif in his tragedy *Troilus and Cressida* (a love story set in Troy, in which neither lover dies), in his erotic allegorical narrative poem "Venus and Adonis" (where Adonis dies but not Venus; see Shakespeare 1989) as well as in the comically rendered play-within-a-play based on Pyramus and Thisbe in *A Midsummer Night's Dream* (V.i). If you continue to pursue Shakespeare's sources, you will notice that both the stories of Pyramus and Thisbe and of Venus and Adonis derive from Ovid's (1986/2008: 76–79, 241–248) classic narrative poem *Metamorphoses* (Books IV and X, respectively).

The search for sources could go on, but even with these findings, some conclusions can be drawn. The star-crossed love motif has been used in a variety of genres, from narrative poems to tragedy to comedy. Both lovers, one of them or neither may die and they may consummate their love, as in *Venus and Adonis*, or not. In broader terms, it may be helpful to understand that the motif of star-crossed lovers is a sub-motif of the main literary theme of human or human-like relation and that it is so popular and effective, since it usually combines the two kinds of basic relation: cordial (love, often heterosexual, but not necessarily so)[1] and hostile (warring clans or the like that make the love doomed).[2] Also, the very fact that the love is obstructed implies a major challenge, thus making use of another major theme of literary world-making, in this case to perform a task, that is, to fulfil their love by marriage and/or sexual intercourse. In the course of doing so, the lovers often portray their love in highly perceptive and metaphorical terms, as in the famous balcony scene in *Romeo and Juliet* (II.ii), which draws on the third main theme of literature: perception, both as such and figuratively rendered (Juliet as the sun). Moreover, understanding the generic, formal and thematic differences of various versions can help us understand what makes, say, Romeo and Juliet so different from Ovid's Pyramus and Thisbe and from Italian versions of Romeo and Juliet. Then one can go into greater detail what is original in motif (say, the mulberry tree as a symbol for forbidden love in Ovid), form (the greater emphasis on other members of the rivalling clans in Shakespeare) and moral (the rivalling clans are expressly reconciled in Shakespeare but only implicitly in Ovid).

As for the connection between star-crossed love and the fable, it is central in Ovid, since the blood of the lovers forever colours the mulberry bush purple and Venus sprinkles nectar on the blood of the deceased Adonis and it becomes a "blood-red flower", the anemone (Ovid 1986/2008: 78, 248 quote). In Shakespeare's (1989: 103; l. 1168) *Venus and Adonis* a "purple flower sprung up" of Adonis' blood, but in his plays with star-crossed love mainly Puck's fleeting transformation of Bottom's head into that of a donkey in *A Midsummer Night's Dream* is a comic reminder of the metamorphoses in Ovid.[3]

---

[1] For instance, Annie Proulx's (1999/2006) short story "Brokeback Mountain" (made into a famous film in 2005 by Ang Lee) is an example of how the homosexual love between Ennis and Jack, two latter-day cowboys, is thwarted by a homophobic society, not by a clash of allegiance to clans or the like.

[2] That is, the love depicted is often more than simply star-crossed, since human intentions actively go against the lovers' relationship.

[3] Often humans turn into animals, birds or plants, but in the classic Chinese novel *A Dream of Red Mansions* a goddess makes a stone acquire "spiritual understanding" in the first pages and then the stone becomes the narrator. Some pages later a plant becomes human (see Cao and Gao 1978/2008: Vol. I: 2, 8–9).

Such comparative analysis can be pursued at length. Thus, a broader view of literature encompassing modal, thematic and formal aspects can give a range of insights into how literary worlds are shaped.

(2) *Helps to avoid (Western) cultural bias.* Much of what is taught in literary studies, at least in the Western world, has, understandably perhaps, a rather strong Western bias, both in the primary and secondary material. The reading lists are seldom very surprising. Few scholars or students of literature are as enterprising as John Barth (1984: 9), who besides studying literature botanised avidly in Classics and Oriental Studies at Johns Hopkins University, so that he later was able to state: "I was permanently impressed with the *size* of literature and its wild variety". To be sure, few have the benefit of a university of such distinction, but many universities have fairly decent university libraries. Still, it should not be the students' responsibility to search out non-Western classics, which ought to be part of the curriculum in one way or another, if for nothing else, in order for students to understand what is truly original in Western literature. The real reason is of course that classics of the East, ancient and modern, are among the greatest literary riches.

So how can Western literature better be understood by reading non-Western literary works – and the other way around? Tristan (Tristram) and Yseut (Iseult, in later versions Isolde) is among the most widespread tales of star-crossed love in the West. Versions are found in a great number of European languages after the French poems from the twelfth century by Thomas of Britain (or Brittany) and Béroul. For centuries, this love story has spawned so many different versions in literature (most recently perhaps, John Updike's novel *Brazil* from 1994), music and art that it has also informed Western views of love. The story itself is based on a Celtic romance, but recently many critics, most notably Dick Davis (2008/2009: xxxii–xlii), have on good grounds argued that it draws heavily on the mid-eleventh-century Persian epic poem *Vis and Ramin* by Fakhraddin Gorgani. Davis (2008/2009: xxxi–xxxiii) also shows how *Vis and Ramin* influenced Nizami (or Nezami) Ganjavi, a twelfth-century Persian romance author, who was to be highly influential for Persian and Near Eastern literature. But to the best of my knowledge nobody has been able to fully explain what even in the twelfth-century versions – such as that the anonymous verse narrative called "The Tale of Tristan's Madness" (*Folie Tristan*) – seems like rather unwarranted madness, apparently only feigned in part (see Beroul 1970: 151–164). That is, for no apparent reason, Tristan disguises himself as a madman and enters the court and raves in front of King Mark about his love for his wife, Yseut the queen.

Nizami's (1997/2011) verse romance *The Story of Layla and Majnun* from 1188 about a pair of star-crossed lovers of so-called virgin love (in which the love is not consummated) was published too late to be able to influence "The Tale of

Tristan's Madness". But it was based on a well-known and widespread Bedouin tale of a youth called Qays, who may have lived in North Africa in the seventh century. According to legend, Qays fell so madly in love with a girl called Layla that he was called Majnun (Madman). Together with Ovid, who has been called "the most popular writer throughout the twelfth century [in Europe]" (Kibler 1991/2004: 7), *Vis and Ramin* and the legend of Layla and Majnun may – by oral transmission, perhaps – have affected the medieval retellings of the Celtic legend, thus perhaps prompting Tristan's raving. In Persian literature (as well as that of other countries in the Near East and beyond), on the other hand, the tale of Layla's and Majnun's unconsummated love became a suitable topic for other Sufi mystics, who read Nizami's allegorical combination of love, madness and poetic genius in Majnun as an Islamic tale of divine love, only to be consummated in Heaven (see e.g. Gelpke 1966/2011). In fact, it may in part have been intended as such, much like Farid ud-Din Attar's *The Conference of the Birds* written at about the same time in Persia, an allegorical tale of how the various birds led by the hoopoe, after some quibble and hardships, find their ideal king, the Simorgh bird, by becoming and constituting Simorgh themselves (see below). This work may in turn be informed by bird descriptions in the ancient Indian collection of fables *The Pañcatantra* (especially the fight between crows and owls in Book III); by the heavenly city built by the birds, led by the hoopoe in Aristophanes' *The Birds*; as well as by the bird metamorphoses in Ovid's (1986/2008: 142) *Metamorphoses* (especially the tale of Tereus, Procne and Philomela in Book VI, in which they all turn into birds, with King Tereus turning into a hoopoe). Or we can go back to Western Europe and think of how Chaucer's "The Parliament of Fowls" (discussed in 4.4) and *The Canterbury Tales* may both draw on motifs from *The Conference of the Birds*.[4]

To take a more modern example, in the Argentinian author Adolfo Bioy Casares's (1940/2003) Kafkaesque science-fiction classic *The Invention of Morel*, the narrator on a faraway island falls in love with a girl called Faustine, only to realize that she and her friends visiting the island are reproductions of people who once spent a week there. As he learns to use the machine projecting the reproductions, the narrator can insert himself into the projection, even if it entails that he will never be able to actually talk to, let alone touch, Faustine, which makes it a rather original version of star-crossed love. Such Wellsian[5] thematics of humans living in technological illusions produced by people with Faust-like hu-

---

[4] For a comparative study of *The Canterbury Tales* and *The Conference of the Birds* see Khoshbakht, Ahmadian and Hekmat (2013).
[5] The questionable use of science by the reproduction machine invented by a man called Morel on a remote island draws on H. G. Wells's novel *The Island of Doctor Moreau* (1896).

bris has exerted a considerable influence on Latin American fiction and European art film, not least by Alain Robbe-Grillet's script for Alain Resnais's *Last Year in Marienbad* (1961), as well as on works in different media thematizing reproduced life, from Philip K. Dick's novel *Ubik* (1969) to Christopher Nolan's film *Inception* (2010).

My point is not just that there is influence from East to West and West to East but rather to recognize how widespread common themes have been and how they cross genres and media. As John Barth (1984: 9) puts it, the sheer size and variety of literature is bound to astonish. Still, for literary scholars and students such astonishment should be the starting-point for deeper study. In terms of more recent literature, this means that, say, the motif of star-crossed lovers must be looked into in detail. In Mo Yan's (1988/2006) novel *The Garlic Ballads* the main plot is about the actual farmers' uprising in the spring of 1987 against officials who told them to grow garlic, but then refused to buy it in Mo Yan's childhood hometown of Gaomi in Eastern China. In fact, uprisings are a traditional theme in Chinese literature, as old as *Tso Chuan* (or *Zuo Zhuan*) (1989: 5–16 *et passim*), the oldest extant Chinese prose collection from the fourth century BCE and the classic fourteenth-century novel *Outlaws of the Marsh* (or *Water Margin*). The subplot of *The Garlic Ballads* is about how one of the rebels, the poor young ex-soldier Gao Ma, falls in love with the girl next door, Jinju, whom her family, against current regulations, has decided to marry off to someone else as a kind of barter marriage. This motif of star-crossed lovers with at least one family going against the marriage (both lovers are badly beaten and finally die) is mainly used to illustrate the clash between tradition and modernization in contemporary China, thus reinforcing the main theme. In fact, since the clash between divinely inspired love and arranged marriages is to be found in classic Asian tales of star-crossed love, such as "The Butterfly Lovers" (see below) and "Heer Ranjha", the Punjabi legend of star-crossed love, Mo Yan may have drawn on both Eastern and Western sources for his motif.[6]

(3) *Provides contextualization*. As we have just seen, the avoidance of cultural bias can easily lead not only to better contextualization in terms of world literature but also to a more specific understanding of the work in the field of indigenous (or related) literature. If the previous section showed how a broad intercultural view can be of use when analysing literary works, I now try to show that a more detailed contextualization in terms of indigenous (or neighbouring) cul-

---

[6] For a retelling of Waris Shah's classic version of "Heer Ranjha" (1766) and some comments on its critical view of arranged marriages see Gill (2003: 3–35, esp. 11–12).

tures can help to identify the sources of what may look like variations on widespread Western motifs. One example is ancient, the other contemporary.

When the medieval Indian classic story collection *Vetālapañćaviṁśati* was first translated into English, it was called *Vikram and the Vampire or Tales of Hindu Devilry* (by Sir Richard Burton in 1870) and later *Twenty-Two Goblins* (by Arthur William Ryder in 1917). Burton may have had in mind John Polidori's well-known novella *The Vampyre* from 1819 and thought the Indian collection would be more easily understood or be more popular, if he used "vampire" in the title. However, like "goblin", "vampire" is rather misleading, since the being in question is a *vetāla* or genie, "a suprahuman being similar to the djinn", according to a more recent translator (Rajan 1995/2006: xvii). Domesticating the *vetāla* into a vampire or a goblin thus simply misses the point of the much more versatile spirit creature, and in fact later translations, in the recension by Śivadāsa (1995/2006), is called *The Five-and-Twenty Tales of the Genie*. By a better indigenous contextualization of *vetāla*, readers understand their nature and the *Vetālapañćaviṁśati* better.

Another novel by Mo Yan, *Life and Death Are Wearing Me Out*, tells the story of a respectable landowner, Ximen Nao, who dies, goes to hell and is reborn as a donkey, an ox, a pig, a dog, a monkey and finally as a boy with a big head and a gift for memorizing and writing. It is evident from the start that the metamorphoses do not draw on the Ovidian tradition but on Buddhist reincarnation, more precisely a mural version of "The Six Stages of Samsara" that the author happened to come across in 2005 (see Mo Yan 2012). As Ximen Nao's various animal reincarnations imply, the animal realm of the Samsara is represented by five reincarnations and a human in one, and the hell realm by Ximen Nao's brief visits there between most of his reincarnations. What is more, the title of the novel implies that the novel is a satire of reincarnation. However, through the various animals Mo Yan tells the story of China from the late 1940s, when Ximen Nao is executed during the Communist takeover, to the end of the year 2000, when neo-capitalist tendencies are evident. In other words, the story reflects the various stages of the Communist regime by Ximen Nao's reincarnations and the lives of his relatives, friends, employees and offspring.

But this modern history is given a historical and literary frame in that at the start of the novel some villagers are staging *Journey to the West* (Mo Yan 2006/2012: 8). This classic Chinese novel that portrays the journey of the monk Tripitaka, Monkey and Pigsy to India to find the ancient Buddhist scripture is an allegorical story of spiritual quest, in which Monkey and Pigsy undergo a number of transformations. Finally, as Ximen Nao is reborn as a monkey and then as a big-headed boy telling the story (that is, the novel) its readers are just about to finish, the connection is corroborated in a metafictional way. Formally too, Mo

Yan follows the classic Chinese novel form: all chapters, except the epilogue, have double titles that mirror their double contents. In this way, Mo Yan's novel is steeped in the (Chinese) Buddhist tradition and the classic Chinese novel, while at the same time renewing them through satire and offering an oblique history of Communist China.

What is more, Mo Yan makes use of classic Chinese legends and foktales, most memorably perhaps the tragic one of star-crossed love called "The Butterfly Lovers",[7] set in the Jin Dynasty (265–420 CE). But Mo Yan (2006/2012: 308–314) gives the story a few twists: Ximen Nao is now a pig and Butterfly Lover is the name of a sow he has set his eyes on; he fights the leading pig for her, wins the scuffle and mounts her. Later, still as a pig, he meets another sow called Little Flower whom he loves dearly and who tragically dies in his hoofs having been bitten on the rump by a savage boar (Mo Yan 2006/2012: 337–343). Hence, even in his pig reincarnation Ximen Nao tells two versions of star-crossed love, one comic and one tragic. In fact, in the classic Chinese realist novel *A Dream of Red Mansions* the main plot turns on the protagonist Jia Baoyu's love of two women, but he leaves one and marries the other, only to leave her in turn and become a monk (see Cao and Gao 1978/2008), thus exemplifying doubly star-crossed love that Ximen Nao's love for two sows may parody. In other words, Mo Yan makes use of both the motif of star-crossed love and animal transformations, but in ways that mainly draw on indigenous themes and genres, which makes his novel better understood if contextualized accordingly.

(4) *Eschews chronological (modern) bias.* If you play the role-playing video game *Final Fantasy VII*, if you watch the television series *Buffy the Vampire Slayer*, or if you read any book or watch any film of the *Twilight* (originally by Stephenie Meyer) or *Hunger Games* series (originally by Suzanne Collins), you come across star-crossed lovers. This goes for major characters in *Superman*, *Star Wars*, *Titanic*, *Brokeback Mountain* and *Avatar* as well – and the list can be extended at will.[8] That is, contemporary popular narratives in different genres and media – comic books, science fiction, adventure and vampire stories, romance and cowboy fiction and film – usually focus on or spice up their plots by star-crossed love.

Similarly, fables and metamorphoses come in a number of guises in recent popular culture: in the anime series *Pokémon* and *Digimon* the characters evolve

---

[7] For four different versions of the Chinese legend of "The Butterfly Lovers" see Idema (2010). In fact, Idema (2010: xiin1) notes that a survey in 2007 found 878 different adaptations in different media in China alone. Multiple versions are also found in South Korea, North Korea and Indonesia.
[8] For more examples see for instance the Wikipedia article "Star-crossed".

and take different shapes; in Bill Willingham's comic-book series *Fables* classic fairytale characters have been forced to move to New York City; and in David Sedaris's short-story collection *Squirrel Seeks Chipmunk. A Wicked Bestiary* (2010) animals take on contemporary human roles in delightfully humorous and amoral upgradings of La Fontaine's verse fables from the seventeenth century.⁹

In order to understand the functions of an early fable, it can be enlightening to consider one of the first fantastic stories, *The Tale of the Shipwrecked Sailor* (1998/2009: 92–98), written about four thousand years ago in Egypt. The frame tale is entirely realistic: in a dialogue a sailor tries to console a count who has returned with an empty ship and worries about how he will be received by the king. The way he does it is by telling, supposedly "free <from> exaggeration" (l. 14), the tale of how he was in even worse circumstances, facing a dragon-like serpent with magical powers, who in turn, in a doubly embedded story, tells how he in turn faced an even greater calamity, a kind of apocalypse. Thus, the embedded stories are fantastic, but the frame story is entirely realistic, so much so that the sailor early on tells the count: "A man's utterance saves him. / His speech turns anger away from him" (ll. 18–19). When the sailor has finished his tale, the count dismisses his tale as mere fanciful yarns as he is about to have his reckoning with the king. Here ends the tale, but the ones who heard or read it may understand the sailor's point: you can learn something by narratives (whether fantastic or not), so that even though the count does not learn anything from the sailor's tale, readers do (that is, the count should come up with a colourful subterfuge to tell the king). In this tale from the Middle Kingdom in Egypt, at the very beginnings of written literature, we can see that realism and fable, dialogue and narration, are blended, that unreliable narration can teach important morals and that stories can be multiply embedded.¹⁰ Often such features are considered modern, even postmodern, but in fact they occur even in the first extant written literature.

Not knowing anything about the history of star-crossed love or of fables leads to a rather skewed perspective of literature and film and makes it impossible to eval-

---

9 See Mikkonen (1997) for readings of metamorphoses in postwar fiction.
10 I am no Egyptologist, but still I am rather surprised when reading the comments on *The Tale of the Shipwrecked Sailor* by some leading names in ancient Egyptian literary studies: Miriam Lichtheim (1973/2006: 10) speaks of "the simply told tale of the shipwrecked sailor" and R. B. Parkinson (1998/2009: 91) claims that the count's "dismissal casts doubt on [the sailor's] moral, on the capacity of speech to change things", a moral that to me seems the very point of the story.

uate the extent to which they are novel in character and plot and in what sense they in fact adhere to or combine existing genres, motifs and techniques.

(5) *Facilitates understanding generic features.* Comparative and detailed study of literary themes and techniques and their relation to each other can clarify their generic features, just as genres can help to explain particular features in literary works. Shakespeare's (1987: 728) *Romeo and Juliet* is a tragedy, so the fate of the lover can be summed up by the Prince of Verona in the last famous lines: "For never was a story of more woe, / Than this of Juliet and her Romeo". But in Ovid (1986/2008: 193), in keeping with his focus on metamorphoses, the faithful lovers Philemon and Baucis turn to "Two trees from one twin trunk grown side by side" (metamorphosis and union in one). In yet another version, by La Fontaine (2007: 358), their passionate love slowly turns into friendship, so that at death they simply turn to oak and linden, respectively, and the speaker sighs about true love: "Alas! For me, too late!" Hence, the genres – from mythical narrative (Ovid) to fable (La Fontaine) to tragedy (Shakespeare) – has particular versions of the motif, possibly owing to the demands of each genre.

On the face of it, the stories of the Persian *Vis and Ramin* by Gorgani and *The Story of Layla and Majnun* by Nizami have much in common: the lovers go through many hardships before they are united in the afterlife. But most importantly perhaps, Vis and Ramin consummate their love, both when married to others and finally when married to each other, while Layla and Majnun do not, even if they could have. In fact, there is a long line of wives (or fiancées-to-be) who have lovers, from ancient to Renaissance literature: not just Vis and Layla, but also Helen (of *The Iliad*), Zhu Yingtai (of "The Butterfly Lovers"), Iseut/Isolde and Criseyde/Cressida. Thus, in this sense it is rather strange that Gustave Flaubert's Madame Bovary and Kate Chopin's Edna Pontellier as well as hundreds of female characters in lesser novels had to fight such fierce fights as "fallen women" even in the nineteenth century.

But the fact that the love is unconsummated in Nizami's work is only a symptom of its change in genre: it may be a romance like Gorgani's work, but it turns love into a Sufi allegory of the human soul. The final dream by a character called Zayd, even if left out in some editions of *Layla and Majnun*, clarifies the Sufi teaching: "This world is dust and perishable. That world is pure and eternal. [---] Commit yourself to love's sanctuary and at once find freedom from your ego" (Nizami 1997/2011: 176). In Nizami, love is merely means to the end of reaching Heaven, while in Gorgani it is an end in itself. In fact, *Vis and Ramin* reads like a surprisingly modern love story, albeit with a mythical touch: both get married to others while the love story goes on, even if they finally are married and live for over eighty years as King and Queen. Still, even Gorgani (2008/2009: 497) ends on a devout note: "We live in two worlds, one flies quickly past / The other one's the one we know will last". But having savoured thousands of lines about the joys of this world, many readers may not be convinced by such a pious stand on the supposed bliss of that world. This shows how understanding the genre and the literary work is co-dependent: when you recognize the genre you grasp the meaning of the work, and the other way around. But you need not be fooled by the alleged intention of the author or narrator.

(6) *Pinpoints specific and innovative aspects of literary works* by (7) *analysing it thematically* and/or (8) *formally*. In the previous points some unrecognized aspects of literary works have been discussed, in both theme and form. Many instances of thematic analysis of star-crossed love have already been touched on, and even classics, we have seen, can be viewed in a new light. Another example is Dante Alighieri, whose semi-autobiographical prosimetrum (combining prose and verse) work *The New Life* (*La Vita Nuova*) from 1295 is, like so much courtly love poetry, an instance of star-crossed love: Dante's love for Beatrice is never consummated. What may be less readily recognized is that his *The Divine Comedy*, in which Beatrice is his guide from Purgatory to Heaven, can be read as a religious allegory of not only divine love but also courtly love. It is by now well-known that Dante was influenced by Islamic philosophy, but it may be less acknowledged that his Christian allegory is much like the Sufi allegories of divine love.[11] Still, there is some discrepancy: Majnun is mad with love for Layla and their love takes them to Heaven, whereas Dante is much more rational and is guided, by Virgil and Beatrice, all the way to Heaven. Yet as the persona in *The Divine Comedy*, Dante too may represent the human soul making its anagogical way up to the stars (which are mentioned in the last line of all three parts, Inferno, Purgatorio and Paradiso), but it is his love for Beatrice that ultimately guides him to Heaven. That is, just as Layla and Majnun, Dante reaches Heaven by means of his (unconsummated) love. At the end of Paradiso, Dante's (1993/2008: 499) human love has brought him to divine love, as his desire and his will "Were being turned like a wheel, all at one speed, // By the love which moves the sun and the other stars". Dante's star-crossed love for Beatrice in *The New Life* has finally been divinely consummated, as he reaches the stars symbolizing Heaven in *The Divine Comedy*.

A twist in the use of a motif, such as star-crossed love, can change its import, also generically. In chapter XVIII of Twain's (1884/1988: 142–155) *Adventures of Huckleberry Finn* there is the story of a family feud between the Shepherdsons and the Grangerfords, but the children of those families, Miss

---

11 Dick Davis (2011: xix) also detects a number of affinities between *The Divine Comedy* and another Sufi classic, Attar's *The Conference of the Birds*, which is discussed below.

Sophia and Harney, have fallen in love with each other. Twain's take on star-crossed love is rather Swiftian, since no-one in the family seems to remember exactly how the feud started, and the young lovers are about to elope when Huck moves on. In other words, as motifs, feuding is satirized and star-crossed love à la *Romeo and Juliet* is given a happy ending in keeping with the (mainly) comic novel in which it is included. The novel form thus requires a change from tragedy to comedy (with a touch of satire) in these motifs, which in turn reinforce the light-hearted down-to-earth character of Huck Finn as a fallible but morally upright narrator, since the feud makes him "sick", his characteristic reaction to immoral behaviour.

A comparative view of literary world-making can even on a formal level easily discern how differently fables work. An easy way to check a focal point of the fable is to locate its moral: it either comes across as a *promythium* (before the tale), *epimythium* (after) or *endomythium* (inside). The *Pañćatantra* by Visnu Śarma (1993) makes use of promythium, since the point is told so as to lure readers into the story, but it also has a frame story of how three princes through the stories should learn to use their brains. Aesop's *Fables* has no frame story, but offers a moral in an epimythium or, at times, a promythium for each story. In his *Fables* La Fontaine (2007) draws on both Aesop and Indian stories,[12] but lodges the moral as an endomythium, usually close to the end of the fable. In his versions of classic fairytales Charles Perrault (2009/2010), La Fontaine's contemporary, usually provides two different epimythical morals, hence suggesting that the moral of a story can be multiple.

However, fables and especially their pointed morals already irritated Jean-Jacques Rousseau in his *Émile or On Education* (1762), a view that has become more widespread ever since.[13] In fact, as Annabel Patterson (1991: 5) shows at length, fables have always included endomythical morals, especially politically subversive ones: "Built into the poetics of the fable [...] is the notion that the fable had from its origins functioned as a self-protective way of communication, whether by a slave addressing the Master society, or by an aristocrat whose political party is currently in defeat". Her view may be most apposite for the Renaissance and sixteenth- and seventeenth-century authors she primarily discusses, but she makes a convincing case that fables often have been endomythical, more recently by allegory, as in Orwell's *Animal Farm*, or by less pointed morals. It is common knowledge that by sentimentalizing politics, sex and vio-

---

12 La Fontaine read a French translation of fables by Pilpay (aka Bidpai), evidently an apocryphal author standing for a collection of stories mostly from *The Pañćatantra*.
13 See Lewis (2012) for an analysis of how Rousseau despite his critical view of fables in fact was informed by them.

lence, Walt Disney and his collaborators have for over half a century made fables palatable for a family audience. But not all recent fables are thus "disneyfied". James Thurber's (1945/1954: esp. 205–231) fables with new twists to explicitly stated morals are a case in point, as are David Sedaris's (2010/2012: 15–21) recent implicitly moral fables, not least "The Squirrel and the Chipmunk". This story makes use of the star-crossed lovers theme in that the chipmunk leaves her lover (egged on by her mother), owing to the fact that she is prejudiced enough to think that the squirrel's interest in "jazz", which she has never heard or even heard of, must be immoral. The moral is there, if only implied: prejudice may preclude personal happiness.

Thus, specific and innovative uses of the themes and techniques shaping literary worlds can be better distinguished through a comparative view. Now let us see how this is done by two further examples of how theme and form can be tightly linked. A complex instance of plot and character merging is to be found in *The Conference of the Birds*, Farid ud-Din Attar's Sufi masterpiece from the twelfth century. Here, a variety of birds come together to search for their ideal king, the imaginary Simorgh bird from ancient Persian mythology.[14] Thirty of Attar's birds finally reach a herald who tells them to read the story of how Joseph in Genesis (37:2–36) is sold into slavery by his brothers envying the prophetic dreams he has (*The Holy Bible* 1980/1987: 41–42). The birds realize that they, like Joseph's brothers, have sinned and by acknowledging their shame, they perceive the "ever-living Light" of their illusory king:

> There in the Simorgh's radiant face they saw
> Themselves, the Simorgh of the world – with awe
> They gazed, and dared at last to comprehend
> They were the Simorgh at the journey's end.
> They see the Simorgh – at themselves they stare,
> And see a second Simorgh standing there;
> They look at both and see the two are one,
> That this is that, that this, the goal is won.
> (Attar 1984/2011: 234; ll. 4234–4241)

In terms of world-making, this must be one of the most carefully planned climaxes in any literature, especially if you get the pun in Persian: *si* means 'thirty' and *morgh* 'bird(s)' (see Attar 1986/2011: 268n25). It combines all three major literary

---

[14] This joint avian effort may well in part have been inspired by Aristophanes' (2005: 333–414) delightfully absurd comedy *The Birds* from 414 BCE, in which various species of birds band together to build a city in the sky called Cloudcuckooland and the human protagonist Peisetairus, dressed up as a bird, finally weds a princess in heaven.

themes: the birds have met the *challenge* of seeking out the Simorgh; they finally *perceive* – see, gaze, stare at – the Simorgh, thus ending their quest; and they themselves make up the Simorgh. It is their mutual *relation* and combined effort that accomplishes the task: they themselves are the very essence of the Simorgh.[15] Moreover, the entire allegorical plot – or extended metaphor turned into narrative, if you like – comes together as *this* (the thirty birds) and *that* (the Simorgh) become one, after over four thousand lines. This union of course entails merging the earthly realm with Heaven, and completes the Sufi allegory of *The Conference of the Birds*. At this point, as readers we have finished reading the allegory, just as the thirty birds fulfil their dream of finding the Simorgh by having read Genesis, in which Joseph eventually was to fulfil his dreams. Like the birds, we feel a sense of wonder as the creation of a literary – and spiritual – world is completed.

(9) *Contributes to literary theory.* As a term, *theory* comes from the Greek *theōrein*, 'to view', just as *method* has its root in the Greek *méthodos*, 'course', 'way' or 'road'. So when you use a theory and apply it as a method in literary studies, what you are doing, in somewhat simplified metaphorical terms, is that you survey your material from one or more points of view and then take the path or paths that you find most rewarding when analysing it. As the above points have suggested, what focusing on how literary worlds are shaped contributes to literary theory is to afford both comparative and analytical perspectives that may enrich the insights along the methodological paths taken. It can be used by comparativists examining literature from various cultures, but since such comparative efforts, however commendable, are rather rare, it may be of even more use to students and scholars working in the literature of particular languages.

As the term implies, then, theory often provides a particular perspective. In literary theory such perspectives often focus on some aspects of literary communication, including the intentions of the author (biographical), the form and contents of the literary work (Russian formalist, new critical, narratological, structuralist), social or ideological thematics (Marxist, feminist, postcolonial, gay, lesbian and queer, ecocritical) or interpretation (poststructuralist, hermeneutic and reader-oriented theories). I would suggest, then, that analysing literary worlds, their origins in the human imagination and literary representation, their thematic and formal features and their relations to the actual world in

---

15 In his *The Masnavi*, at times called the Persian *Qur'an*, Attar's younger contemporary Jalal al-Din Rumi (2004/2008, 2007/2008) makes central use of the mirror metaphor suggested here: the soul or heart as a reflection of heaven or eternity. By the way, some of the Sufi wisdom in *The Masnavi* is expressed in fables.

which they have been created, can be of use as such or as an aid to any literary theory. Since I have mainly focused on literary worlds as such, it is evident that the approach presented here is most useful in textual and contextual study, even though how they are created and interpreted of course can be part and parcel of any broader view of literary communication.

The works discussed in this chapter might give rise to questions throughout the spectrum of literary theory: How aware were the authors of the motifs they were using or the genre or genres they were writing in? What forms have the fable or the motif of star-crossed love had in various cultures? What do cordial and hostile relations in literature tell us about the societies at the time it was written, also in terms of the history of colonialism? How are gender roles in star-crossed love portrayed in different literatures at different times? What can fables – especially animal fables – convey about the relations between humans, animals and plants? And by what means can we as scholars come to some kind of interpretive validity, however relative, in trying to answer such questions? In other words, all existing literary theories can make use of, build on and develop a comparative study of literary worlds.

(10) *Revives literary studies*. In chapter 4 we saw that the three major themes of literature in different modes and genres through the ages are (variations of) human or human-like *challenge*, *perception* and *relation*. Thus, as a mnemonic and pedagogical aid, however facetious, we could speak of *CPR*. That is, even if not in an acute danger of expiring, literary studies may be in need of some sort of cardiopulmonary resuscitation to revive them. But the CPR that this study offers is not just based on its three main themes but on the comparative poetics it has presented of how literary worlds are shaped. This broad view of literature across ages and cultures is intended as a starting-point for more detailed studies of particular literatures and authors. And literary imagination matters because it is all about what it means to be human and living together with other organisms on this planet. It is apparent that it continues to do so, also through new genres and media. So evidently literature continues to matter, but it is up to us as literary scholars to show that literary studies are able to provide an enriching understanding of it, which in turn throws light on the plight of some conscious pieces of matter on this blob of mud called earth. Hence, literary studies too should matter, both to students, scholars and the general public.

Conclusion

Having considered how literary worlds are shaped by imaginative uses of mimesis, how they are made up of different themes and techniques and how we in turn are shaped by them while they provide us with delight, benefit and wonder, we can see that the account presented here offers a comparative poetics, that is, encompasses some of the most salient means of which literature is made – in the Greek sense of *poieîn* – in various cultures.

The makings, I maintain, are the individual and shared human imagination, which creates literary worlds that blend the real and the fantastic, mimesis and genre (chapters 1 and 2). In their narration, characterization and exposition such worlds are often modulated by different kinds of unreliability (chapter 3). The main building blocks of literary worlds are three modes – the oral, the visual and the written – and three themes: challenge, perception and relation (chapter 4). Excepting unreliability, these modes and themes are combined and inflected in different ways by combinations of narratives and figures as well as by indirection, thwarted aspirations, meta-usages, hypothetical action and hierarchies and blends of genre and text type (chapters 5 and 6). Moreover, literary worlds are not only constructed by human beings but also shape their lives and the world they inhabit (chapter 7). And literature matters because it gives benefit as well as delight and strengthens the sense of wonder of being alive (chapter 8). Finally, ten reasons are given to show how this comparative view of the makings of literary worlds can be useful for literary studies (chapter 9).

In the introduction I grouped these chapters into three clusters: a general one on imagination, literary imagination, mimesis and unreliability (chapters 1 to 3), a specific one on literary worlds and their inflections (chapters 4 to 6) and a world-oriented one on the effects of literary worlds on the real world (chapters 7 to 9). By way of conclusion, let me now consider what more we can learn about those three aspects and the uses of literary imagination in broader terms by commenting on some mythical and literary works from different times and cultures: Australian aboriginal myths and pre-Columbian Mesoamerican literature, the utopian novella *The Description of a New World, Called the Blazing World* (1666) by Margaret Cavendish, Duchess of Newcastle, and Siri Hustvedt's postmodern take on its theme in her novel *The Blazing World* (2014) as well as two other rather dissimilar contemporary authors, the Russian concrete poet Lev Rubinstein (b. 1947) and the American horror fiction author Thomas Ligotti (b. 1953).

In fact, surprisingly perhaps, the literary worlds of this disparate material seem to make use of some related features. In terms of the first cluster of imagination, mimesis and unreliability, it spans imagination and popular imagination in various ways. Understandably, in being oral, indigenous Australian myths draw on the popular imagination of mythical "Dreaming", which unites the mythic past with the present by grounding it in location.[1] The extant ancient Mesoamerican literature has a broad range of genres, in which some of the texts can be attributed to specific authors, while others have been orally transmitted for centuries before having been written down, often originally by Spanish clergymen (which may colour the rendition). But texts by specific authors can also draw on popular imagination or genres, however idiosyncratic they may seem. Cavendish's fantastic *The Blazing World* clearly makes use of the utopian tradition from Plato's *Republic* to Thomas More's *Utopia*, but also of romances and travelogues, especially parodies on travelogues, such as Lucian's *A True Story*. Hustvedt, of course, follows in Cavendish's footsteps, but adds features of the postmodern novel, fictional biography and the realist novel (of the New York art world) in her composite construction of notebook fragments, articles, interviews, written statements and edited transcripts. Rubinstein renews the Russian Oberiu avant-garde of the 1920s and 1930s and Ligotti the horror fiction tradition, especially that of the philosophical and largely psychological horror of Edgar Allan Poe and H. P. Lovecraft.

As this may suggest, all these texts and their authors are rather differently situated on the spectrum of literary mimesis from the real to the fantastic. Still, even what may seem closer to the latter end often has a grounding in the life world of its culture. Ronald M. Berndt and Catherine H. Berndt (1994: 4), compilers of a prodigious anthology of indigenous Australian myths, claim that for Aboriginal people, their mythology "was and is like a huge mirror that reflected – sometimes dimly, sometimes in an exaggerated way, sometimes phantasmagorically – what was familiar to them, something they expected to see and something that they could identify". Traditional Mesoamerican literature was evidently part and parcel of the social life: sacred narratives, hymns, prayers and ceremonies served to strengthen the devotion and pass on its traditions; metaphysical, war and bawdy poems had their respective uses; and so did dramatic, political, prophetic and historical literature as well as proverbs and conundrums (see Léon-Portilla and Shorris 2001). In hindsight, we can say that Cavendish, her gender-bending personality and her novella portraying an allegorical feminist utopia with hybrid species have had a significant effect on fem-

---

[1] For an informed reading of "Dreaming" (or rather "Dreamings") see Swain (1993/1997: 14–28, esp. 21), who shows that the common synonymous epithet "Dreamtime" is based on a mistranslation. Even the indigenous activist and author Oodgeroo Noonuccal (1990: 8) at times uses it in her writings, even though she is aware that the notion it is based on (*Alcheringa* or *Altjiringa*) is "renamed 'Dreamtime' without our permission".

inism, which is evident not only in Hustvedt's portrayal of the misogynistic art world but also in the use Virginia Woolf (1928/2000: 62) makes of her in *A Room of One's Own* as a precursor – the "hare-brained, fantastical Margaret of Newcastle" – as well as a possible inspiration for the speculation on the fate of Shakespeare's hypothetical sister Judith. When launching her fantastic voyage, Cavendish (1666/2004: 123, 124, 224) maintains that "fancy creates of its own accord whatsoever it pleases", so she decides to make "a world of [her] own", and ends by stating that her "ambition is not only to be Empress", like her fictional character, "but Authoress of a whole world".

Rubinstein (2004: v), an ex-librarian, creates not poems or poetry collections but card decks consisting of library file cards in what he terms "meta-texts" that seem to X-ray the contemporary Russian psyche and society. The intensely personal deck of cards called "This Is Me" shows his alter ego contemplating himself, his family and friends. The first five cards read: "This is me. // This is also me. // And this is me. // These are my parents. It looks like... Kislovodsk. The inscription: "1952." // Misha with a volleyball" (Rubinstein 2004: n.p.).[2] As the cards pile up, we get the point: they are simulating photographs, even though further on in the deck Rubinstein's ruminations go on to include dialogue and all sorts of references to books, articles, novels, animals and objects. In Mikhail N. Epstein's (1995: 35) words, "it all appears as merely an imitation of someone – no one – else's speech; it is not 'we' who speak this way, this is how 'they' speak 'us'". The texts on Rubinstein's cards are so suffused with Russian culture, literature and vernacular that the view of their translators hit the mark: they are "vividly futurist yet haunted by ghosts" (Metres and Tulchinsky 2004: xiii).

Not surprisingly, in a horror writer like Ligotti ghosts and other supernatural creatures appear frequently. But more importantly, his characters are uncertain whether they or their world are real or imitations, which in some sense resembles Rubinstein's reciprocal imitating. Am "I" or are "we" informed or mirrored by "them" or is it the other way around? If so, who is real? In an early credo-like short story, Ligotti (1986/2015: 103) states that "the proper voice of horror is really that of the *personal confession*", which comes across in his frequent use of first-person narration, usually singular but also plural. This means that most of his stories are unreliable: whether the character narrators are deranged is left open. What is appearance or dream is often unclear to them, just as one of Rubinstein's speakers "dreamt as if we were sitting here and doing the same thing that we're doing now" (card 40 in the deck "Thursday Night [When Dreams Come True]"). The

---

2 Rubinstein's translators Philip Metres and Tatiana Tulchinsky (2004: xiii) have decided not to paginate their collection, "as a gesture towards the non-book that these texts represent".

other texts are less forthrightly unreliable, but offer different subjective stands pitted against each other: views by and of the unreliable protagonist Harriet "Harry" Burden (Hustvedt); romance, science, philosophy and imaginary journeys parodied (Cavendish); and different and often interrelated takes on religious, fantastic and real phenomena (Mesoamerican and Australian indigenous literature).

As for more specific themes and techniques, many seem to recur. Dual deities are a staple in many mythologies. In Mesoamerican mythology, there are divine pairs, including Our Mother / Our Father, the dual god Ometeotl and the hero twins Hunahpu and Xabalanque of the Mayan sacred narrative *Popol Vuh* (see Léon-Portilla and Shorris 2001: 16–19, The *Popol Vuh* c. 1550–1555/2001: 423–438). In Australian myth, where there is no divinity as such, two shape-changing human siblings Aidjumala and Maidjuminmag incestuously people the land or, in other stories, two brothers fight each other (see Berndt and Berndt 1994: 29–34, 252–256). The Empress of Cavendish's Blazing World is in many ways mirrored by the Duchess, both of whom seem to represent features of Cavendish herself. The world they inhabit is full of hybrid species, including "the worm-, bear- and fly-men, the ape-men, the satyrs, the spider-men, and all others of such sorts", who have their "contentions and divisions" (Cavendish 1666/2004: 201). In Hustvedt (2014: 1–11 *et passim*), Burden admits she is "a trickster", who produces art (and art criticism on it) under a number of male aliases, all of which she gathers under the umbrella title "*Maskings*". Rubinstein speaks through a number of voices and characters, on which tables are turned in different ways, as "when you think you're pretending to be asleep, but in fact you really are sleeping" (card 69 in the deck "Here I Am"). In Ligotti's (1986 and 1991/2015) stories, characters shift shapes and change roles (especially master and disciple, the dead and the living), strange creatures emanate from earth, people seem to wear masks or turn out to be puppets,[3] and art and life are deceptive in a number of ways. Thus, most of these texts exhibit a number of genres and the main themes of challenge, perception and relation, but they also include different text types and blends of narratives, figures and meta-usages. Also, there are many instances of inversion and hypothetical action, as in Ligotti's (1991/2015: 239) story "Vastarien", where worlds in books are "impostors of the authentic unreality which was the only redemption", Rubinstein's card deck "Catalogue of

---

[3] For instance, on changing roles see "The Spectacles in the Drawer", on creatures emanating from earth see "The Shadow at the Bottom of the World" (Ligotti's favourite story) and on masks and puppets see "The Last Feast of Harlequin" (all in Ligotti 1991/2015). If conflating humans and puppets seems a modern, perhaps even postmodern, notion, we can think of how the earth in the *Popol Vuh* (c. 1550–1555/2001: 406–409) during its third creation (the one preceding humans) was populated by wooden manikins.

Comic Novelties", in which all cards start with "You could...", and Hustvedt's tongue-in-cheek speculations as to Burden's identity.

Even more interesting, perhaps, are the world-oriented aspect of the texts. However different, they all make or seek to make an impact on the world. In that they also employ literary representation in order to do so, we have in part come back to the general aspects of literary worlds, that is, imagination, mimesis and unreliability. The Mesoamerican and indigenous Australian myths and literary genres contain much of the essential knowledge of the life world informing listeners how to survive in nature and society. The teachings of Australian indigenous myths are often ambiguous, open-ended or indirect (as in warnings that evil spirits reside by water holes, that is, you should not go there alone, because you might drown), so that listeners may ponder on the best course of action in the situations and conflicts portrayed (see Noonuccal 1990: 8–9 and Berndt and Berndt 1994: 3, 256). Traditional Mesoamerican literature (or, more precisely, what today is considered as such) embraced all facets of learning, including science (e.g. calendars based on stargazing), society and culture. In other words, the literary form – just as the suspenseful narrative format of Australian indigenous myths – was important because it facilitated memorizing.

The individual authors are also prone to make an impact. Cavendish blazes a hole through the complacent patriarchy of her time by her feminist utopia and Hustvedt (2014: 357) shows that such works of art are still needed and can remain "blazing hot and bright" even after the death of their creators. Rubinstein, who started his literary career in the early 1970s, has had to contend with the abiding political forces in the Soviet Union and later Russia, so that his note cards from four decades both draw on and satirize life and culture Russia. Ligotti, one of the most outspoken anti-natalists of our time, offers his bleak visions of humankind in order for his readers to learn – or at least consider – that human life on earth might be discontinued (see Ligotti 2010). But, of course, they also delight in his wonderfully well-wrought and bizarre creations.

I must confess that I in part at least chose the above texts at random but with as wide a spread as possible in order to see whether the views put forth in this study could be employed to analyse some vastly disparate material. The comments I have made above may suggest that they can be of use – even if much more work should be done in order to amend and strengthen, broaden and specify the comparative poetics of literary imagination presented.

Still, from a wider perspective, literary studies can inform other sciences as well. As David Lodge (2002: 16) has noted, "Literature constitutes a kind of knowledge about consciousness which is *complementary* to scientific knowledge". As for literary studies and the humanities in general, Rens Bod (2013) in his *A New History of the Humanities* shows that the humanities have always looked for principles and patterns and that those principles and patterns have also benefited other sciences.[4] But what is more, as we have seen, literature can give us enchanting, edifying and wondrous experiences, and literary studies can also study meanings in literature in ways that go beyond principles and patterns. In sum, I think Lodge (2002: 10) is right in claiming that "literature is a record of human consciousness, the richest and most comprehensive we have". That is why we are fortunate to be able to delight in, benefit from and, if we like, study the treasure trove of literary worlds that imagination has produced.

My hope is that the comparative and analytical views presented in this study might help to reinvigorate literary studies, where in the last half a century or so some rather narrow, even abstruse, theoretical perspectives have been championed (see Pettersson 1999b, 2005a, 2008, 2012b). Literature can be complex, ambiguous and vague, its narrators, speakers or characters unreliable, fantastic or seemingly real, its worlds inflected by expositional manipulation, inversion, thwarted aspirations, meta-usages, genre, text type, hypothetical action or other means. But even such – and other – features can be studied in considerable detail by a focus on the manifold imaginative aspects of literary worlds.

To go beyond literary studies: what might literary imagination or a poetics based on it be able to offer twenty-first-century humankind? As I noted in chapter 8, much of what we as listeners or readers learn from literature can be oblique or subjective, perhaps even the opposite of what authors may have intended. Stephen K. Levine (1992/1997, 2009) has shown that on an individual level the creative act or *poiesis* in all kinds of art is an effective tool in psychotherapy, which could be developed and used more widely. But in a global situation where what we are is being curtailed by where we live, by the air that we breathe, the climate change and the toxic substances in our earth, water and food, we might also pause to consider whether the treasure trove we call literature might give us any clues what to do. Perhaps the contemporary German philosopher Peter Sloterdijk (1999/2014: 966) is right: in this situation "solidarity can only be achieved by transferring early cultural forms of shared existence to large-scale societies". The point of his major *Spheres* trilogy is to focus on the spatial metaphors of bubbles (identity), globes (the process of globalization)

---

4 In contrast, *The Fontana History of the Human Sciences* (*The Norton History of the Human Sciences* in the United States) by Roger Smith (1997) views the human sciences as a self-reflexive and dialogical process (even more explicitly in Smith 2007). To be sure, Bod discusses the humanities (starting in antiquity) and Smith the human sciences (starting with the Renaissance), but much of their difference of focus may owe to their original disciplinary interests: for Bod, computational linguistics; for Smith, the biological sciences and the history and philosophy of science.

and foam (the current result of globalization) instead of chronological ones (see Sloterdijk 1998/2011: 62–77). Philosophically, it can be seen as a countermove to Martin Heidegger's (1927/1996) *Being and Time*, but its aim seems much broader: to question the time- and technology-ridden culture that has taken us where we are now. One need not agree with all of his assessment of the past or the present world, but perhaps his plea for global solidarity should touch us enough to make us act in some way – possibly inspired by what we might salvage from "early cultural forms of shared existence".

If you think I am straying from my subject, I shall try to show that I am not. I started out this study by quoting Fredric Brown's extended defamiliarizing metaphor of what it is to be a creature aware of "standing on [a] blob of mud". Well, now that blob and the creatures who inhabit it are in peril. Perhaps imagination, the impetus behind so much science, technology and art, can help us. For instance, we might learn from what literary imagination has produced. In fact, I want to take up Sloterdijk's challenge by considering what we might salvage from two of the oldest human cultures, the indigenous ones in Australia and Mesoamerica.

Just as in ancient Greece, in both cultures the bond between mythical personages (and divinities in the latter) and humans is never severed. If Ernst Cassirer (1945/1979: 245, 246) is right in stating that myth (from *mythos*, story or plot) is "not an outgrowth of primitive mentality", but "a permanent element in human culture", which has given language its "metaphorical and figurative elements", then it is evident that literary imagination through the ages draws on the complexity inherent in myth. In both Australian and Mesoamerican myth and literature, humans are sustained by the very nature they inhabit, literally and spiritually. For Berndt and Berndt (1994), drawing on half a century of research, the fundamental metaphor for Australian indigenous myth is *the speaking land*. Or, as Swain (1993/1997: 25) puts it, the pervasive Aboriginal principle is "*geosophy:* all knowledge and wisdom derives, through Abiding Events (Dreamings [emphasis original]), from place", on which the spatial memorizing of the "songlines" or "dreaming tracks" in the myths and legends are based.[5] In ancient Mesoamerican culture, on the other hand, what is central is not the land as such, but the mythical, metaphorical and actual creatures (often occuring

---

[5] Thus, I gather that the non-indigenous informant in Bruce Chatwin's (1987/1998: 14) Australian travelogue *The Songlines* is somewhat misinformed when claiming that "[b]y singing the world into existence […], the [Aboriginal] Ancestors had been poets in the original sense of *poesis*, meaning 'creation'". Rather, it is the land that speaks – or sings – through mythical characters and past and present Aborigines. In fact, the spatially memorizing songlines should rightly be understood as precursors of the Western art of memory so thoroughly studied by e.g. Frances Yates (1966/2014) and Mary Carruthers (1990/2013).

as twins) that inhabit it. The name of many deities end with -*coatl*, meaning both 'twin' and 'serpent', and, as noted in 1.5, the metaphor for poetry and art in general is "flower and song", often conflating bird song and human song (see Léon-Portilla-Shorris 2001: 17, 31). Thus, the metaphor "flower and song" serves to substantiate the bond between nature and humans, just as the act of singing strengthens the friendship between the singer and his listeners (see Tecayehuatzin c. 1490/2001: 91 and Léon-Portilla and Shorris 2001: 31, 151).

We can see that in both cultures there is an awareness of the relations of humans to the past as well as an emphasis on the natural life world they inhabit. In literary studies perhaps the best-known treatise combining time and space is Bakhtin's (1937–1938, 1973/2001) long essay "Forms of Time and of the Chronotope in the Novel". In a recent study of Anton Chekhov, the Finnish scholar Tintti Klapuri (2015: 25–31, 26n53 *et passim*) has viewed Bakhtin's rather text-centred concept of chronotope in contextual and ethical terms, noting in passing that Bakhtin in fact draws on Cassirer's view of language and myth in developing his concept. In other words, in literature, literary studies and beyond we might benefit from considering what we are as a species, where we come from and where we live. In fact, one reason why I discussed animal fables in relation to (human) star-crossed love in the previous chapter is that together they suggest the close relation between humans and other living organisms, not least by metaphorical usages and metamorphoses of humans into animals and plants.[6]

As we saw in 1.4, Richard Kearney has noted that the first step in changing the world is to *imagine* that things can be different than they are. A sustaining glocal view of who and where we are might build on the Estonian ethologist and biologist Jakob von Uexküll's (2010) notion of *Umwelt*, which regards the environment from the point of view of (each individual in) each species. Through the respect for nature and its variety of species that this notion entails, we could learn to be more aware of *the perception world* (*Merkwelt*) and *the effect world* (*Wirkwelt*) of different species, especially the detrimental effects of humans, so that our planet might thrive (see Uexküll 2010: 42). Hence, scientific, mythical and literary imagination can indeed teach "large-scale societies" about "shared existence". If we do not take this or some other compassionate path, we will soon have no blob of mud and no creatures with higher awareness delighting in imaginative artefacts "blazing hot and bright".

---

6 In fact, some advances in neurophysiology and biology suggest as much. Jaak Panksepp and Lucy Biven (2012: 1–2) claim that "across many species of warm-blooded vertebrates [mammals and birds], a variety of basic emotional networks are anatomically situated in similar brain regions, and these networks serve remarkably similar functions" and Daniel Chamowitz (2012: 137–138) that plants not only have different kinds of sentience, but awareness.

Appendix 1

The Tyger

Tyger Tyger, burning bright,   [1]
In the forests of the night;
What immortal hand or eye.
Could frame thy fearful symmetry?

In what distant deeps or skies,   [2]
Burnt the fire of thine eyes?
On what wings dare he aspire?
What the hand, dare sieze the fire?

And what shoulder, & what art,   [3]
Could twist the sinews of thy heart?
And when thy heart began to beat,
What dread hand? & what dread feet?

What the hammer? what the chain,   [4]
In what furnace was thy brain?
What the anvil? what dread grasp,
Dare its deadly terrors clasp?

When the stars threw down their spears   [5]
And water'd heaven with their tears:
Did he smile his work to see?
Did he who made the Lamb make thee?

Tyger Tyger, burning bright,   [6]
In the forests of the night:
What immortal hand or eye,
Dare frame thy fearful symmetry?

Text on plate of "*The* Tyger" in Blake (2009: 84)

Appendix 2

I cannot live with You –   [1]
It would be Life –
And Life is over there –
Behind the Shelf

The Sexton keeps the Key to –   [2]
Putting up
Our Life – His Porcelain –
Like a Cup –

Discarded of the Housewife –   [3]
Quaint – or Broke –
A newer Sevres pleases –
Old Ones crack –

I could not die – with You –   [4]
For One must wait
To shut the Other's Gaze down –
You – could not –

And I – Could I stand by   [5]
And see You – freeze –
Without my Right of Frost –
Death's privilege?

Nor could I rise – with You –   [6]
Because Your Face
Would put out Jesus' –
That New Grace

Glow plain – and foreign   [7]
On my homesick Eye –
Except that You than He
Shone closer by –
They'd judge Us – How –
For You – served Heaven – You know,   [8]

Or sought to –
I could not –

Because You saturated Sight –   [9]
And I had no more Eyes
For sordid excellence
As Paradise

And were You lost, I would be –   [10]
Though My Name
Rang loudest
On the Heavenly fame –

And were You – saved –   [11]
And I – condemned to be
Where You were not –
That self – were Hell to Me –

So We must meet apart –   [12]
You there – I – here –
With just the Door ajar
That Oceans are – and Prayer –
And that White Sustenance –
Despair –

Poem 640 in Dickinson (1960: 317–318)

Bibliography

Primary Sources

1000 Poems from the Manyōshū. 2005. Trans. Japanese Classic Translation Committee. Mineola, NY: Dover.
Achebe, Chinua. 1958/1984. *Things Fall Apart*. New York: Fawcett Crest.
Aesop. 2002/2008. *Aesop's Fables*. Trans. Laura Gibbs. Oxford et al.: Oxford University Press.
Akutagawa, Ryonosuke. 1915/1959. "Rashomon". In *Rashomon and Other Stories*. Trans. Takashi Kojima. New York: Bantam. 29–39.
Akutagawa, Ryonosuke. 1922/1959. "In a Grove". In *Rashomon and Other Stories*. Trans. Takashi Kojima. New York: Bantam. 13–28.
Apuleius. 1994/2008. *The Golden Ass*. Trans. P. G. Walsh. Oxford et al.: Oxford University Press.
The Arabian Nights. Tales from A Thousand and One Nights. 2001/2004. Trans. Sir Richard F. Burton. New York: The Modern Library. "The Tale of the Three Apples". 145–154.
Aristophanes. 2005. *The Complete Plays*. Trans. Paul Roche. New York: New American Library.
Ashbery, John. 2002. *Chinese Whispers*. Manchester: Carcanet.
Attar, Farid ud-Din. 1984/2011. *The Conference of the Birds*. Trans. Afkham Darbandi and Dick Davis. London et al.: Penguin.
Baker, Nicholson. 1988/1989. *The Mezzanine*. Cambridge: Granta.
Baker, Nicholson. 1990/1991. *Room Temperature*. London: Granta.
Baker, Nicholson. 2003/2004. *A Box of Matches*. London: Vintage.
Banville, John. 1989/1990. *The Book of Evidence*. London: Minerva.
Banville, John. 2002/2003. *Shroud*. London: Picador.
Barnes, Julian. 2005/2006. *Arthur & George*. London: Vintage.
Bashō, Matsuo. 1966. *The Narrow Road to the Deep North and Other Travel Sketches*. Trans. Noboyuki Yuasa. London et al.: Penguin.
Beckett, Samuel. 1986/1990. *The Complete Dramatic Works*. London: Faber and Faber.
Berndt, Ronald M. and Catherine H. Berndt. 1994. *The Speaking Land. Myth and Story in Aboriginal Australia*. Rochester, VT: Inner Traditions International.
Beroul. 1970. *The Romance of Tristan and The Tale of Tristan's Madness*. Trans. Alan S. Fedrick. Harmondsworth: Penguin.
Betjeman, John. *Collected Poems*. Enlarged ed. London: John Murray.
Blake, William. 1956/1968. *The Letters of William Blake*. Ed. Geoffrey Keynes. 2nd rev. ed. London: Rupert Hart-Davis.
Blake, William. 1967/1982. *Songs of Innocence and of Experience*. Ed. Sir Geoffrey Keynes. Oxford et al.: Oxford University Press.
Blake, William. 1977. *The Complete Poems*. Ed. Alicia Ostriker. London et al.: Penguin.
Blake, William. 2000/2009. *The Complete Illuminated Books*. Ed. David Bindman. London: Thames & Hudson.
The Book of Songs. 1937/1996. Trans. Arthur Waley. New York: Grove Press.
Bowers, Faubion (ed.). 1996. *The Classic Tradition of Haiku. An Anthology*. Various trans. Mineola, NY: Dover.
Bristow, Michael Jamieson (ed.). 2006. *National Anthems of the World*. 11th ed. London: Weidenfeld & Nicolson.

Brontë, Charlotte. 1847/1953. *Jane Eyre*. New York: Pocket Books.
Brown, Fredric. 1955/2007. "Imagine". In *From These Ashes. The Complete Short SF of Fredric Brown*. Ed. Ben Yalow. Framingham, MA: The NESFA Press. 565.
Buber, Martin (ed.). 1910/1998. *Zhuangzi: Sayings and Parables*. In Buber 1991/1998: 1–107.
Buber, Martin (ed.). 1911/1998. *Chinese Ghost and Love Stories* [by Pu Songling]. In Buber 1991/1998: 109–211.
Buber, Martin (ed.). 1991/1998. *Chinese Tales*. Trans. Alex Page. New York: Humanity Books.
Calderón de la Barca, Pedro. c. 1635/2002. *Life Is a Dream / La vida es sueño*. Ed. and trans. Stanley Appelbaum. Mineola, NY: Dover.
Cao Xueqin and Gao E. 1978/2008. *A Dream of Red Mansions*. Trans. Yang Xianyi and Gladys Yang. Beijing: Foreign Languages Press.
Carver, Raymond. 1988/1989. "Blackbird Pie". In *Elephant and Other Stories*. London: Collins Harvill. 91–109.
Casares, Adolfo Bioy. 1940/2003. *The Invention of Morel*. Trans. Ruth L. C. Simms. Ill. Norah Borges de Torre. New York: The New York Review of Books.
Cavendish, Margaret, Duchess of Newcastle. 1666/2004. *The Description of a New World, Called The Blazing World*. In *The Blazing World and Other Writings*. Ed. Kate Lilley. London et al.: Penguin, 1992/2004. 119–225.
Cervantes, Miguel de. 2003/2005. *Don Quixote*. Trans. Edith Grossman. London: Vintage.
Chatwin, Bruce. 1987/1998. *The Songlines*. London: Vintage.
Chaucer, Geoffrey. 1964/1979. *Canterbury Tales / Tales of Caunterbury*. Eds A. Kent Hieatt and Constance Hieatt. New York: Bantam.
Chaucer, Geoffrey. 2007. *Dream Visions and Other Poems*. Ed. Kathryn L. Lynch. New York and London: W. W. Norton.
Chesney, George Tomkyns. 1871/1914. *The Battle of Dorking*. London: Grant Richards.
Cicero, Marcus Tullius. 2007. "From *Scipio's Dream*". In Chaucer 2007: 258–264.
Conrad, Joseph 1902/1976: *Heart of Darkness*. Harmondsworth: Penguin.
Cooder, Ry. 2011. *Los Angeles Stories*. San Francisco, CA: City Lights.
Dante Alighieri. 1993/2008. *The Divine Comedy*. Trans. C. H. Sisson. Oxford et al.: Oxford University Press.
Defoe, Daniel. 1722/1972. [*The Fortunes and Misfortunes of the Famous*] *Moll Flanders*. London/New York: Dent/Dutton.
Díaz, Junot 2007/2008: *The Brief Wondrous Life of Oscar Wao*. New York: Riverhead Books.
Dick, Philip K. 1986/2008. *Humpty Dumpty in Oakland*. New York: Tor.
Dick, Philip K. 2002. "The Electric Ant". In *Selected Stories of Philip K. Dick*. New York: Pantheon. 382–400.
Dickinson, Emily. 1960. *The Complete Poems of Emily Dickinson*. Ed. Thomas H. Johnson. Boston: Little, Brown and Company.
Diski, Jenny. 1988/1990. *Like Mother*. London: Vintage.
Eggers, Dave. 2005. *How We Are Hungry. Stories*. London et al.: Penguin.
Eliot, George. 1874/2000. *Middlemarch*. Ware, Hertfordshire: Wordsworth.
Eliot, T. S. 1915/2015. "The Love Song of J. Alfred Prufrock". In Eliot 2015: 5–9.
Eliot, T. S. 1922/2015. *The Waste Land*. In Eliot 2015: 53–71.
Eliot, T. S. 2015. *The Poems of T. S. Eliot. Volume I. Collected and Uncollected Poems*. Eds Christopher Ricks and Jim McCue. Baltimore, MD: Johns Hopkins University Press.
Ellis, Bret Easton. 1991. *American Psycho. A Novel*. London: Picador.

Ellmann, Richard and Robert O'Clair (eds). 1988. *The Norton Anthology of Modern Poetry*. 2nd ed. New York and London: W. W. Norton.
Enright, D. J. 1987. *Collected Poems 1987*. Oxford and New York: Oxford University Press.
The Epic of Gilgamesh. 1999/2000. Trans. Andrew George. London: Penguin.
Everyman (*The Moral Play of Everyman*). 1956/2000. In *Everyman and Medieval Miracle Plays*. Ed. A. C. Cawley. London: J. M. Dent. 195–225.
Faulkner, William. 1930/1995. "A Rose for Emily". In *Collected Stories*. London: Vintage. 119–130.
Fielding, Henry. 1749/1963. *The History of Tom Jones. A Foundling*. New York, Scarborough, ON, and London: Signet / The New English Library.
Filson, John. 1784/2007. *The Discovery, Settlement and Present State of Kentucke*. Facsimile rpt. Westminster, MD: Heritage Books.
Flynn, Gillian. 2012. *Gone Girl*. London: Phoenix.
Ford, Ford Madox. 1915/1995. *The Good Soldier*. Ed. Martin Stannard. New York and London: W. W. Norton.
Ford, Ford Madox. 1924–1928/2013. *Parade's End*. Ware, Hertfordshire: Wordsworth.
Fowler, Karen Joy. 1991/2012. *Sarah Canary*. London: Gollancz.
Frayn, Michael, 2002. *Spies*. London: Faber and Faber.
Gaige, Amity. 2013. *Schroder. A Novel*. London: Faber and Faber.
Geyh, Paula, Fred G. Leebron and Andrew Levy (eds). 1998. *Postmodern American Fiction. A Norton Anthology*. New York and London: W. W. Norton.
Gibson, William. 1984 rpt. *Neuromancer*. New York: Ace Books.
Gill, Harjeet Singh. 2003. "Heer Ranjha: The Cosmology of Heer". In *Heer Ranjha and Other Legends of the Punjab*. Ill. Eric Vikramjeet Singh Gill. New Delhi: Harman. 1–35.
Goethe, Johann Wolfgang von. 1819?/1969. "Parabase [Parabasis]". In *Goethe* [Selected Verse in German with Prose Translations]. Trans. David Luke. Harmondsworth: Penguin. 272.
Gogol, Nikolai. "Nevsky Prospect". 1835/1998. In Gogol 1998: 245–278.
Gogol, Nikolai. 1998. *The Collected Tales of Nikolai Gogol*. Trans. Richard Pevear and Larissa Volokhonsky. London: Granta.
Gorgani, Fakhraddin. 2008/2009. *Vis and Ramin*. Trans. Dick Davis. New York et al.: Penguin.
Groom, Winston. 1986/1995. *Forrest Gump*. London: Black Swan.
Guillame de Lorris and Jean de Meun. 1994/2008. *The Romance of the Rose*. Trans. Frances Horgan. Oxford et al.: Oxford University Press.
Haddon, Mark. 2003/2004. *The Curious Incident of the Dog in the Night-Time*. London: Vintage.
Hardy, Thomas. 1891/1983. *Tess of the d'Urbervilles. A Pure Woman*. Ed. David Skilton. Harmondsworth et al.: Penguin.
Harris, Joanne. 2010/2011. *blueeyedboy*. London: Black Swan.
Harrison, Harry (ed.). 1971. *The Light Fantastic. Science Fiction Classics in the Mainstream*. New York: Charles Scribner's Sons.
Haslett, Adam. 2002/2003. "The Good Doctor". In *You Are Not a Stranger Here*. London: Vintage. 24–47.
Hawkins, Paula. 2015. *The Girl on the Train*. London et al.: Doubleday.
Hawthorne, Nathaniel. 1835/1987. "Wakefield". In *Nathaniel Hawthorne's Tales*. Ed. James McIntosh. New York and London: W. W. Norton. 75–82.
Heliodorus. 1989/2008. *An Ethiopian Story*. Trans. J. R. Morgan. In Reardon 1989/2008: 349–588.

Heller, Joseph. 1961/1978. *Catch-22*. London: Corgi.
Heyman, Michael with Sumanyu Satpathy and Anushka Ravishankar (eds). 2007. *The Tenth Rasa. An Anthology of Indian Nonsense*. Various trans. New Delhi et al.: Penguin.
Hinton, David (ed. and trans.). 2008. *Classical Chinese Poetry. An Anthology*. New York: Farrar, Straus and Giroux.
The Holy Bible. 1980/1987. New International Version. Trans. The Committee on Bible Translation. London et al.: Hodder and Stoughton.
Homer. 1951/2011. *The Iliad*. Trans. Richmond Lattimore. Chicago and London: The University of Chicago Press.
Homer. 1967/2007. *The Odyssey*. Trans. Richmond Lattimore. New York et al.: Harper Perennial Modern Classics.
Homer. 1990/1991. *The Iliad*. Trans. Robert Fagles. Harmondsworth: Penguin.
Homer. 1996/2006. *The Odyssey*. Trans. Robert Fagles. London: Penguin.
Hustvedt, Siri. 2014. *The Blazing World. A Novel*. New York et al.: Simon and Schuster.
Idema, Wilt L. (ed. and trans.). 2010. *The Butterfly Lovers. The Legend of Liang Shanbo and Zhu Yingtai. Four Versions, with Related Texts*. Indianapolis, IN, and Cambridge: Hackett.
The Ise Stories [aka *The Tales of Ise*]. *Ise Monogatari*. 2010. Trans. Joshua S. Mostow and Royall Tyler. Honolulu: University of Hawai'i Press.
Ishiguro, Kazuo. 1989/1996. *The Remains of the Day*. London: Faber and Faber.
Jacobsen, Thorkild (ed. and trans.). 1987. *The Harps That Once... Sumerian Poetry in Translation*. New Haven, CT, and London: Yale University Press.
James, Henry. 1878/1974. *Daisy Miller: A Study*. In Daisy Miller *and* The Turn of the Screw. New York et al.: Scholastic Book Services. 157–243.
James, Henry. 1898/1974. *The Turn of the Screw*. In Daisy Miller *and* The Turn of the Screw. New York et al.: Scholastic Book Services. 1–155.
James, Henry. 1903/2001. "The Beast in the Jungle". In *Selected Tales*. Ed. John Lyon. London: Penguin. 426–461.
Jemie, Onwuchekwa. 1971/1998. "Toward a Poetics". In Gerald Moore and Ulli Beier (eds), *The Penguin Book of Modern African Poetry*. 4th ed. London et al.: Penguin. 277–278.
Johnson, Adam. 2012/2013. *The Orphan Master's Son*. London: Black Swan.
Kafka, Franz. 1930/2005. *The Castle*. Trans. Willa and Edwin Muir; additional material trans. Eithne Wilkins and Ernst Kaiser. London: Vintage.
Kafka, Franz. 1983/2005. *The Complete Short Stories*. Ed. Nahum E. Glatzer. Various trans. London: Vintage.
The Kalevala. 1990. Ed. Elias Lönnrot. Trans. Keith Bosley. Oxford and New York: Oxford University Press.
Kālidāsa. 1986/2006. *Abhijñānaśākuntalam (The Recognition of Śakuntalā)*. In *The Loom of Time. A Selection of His Plays and Poems*. Trans. Chandra Rajan. London et al.: Penguin. 165–281.
Karadžić, Vuk. 1997. *Songs of the Serbian People. From the Collections of Vuk Karadžić*. Ed. and trans. Milne Holton and Vasa D. Mihailovich. Pittsburgh, PA: University of Pittsburgh Press.
Kivi, Aleksis. 1870/1984. *Seitsemän veljestä. Kertomus* [Seven Brothers. A Tale]. In *Teokset* [Works]. Helsinki: Otava. 451–678.
The Kokinshū [*Kokin Wakashū*]. *A Collection of Poems Ancient and Modern*. 1984/2012.Trans. Laurel Rasplica Rodd with Mary Catherine Henkenius. Boston, MA: Cheng & Tsui.
Kosinski, Jerzy. 1970/1996. *Being There*. London: Black Swan.

Kuan Han-ch'ing. 1972. *The Injustice Done to Tou Gno*. In *Six Yüan Plays*. Trans. Liu Jung-en. Harmondsworth, Baltimore, Victoria: Penguin. 115–158.

La Fontaine, Jean de. 2007. *The Complete Fables of Jean de La Fontaine*. Trans. Norman R. Shapiro. Ill. David Shorr. Urbana and Chicago: University of Illinois Press.

Lem, Stanislaw. 1961/1991. *Solaris*. Trans. Joanna Kilmartin and Steve Cox. London and Boston: Faber and Faber.

Lennon, John. 1997. *In His Own Write* & *A Spaniard in the Works*. London: Pimlico. (Originally published 1964 and 1965)

León-Portilla, Miguel and Earl Shorris (eds). 2001. *In the Language of Kings. An Anthology of Mesoamerican Literature – Pre-Columbian to the Present*. New York and London: W. W. Norton.

Lichtheim, Miriam (ed.). 1973/2006. *Ancient Egyptian Literature. A Book of Readings. Volume I: The Old and Middle Kingdoms*. Berkeley, Los Angeles, London: University of California Press.

Ligotti, Thomas. 1986 and 1991/2015. *Songs of a Dead Dreamer* and *Grimscribe. His Lives and Works*. New York: Penguin.

Lu Xun. 1918/2009. "Diary of a Madman". In Lu Xun 2009: 21–31.

Lu Xun. 1921/2009. The Real Story of Ah-Q". In Lu Xun 2009: 79–123.

Lu Xun. 1936/2009. "Bringing Back the Dead". In Lu Xun 2009: 393–402.

Lu Xun. 2009. *The Real Story of Ah-Q and Other Tales of China. The Complete Fiction of Lu Xun*. Trans. Julia Lovell. London: Penguin.

Lucian. 1989/2008. *A True Story*. Trans. B. P. Reardon. In Reardon 1989/2008: 619–649.

The Mahābhārata. 2009. Abridged and trans. John D. Smith. London et al.: Penguin.

de Maistre, Xavier. 2006. *A Journey around My Room* and *A Nocturnal Expedition around My Room*. Trans. Andrew Brown. London: Hesperus Press, 2006. (Originally published 1794 and 1825)

Mao Zedong. 1972/2008. *The Poems of Mao Zedong*. Trans. Willis Barnstone. Berkeley, Los Angeles, London: University of California Press.

Maupassant, Guy de. 1885/1997. "The Diary of a Madman". In *The Dark Side. Tales of Terror and the Supernatural*. Trans. Arnold Kellett. New York: Carroll and Graf. 113–119.

Melville, Herman. 1851/2002. *Moby-Dick*. A Norton Critical Edition. 2nd ed. Eds Hershel Parker and Harrison Hayford. New York and London: W. W. Norton.

Mills, Magnus. 1998/1999. *The Restraint of Beasts*. London: Flamingo.

Mills, Magnus. 1999/2004. "Only When the Sun Shines Brightly." In *Only When the Sun Shines Brightly*. Tadworth, Surrey: Acorn, 2004. 25–38.

Mills, Magnus. 1999/2004. *All Quiet on the Orient Express*. London: Harper Perennial.

Mills, Magnus. 2001/2002. *Three to See the King*. London: Flamingo.

Mills, Magnus. 2003/2004. *The Scheme for Full Employment*. London: Harper Perennial.

Mills, Magnus. 2005/2006. *Explorers of the New Century*. London: Bloomsbury.

Mills, Magnus. 2009. *The Maintenance of Headway*. London, Berlin, New York: Bloomsbury.

Mills, Magnus. 2011. *A Cruel Bird Came Into the Nest and Looked In*. London et al.: Bloomsbury.

Mills, Magnus. 2015. *The Field of the Cloth of Gold*. London et al.: Bloomsbury.

Minford, John and Joseph S. M. Lau (eds). 2000. *Classical Chinese Literature. An Anthology of Translations. Volume I: From Antiquity to the Tang Dynasty*. Trans. Richard Wilbur and Alan Drury. New York/Hong Kong: Columbia University Press/The Chinese University Press.

Mo Yan. 1988/2006. *The Garlic Ballads*. Trans. Howard Goldblatt. York, UK: Methuen.
Mo Yan. 2006/2012. *Life and Death Are Wearing Me Out. A Novel*. Trans. Howard Goldblatt. New York: Arcade.
Molière [Jean-Baptiste Poquelin]. 1982. *Five Plays. The School for Wives, Tartuffe, The Misanthrope, The Miser, The Hypochondriac*. Various trans. London: Methuen.
Moore, Alan and Dave Gibbons 1986/2005: *Watchmen*. New York: DC Comics.
More, Thomas. 1999/2008. *Utopia*. Trans. Ralph Robinson. In *Three Early Modern Utopias*. Thomas More, *Utopia*, Francis Bacon, *New Atlantis*, Henry Neville, *The Isle of Pines*. Ed. Susan Bruce. Oxford et al.: Oxford University Press. 1–148.
Morrison, Toni. 1987/1988. *Beloved*. New York: Plume/Penguin.
Munro, Alice. 2001/2002. "Hateship, Friendship, Courtship, Loveship, Marriage". In *Hateship, Friendship, Courtship, Loveship, Marriage*. London, Vintage, 2002. 3–54.
Murasaki Shikibu [Lady Murasaki]. 1976/1985. *The Tale of Genji*. Abridged trans. Edward G. Seidensticker. New York: Vintage.
Murasaki Shikibu. 2001/2003. *The Tale of Genji*. Trans. Royall Tyler. New York et al.: Penguin.
Nabokov, Vladimir. 1938/1961. *Laughter in the Dark*. Harmondsworth: Penguin. (Originally in Russian in 1933)
Nabokov, Vladimir. 1955/1962. *Lolita*. New York: Crest.
Nash, Ogden. 1994/2001. *Candy Is Dandy. The Best of Ogden Nash*. London: André Deutsch.
Niane, D. T. 2006/2007. *Sundiata. An Epic of Mali*. Rev. ed. Trans. G. D. Pickett. Harlow, Essex: Pearson/Longman.
Nizami [Nezami] Ganjavi. 1997/2011. *The Story of Layla and Majnun*. Trans. Rudolph Gepke; final chapter trans. Zia Inayat and Omid Safi. New Lebanon, NY: Omega.
Opie, Iona and Peter Opie (eds). 1997. *The Oxford Dictionary of Nursery Rhymes*. Oxford et al.: Oxford University Press.
Ovid. 1986/2008. *Metamorphoses*. Trans. A. D. Melville. Oxford et al.: Oxford University Press.
Owen, Wilfred. 1920/1973. "Dulce et Decorum Est". In Frank Kermode and John Hollander (eds), *Modern British Literature*. New York, London, Toronto: Oxford University Press. 542–543.
Parker, Dorothy. 1999. *Complete Poems*. New York et al.: Penguin.
Parkinson, R. B. (ed. and trans.). 1998/2009. *The Tale of Sinuhe and Other Ancient Egyptian Poems 1940–1640 BC*. Oxford et al.: Oxford University Press.
Perrault, Charles. 2009/2010. *The Complete Fairy Tales*. Trans. Christopher Betts. Oxford et al.: Oxford University Press.
Plato. 1994/2008. *Republic*. Trans. Robin Waterfield. Oxford et al.: Oxford University Press.
Poems on Life and Love in Ancient India. Hāla's Sattasaī. Trans. Peter Khoroche and Herman Tieken. Albany: State University of New York Press.
The *Popol Vuh*. c. 1550–1555/2001. In Léon-Portilla and Shorris 2001: 397–451.
Pound, Ezra. 1913. "IN A STATION OF THE METRO". *Poetry Magazine* (April 1913): 12. http://www.poetryfoundation.org/poetrymagazine/browse/2/1#20569747 (accessed 5 September 2012)
Pound, Ezra. 1916/1988. "In a Station of the Metro". In Ellmann and O'Clair 1988: 381.
Powys, T. F. 1931/2011. *Unclay*. Sherborne, Dorset: The Sundial Press.
Pratchett, Terry. 1994/1995. *Soul Music*. London: Corgi Books.
Pratchett, Terry. 1996/1997. *Hogfather*. London: Corgi Books.

Proulx, Annie. 1999/2006. "Brokeback Mountain". In *Close Range: Brokeback Mountain and Other Stories*. London et al.: Harper Perennial. 281–318.
Pu Songling. 2006. *Strange Tales from a Chinese Studio*. Ed. and trans. John Minford. London et al.: Penguin.
Pullman, Philip. 1995/2007. *Northern Lights*. Book I in *His Dark Materials*. London: Scholastic.
Pynchon, Thomas. 1966/1974. *The Crying of Lot 49*. Harmondsworth: Penguin.
Racine, Jean. 1677/1987. *Phaedra*. In *Iphigenia / Phaedra / Athalia*. Trans. John Cairncross. Harmondsworth et al.: Penguin. 127–214.
Ramanujan, A. K. (ed. and trans.). 1985. *Poems of Love and War. From the Eight Anthologies and the Ten Long Poems of Classical Tamil*. New Delhi: Oxford University Press.
Reardon, B. P. (ed.). 1989/2008. *Collected Ancient Greek Novels*. Berkeley, Los Angeles, London: University of California Press.
Reza, Yasmina. 1994/2005. *"Art"*. In *Plays One*. Trans. Christopher Hampton. London: Faber and Faber. 1–69.
Rhys, Ernest (ed.). 1927/1961. *A Book of Nonsense*. London/New York: Dent/Dutton.
The Rig Veda. An Anthology. 1981. Ed. and trans. Wendy Doniger. London et al.: Penguin.
Rowling, J. K. 1997. *Harry Potter and the Philosopher's Stone*. London: Bloomsbury.
Rubinstein, Lev. 2004. *Catalogue of Comedic Novelties. Selected Poems*. Eastern European Poets Series 4. Trans. Philip Metres and Tatiana Tulchinsky. New York: Ugly Duckling Presse.
Rumi, Jalal al-Din. 2004/2008. *The Masnavi. Book One*. Trans. Jawid Mojaddedi. Oxford et al.: Oxford University Press.
Rumi, Jalal al-Din. 2007/2008. *The Masnavi. Book Two*. Trans. Jawid Mojaddedi. Oxford et al.: Oxford University Press.
Runeberg, Johan Ludvig. 1952. *The Tales of Ensign Stål*. Trans. Charles Wharton Stork, Clement Burbank Shaw and C. D. Broad. Helsinki: Söderström & Co. (Originally published 1848 and 1860)
Sedaris, David. 2010/2012. *Squirrel Seeks Chipmunk. A Wicked Bestiary*. Ill. Ian Falconer. London: Abacus.
Service, Robert. *Collected Poems*. New York: Putnam, 1940 rpt.
Shakespeare, William. 1982/1987. *The Illustrated Stratford Shakespeare*. London: Chancellor Press.
Shakespeare, William. 1989. "Venus and Adonis". In *The Narrative Poems*. Ed. Maurice Evans. London: Penguin. 69–104.
Silliman, Ron. 2007. "Sunset Debris". In *The Age of Huts (compleat)*. Berkeley, Los Angeles, London: University of California Press. 103–145.
Śivadāsa. 1995/2006. *The Five-and-Twenty Tales of the Genie (Vetālapañcaviṃśati)*. Trans. Chandra Rajan. London et al.: Penguin.
Somadeva. 1994/1996. *Tales from the Kathāsaritsāgara*. Trans. Arshia Sattar. London et al.: Penguin.
Sophocles. 2001/2010. *Oedipus the King*. In *The Complete Plays*. Trans. Paul Roche. New York: Signet. 209–263.
Stoppard, Tom. 1967/1974. *Rosencrantz and Guildenstern Are Dead*. London: Faber and Faber.
Swift, Jonathan. 1726/1960. *Gulliver's Travels*. New York: Signet.
The Tale of King Cheops' Court. 1998/2009. In Parkinson 1998/2009: 102–127.

The Tale of Sinuhe. 1998/2009. In Parkinson 1998/2009: 21–53.
The Tale of the Shipwrecked Sailor. 1998/2009. In Parkinson 1998/2009: 89–101.
Tan, Shaun. 2006/2007. *The Arrival*. London and Sydney: Hodder.
Tecayehuatzin of Huexotzinco. c. 1490/2001. "Poetics: A Dialogue of Flower and Song". Trans. Sylvia and Earl Shorris. In León-Portilla and Shorris 2001: 81–91.
Thurber, James. 1942/1954. "The Secret Life of Walter Mitty". In Thurber 1945/1954: 37–42.
Thurber, James. 1945/1954. *The Thurber Carnival*. Harmondsworth: Penguin.
Tiptree, James, Jr. [Alice B. Sheldon]. 1971/2014. "Love Is the Plan the Plan Is Death". In Tiptree 1990/2014: 403–419.
Tiptree, James, Jr. [Alice B. Sheldon]. 1972/2014. "The Women Men Don't See". In Tiptree 1990/2014: 115–143.
Tiptree, James, Jr. [Alice B. Sheldon]. 1990/2014. *Her Smoke Rose Up Forever*. London: Gollancz.
Tolkien, J. R. R. 1954–1955/1976. *The Lord of the Rings*. London: George Allen and Unwin.
The Tso Chuan. Selections from China's Oldest Narrative History. 1989. Trans. Burton Watson. New York and Chichester, West Sussex: Columbia University Press.
Twain, Mark. 1884/1988. *Adventures of Huckleberry Finn. The Works of Mark Twain 8*. Eds Walter Blair and Victor Fischer. Berkeley: University of California Press.
Tzara, Tristan. 1977/1992. *Seven Dada Manifestos* and *Lampisteries*. Ill. Francis Picabia. Trans. Barbara Wright. London, Paris, New York: Calder/Riverrun.
Virgil. 1968. *Virgil's Aeneid*. Trans. John Dryden. New York: Airmont.
Visnu Śarma. 1993. *The Pañcatantra*. Trans. Chandra Rajan. New Delhi et al.: Penguin.
Vonnegut, Kurt. 1989/1990. *Jailbird*. Frogmore, St Albans: Granada/Panther.
Waters, Sarah. 2009/2010. *The Little Stranger*. London: Virago.
Wells, H. G. 1898/2005: *The War of the Worlds*. London et al.: Penguin.
Wister, Owen. 1902/2009. *The Virginian. A Horseman of the Plains*. Ed. Robert Shulman. Oxford et al.: Oxford University Press.
Woolf, Virginia. 1944a/1989. "Together and Apart". In Woolf 1985/1989: 189–194.
Woolf, Virginia. 1944b/1989. "The Mark on the Wall". In Woolf 1985/1989: 83–89.
Woolf, Virginia. 1985/1989. *The Complete Shorter Fiction*. 2nd ed. Ed. Susan Dick. Orlando, FL, et al.: Harvest/Harcourt.
Zeami Motokiyo. 1992/2004. *Matsukaze*. In Royall Tyler (ed. and trans.), *Japanese Nō Dramas*. London et al.: Penguin. 183–204.
Zhuangzi. 2009. *The Essential Writings*. Trans. Brook Ziporyn. Indianapolis, IN, and Cambridge: Hackett.
Zusak, Markus. 2005/2007. *The Book Thief*. London: Black Swan.

Secondary Sources

Abel, Reuben. 1976/1997. *Man Is the Measure. A Cordial Invitation to the Central Problems of Philosophy*. New York et al.: The Free Press.
Abrams, M. H. 1953/1971. *The Mirror and the Lamp. Romantic Theory and the Critical Tradition*. London, Oxford, New York: Oxford University Press.
Achebe, Chinua. 1977/1990. "An Image of Africa: Racism in Conrad's *Heart of Darkness*". In *Hopes and Impediments. Selected Essays*. New York et al.: Anchor Books. 1–20.

Ackroyd, Peter. 1995/1996. *Blake*. London: Minerva.
Alber, Jan, Stefan Iversen, Henrik Skov Nielsen and Brian Richardson. 2010. "Unnatural Narratives, Unnatural Narratology: Beyond Mimetic Models". *Narrative* 18.2: 113–36.
Alber, Jan. 2012. "What Is Unnatural about Unnatural Narratology?: A Response to Monika Fludernik". *Narrative* 20.3: 371–382.
Aldiss, Brian. 2005. "Introduction". In Wells 1898/2005: xiii–xxix.
Alexander, Gavin. 2004a. "Introduction". In Alexander 2004b: xvii–lxxix.
Alexander, Gavin (ed.). 2004b. *Sidney's 'The Defence of Poesy' and Selected Renaissance Criticism*. London et al.: Penguin.
Alm-Arvius, Christina. 2003. *Figures of Speech*. Lund, Sweden: Studentlitteratur.
Altman, Charles F. 1986. "The Medieval Marquee: Church Portal Sculpture as Publicity". In Campbell 1986: 6–15.
Ānandavardhana, Rājānaka and Abhinavagupta. 1990. *The Dhvanyāloka of Ānandavardhana with the Locana of Abhinavagupta*. Ed. Daniel H. H. Ingalls. Trans. Daniel H. H. Ingalls, Jeffrey Moussaieff Masson and M. V. Pathwardhan. Cambridge, MA, and London: Harvard University Press.
Anderson, Benedict. 1983/2006. *Imagined Communities. Reflections on the Origin and Spread of Nationalism*. Rev. ed. London and New York: Verso.
Anderson, Marsten. 1990. *The Limits of Realism. Chinese Fiction in the Revolutionary Period*. Berkeley, Los Angeles, London: University of California Press.
Aristotle. 1941/2001a. *De poetica (Poetics)*. Trans. Ingram Bywater. In *Basic Works of Aristotle*. Ed. Richard McKeon. New York: The Modern Library. 1453–1487.
Aristotle. 1941/2001b. *Metaphysica (Metaphysics)*. Trans. W. D. Ross. In *Basic Works of Aristotle*. Ed. Richard McKeon. New York: The Modern Library. 681–926.
Aristotle. 1986. *De Anima (On the Soul)*. Trans. Hugh Lawson-Tancred. Harmondsworth: Penguin.
Aristotle. 1991. *The Art of Rhetoric*. Trans. H. C. Lawson-Tancred. Harmondsworth: Penguin.
Armstrong, Paul B. 1987/1995. "[Dowell as Trustworthy Narrator]". In Ford 1915/1995: 388–391.
Auerbach, Erich. 1938/2014. "*Figura*". In Auerbach 2014: 65–113.
Auerbach, Erich. 1946/1991. *Mimesis. The Representation of Reality in Western Literature*. Trans. Willard R. Trask. Princeton, NJ: Princeton University Press.
Auerbach, Erich. 1952/2014. "The Philology of World Literature". In Auerbach 2014: 253–265.
Auerbach, Erich. 2014. *Time, History, and Literature. Selected Essays of Erich Auerbach*. Trans. Jane O. Newman. Ed. James I. Porter. Princeton, NJ, and Oxford: Princeton University Press.
Bachelard, Gaston. 1958/1994. *The Poetics of Space*. Trans. Maria Jolas. Boston, MA: Beacon Press.
Bachelard, Gaston. 1987/1989. *On Poetic Imagination and Reverie*. Selection and trans. Colette Gaudin. Dallas, TX: Spring.
Bacon, Francis. 1605/1996. *The Advancement of Learning*. In Brian Vickers (ed.), *Francis Bacon*. The Oxford Authors. Oxford and New York: Oxford University Press. 120–299.
Bakeless, John. 1939/1989. *Daniel Boone. Master of the Wilderness*. Lincoln and London: University of Nebraska Press.
Bakhtin, M. M. 1937–1938, 1973/2001. "Forms of Time and of the Chronotope in the Novel. Notes toward a Historical Poetics". In *The Dialogic Imagination: Four Essays*. Ed. Michael

Holquist. Trans. Michael Holquist and Caryl Emerson. Austin and London: University of Texas Press, 1981/2001. 84–258.
Bakhtin, M. M. 1986/2006. *Speech Genres and Other Late Essays*. Trans. Vern W. McGee. Austin: University of Texas Press.
Bal, Mieke. 1977/1985. *Narratology. Introduction to the Theory of Narrative*. Trans. Christine van Boheemen. Toronto, Buffalo and London: University of Toronto Press.
Banfield, Ann. 1982. *Unspeakable Sentences. Narration and Representation in the Language of Fiction*. Boston et al.: Routledge & Kegan Paul.
Barnstone, Willis. 1972/2008. "Introduction". In Mao 1972/2008: 1–27.
Barth, John. 1984. *The Friday Book. Essays and Other Nonfiction*. New York: G. P. Putnam's Sons.
Bateson, Gregory. 1955/2000. "A Theory of Play and Fantasy". In *Steps to an Ecology of Mind*. Chicago and London: The University of Chicago Press. 177–193.
Beecroft, Alexander. 2010. *Authorship and Cultural Identity in Early Greece and China. Patterns of Literary Circulation*. Cambridge et al.: Cambridge University Press.
Bell, Michael J. 1982. "The Study of Popular Culture". In M. Thomas Inge (ed.), *Concise Histories of American Popular Culture*. Westport, CT: Greenwood Press. 443–465.
Berlin, Isaiah. 1953/1998. "The Hedgehog and the Fox. An Essay on Tolstoy's View of History". In Berlin 1998: 436–498.
Berlin, Isaiah. 1979/1998. "The Divorce between the Sciences and the Humanities". In Berlin 1998: 326–358.
Berlin, Isaiah. 1998. *The Proper Study of Mankind. An Anthology of Essays*. Eds Henry Hardy and Roger Hausheer. London: Pimlico.
Bernaerts, Lars, Dirk De Geest, Luc Herman and Bart Vervaeck. 2013a. "Introduction: Cognitive Narrative Studies: Themes and Variations". In 2013b: 1–20.
Bernaerts, Lars, Dirk De Geest, Luc Herman and Bart Vervaeck (eds). 2013b. *Stories and Minds. Cognitive Approaches to Literary Narrative*. Lincoln and London: University of Nebraska Press.
Bod, Rens. 2013. *A New History of the Humanities. The Search for Principles and Patterns from Antiquity to the Present*. Oxford: Oxford University Press.
Boitani, Piero. 2003. "Old Books Brought to Life in Dreams: the *Book of Duchess*, the *House of Fame*, the *Parliament of Fowls*". In Piero Boitani and Jill Mann (eds), *The Cambridge Companion to Chaucer*. Cambridge et al.: Cambridge University Press. 58–77.
Booker, Christopher. 2004/2012. *The Seven Basic Plots. Why We Tell Stories*. London and New York: Continuum.
Booth, Wayne C. 1961/1983. *The Rhetoric of Fiction*. 2nd ed. Chicago and London: The University of Chicago Press.
Booth, Wayne C. 1988. *The Company We Keep. An Ethics of Fiction*. Berkeley et al.: University of California Press.
Botton, Alain de. 2006. "Foreword". In de Maistre 2006: vii–ix.
Bourg, Tammy. 1996. "The Role of Emotion, Empathy, and Text Structure in Children's and Adults' Narrative Text Comprehension". In Roger J. Kreuz and Mary Sue MacNealy (eds), *Empirical Approaches to Literature and Aesthetics*. Norwood, NJ: Ablex. 241–260.
Boyd, Brian. 2009. *On the Origin of Stories. Evolution, Cognition, and Fiction*. Cambridge, MA, and London: The Belknap Press of Harvard University Press.
Boyd, Brian. 2012. *Why Lyrics Last. Evolution, Cognition, and Shakespeare's Sonnets*. Cambridge, MA, and London: Harvard University Press.

Boys-Stones, G. R. (ed.), *Metaphor, Allegory and the Classical Tradition*. Oxford et al.: Oxford University Press.
Brann Eva T. 1991. *The World of the Imagination. Sum and Substance*. Lanham, MD: Rowman & Littlefield.
Bråten, Stein (ed.). 1998a. *Intersubjective Communication and Emotion in Early Ontogeny*. Cambridge and Paris: Cambridge University Press and Editions de la Maison des Sciences de l'Homme.
Bråten, Stein. 1998b. "Infant Learning by Altercentric Participation: The Reverse of Egocentric Observation in Autism". In Bråten 1998a: 105–124.
Bråten, Stein. 1998c. "Intersubjective Communion and Understanding: Development and Perturbation". In Bråten 1998a: 372–382.
Brecht, Bertolt. 1964/1987. *Brecht on Theatre. The Development of an Aesthetic*. Ed. and trans. John Willett. London et al.: Methuen.
Brentano, Franz. 1973/1995. *Psychology from an Empirical Standpoint*. Eds Oskar Kraus and Linda L. McAlister. Trans. Antos C. Rancurello, D. B. Terrell and Linda L. McAlister. London and New York: Routledge. (Originally published 1874)
Brett, R. L. 1969. *Fancy and Imagination*. The Critical Idiom. London: Methuen.
Bridgham, Fred (ed.). 2006. *The First World War as a Clash of Cultures*. Rochester, NY, and Woodbridge, Suffolk: Camden House.
Brooke-Rose, Christine. 1981/1983. *A Rhetoric of the Unreal. Studies in Narrative Structure, Especially of the Fantastic*. Cambridge et al.: Cambridge University Press.
Brooke-Rose, Christine. 1991/2009. *Stories, Theories and Things*. Cambridge et al.: Cambridge University Press.
Brown, Andrew. 2006. "Introduction". In de Maistre: xi–xv.
Brown, Richard Harvey. 1977/1989. *A Poetic for Sociology. Toward a Logic of Discovery for the Human Sciences*. Chicago and London: The University of Chicago Press.
Bruner, Jerome. 1986. *Actual Minds, Possible Worlds*. Cambridge, MA, and London: Harvard University Press.
Bruner, Jerome. 1990/1994. *Acts of Meaning*. Cambridge, MA, and London: Harvard University Press.
Bruner, Jerome. 1991. "The Narrative Construction of Reality". *Critical Inquiry* 18.1: 1–21.
Bruner, Jerome. 1996. *The Culture of Education*. Cambridge, MA, and London: Harvard University Press.
Bruner, Jerome. 2002/2003. *Making Stories. Law, Literature, Life*. Cambridge, MA, and London: Harvard University Press.
Bruno, Giordano. 1998. *Cause, Principle and Unity. Essays on Magic*. Eds and trans. Robert de Lucca and Richard J. Blackwell. Cambridge et al.: Cambridge University Press.
Bryant, Mark L. 1983. *Riddles Ancient and Modern*. London et al.: Hutchinson.
Buber, Martin. 1952. *Images of Good and Evil*. Trans. Michael Bullock. London: Routledge & Kegan Paul.
Burke, Kenneth. 1941/1961. *The Philosophy of Literary Form. Studies in Symbolic Action*. New York: Vintage.
Burke, Kenneth. 1945/1969. *A Grammar of Motives*. Berkeley, Los Angeles, London: University of California Press.
Burke, Kenneth. 1950. *A Rhetoric of Motives*. New York: Prentice-Hall.
Burke, Michael. 2011. *Literary Reading, Cognition and Emotion. An Exploration of the Oceanic Mind*. New York and London: Routledge.

Butler, Christopher. 2005. *Pleasure and the Arts. Enjoying Literature, Painting, and Music*. Oxford et al.: Oxford University Press.
Buxton, Richard. 2004/2011. "Similes and Other Likenesses". In Robert Fowler (ed.), *The Cambridge Companion to Homer*. Cambridge et al.: Cambridge University Press. 139–155.
Callois, Roger. 1958/2001. *Man, Play and Games*. Trans. Meyer Barash. Urbana and Chicago: University of Illinois Press.
Campbell, Joseph. 1949/1988. *The Hero with a Thousand Faces*. London: Paladin.
Campbell, Josie P. (ed.). 1986. *Popular Culture in the Middle Ages*. Bowling Green, OH: Bowling Green State University Popular Press.
Caracciolo, Marco. 2013. "Blind Reading: Toward an Enactivist Theory of the Reader's Imagination". In Bernaerts et al. 2013b: 81–105.
Carroll, Joseph. 1995. *Evolution and Literary Theory*. Columbia and London: University of Missouri Press.
Carroll, Joseph. 2004. *Literary Darwinism. Evolution, Human Nature, and Literature*. New York and London: Routledge.
Carroll, Noël. 1998. *A Philosophy of Mass Art*. Oxford: Clarendon Press.
Carruthers, Mary. 1990/2013. *The Book of Memory. A Study of Memory in Medieval Culture*. 2nd ed. Cambridge: Cambridge University Press.
Carter, Rita. 1998. *Mapping the Mind*. London: Phoenix.
Cassirer, Ernst. 1944/1974. *An Essay on Man*. New Haven, CT, and London: Yale University Press.
Cassirer, Ernst. 1945/1979. "The Technique of Our Modern Political Myths". In *Symbol, Myth, and Culture. Essays and Lectures of Ernst Cassirer*. Ed. Donald Phillip Verene. New Haven, CT, and London: Yale University Press. 242–267.
Castoriadis, Cornelius. 1975/1987. *The Imaginary Institution of Society*. Trans. K. Blamey. Cambridge: Polity Press.
Cawelti, John G. 1999. *The Six-Gun Mystique Sequel* [rev. ed. of *The Six-Gun Mystique*, 1970]. Bowling Green, OH: Bowling Green State University Press.
Chamowitz, Daniel. 2012. *What a Plant Knows. A Field Guide to the Senses*. New York: Scientific American / Farrar, Straus and Giroux.
Chan, Shelley W. 2011. *A Subversive Voice in China. The Fictional World of Mo Yan*. Amherst, NY: Cambria Press.
Chase, Richard. 1957. *The American Novel and Its Tradition*. New York: Doubleday Anchor.
Chase, Richard. 1960/1961. "Myth as Literature". In James E. Miller, Jr. (ed.), *Myth and Method. Modern Theories of Fiction*. n.p.: University of Nebraska Press/Bison. 127–143. (Original work published 1949)
Chatman, Seymour. 1990. *Coming to Terms. The Rhetoric of Narrative in Fiction and Film*. Ithaca, NY, and London: Cornell University Press.
Chesterman, Andrew. 1998. "Causes, Translations, Effects". *Target* 10.2: 201–230.
Cicero, Marcus Tullius. 2001. *On the Ideal Orator*. Trans. James M. May and Jakob Wise. New York and Oxford: Oxford University Press.
Clark, Herbert H. and Richard J. Gerrig. 1984/2007. "On the Pretense Theory of Irony". In Gibbs and Colston 2007: 25–33.
Clarke, I. F. 1992. *Voices Prophesying War. Future Wars 1763–3749*. 2nd ed. Oxford and New York: Oxford University Press.

Clarke, I. F. (ed.). 1995. *The Tale of the Next Great War, 1871–1914. Fictions of Future Warfare and Battles Still-to-come.* Liverpool: Liverpool University Press.
Cohn, Dorrit. 1978/1983. *Transparent Minds. Narrative Modes for Presenting Consciousness in Fiction.* Princeton, NJ: Princeton University Press.
Cohn, Dorrit. 1999/2000. *The Distinction of Fiction.* Baltimore and London: The Johns Hopkins Uniersity Press.
Cole, Michael. 1996. *Cultural Psychology. A Once and Future Discipline.* Cambridge, MA, and London: The Belknap Press of Harvard University Press.
Coleridge, Samuel Taylor. 1816/2000. "Lay Sermons, I". In Coleridge 2000. 660–662.
Coleridge, Samuel Taylor. 1817/2000. *Biographia Literaria; or Biographical Sketches of My Literary Life and Opinions.* In Coleridge 2000. 155–482.
Coleridge, Samuel Taylor. 2000. *The Major Works.* Ed. H. J. Jackson. Oxford et al.: Oxford University Press.
Collingwood, R. G. 1938/1970. *The Principles of Art.* London et al.: Oxford University Press.
Collingwood, R. G. 1946/1993. *The Idea of History.* Rev. ed. Oxford et al.: Clarendon Press.
Collingwood, R. G. 2005/2007. "The Philosophy of Art". In *The Philosophy of Enchantment. Studies in Folktale, Cultural Criticism, and Anthropology.* Eds David Boucher, Wendy James and Philip Smallwood. Oxford et al.: Oxford University Press. 49–80. (Written in 1930)
Collins, Christopher. 1991. *The Poetics of the Mind's Eye. Literature and the Psychology of Imagination.* Philadelphia: University of Pennsylvania Press.
Collins, Christopher. 2013. *Paleopoetics. The Evolution of the Preliterate Imagination.* New York and Chichester, West Sussex: Columbia University Press.
Collins, Randall. 1998. *The Sociology of Philosophies. A Global Theory of Intellectual Change.* Cambridge, MA, and London: The Belknap Press of Harvard University Press.
Corballis, Michael. 1999. "The Gestural Origins of Language". *American Scientist* 87.2, March–April. 138–145.
Cornoldi, Cesare, Robert H. Logie, Maria A. Brandimonte, Geir Kaufmann and Daniel Reisberg. 1996. *Stretching the Imagination. Representation and Transformation in Mental Imagery.* New York and Oxford: Oxford University Press.
Crisp, Peter. 2008. "Between Extended Metaphor and Allegory: Is Blending Enough?" *Language and Literature* 17.4: 291–308.
Croce, Benedetto. 1902/1922. *Aesthetic as Science of Expression and General Linguistic*, 2nd ed. Trans. Douglas Ainslie. London: Macmillan.
Crumbley, Paul. 1996. *Inflections of the Pen. Dash and Voice in Emily Dickinson.* Lexington, KY: The University Press of Kentucky.
Csicsery-Ronay, Istvan, Jr. 2008. *The Seven Beauties of Science Fiction.* Middletown, CT: Wesleyan University Press.
Cunliffe, Richard John. 1924/1977. *A Lexicon of the Homeric Dialect.* New ed. Norman: University of Oklahoma Press.
Currie, Gregory. 1995. *Image and Mind. Film, Philosophy and Cognitive Science.* Cambridge et al.: Cambridge University Press.
Currie, Gregory and Ian Ravenscroft. 2002. *Recreative Minds. Imagination in Philosophy and Literature.* Oxford et al. Oxford University Press.
Curtius, Ernst Robert. 1948/1990. *European Literature and the Latin Middle Ages.* Bollingen Series XXXVI. Trans. Willard R. Trask. Princeton: Princeton University Press.

Damasio, Antonio. 1999/2000. *The Feeling of What Happens. Body and Emotion in the Making of Consciousness*. London: William Heinemann.
Damrosch, David (ed.). 2014. *World Literature in Theory*. Malden, MA, Oxford and Chichester: Wiley-Blackwell.
D'Andrade, Roy. 1995. *The Development of Cognitive Anthropology*. Cambridge et al.: Cambridge University Press.
Danesi, Marcel (ed.). 1995. *Giambattista Vico and Anglo-American Science. Philosophy and Writing*. Berlin and New York: Mouton de Gruyter.
Danesi, Marcel. 2002. *The Puzzle Instinct. The Meaning of Puzzles in Human Life*. Bloomington and Indianapolis: Indiana University Press.
Danesi, Marcel and Frank Nuessel. 1994a. "Preface". In Danesi and Nuessel 1994b: iii–v.
Danesi, Marcel and Frank Nuessel (eds). 1994b. *The Imaginative Basis of Thought and Culture: Contemporary Perspectives on Giambattista Vico*. Toronto: Canadian Scholars' Press.
Davies, Stephen. 2012. *The Artful Species. Aesthetics, Art, and Evolution*. Oxford: Oxford University Press.
Davis, Dick. 2008/2009. "Introduction". In Gorgani 2008/2009: ix–xlvi.
Davis, Dick. 2011. "Introduction". In Attar 1984/2011: ix–xxiii.
Davis, Todd F. and Kenneth Womack (eds). 2001. *Mapping the Ethical Turn. A Reader in Ethics, Culture, and Literary Theory*. Charlottesville and London: University of Virginia Press.
Deacon, Terrence. 1997/1998. *The Symbolic Species. The Co-Evolution of Language and the Human Brain*. Harmondsworth: Penguin.
De Jong, Irene J. F. 1987. *Narrators and Foclizers. The Presentation of the Story in The Iliad*. Amsterdam: Grüner.
Delany, Samuel R. 1971. "About Five Thousand One Hundred and Seventy Five Words". In Thomas D. Clareson (ed.), *SF: The Other Side of Realism*. Bowling Green, OH: Bowling Green University Popular Press. 130–146.
Dennett, Daniel C. 1991/1993. *Consciousness Explained*. Harmondsworth: Penguin.
Descartes, René. 1637/1968. *Discourse on the Method of Properly Conducting One's Reason and of Seeking the Truth in the Sciences*. In *Discourse on Method and The Meditations*. Trans. F. E. Sutcliffe. Harmondsworth: Penguin. 25–91.
Dewey, John. 1916/1980. *The Middle Works, 1899–1924. Vol. 9: 1916. Democracy and Education*. Ed. Jo Ann Boydston. Carbondale and Edwardsville: Southern Illinois University Press.
Dewey, John. 1934/1987. *The Later Works, 1925–1953. Vol. 10: 1934. Art as Experience*. Ed. Jo Ann Boydston. Carbondale and Edwardsville: Southern Illinois University Press.
D'haen, Theo, César Domínguez and Mads Rosendahl Thomsen (eds). 2013. *World Literature. A Reader*. London and New York: Routledge.
D'hoker, Elke, and Gunther Martens (eds). 2008. *Narrative Unreliability in the Twentieth Century First-Person Novel*. Berlin and New York: Walter de Gruyter.
Diamond, Jared. 1997/1998. *Guns, Germs and Steel. A Short History of Everybody for the Last 13,000 Years*. London: Vintage.
Dilthey, Wilhelm. 1860/1996. "Schleiermacher's Hermeneutical System in Relation to Earlier Protestant Hermeneutics". Trans. Theodore Nordenhaug. In Dilthey 1996: 33–227.

Dilthey, Wilhelm. 1883/1988. *Introduction to the Human Sciences. An Attempt to Lay a Foundation for the Study of Society and History.* Trans. Ramon J. Betanzos. London: Harvester Wheatsheaf.
Dilthey, Wilhelm. 1887/1985. "The Imagination of the Poet: Elements for a Poetics". Trans. Louis Agosta and Rudolf A. Makkreel. In Dilthey 1985: 29–173.
Dilthey, Wilhelm. 1900/1972. "The Rise of Hermeneutics". Trans. Fredric Jameson. *New Literary History* III: 2. 229–244.
Dilthey, Wilhelm. 1907–08/1985. "Fragments for a Poetics". Trans. Rudolf A. Makkreel. In Dilthey 1985: 223–231.
Dilthey, Wilhelm. 1910/1985. "Goethe and the Poetic Imagination". Trans. Christopher Rodie. In Dilthey 1985: 235–302.
Dilthey, Wilhelm. 1985. *Poetry and Experience. Selected Works Vol. V.* Eds Rudolf A. Makkreel and Frithjof Rodi. Princeton: Princeton University Press.
Dilthey, Wilhelm. 1996. *Hermeneutics and the Study of History. Selected Works Vol. IV.* Eds Rudolf A. Makkreel and Frithjof Rodi. Princeton: Princeton University Press.
Dissanayake, Ellen. 1988. *What Is Art For?* Seattle and London: University of Washington Press.
Dissanayake, Ellen. 1992. *Homo Aestheticus. Where Art Comes From and Why.* New York: The Free Press.
Dissanayake, Ellen. 2000. *Art and Intimacy. How the Arts Began.* Seattle and London: University of Washington Press.
Dissanayake, Ellen and David S. Miall. 2003. "The Poetics of Babytalk". *Human Nature* 14.4: 337–364.
Doležel, Lubomír. 1998. *Heterocosmica. Fiction and Possible Worlds.* Baltimore and London: The Johns Hopkins University Press.
Donald, Merlin. 1991. *Origins of the Modern Mind. Three Stages in the Evolution of Culture and Cognition.* Cambridge, MA, and London: Harvard University Press.
Donald, Merlin. 2001/2002. *A Mind So Rare. The Evolution of Human Consciousness.* New York and London: W. W. Norton.
Doody, Margaret Anne. 1996/1998. *The True Story of the Novel.* London: Fontana Press.
Dundes, Alan. 1964. *The Morphology of North American Indian Folktales.* Helsinki: Acta Scientiarum Fennica.
Durix, Jean-Pierre. 1998. *Mimesis, Genres and Post-Colonial Discourse. Deconstructing Magic Realism.* Houndmills, Basingstoke, and London/New York: Macmillan/St. Martin's Press.
Dutton, Denis. 2009. *The Art Instinct. Beauty, Pleasure and Human Evolution.* Oxford et al.: Oxford University Press.
Easterlin, Nancy. 1999. "Making Knowledge: Bioepistemology and the Foundations of Literary Theory". *Mosaic* 32.1: 131–147.
Easterlin, Nancy. 2012. *A Biocultural Approach to Literary Theory and Interpretation.* Baltimore, MD: The Johns Hopkins University Press.
Egan, Kieran. 1992. *Imagination in Teaching and Learning. Ages 8 to 15.* London: Routledge.
Eichenbaum, Boris. 1965. "The Theory of the 'Formal Method'". In Lee T. Lemon and Marion J. Reis (eds and trans. from Russian), *Russian Formalist Criticism. Four Essays.* Lincoln and London: University of Nebraska Press. 99–139. (Originally in Ukrainian in 1926)
Einstein, Albert. 1931/2009. *Einstein on Cosmic Religion and Other Opinions and Aphorisms.* Mineola, NY: Dover.

Elias, Norbert. 1983/1987. *Involvement and Detachment*. Trans. Edmund Jephcott. Oxford: Basil Blackwell.
Elias, Norbert. 1991/1995. *The Symbol Theory*. London: Sage.
Elias, Norbert. 1998. *On Civilization, Power and Knowledge. Selected Writings*. Eds Stephen Mennell and Johan Goudsblom. Chicago and London: The University of Chicago Press.
Ellis, Ralph D. 1995a. *Questioning Consciousness. The Interplay of Imagery, Cognition, and Emotion in the Human Brain*. Amsterdam and Philadelphia: John Benjamins.
Ellis, Ralph D. 1995b. "The imagist approach to inferential thought patterns: The crucial role of rhythm pattern recognition". *Pragmatics & Cognition* 3.1: 75–109.
Engel, Susan. 1999. *Context Is Everything. The Nature of Narrative*. New York and Houndmills, Basingstoke: W. H. Freeman.
Enkvist, Nils Erik. 1994. "Context." In Roger D. Sell and Peter Verdonk (eds), *Literature and the New Interdisciplinarity*. Amsterdam and Atlanta: Rodopi. 45–60.
Epstein, Mikhail N. 1995. *After the Future. The Paradoxes of Postmodernism and Contemporary Russian Culture*. Amherst: The University of Massachusetts Press.
Esrock, Ellen J. 1994. *The Reader's Eye. Visual Imaging as Reader Response*. Baltimore and London: The Johns Hopkins University Press.
Esslin, Martin. 1976/1996. *An Anatomy of Drama*. New York: Hill and Wang.
Esslin, Martin. 1987/1996. *The Field of Drama. How the Signs of Drama Create Meaning on the Stage and Screen*. London et al.: Methuen.
Faragher, John Mack. 1992/1993. *Daniel Boone. The Life and Legend of an American Pioneer*. New York: Henry Holt.
Fauconnier, Gilles. 1997/1999. *Mappings in Thought and Language*. Cambridge: Cambridge University Press.
Fauconnier, Gilles and Mark Turner. 2002/2003. *The Way We Think. Conceptual Blendings and the Mind's Hidden Complexities*. New York: Basic Books.
Felski, Rita. 2008. *Uses of Literature*. Malden, MA, and London: Blackwell.
Fenollosa, Ernest and Ezra Pound. 2008/2010. *The Chinese Written Character as a Medium for Poetry*. Eds Haun Saussy, Jonathan Stalling and Lucas Klein. New York: Fordham University Press.
Fernandez, James W. (ed.). 1991. *Beyond Metaphor. The Theory of Tropes in Anthropology*. Stanford: Stanford University Press.
Ferris, Marc. 2014. *Star-Spangled Banner. The Unlikely Story of America's National Anthem*. Baltimore, MD, and London: Johns Hopkins University Press.
Fichte, Johann Gottlieb. 1797–1800/1994. *Introductions to the Wissenschaftslehre and Other Writings (1797–1800)*. Ed. and trans. Daniel Breazeale. Indianapolis, IN, and Cambridge: Hackett.
Fields, Kenneth. 2009. "The Pleasures of Lying". In Harrington 2009: 275–288.
Fisch, Max Harold. 1984. "Introduction". In Vico 1744/1984: xix–xlv.
Fischer, Steven Roger. 2003. *A History of Writing*. New ed. London: Reaktion.
Fiske, John. 1989/1990. *Understanding Popular Culture*. Boston et al.: Unwin Hyman.
Fletcher, Angus 1964: *Allegory. The Theory of a Symbolic Mode*. Ithaca, NY: Cornell University Press.
Fludernik, Monika. 1993. *The Fictions of Language and the Languages of Fiction. The Linguistic Representation of Speech and Consciousness*. London and New York: Routledge.
Fludernik, Monika. 1996. *Towards a 'Natural' Narratology*. London and New York: Routledge.

Fludernik, Monika (ed.). 2011. *Beyond Cognitive Metaphor Theory. Perspectives on Literary Metaphor.* New York and London: Routledge/Taylor and Francis Group.
Fludernik, Monika. 2012. "How Natural Is 'Unnatural Narratology'; or, What Is Unnatural about Unnatural Narratology?" *Narrative* 20.3: 357–370.
Fokkema, Aleid. 1991. *Postmodern Characters. A Study of Characterization in British and American Postmodern Fiction.* Amsterdam and Atlanta: Rodopi.
Fokkema, Aleid. 1999. "The Author: Postmodernism's Stock Character". In Franssen and Hoenselaars 1999: 39–51.
Forceville, Charles. 2008. "Metaphor in Pictures and Multimodal Representations". In Gibbs 2008a: 462–82.
Ford, Ford Madox. 1915/1995. "On Impressionism". In Ford 1915/1995: 257–274.
Fowler, Alastair. 1982. *Kinds of Literature. An Introduction to the Theory of Genres and Modes.* Oxford et al.: Oxford University Press.
Franssen, Paul and Ton Hoenselaars (eds). 1999. *The Author as Character. Representing Historical Writers in Western Literature.* Madison and Teaneck, NJ/London: Fairleigh Dickinson University Press/Associated University Presses.
Freeman, Margaret H. 2005. "Poetry as Power: The Dynamics of Cognitive Poetics as a Scientific and Literary Paradigm". In Veivo et al. 2005: 31–57.
Freud, Sigmund. 1929/1961. *Civilization and Its Discontents.* Trans. James Strachey. New York and London: W. W. Norton.
Frow, John. 2005. "Genre Worlds: The Discursive Shaping of Knowledge". *Arena Journal* 23: 129–146.
Frow, John. 2006. *Genre.* London and New York: Routledge.
Frye, Northrop. 1947/1949. *Fearful Symmetry. A Study of William Blake.* Princeton, NJ: Princeton University Press.
Frye, Northrop. 1957/1973. *Anatomy of Criticism. Four Essays.* Princeton, NJ: Princeton University Press.
Frye, Northrop. 1964. *The Educated Imagination.* Bloomington and Indianapolis: Indiana University Press.
Frye, Northrop. 1981/1983. *The Great Code. The Bible and Literature.* London, Melbourne, Henley: Ark.
Furniss, Thomas. 2012. "CONNOTATION AND DENOTATION". In Roland Greene and Stephen Cushman et al. (eds), *The Princeton Encyclopedia of Poetry and Poetics.* 4th ed. Princeton, NJ: Princeton University Press. 298–299.
Furst, Lilian R. 1995. *All Is True. The Claims and Strategies of Realist Fiction.* Durham, NC, and London: Duke University Press.
Fussell, Paul. 1975. *The Great War and Modern Memory.* New York: Oxford University Press.
Fussell, Paul. 1989. *Wartime. Understanding Behavior in the Second World War.* New York and London: Oxford University Press.
Fussell, Susan R. and Roger J. Kreuz (eds). 1998. *Social and Cognitive Approaches to Interpersonal Communication.* Mahwah, NJ, and London: Lawrence Erlbaum.
Gadamer, Hans-Georg. 1975/1989. *Truth and Method.* 2nd, rev. ed. Trans. W. Glen-Doepel; rev. trans. Joel Weinsheimer and Donald G. Marshall. London: Sheed & Ward. (Original work published 1960)
Gavins, Joanna. 2007. *Text World Theory. An Introduction.* Edinburgh: Edinburgh University Press.

Gebauer, Gunter and Christoph Wulf. 1992/1995. *Mimesis. Culture – Art – Society*. Trans. Don Reneau. Berkeley, Los Angeles, London: University of California Press.
Geertz, Clifford. 1973/1993. *The Interpretation of Cultures. Selected Essays*. London: Fontana.
Geertz, Clifford. 1983/1993. *Local Knowledge. Further Essays in Interpretive Anthropology*. London: Fontana.
Geertz, Clifford. 2000. *Available Light. Anthropological Reflections on Philosophical Topics*. Princeton: Princeton University Press.
Gelpke, Rudolph. 1997/2011. "Translator's Preface". In Nizami 1997/2011: xi–xvii.
Genette, Gérard. 1972/1980. *Narrative Discourse*. Trans. Jane E. Lewin. Oxford: Basil Blackwell.
Genette, Gérard. 1979/1992: *The Architext. An Introduction*. Trans. Jane E. Lewin. Berkeley, Los Angeles, London: University of California Press.
Genette, Gérard. 1982. *Figures of Literary Discourse*. Trans. Alan Sheridan. New York: Columbia University Press.
Genette, Gérard. 1983/1988. *Narrative Discourse Revisited*. Trans. Jane E. Lewin. Ithaca, NY: Cornell University Press.
Genette, Gérard. 1987/1997. *Paratexts. Thresholds of Interpretation*. Trans. Jane E. Lewin. Cambridge, New York, Melbourne: Cambridge University Press.
Germer, Rudolf. 1966. *T. S. Eliots Anfänge als Lyriker (1905–1915)*. Heidelberg: Carl Winters Universitätsverlag.
Gerrig, Richard J. 1993. *Experiencing Narrative Worlds. On the Psychological Activities of Reading*. New Haven, CT, and London: Yale University Press.
Gibbs, Raymond W., Jr. 1994. *The Poetics of Mind. Figurative Thought, Language, and Understanding*. Cambridge et al.: Cambridge University Press.
Gibbs, Raymond W., Jr. 1999. *Intentions in the Experience of Meaning*. Cambridge et al.: Cambridge University Press.
Gibbs, Raymond W., Jr. (ed.). 2008a. *The Cambridge Handbook of Metaphor and Thought*. Cambridge et al.: Cambridge University Press.
Gibbs, Raymond W., Jr. 2008b. "Metaphor and Thought: The State of the Art". In Gibbs 2008a: 5–13.
Gibbs, Raymond W., Jr. and Herbert L. Colston (eds). 2007. *Irony in Language and Thought. A Cognitive Science Reader*. New York and London: Lawrence Erlbaum.
Gibbs, Raymond W., Jr. and Teenie Matlock. 2008. "Metaphor, Imagination, and Simulation: Psycholinguistic Evidence". In Gibbs 2008a: 161–76.
Goldblatt, Howard. 2000. "The 'Saturnicon'. Forbidden Food of Mo Yan". *World Literature Today* 74.3: 477–485.
Goldman, Jane. 2006. *The Cambridge Introduction to Virginia Woolf*. Cambridge et al.: Cambridge University Press.
Goldman, L. R. 1998. *Child's Play. Myth, Mimesis and Make-Believe*. Oxford and New York: Berg.
Goldman, Merle. 1985. "The Political Use of Lu Xun in the Cultural Revolution and After". In Lee 1985: 180–196.
Goodheart, Eugene. 1986/1995. "What Dowell Knew". In Ford 1915/1995: 375–384.
Goodman, Nelson. 1976. *Languages of Art. An Approach to a Theory of Symbols*. 2nd ed. Indianapolis, IN, and Cambridge: Hackett.
Goodman, Nelson. 1978. *Ways of Worldmaking*. Indianapolis, IN: Hackett.

Goodman, Nelson. 1984. *Of Mind and Other Matters*. Cambridge, MA, and London: Harvard University Press.
Gopnik, Alison, Andrew N. Meltzoff and Patricia K. Kuhl. 1999. *The Scientist in the Crib. Minds, Brains, and How Children Learn*. New York: William Morrow.
Gottschall, Jonathan. 2012. *The Storytelling Animal. How Stories Make Us Human*. Boston and New York: Houghton Mifflin Harcourt.
"The 'Great Preface'" [to *The Book of Songs*]. 1992. In Owen 1992: 37–56.
Green, Melanie C., Jennifer Garst and Timothy C. Brock. 2004. "The Power of Fiction: Determinants and Boundaries". In L. J. Shrum (ed.), *The Psychology of Entertainment Media*. Mahwah, NJ, and London: Lawrence Erlbaum. 161–176.
Green, Melanie C., Jeffrey J. Strange and Timothy C. Brock (eds). 2002/2013. *Narrative Impact. Social and Cognitive Foundations*. New York and Hove, East Sussex: Psychology Press.
Gregory, Derek. 1994. *Geographical Imaginations*. Cambridge, MA: Blackwell.
Greimas, A. J. 1966/1983. *Structural Semantics. An Attempt at a Method*. Trans. Daniele McDowell, Ronald Schleifer and Alan Velie. Lincoln: University of Nebraska Press.
Gu, Ming Dong. 2005. "Mimetic Theory in Chinese Literary Thought". *New Literary History* 36: 403–424.
Halliwell, Stephen. 2002. *The Aesthetics of Mimesis. Ancient Texts and Modern Problems*. Princeton, NJ: Princeton University Press.
Halliwell, Stephen. 2012. "Aristotelian Mimesis between Theory and Practice". In Isomaa et al. 2012: 3–24.
Hamburger, Käte. 1957/1993. *The Logic of Literature*. 2nd, rev. ed. Trans. Marilynn J. Rose. Bloomington and Indianapolis: Indiana University Press.
Hamon, Philippe. 1973. "Un discours constraint". *Poétique* 16: 411–445.
Hansen, Per Krogh. 2005. "When Facts Become Fiction: Facts, Fiction and Unreliable Narration". In Lars-Åke Skalin (ed.), *Fact and Fiction in Narrative: An Interdisciplinary Approach*. Örebro, Sweden: Örebro University, University Library. 283–307.
Harrington, Brooke (ed.). 2009. *Deception. From Ancient Empires to Internet Dating*. Stanford, CA: Stanford University Press.
Harris, Paul L. 1998. "Fictional absorption: emotional responses to make-believe". In Bråten 1998a: 336–353.
Harris, Paul L. 2000. *The Work of the Imagination*. Oxford and Malden, MA: Blackwell.
Hart, F. Elizabeth. 2012. "Foreword". In Jaén and Simon 2012: vii–xiii.
Haugeland, John. 1995. "Mind Embodied and Embedded". In Leila Haaparanta and Sara Heinämaa (eds), *Mind and Cognition. Philosophical Perspectives on Cognitive Science and Artificial Intelligence*. Acta Philosophica Fennica 58. Helsinki: The Philosophical Society of Finland. 233–267.
Hawking, Stephen. 1988/1989. *A Brief History of Time. From the Big Bang to Black Holes*. Toronto et al.: Bantam.
Hawking, Stephen. 1993/1994. *Black Holes and Baby Universes and Other Essays*. Toronto et al.: Bantam.
Hayot, Eric. 2012. *On Literary Worlds*. Oxford et al.: Oxford University Press.
Hegerfeldt, Anne C. 2005. *Lies that Tell the Truth. Magic Realism Seen through Contemporary Fiction from Britain*. Amsterdam and New York: Rodopi.
Heidegger, Martin. 1927/1996. *Being and Time. A Translation of* Sein und Zeit. Trans. Joan Stambaugh. Albany: State University of New York Press.

Herman, David. 2002/2004. *Story Logic. Problems and Possibilities of Narrative*. Lincoln and London: University of Nebraska Press.
Herman, David (ed.). 2003. *Narrative Theory and the Cognitive Sciences*. Stanford, CA: CSLI Publications.
Herman, David. 2009. *Basic Elements of Narrative*. Malden, MA, Oxford, Chichester: Wiley-Blackwell.
Herman, David. 2010. "Directions in Cognitive Narratology: Triangulating Stories, Media, and the Mind". In Jan Alber and Monika Fludernik (eds), *Postclassical Narratology*. Columbus: The Ohio State University Press. 137–162.
Herman, David (ed.). 2011. *The Emergence of Mind. Representations of Consciousness in Narrative Discourse in English*. Lincoln and London: University of Nebraska Press.
Herman, David. 2013. *Storytelling and the Sciences of the Mind*. Cambridge, MA, and The MIT Press.
Herman, David, Manfred Jahn and Marie-Laure Ryan (eds). 2005. *Routledge Encyclopedia of Narrative Theory*. London and New York: Routledge.
Hernadi, Paul. 2001. "Literature and Evolution". *SubStance* 30.1&2: 55–71.
Hernadi, Paul. 2002. "Why Is Literature: A Coevolutionary Perspective on Imaginative Worldmaking". *Poetics Today* 23.1: 22–44.
Hester, Marcus B. 1967. *The Meaning of Poetic Metaphor. An Analysis in the Light of Wittgenstein's Claim that Meaning Is Use*. The Hague and Paris: Mouton.
Hertzberg, Lars. 1991. "Imagination and the Sense of Identity". In David Cockburn (ed.), *Human Beings*. Royal Institute of Philosophy Supplement: 29. Cambridge et al.: Cambridge University Press. 143–155.
Heyman, Michael. 2007. "Uncovering the Tenth Rasa: An Introduction. An Indian Nonsense Naissance". In Heyman with Satpathy and Ravishankar 2007: xix–xliii.
Hirn, Yrjö. 1900. *The Origins of Art. A Psychological and Sociological Inquiry*. London and New York: Macmillan.
Hjort, Mette, and Sue Laver (eds). *Emotion and the Arts*. New York and Oxford: Oxford University Press.
Hobbes, Thomas. 1651/2008. *Leviathan*. Ed. by J. C. A. Gaskin. Oxford and New York: Oxford University Press.
Hochman, Baruch. 1985. *Character in Literature*. Ithaca, NY, and London: Cornell University Press.
Hogan, Patrick Colm. 2003/2009. *The Mind and Its Stories. Narrative Universals and Human Emotion*. Cambridge and New York: Cambridge University Press.
Hogan, Patrick Colm. 2011. *Affective Narratology. The Emotional Structure of Stories*. Lincoln and London: University of Nebraska Press.
Holm, David. 1985. "Lu Xun in the Period of 1936–1949: The Making of a Chinese Gorki". In Lee 1985: 153–179.
Horace. 1929/2005. "Ars Poetica [or Epistle to the Pisos]". In *Satires, Epistles and Ars Poetica*. The Loeb Classical Library. In Latin with trans. H. Rushton Fairclough. Cambridge, MA, and London: Harvard University Press. 450–489.
Horgan, Terence and John Tienson. 1996. *Connectionism and the Philosophy of Psychology*. Cambridge, MA, and London: The MIT Press.
Huizinga, Johan. 1950/1992. *Homo Ludens. A Study of the Play-Element in Culture*. Trans. author and R. F. C. Hull. Boston, MA: The Beacon Press.

Hume, David. 1758/1999. *An Enquiry Concerning Human Understanding*. Ed. Tom L. Beauchamp. Oxford: Oxford University Press.
Hundert, Edward M. 1995. *Lessons from an Optical Illusion. On Nature and Nurture, Knowledge and Values*. Cambridge, MA; and London: Harvard University Press.
Husserl, Edmund. 1999. *The Essential Husserl. Basic Writings in Transcendental Phenomenology*. Ed. Donn Welton. Various trans. Bloomington and Indianapolis: Indiana University Press.
Hutcheon, Linda, with Siobhan O'Flynn. 2013. *A Theory of Adaptation*. 2nd ed. Milton Park, Oxfordshire, and New York: Routledge.
Hutcheon, Pat Duffy. 1999. *Building Character and Culture*. Westport, CT, and London: Praeger.
Hühn, Peter. 2015. "Unreliability in Lyric Poetry". In Nünning 2015: 173–187.
Idema, Wilt L. 2010. "Introduction". In Idema 2010: xi–xxxvi.
Ingalls, Daniel H. H. 1990. "Introduction". In Ānandavardhana and Abhinavagupta 1990: 1–39.
Iser, Wolfgang. 1978/1984. *The Act of Reading. A Theory of Aesthetic Response*. Baltimore and London: The Johns Hopkins University Press.
Iser, Wolfgang. 1989. *Prospecting. From Reader Response to Literary Anthropology*. Baltimore and London: The Johns Hopkins University Press.
Isomaa, Saija, Sari Kivistö, Pirjo Lyytikäinen, Sanna Nyqvist, Merja Polvinen and Riikka Rossi (eds). 2012. *Rethinking Mimesis. Concepts and Practices of Literary Representation*. Cambridge: Cambridge Scholars Press.
Jaén, Isabel and Julien Jacques Simon (eds). 2012. *Cognitive Literary Studies. Current Themes and New Directions*. Austin: University of Texas Press.
Jahn, Manfred. 2005. "Cognitive Narratology". In Herman et al. 2005: 67–71.
Jakobson, Roman. 1956/1987. "Two Aspects of Language and Two Types of Aphasic Disturbances". In *Language in Literature*. Ed. Krystyna Pomorska and Stephen Rudy. Cambridge, MA, and London: The Belknap Press of Harvard University Press. 95–119.
Jakobson, Roman. 1960/1987. "Linguistics and Poetics". In *Language in Literature*. Ed. Krystyna Pomorska and Stephen Rudy. Cambridge, MA, and London: The Belknap Press of Harvard University Press. 62–94.
James, D. G. 1937. *Scepticism and Poetry. An Essay on the Poetic Imagination*. London: George Allen & Unwin.
James, D. G. 1948/1963. *The Romantic Comedy. An Essay on English Romanticism*. London: Oxford University Press.
Johansen, Jørgen Dines. 2002. *Literary Discourse. A Semiotic-Pragmatic Approach to Literature*. Toronto et al.: University of Toronto Press.
Johansen, Jørgen Dines. 2005. "Theory and/vs. Interpretation in Literary Studies". In Veivo et al. 2005: 241–266.
Johnson, Anthony W. 2005. "Notes Towards a New Imagology". *The European English Messenger* 14.1: 50–58.
Johnson, Dominic. 2012. *Theatre & the Visual*. Houndmills, Basingstoke: Palgrave Macmillan.
Johnson, Mark. 1987. *The Body in the Mind. The Bodily Basis of Meaning, Imagination, and Reason*. Chicago and London: The University of Chicago Press.
Johnson, Mark. 1993. *Moral Imagination. Implications of Cognitive Science for Ethics*. Chicago and London: The University of Chicago Press.

Joughin, John J. and Simon Malpas. 2003. "The New Aestheticism: An Introduction". In Joughin and Malpas (eds), *The New Aestheticism*. Manchester and New York: Manchester University Press. 1–19.
Jullien, François. 1995/2000. *Detour and Access. Strategies of Meaning in China and Greece*. Trans. Sophie Hawkes. New York: Zone Books.
Kant, Immanuel. 1781–1787/1996. *Critique of Pure Reason. Unified Edition*. Trans. Werner S. Pluhar. Indianapolis, IN, and Cambridge: Hackett.
Karlsson, Jonas. 2012. "'In that hour it began'? Hitler, Rienzi, and the Trustworthiness of August Kubizek's *The Young Hitler I Knew*". *The Wagner Journal* 6.2: 33–47.
Karttunen, Laura. 2015. *The Hypothetical in Literature. Emotion and Emplotment*. Tampere, Finland: Suomen Yliopistopaino/Juvenes Print.
Kasten, Madeleine. 2005. "Allegory". In Herman, Jahn and Kasten 2005: 10–2.
Katz, Alfred N., Christina Cacciari, Raymond W. Gibbs, Jr. and Mark Turner. 1998. *Figurative Language and Thought*. New York and Oxford: Oxford University Press.
Kearney, Richard. 1988. *The Wake of Imagination. Toward a Postmodern Culture*. Minneapolis: University of Minnesota Press.
Kearney, Richard. 1998. *Poetics of Imagining. Modern to Post-modern*. Edinburgh: Edinburgh University Press.
Kearney, Richard. 2004. *On Paul Ricoeur. The Owl of Minerva*. Aldershot and Burlington, VT: Ashgate.
Keen, Suzanne. 2007. *Empathy and the Novel*. Oxford et al.: Oxford University Press.
Kennedy, George A. 1998. *Comparative Rhetoric. An Historical and Cross-Cultural Introduction*. New York and London: Oxford University Press.
Kenny, Anthony. 1989/1992. *The Metaphysics of Mind*. Oxford and New York: Oxford University Press.
Khoshbakht, Maryam, Moussa Ahmadian and Shahrukh Hekmat. 2013. "A Comparative Study of Chaucer's *The Canterbury Tales* & Attar's *The Conference of the Birds*". *International Journal of Applied Linguistics & English Literature* 2.1: 90–97.
Kibler, William W. 1991/2004. "Introduction". In Chrétien de Troyes, *Arthurian Romances*. Trans. Kibler. London et al.: Penguin. 1–22.
Klapuri, Tintti. 2015. *Chronotopes of Modernity in Chekhov*. Annales Universitatis Turkuensis B 409. Turku, Finland: University of Turku.
Klinkmann, Sven-Erik (ed.). 2002. *Popular Imagination. Essays on Fantasy and Cultural Practice*. Turku, Finland: Nordic Network of Folklore.
Knight, Sabina. 2012. *Chinese Literature. A Very Short Introduction*. Oxford and New York: Oxford University Press.
Koch, Sigmund. 1999. *Psychology in Human Context. Essays in Dissidence and Reconstruction*. Eds David Finkelman and Frank Kessel. Chicago and London: The University of Chicago Press.
Koestler, Arthur. 1964/1989. *The Act of Creation*. London: Penguin/Arkana.
Kövecses, Zoltán. 2005. *Metaphor in Culture. Universality and Variation*. Cambridge et al.: Cambridge University Press.
Krausz, Michael (ed.). 2002. *Is There a Single Right Interpretation?* University Park: The Pennsylvania State University Press.
Kuzmičová, Anežka. 2013. "The Words and Worlds of Literary Narrative: The Trade-off between Verbal Presence and Direct Presence in the Activity of Reading". In Bernaerts et al. 2013b: 107–128.

Lakoff, George. 1987. *Women, Fire, and Dangerous Things. What Categories Reveal about the Mind*. Chicago and London: The University of Chicago Press.
Lakoff, George and Mark Johnson. 1980. *Metaphors We Live By*. Chicago and London: The University of Chicago Press.
Lakoff, George and Mark Johnson. 1999. *Philosophy in the Flesh. The Embodied Mind and Its Challenge to Western Thought*. New York: Basic Books.
Lakoff, George and Mark Turner. 1989. *More than Cool Reason. A Field Guide to Poetic Metaphor*. Chicago and London: The University of Chicago Press.
Lamarque, Peter, and Stein Haugom Olsen. 1994/1996. *Truth, Fiction, and Literature. A Philosophical Perspective*. Oxford: Oxford University Press.
Lane, Richard J. (ed.). 2013. *Global Literary Theory. An Anthology*. New York and London: Routledge.
Langer, Susanne K. 1942/1956. *Philosophy in a New Key. A Study in the Symbolism of Reason, Rite, and Art*. New York: Mentor.
Langer, Susanne K. 1953/1963. *Feeling and Form. A Theory of Art Developed from* Philosophy in a New Key. London: Routledge & Kegan Paul.
Langer, Susanne K. 1962. *Philosophical Sketches*. Baltimore: The Johns Hopkins Press.
Langer, Susanne K. 1988. *Mind: An Essay on Human Feeling*. Abridged ed. Ed. Gary Van Den Heuvel. Baltimore and London: The Johns Hopkins University Press.
Lanham, Richard A. 1991. *A Handlist of Rhetorical Terms*. 2nd ed. Berkeley, Los Angeles, London: University of California Press.
Laughlin, Charles. 2008. "The Revolutionary Tradition in Modern Chinese Literature". In Kam Louie (ed.), *The Cambridge Companion to Modern Chinese Culture*. Cambridge et al.: Cambridge University Press. 218–234.
Lawson-Tancred, Hugh. 1986. "Introduction". In Aristotle 1986: 11–116.
LeDoux, Joseph. 1996/1998. *The Emotional Brain. The Mysterious Underpinnings of Emotional Life*. New York et al.: Simon & Schuster.
Lee, Leo Ou-fan (ed.). 1985. *Lu Xun and His Legacy*. Berkeley, Los Angeles, London: University of California Press.
Le Goff, Jacques. 1977/1980. *Time, Work, & Culture in the Middle Ages*. Trans. Arthur Goldhammer. Chicago and London: The University of Chicago Press.
Le Goff, Jacques. 1981/1986. *The Birth of Purgatory*. Trans. Arthur Goldhammer. Chicago and London: The University of Chicago Press.
Lehtimäki, Markku. 2005. *The Poetics of Norman Mailer's Fiction. Self-Reflexivity, Literary Form, and the Rhetoric of Narrative*. Tampere, Finland: Tampere University Press.
Leidl, Christoph G. 2003. "The Harlot's Art: Metaphor and Literary Criticism". In Boys-Stones 2003: 31–54.
Lem, Stanisław. 1981/1984. "Metafantasia: The Possibilities of Science Fiction". Trans. Etelka de Laczay and Istvan Csicsery-Ronay, Jr. In *Microworlds. Writings on Science Fiction and Fantasy*. Ed. Franz Rottensteiner. San Diego, New York, London: Harvest / Harcourt Brace. 161–199.
Lem, Stanisław. 2002. "The Solaris Station". On *Stanisław Lem – The Official Site*. Accessed 13 December 2012.
http://english.lem.pl/arround-lem/adaptations/soderbergh/147-the-solaris-station?start=1
Levin, Samuel. 1977. *The Semantics of Metaphor*. Baltimore and London: The Johns Hopkins University Press.

Levine, Stephen K. 1992/1997. *Poiesis. The Language of Psychology and the Speech of the Soul*. London and Philadelpia, PA: Jessica Kingsley Publishers.
Levine, Stephen K. 2009. *Trauma, Tragedy, Therapy. The Arts and Human Suffering*. London and Philadelpia, PA: Jessica Kingsley Publishers.
Levinson, Jerrold. 1997. "Emotion in Response to Art: A Survey of the Terrain". In Hjort and Laver 1997: 20–34.
Lewis, Tyson E. 2012. "Rousseau and the Fable: Rethinking the Fabulous Nature of Educational Philosophy". *Educational Theory* 62.3: 323–341.
Lieberman, Philip. 1998. *Eve Spoke. Human Language and Human Evolution*. New York and London: W. W. Norton.
Ligotti, Thomas. 2010. *The Conspiracy against the Human Race. A Contrivance of Horror*. New York: Hippocampus Press.
Lindberg-Wada, Gunilla (ed.). 2006. *Literary History: Towards a Global Perspective*, Volumes 1–4. Berlin and New York: Walter de Gruyter.
Liu Hsie/Xie. 1959. *The Literary Mind and the Carving of Dragons*. Trans. Vincent Yu-chung Shih. New York: Columbia University Press.
Liu Hsie/Xie. 2000. "On Imagination. Chapter 26 of *Literary Mind and the Carving of Dragons*". Trans. Siu-kit Wong. In Minford and Lau 2000: 645–650.
Ljungberg, Christina. 2005. "Models of Reading: Diagrammatic Aspects of Literary Texts". In Veivo et al. 2005: 105–125.
Lloyd, G. E. R. 1990. *Demystifying Mentalities*. Cambridge et al.: Cambridge University Press.
Lloyd, G. E. R. 2003. "The Problem of Metaphor: Chinese Reflections". In Boys-Stones 2003: 101–114.
Lloyd, G. E. R. 2012. *Being, Humanity, and Understanding*. Oxford: Oxford University Press.
Locke, John. 1690/2004. *An Essay Concerning Human Understanding*. London et al.: Penguin.
Locke, John. 1693/1996. *Some Thoughts Concerning Education*. In *Some Thoughts Concerning Education and Of the Conduct of Understanding*. Eds Ruth W. Grant and Nathan Tarcov. Indianapolis, IN, and Cambridge: Hackett. 1–161.
Lodge, David. 2002. *Consciousness and the Novel. Connected Essays*. London: Secker & Warburg.
Lotman, Yuri M. 1990/2000. *Universe of the Mind. A Semiotic Theory of Culture*. Bloomington and Indianapolis: Indiana University Press.
Lovell, Julia. 2009. "Introduction". In Lu Xun 2009: xiii–xxxix.
Lu Xun. 1923/1973. "What Happens after Nora Leaves Home?". In Lu Xun 1973: 148–154.
Lu Xun. 1923/2009. "Preface". In Lu Xun 2009: 15–20.
Lu Xun. 1927/1973. "Silent China". In Lu Xun 1973: 163–167.
Lu Xun. 1973. *Silent China. Selected Writings*. Ed. and trans. Gladys Yang. London, Oxford, New York: Oxford University Press.
Lynch, Kathryn L. 2007. "The Parliament of Fowls". In Chaucer 2007: 93–96.
McCormick, Paul. 2009. "Claims of Stable Identity and (Un)reliability in Dissonant Narration". *Poetics Today* 30.2: 317–352.
McGann, Jerome J. 1973. "The Aim of Blake's Prophecies and the Uses of Blake Criticism". In Stuart Curran and Joseph Anthony Wittreich, Jr. (eds), *Blake's Sublime Allegory. Essays on The Four Zoas, Milton, Jerusalem*. Madison, WI, and London: The University of Wisconsin Press. 3–21.
McHale, Brian. 1982. "Writing about Postmodernist Writing". *Poetics Today* 3.3: 211–227.
McHale, Brian. 1987. *Postmodernist Fiction*. New York and London: Methuen.

McHale, Brian. 2001. "Weak Narrativity: The Case of Avant-Garde Narrative Poetry". *Narrative* 9.2: 161–167.
McHale, Brian. 2005. "Poetry under Erasure". In Eva Müller-Zettelmann and Margarete Rubik (eds), *Theory into Poetry. New Approaches to the Lyric*. Amsterdam and New York: Rodopi. 277–301.
McHale, Brian. 2010. "Science Fiction, or, the Most Typical Genre in World Literature". In Pirjo Lyytikäinen, Tintti Klapuri and Minna Maijala (eds), *Genre and Interpretation*. Helsinki: Department of Finnish, Finno-Ugrian and Scandinavian Studies, University of Helsinki, and The Finnish Graduate School of Literary Studies. 11–27.
Madsen, Deborah L. 1996. *Allegory in America. From Puritanism to Postmodernism*. Houndmills, Basingstoke, and London: Macmillan / New York: St. Martin's Press.
Makkreel, Rudolf A. 1975/1992. *Dilthey. Philosopher of the Human Studies*. Princeton: Princeton University Press.
Mao Zedong [Tse-Tung/Tsetung]. 1937/1967. "Myth and Reality". In Mao 1960/1967: 46.
Mao Zedong [Tse-Tung/Tsetung]. 1940/1967. "The Culture of New Democracy". In Mao 1960/1967: 58–79.
Mao Zedong [Tse-Tung/Tsetung]. 1942/1967. "Talks at the Yenan Forum on Literature and Art". In Mao 1960/1967: 1–43.
Mao Zedong [Tse-Tung/Tsetung]. 1957/1967. "Speech at the Chinese Communist Party's National Conference on Propaganda Works". In Mao 1960/1967: 142–162.
Mao Zedong [Tse-Tung/Tsetung]. 1960/1967. *On Literature and Art*. Peking [Beijing]: Foreign Languages Press.
Mao Zedong [Tse-Tung/Tsetung]. 1966/1976. *Quotations from Chairman Mao Tsetung*. Peking [Beijing]: Foreign Languages Press.
Matthiessen, C. M. I. M. 1998. "Construing processes of consciousness: From the commonsense model to the uncommonsense model of cognitive science". In J. R. Martin and Robert Veel (eds), *Reading Science. Critical and Functional Perspectives on Discourses of Science*. London and New York: Routledge. 327–356.
Mee, Jon. 1998. "The 'Insidious Poison of Secret Influence': A New Historical Context for Blake's 'The Sick Rose'". *Eighteenth Century Life* 22.1: 111–122.
Mendlesohn, Farah. 2003. "Introduction: Reading Science Fiction". In Edward James and Farah Mendlesohn (eds), *The Cambridge Companion to Science Fiction*. Cambridge et al.: Cambridge University Press. 1–12.
Mennell, Stephen and Johan Goudsblom. 1998. "Introduction". In Elias 1998: 1–45.
Metres, Philip and Tatiana Tulchinsky. 2004. "Translators' Introduction". In Rubinstein 2004: vi–xiii.
Miall, David S. 2006. *Literary Reading. Empirical and Theoretical Studies*. New York et al.: Peter Lang.
Miall, David S. 2011. "Emotions and the Structuring of Narrative Response". *Poetics Today*, 32.2: 323–348.
Mikkonen, Kai. 1997. *The Writer's Metamorphosis. Tropes of Literary Reflection and Revision*. Tampere Studies in Literature and Textuality. Tampere, Finland: Tampere University Press.
Milech, Barbara H. 1991. "Poetry and Gender". Chapter in David Buchbinder, *Contemporary Theory and the Reading of Poetry*. Melbourne: Macmillan. 120–141.
Miller, Arthur I. 1984/1986. *Imagery in Scientific Thought. Creating 20th-Century Physics*. Cambridge, MA, and London: The MIT Press.

Miller, Arthur I. 1996. *Insights of Genius. Imagery and Creativity in Science and Art*. New York: Copernicus / Springer-Verlag.
Miner, Earl. 1990. *Comparative Poetics. An Intercultural Essay on Theories of Literature*. Princeton, NJ, and Oxford: Princeton University Press.
Minford, John. 2006. "Introduction". In Pu Songling 2006: xi–xxxi.
Mitchell, W. J. T. 1978. *Blake's Composite Art. A Study of the Illuminated Poetry*. Princeton, NJ: Princeton University Press.
Mithen, Steven. 1996. *The Prehistory of the Mind. A Search for the Origins of Art, Religion and Science*. London: Phoenix.
Mithen, Steven. 2001. "The Evolution of Imagination: An Archaeological Perspective". *SubStance* 30. 1&2: 28–54.
Möllering, Guido. 2009. "Leaps and Lapses of Faith: Exploring the Relationship between Trust and Deception". In Harrington 2009: 137–153.
Montaigne, Michel de. 1958/1993. *Essays*. Trans. John M. Cohen. Harmondsworth: Penguin. (Original work published 1580)
Moore, Steven. 2010/2011. *The Novel. An Alternative History. Beginnings to 1600*. New York and London: Continuum.
Moretti, Franco (ed.). 2006a. *The Novel. Volume 1. History, Geography, and Culture*. Princeton and Oxford: Princeton University Press.
Moretti, Franco (ed.). 2006b. *The Novel. Volume 2. Forms and Themes*. Princeton and Oxford: Princeton University Press.
Murray, Nicholas. 2004/2006. *Kafka*. London: Abacus.
Murrin, Michael. 1969. *The Veil of Allegory. Some Notes Toward a Theory of Allegorical Rhetoric in the English Renaissance*. Chicago and London: The University of Chicago Press.
The Nātyaśāstra. 2010. Trans. Adya Rangacharya. New Delhi: Munshiram Manoharlal.
Nichols, Shaun (ed.). 2006. *The Architecture of the Imagination. New Essays on Pretence, Possibility, and Fiction*. Oxford et al.: Oxford University Press.
Noonuccal, Odgeroo [with photographs by Reg Morrison]. 1990. *Australian Legends and Landscapes*. Sydney et al.: Random House Australia.
Norrman, Ralf. 1977. *Techniques of Ambiguity in the Fiction of Henry James*. Åbo/Turku, Finland: Åbo Akademi.
Norrman, Ralf. 1982. *The Insecure World of Henry James's Fiction*. London/New York: Macmillan/St. Martin's Press.
Norrman, Ralf. 1986. *Samuel Butler and the Meaning of Chiasmus*. London/New York: Macmillan/St. Martin's Press.
Norrman, Ralf. 1998. *Wholeness Restored. Love of Symmetry as a Shaping Force in the Writings of Henry James, Kurt Vonnegut, Samuel Butler and Raymond Chandler*. Frankfurt am Main et al.: Peter Lang.
Norton, David L. 1996. *Imagination, Understanding, and the Virtue of Liberality*. Lanham, MD, and London: Rowman & Littlefield.
Novitz, David. 1987. *Knowledge, Fiction, and Imagination*. Philadelphia: Temple University Press.
Novitz, David. 1992. *The Boundaries of Art*. Philadelphia: Temple University Press.
Nuessel, Frank. 1995. "Vico and Current Work in Cognitive Linguistics". In Danesi 1995: 127–145.

Nuessel, Frank. 1998. "Vico's Views on Language and Linguistics". *Romance Languages Annual* IX: 280–287.
Nünning, Ansgar (ed.). 1998. *Unreliable Narration. Studien zur Theorie und Praxis unglaubwürdigen Erzählens in der englischsprachigen Erzählliteratur.* Trier: Wissenschaftlicher Verlag Trier.
Nünning, Ansgar. 1999. "Unreliable, Compared to What? Towards a Cognitive Theory of *Unreliable Narration:* Prolegomena and Hypotheses". In Walter Grünzweig and Andreas Solbach (eds), *Grenzüberschreitungen: Narratologie im Kontext / Transcending Boundaries: Narratology in Context.* Tübingen: Gunter Narr. 53–73.
Nünning, Ansgar. 2007. "Towards a Typology, Poetics and History of Description in Fiction." In Wolf and Bernhart 2007: 91–128.
Nünning, Ansgar. 2008. "Reconceptualizing the Theory, History and Generic Scope of Unreliable Narration: Towards a Synthesis of Cognitive and Rhetorical Approaches". In D'hoker and Martens 2008: 29–76.
Nünning, Ansgar and Christine Schwanecke. 2015. "The Performative Power of Unreliable Narration and Focalisation in Drama and Theatre: Conceptualising the Specificity of Dramatic Unreliability". In Nünning 2015: 189–219.
Nünning, Ansgar and Vera Nünning. 2010. "Ways of Worldmaking as a Model for the Study of Culture: Theoretical Frameworks, Epistemological Underpinnings, New Horizons". In Nünning, Nünning and Neumann 2010: 1–25.
Nünning, Vera. 2004. "Unreliable Narration and the Historical Validity of Values and Norms: *The Vicar of Wakefield* as a Test Case of a Cultural-Historical Narratology". *Style* 38.2: 236–252.
Nünning, Vera. 2010. "The Making of Fictional Worlds: Processes, Features, and Functions". In Nünning, Nünning and Neumann 2010: 215–243.
Nünning, Vera (ed.). 2015. *(Un)reliable Narration and (Un)trustworthiness. Intermedial and Interdisciplinary Perspectives.* Narratologia. Berlin, Munich and Boston: De Gruyter.
Nünning, Vera, Ansgar Nünning and Birgit Neumann (eds). 2010. *Cultural Ways of Worldmaking. Media and Narratives.* Berlin and New York: Walter de Gruyter.
Nussbaum, Martha C. 1990. *Love's Knowledge. Essays on Philosophy and Literature.* New York and Oxford: Oxford University Press.
Nussbaum, Martha C. 1995. *Poetic Justice. The Literary Imagination and Public Life.* Boston: Beacon Press.
Nussbaum, Martha C. 1997. *Cultivating Humanity. A Classical Defense of Reform in Liberal Education.* Cambridge, MA, and London: Harvard University Press.
Nussbaum, Martha C. 2001. *Upheavals of Thought. The Intelligence of Emotions.* Cambridge et al.: Cambridge University Press.
Oatley, Keith. 2002. "Emotions and the Story Worlds of Fiction". In Green, Strange and Brock 2002: 39–69.
Oatley, Keith. 2011. *Such Stuff as Dreams. The Psychology of Fiction.* Malden, MA, Oxford and Chichester: Wiley–Blackwell.
Olsen, Stein Haugom. 2015. "The Concept of Literary Realism". In J. Alexander Bareis and Lene Nordrum (eds), *How to Make Believe. The Fictional Truths of the Representational Arts.* Berlin and Boston: De Gruyter. 15–39.
Olson, David R. 1994/1996. *The World on Paper. The Conceptual and Cognitive Implications of Writing and Reading.* Cambridge, New York, Melbourne: Cambridge University Press.

Olson, David R. and Nancy Torrance (eds). 1996. *Modes of Thought. Explorations in Culture and Cognition.* Cambridge et al.: Cambridge University Press.

Ong, Walter J. 1982/1984. *Orality and Literacy. The Technologizing of the Word.* London and New York: Methuen.

Ortony, Andrew (ed.). 1993/1998. *Metaphor and Thought.* 2nd ed. Cambridge, New York, Melbourne: Cambridge University Press.

O'Sullivan, Maureen. 2009. "Why Most People Parse Palters, Fibs, Lies, Whoppers, and Other Deceptions Poorly". In Harrington 2009: 74–91.

Owen, Stephen (ed. and trans.). 1992. *Readings in Chinese Literary Thought.* Cambridge, MA, and London: Harvard University Press.

Panksepp, Jaak and Lucy Biven. 2012. *The Archaeology of Mind. Neuroevolutionary Origins of Human Emotions.* New York and London: W. W. Norton.

Patterson, Annabel. 1991. *Fables of Power. Aesopian Writing and Political History.* Durham, NC, and London: Duke University Press.

Pavel, Thomas G. 1986. *Fictional Worlds.* Cambridge, MA, and London: Harvard University Press.

Pavel, Thomas G. 2006. "The Novel in Search of Itself: A Historical Morphology". Trans. Carol Rigolot. In Moretti 2006b: 3–31.

Pavel, Thomas G. 2013. *The Lives of the Novel. A History.* Princeton, NJ, and Oxford: Princeton University Press.

Peer, Willie van and Chatman, Seymour (eds). 2001. *New Perspectives on Narrative Perspective.* Albany, NY: State University of New York Press.

Perry, Menakhem. 1979. "Literary Dynamics. How the Order of a Text Creates its Meanings [With an Analysis of Faulkner's 'A Rose for Emily']". *Poetics Today* 1.1–2: 35–64, 311–361.

Pettersson, Bo. 1993. "Redefining Prufrock's 'Overwhelming Question'". In Julian Meldon D'Arcy (ed.), *Proceedings of the Fifth Nordic Conference for English Studies.* Reykjavik: University of Iceland. 415–429.

Pettersson, Bo. 1994. *The World According to Kurt Vonnegut. Moral Paradox and Narrative Form.* Åbo/Turku, Finland: Åbo Akademi University Press.

Pettersson, Bo. 1999a. "On Narrative in Recent Anglo-American Literature, Literary Theory, Historiography and Science: Referential versus Interpretive Attitudes". In Jon Buscall and Outi Pickering (eds), *Approaches to Narrative Fiction.* Anglicana Turkuensia 18. Åbo/Turku, Finland: University of Turku. 1–19.

Pettersson, Bo. 1999b. "The Postcolonial Turn in Literary Translation Studies: Theoretical Frameworks Reviewed". *AE: Canadian Aesthetics Journal / Revue canadienne d'esthétique*, Summer 1999. <http://www.uqtr.uquebec.ca/AE/vol_4/petter.htm>

Pettersson, Bo. 1999c. "Towards a Pragmatics of Literary Interpretation". In Arto Haapala and Ossi Naukkarinen (eds), *Interpretation and Its Boundaries.* Helsinki: Helsinki University Press. 48–65.

Pettersson, Bo. 1999d. "'Would I Lie to You?': Deception, Self-Deception and the Teaching of Literature in Academia". In Sanna-Kaisa Tanskanen and Brita Wårvik (eds), *Proceedings of the 7th Nordic Conference on English Studies.* Anglicana Turkuensia 20. Åbo/Turku, Finland: University of Turku. 397–409.

Pettersson, Bo. 1999e. "Who Is 'Sivilizing' Who(m)?: The Function of Naivety and the Criticism of *Huckleberry Finn* – A Multidimensional Approach". In Irma Taavitsainen, Gunnel Melchers and Päivi Pahta (eds), *Writing in Nonstandard English*. Pragmatics and Beyond NS 67. Amsterdam: Benjamins. 101–122.

Pettersson, Bo. 1999f. "Om Runeberg och mytbildning" [On Runeberg and Myth-Making]. *Finsk Tidskrift* 1: 14–21.

Pettersson, Bo. 2001a. "On LIFE IS A JOURNEY as a Link between Analogy and Narrative". In Martin Gill, Anthony W. Johnson, Lena M. Koski, Roger D. Sell and Brita Wårvik (eds), *Language, Learning, Literature. Studies Presented to Håkan Ringbom*. English Department Publications 4. Åbo/Turku, Finland: Åbo Akademi University. 199–214.

Pettersson, Bo. 2001b. "The Finnish National Anthem in Translation: Deixis and National Sentiment". Pirjo Kukkonen and Ritva Hartama-Heinonen (eds), *Mission, Vision, Strategies, and Values. A Celebration of Translator Training and Translation Studies in Kouvola*. Helsinki: Helsinki University Press. 187–194.

Pettersson, Bo. 2002. "Från babyspråk till litteraturtolkning" [From Motherese to Literary Interpretation]. *Finsk Tidskrift* 2–3: 112–123.

Pettersson, Bo. 2004a. "The Geography of Time Remembered: Richard Brautigan's Autobiographical Fiction". *Helsinki English Studies* 3 / 2004. http://www.eng.helsinki.fi/hes/Literature/geography_of_time1.htm

Pettersson, Bo. 2004b. "Exploring the Common Ground: *Sensus Communis*, Humour and the Interpretation of Comic Poetry". *Journal of Literary Semantics* 33.2. 153–165.

Pettersson, Bo. 2005a. "Literature as a Textualist Notion". In Stein Haugom Olsen and Anders Pettersson (eds), *From Text to Literature. New Analytic and Pragmatic Approaches*. Houndmills, Basingstoke, and New York: Palgrave Macmillan. 128–145.

Pettersson, Bo. 2005b. "Afterword. Cognitive Literary Studies: Where to Go from Here". In Veivo et al. 2005: 307–322.

Pettersson, Bo. 2005c. "The Many Faces of Unreliable Narration: A Cognitive Narratological Reorientation". In Veivo et al. 2005: 59–88.

Pettersson, Bo. 2007. "The Real in the Unreal: Mimesis and Postmodern American Fiction". *The European English Messenger* 16.1: 33–39.

Pettersson, Bo. 2008. "Procrustean Beds and Strange Bedfellows: On Literary Value as Assigned by Literary Theories". *Journal of Literary Theory* 2.1: 19–33.

Pettersson, Bo. 2009a. "Narratology and Hermeneutics: Forging the Missing Link". In Sandra Heinen and Roy Sommer (eds), *Narratology in the Age of Interdisciplinary Narrative Research*. Berlin and New York: Walter de Gruyter. 11–34.

Pettersson, Bo. 2009b. "Three Fallacies in Interpreting Literature". In Jason Finch, Martin Gill, Anthony Johnson, Iris Lindahl-Raittila, Inna Lindgren, Tuija Virtanen and Brita Wårvik (eds), *Humane Readings. Essays on Literary Mediation and Communication in Honour of Roger D. Sell*. Amsterdam and Philadelphia: Benjamins. 145–156.

Pettersson, Bo. 2011. "An Invitation to Imagine: On the Significance of Imagination in Cognition, Literature and Literary Studies". In Stein Haugom Olsen and Anders Pettersson (eds), *Why Literary Studies? Raisons d'Être of a Discipline*. Oslo: Novus. 133–155.

Pettersson, Bo. 2012a. "Beyond Anti-Mimetic Models: A Critique of Unnatural Narratology". In Isomaa et al. 2012: 73–91.

Pettersson, Bo. 2012b. "On the Linguistic Turns in the Humanities and Their Effect on Literary Studies". In Ansgar Nünning and Kai Marcel Sicks (eds), *Turning Points. Concepts and Narratives of Change in Literature and Other Media*. spectrum Literature 33. Berlin and Boston: De Gruyter. 407–423.

Pettersson, Bo. 2012c. "What Happens When Nothing Happens: Interpreting Narrative Technique in the Plotless Novels of Nicholson Baker". In Markku Lehtimäki, Laura Karttunen and Maria Mäkelä (eds), *Narrative, Interrupted. The Plotless, the Disturbing and the Trivial in Literature*. Berlin and Boston: De Gruyter. 42–56.

Pettersson, Bo. 2013. "Hypothetical Action. Poetry under Erasure in Blake, Dickinson and Eliot". In Roger D. Sell, Inna Lindgren and Adam Borch (eds), *The Ethics of Literary Communication. Genuineness, Directness, Indirectness*. Amsterdam and Philadelphia: Benjamins. 129–145.

Pettersson, Bo. 2014. "The Hilarious and Serious Teachings of Lem's Robot Fables: *The Cyberiad*". In Peter Swirski and Waclaw M. Osadnik (eds), *Lemography. Stanislaw Lem in the Eyes of the World*. Liverpool: Liverpool University Press. 93–113.

Pfister, Manfred. 1977/1993. *The Theory and Analysis of Drama*. Trans. John Halliday. Cambridge, New York, Melbourne: Cambridge University Press.

Phelan, James. 2005. *Living to Tell about It. A Rhetoric and Ethics of Character Narration*. Ithaca, NY, and London: Cornell University Press.

Phelan, James. 2006. "Narrative Theory, 1966–2006: A Narrative". In Scholes, Phelan and Kellogg 2006: 283–336.

Phelan, James. 2007. *Experiencing Fiction. Judgments, Progressions, and the Rhetorical Theory of Narrative*. Columbus: The Ohio State University Press.

Phelan, James. 2008. "Estranging Unreliability, Bonding Unreliability, and the Ethics of *Lolita*". In D'hoker and Martens 2008: 7–28.

Pico della Mirandola, Gianfrancesco. 1930. *On the Imagination*. Cornell Studies in English XVI. Trans. Harry Caplan. New Haven, CT: Yale University Press.

Poetics Today. Special issues "Literature and the Cognitive Revolution" 23: 1 (Spring 2002) and "The Cognitive Turn? A Debate on Interdisciplinarity" 24: 2 (Summer 2003).

Polichak, James W. and Richard J. Gerrig. "'Get Up and Win!' Participatory Responses to Narrative". In Green, Strange and Brock 2002: 71–95.

Polvinen, Merja. In press. "Enactive Perception and Fictional Worlds". In Peter Garratt (ed.), *The Cognitive Humanities. Embodied Mind in Literature and Culture*. Palgrave Macmillan.

Popova, Yanna B. 2015. *Stories, Meaning, and Experience. Narrativity and Enaction*. New York and Milton Park, Abingdon: Routledge.

Popper, Karl R. 1945/1983. "The Defence of Rationalism". In David Miller (ed.), *A Pocket Popper*. n.p.: Fontana. 33–45.

Posner, Michael I. and Daniel J. Levitin. 1997/1999. "Imaging the Future". In Robert L. Solso (ed.), *Mind and Brain Sciences in the 21st Century*. Cambridge, MA, and London: The MIT Press. 91–109.

Posner, Michael I. and Marcus E. Raichle. 1994/1997. *Images of Mind*. New York: Scientific American Library.

Potolsky, Matthew. 2006. *Mimesis*. London and New York: Routledge.

Prince, Gerald. 1992. *Narrative as Theme. Studies in French Fiction*. Lincoln and London: University of Nebraska Press.

Propp, Vladimir. 1928/2009. *Morphology of the Folktale*. 2nd rev. ed. Ed. Louis A. Wagner. Trans. Laurence Scott. Austin: University of Texas Press.

Quintilian. 2001. *The Orator's Education [Institutio Oratoria]. Books 1–12*. Volumes I–V. The Loeb Classical Library. Ed. and trans. Donald A. Russell. Cambridge, MA, and London: Harvard University Press.

Raglan, Lord [FitzRoy Richard Somerset]. 1936/1990. *The Hero: A Study in Tradition, Myth, and Drama*. In Rank, Raglan and Dundes 1990: 87–175.
Rajan, Chandra. 1993. "Introduction". In Visnu Śarma 1993: xv–lv.
Rank, Otto. 1909/1990. *The Myth of the Birth of the Hero*. Trans. F. Robbins and Smith Ely Jelliffe. In Rank, Raglan and Dundes 1990: 1–86.
Rank, Otto, Lord Raglan and Alan Dundes. 1990. *In Quest of the Hero*. Princeton: Princeton University Press.
Rees, Thomas R. 1974. *The Technique of T. S. Eliot. A Study in the Orchestration of Meaning in Eliot's Poetry*. The Hague: Mouton.
Reiss, Tom. 2005. "Imagining the Worst. How a Literary Genre Anticipated the Modern World". *The New Yorker* (November 28, 2005). 106–114.
Rhetorica ad Herennium [Cicero] [?]. 1954. In Latin with trans. Harry Caplan. Cambridge, MA, and London: Harvard University Press.
Richards, I. A. 1926/2001. *Principles of Literary Criticism*, 2nd ed. London and New York: Routledge. (Original work published 1924)
Richards, I. A. 1932. *Mencius on the Mind. Experiments in Multiple Definition*. New York/London: Harcourt, Brace and Company/Kegan Paul, Trench, Trubner & Co.
Richards, I. A. 1934/1969. *Coleridge on Imagination*. Bloomington and London: Indiana University Press.
Richards, I. A. 1936/1965. *The Philosophy of Rhetoric*. London, Oxford, New York: Oxford University Press.
Richardson, Alan. 2010. *The Neural Sublime. Cognitive Theories and Romantic Texts*. Baltimore, MD: Johns Hopkins University Press.
Richardson, Alan. 2011. "Defaulting to Fiction: Neuroscience Rediscovers the Romantic Imagination". *Poetics Today* 32.4: 663–692.
Richardson, Alan. 2015. "Imagination. Literary and Cognitive Intersections". In Zunshine 2015. 225–245.
Richardson, Brian. 2006. *Unnatural Voices. Extreme Narration in Modern and Contemporary Fiction*. Columbus: The Ohio State University Press.
Richardson, Nicholas. 1993. *The Iliad: A Commentary. Volume VI: Books 21–24*. Cambridge, New York, Oakleigh, Victoria: Cambridge University Press.
Ricœur, Paul. 1974/2004. "Structure and Hermeneutics". Trans. Kathleen McLaughlin. In *The Conflict of Interpretations. Essays in Hermeneutics*. Ed. Don Ihde. London and New York: Continuum. 27–60.
Ricœur, Paul. 1977/2003. *The Rule of Metaphor. The Creation of Meaning in Language*. Trans. Robert Czerny with Kathleen McLaughlin and John Costello. London and New York: Routledge. (Rev. ed. of the French original from 1975)
Ricœur, Paul. 1983/1990. *Time and Narrative. Volume 1*. Trans. Kathleen McLaughlin and David Pellauer. Chicago and London: The University of Chicago Press.
Ricœur, Paul. 1984/1985. *Time and Narrative. Volume 2*. Trans. Kathleen McLaughlin and David Pellauer. Chicago and London: The University of Chicago Press.
Ricœur, Paul. 1985/1988. *Time and Narrative. Volume 3*. Trans. Kathleen McLaughlin and David Pellauer. Chicago and London: The University of Chicago Press.
Ricœur, Paul. 1991/2008. "Imagination in Discourse and Action". Trans. Kathleen Blamey. In *From Text to Action. Essays in Hermeneutics, II*. London and New York: Continuum. 164–183.

Ridley, Aaron. 1997. "Not Ideal: Collingwood's Expression Theory". *Journal of Aesthetics and Art Criticism* 55.3: 263–272.
Rieder, John. 2008. *Colonialism and the Emergence of Science Fiction*. Middletown, CT: Wesleyan University Press.
Riggan, William. 1981. *Pícaros, Madmen, Naïfs, and Clowns. The Unreliable First-Person Narrator*. Norman: University of Oklahoma Press.
Ritvo, Harriet. 1997. *The Platypus and the Mermaid and Other Figments of the Classifying Imagination*. Cambridge, MA, and London: Harvard University Press.
Robinson, Gillian and John Rundell (eds). 1994. *Rethinking Imagination. Culture and Creativity*. London and New York: Routledge.
Rodi, Frithjof. 1985. "Hermeneutics and the Meaning of Life: A Critique of Gadamer's Interpretation of Dilthey". In Hugh J. Silverman and Don Ihde (eds), *Hermeneutics and Deconstruction*. Albany, NY: State University of New York Press. 82–90.
Rosenberg, Bruce A. 1986. "Was There a Popular Culture in the Middle Ages?" In Campbell 1986: 152–157.
Ryan, Marie-Laure. 1980. "Fiction, Non-Factuals, and the Principle of Minimal Departure". *Poetics Today* 9.4: 403–422.
Ryan, Marie-Laure. 2007. "Toward a Definition of Narrative". In David Herman (ed.), *The Cambridge Companion to Narrative*. Cambridge et al.: Cambridge University Press. 22–35.
Ryan, Marie-Laure. 2009. "Cheap Plot Tricks, Plot Holes, and Narrative Design". *Narrative* 17.1: 56–75.
Ryle, Gilbert. 1949/1990. *The Concept of Mind*. Harmondsworth: Penguin.
Saler, Michael. 2012. *As If. Modern Enchantment and the Literary Prehistory of Virtual Reality*. Oxford et al.: Oxford University Press.
Saltzman, Arthur. 1999. *Understanding Nicholson Baker*. Columbia: University of South Carolina Press.
Sandbacka, Carola. 1987. *Understanding Other Cultures. Studies in the Philosophical Problems of Cross-Cultural Interpretation*. Acta Philosophica Fennica 42. Helsinki: The Philosophical Society of Finland.
Sanford, Anthony J. and Catherine Emmott. 2012. *Mind, Brain and Narrative*. Cambridge et al.: Cambridge University Press.
Sartre, Jean-Paul. 1940/1978. *The Psychology of Imagination*. Trans. Bernard Frechtman. London: Methuen.
Savage-Rumbaugh, Sue, Stuart G. Shanker and Talbot J. Taylor. 1998. *Apes, Language, and the Human Mind*. New York and Oxford: Oxford University Press.
Schaeffer, Jean-Marie. 1999/2010. *Why Fiction?* Trans. Dorrit Cohn. Lincoln and London: University of Nebraska Press.
Schaeffer, Jean-Marie and Ioana Vultur. 2005. "Mimesis". In Herman et al. 2005: 309–310.
Schauer, Frederick and Richard Zeckhauser. 2009. "Paltering". In Harrington 2009: 38–54.
Schleiermacher, Friedrich. 1799/1988. *On Religion. Speeches to Its Cultured Despisers*. Ed. Richard Crouter. Cambridge et al.: Cambridge University Press.
Scholes, Robert, James Phelan and Robert Kellogg. 2006. *The Nature of Narrative*. Fortieth Anniversary Edition, Revised and Expanded. Oxford et al.: Oxford University Press.
Scholes, Robert and Eric S. Rabkin 1977: *Science Fiction. History – Science – Vision*. London, Oxford, New York: Oxford University Press.

Schön, Donald A. 1993/1998. "Generative Metaphor: A Perspective on Problem-Setting in Social Policy." In Ortony 1993/1998: 137–163.
Scruton, Roger. 1974/1982. *Art and Imagination. A Study in the Philosophy of Mind.* London et al.: Routledge & Kegan Paul.
Scruton, Roger. 1983. *The Aesthetic Understanding. Essays in the Philosophy of Art and Culture.* London and New York: Methuen.
Sebeok, Thomas A. 1994. "Some Reflections of Vico in Semiotics". In Danesi and Nuessel 1994b: 113–124.
Segal, Erwin M. 1995. "Narrative Comprehension and the Role of Deictic Shift Theory". In Judith F. Duchan, Gail A. Bruder and Lynne E. Hewitt (eds), *Deixis in Narrative. A Cognitive Science Perspective.* Hillsdale, NJ, and Hove, UK: Lawrence Erlbaum. 3–17.
Segal, Robert A. 1990. "Introduction: In Quest of the Hero". In Rank, Raglan and Dundes 1990: vii–xli.
Seitel, Peter. 2003. "Theorizing Genres – Interpreting Works". *New Literary History* 34: 275–297.
Sell, Roger D. 2002. *Mediating Criticism. Literary Education Humanized.* Amsterdam: Benjamins.
Semino, Elena. 1997/2014. *Language and World Creation in Poems and Other Texts.* London and New York: Routledge.
Semino, Elena and Jonathan Culpeper (eds). 2002. *Cognitive Stylistics. Language and Cognition in Text Analysis.* Amsterdam and Philadelphia: Benjamins.
Semino, Elena and Gerard Steen. 2008. "Metaphor in Literature". In Gibbs 2008a: 232–46.
Shelley, Percy Bysshe. 1840/2002. "A Defence of Poetry". In *The Selected Poetry and Prose of Shelley.* London: Wordsworth. 635–660.
Shklovsky, Viktor. 1917/1998. "Art as Device". In *Theory of Prose.* Trans. Benjamin Sher. Normal, IL: Dalkey Archive Press. 1–14.
Shore, Bradd. 1996. *Culture in Mind. Cognition, Culture, and the Problem of Meaning.* New York and Oxford: Oxford University Press.
Short, Philip. 1999. *Mao. A Life.* London: Hodder and Stoughton.
Shulman, Robert. 1998/2009. "Introduction". In Wister 1902/2009: vii–xxix.
Sidney, Sir Philip. 1595/2004. "The Defence of Poesy". In Alexander 2004b: 1–54.
Silk, Michael. 2003. "Metaphor and Metonymy: Aristotle, Jakobson, Ricœur, and Others". In Boys-Stones 2003: 115–147.
Skalin, Lars-Åke. n.d. "Stories in Disguise: On Odysseus' Ithacan Lies and Their Relevance to the Device of the Unreliable Narrator". http://www.oru.se/PageFiles/5354/Lars-%c3%85ke%20Skalin%20-%20Stories%20in%20Disguise.pdf (accessed on 26 March 2013)
Sloterdijk, Peter. 1998/2011. *Spheres. Volume 1: Bubbles. Microspherology.* Trans. Wieland Hoban. Los Angeles, CA: Semiotext(e).
Sloterdijk, Peter. 1999/2014. *Spheres. Volume 2: Globes. Macrospherology.* Trans. Wieland Hoban. Los Angeles, CA: Semiotext(e).
Slotkin, Richard. 1973/2000. *Regeneration through Violence. The Mythology of the American Frontier, 1600–1860.* Norman: University of Oklahoma Press.
Slotkin, Richard. 1985/1986. *The Fatal Environment. The Myth of the Frontier in the Age of Industrialization, 1800–1890.* Middletown, CT: Wesleyan University Press.
Slotkin, Richard. 1992/1998. *Gunfighter Nation. The Myth of the Frontier in Twentieth-Century America.* Norman: University of Oklahoma Press.

Smith, Henry Nash. 1950/1973. *Virgin Land. The American West as Symbol and Myth.* Cambridge, MA: Harvard University Press.
Smith, John D. 2009. "Introduction". In *The Mahābhārata* 2009: xi–lxx.
Smith, Roger. 1997. *The Fontana History of the Human Sciences.* London: Fontana.
Smith, Roger. 2007. *Being Human. Historical Knowledge and the Creation of Human Nature.* New York: Columbia University Press.
Snow, C. P. 1959/1964. *The Two Cultures: and a Second Look.* Cambridge: Cambridge University Press.
Soja, Edward W. 1996. *Thirdspace. Journeys to Los Angeles and Other Real-and-Imagined Places.* Cambridge, MA: Blackwell.
Spinoza, Benedictus de. 1677/1989. *Ethics.* Ed. and rev. trans. G. H. R. Parkinson. Trans. Andrew Boyle. London: J. M. Dent & Sons.
Stallybrass, Peter and Allon White. 1986. *The Politics and Poetics of Transgression.* London: Methuen.
Stanzel, F. K. 1979/1986. *A Theory of Narrative.* Trans. Charlotte Goedsche. Cambridge et al.: Cambridge University Press.
Steen, Gerard. 2005. "Parable". In Herman, Jahn and Ryan 2005: 418–9.
Stern, J. P. 1973. *On Realism.* London and Boston: Routledge & Kegan Paul.
Sternberg, Meir. 1978. *Expositional Modes and Temporal Ordering in Fiction.* Baltimore and London: The Johns Hopkins University Press.
Sternberg, Meir. 2003a. "Universals of Narrative and Their Cognitivist Fortunes (I)". *Poetics Today* 24.2: 297–395 and 517–638.
Sternberg, Meir. 2003b. "Universals of Narrative and Their Cognitivist Fortunes (II)". *Poetics Today* 24.3: 517–638.
Stevenson, Robert Louis. 1883/1925. "A Note on Realism". In *Essays in the Art of Writing.* London: Chatto & Windus. 95–111.
Stockwell, Peter. 2002. *Cognitive Poetics.* London: Routledge.
Storey, Robert. 1996. *Mimesis and the Human Animal. On the Biogenetic Foundations of Literary Representation.* Evanston, IL: Northwestern University Press.
Strange, Jeffrey J. 2002/2013. "How Fictional Tales Wag Real-World Beliefs". In Green, Strange and Brock 2002/2013: 263–286.
Struck, Peter T. 2004. *Birth of the Symbol. Ancient Readers at the Limits of Their Texts.* Princeton, NJ, and Oxford: Princeton University Press.
Suddendorf, Thomas. 2013. *The Gap. The Science of What Separates Us from Other Animals.* New York: Basic Books.
Suvin, Darko. 1974/1988. "Science Fiction and Utopian Fiction: Degrees of Kinship". In Suvin 1988: 33–43.
Suvin, Darko. 1982/1988. "The SF Novel as Epic Narration: For a Fusion of 'Formal' and 'Sociological' Analysis". In Suvin 1988: 74–85.
Suvin, Darko. 1988. *Positions and Presuppositions in Science Fiction.* Kent, OH: Kent State University Press.
Svensson, Martin. 1999. "A Second Look at the *Great Preface* on the Way to a New Understanding of Han Dynasty Poetics". *Chinese Literature, Essays, Articles, Reviews* [CLEAR] 21: 1–33.
Svensson Ekström, Martin. 2006. "One Lucky Bastard: On the Hybrid Origins of Chinese 'Literature'". In Gunilla Lindberg-Wada (ed.), *Literary History: Towards a Global*

Perspective, Volume 1. *Notions of Literature Across Times and Cultures*. Ed. Anders Pettersson. Berlin and New York: Walter de Gruyter. 70–110.
Swain, Tony. 1993/1997. *A Place for Strangers. Towards a History of Australian Aboriginal Being*. Cambridge et al.: Cambridge University Press.
Swirski, Peter. 2005. *From Lowbrow to Nobrow*. Montreal and London: McGill-Queen's University Press.
Swirski, Peter. 2007. *Of Literature and Knowledge. Explorations in Narrative Thought Experiments, Evolution, and Game Theory*. London and New York: Routledge.
Tagliacozzo, Giorgio and Donald Phillip Verene (eds). 1976. *Giambattista Vico's Science of Humanity*. Baltimore and London: The Johns Hopkins University Press.
Tallis, Raymond. 1995. *Newton's Sleep. Two Cultures and Two Kingdoms*. Houndmills, Basingstoke, and London / New York: Macmillan / St. Martin's Press.
Tallis, Raymond. 2000. "The Difficulty of Arrival: Reflections on the Function of Art". In Michael Grant (ed.), *The Raymond Tallis Reader*. Houndmills, Basingstoke, and New York: Palgrave. 354–61.
Tallis, Raymond. 2012a. "Zhuangzi and that Bloody Butterfly". In Tallis 2012c: 30–35.
Tallis, Raymond. 2012b. "In Defence of Wonder". In Tallis 2012c: 1–22.
Tallis, Raymond. 2012c. *In Defence of Wonder and Other Philosophical Reflections*. Durham and Bristol, CT: Acumen.
Tate, Aaron. 2005. "Fable". In Herman, Jahn and Ryan 2005: 157.
Taylor, Mark C. and Esa Saarinen. 1994. *Imagologies. Media Philosophy*. London: Routledge.
Todorov, Tzvetan. 1971/1977. *The Poetics of Prose*. Trans. Richard Howard. Ithaca, NY: Cornell University Press.
Tomasello, Michael. 1999a. *The Cultural Origins of Human Cognition*. Cambridge, MA, and London: Harvard University Press.
Tomasello, Michael. 1999b. "Having Intentions, Understanding Intentions, and Understanding Communicative Intentions". In Philip David Zelaso, Janet Wilde Astington and David R. Olson (eds), *Developing Theories of Intention. Social Understanding and Self-Control*. Mahwah, NJ, and London: Lawrence Erlbaum Associates. 63–75.
Tomasello, Michael. 2008/2010. *Origins of Human Communication*. Cambridge, MA, and London: The MIT Press.
Tomasello, Michael. 2014. *A Natural History of Human Thinking*. Cambridge, MA, and London: Harvard University Press.
Tompkins, Jane. 1992. *West of Everything. The Inner Life of Westerns*. New York and Oxford: Oxford University Press.
Tooby, John and Leda Cosmides. 1992. "The Psychological Foundations of Culture". In Jerome H. Barkow, Leda Cosmides and John Tooby (eds), *The Adapted Mind. Evolutionary Psychology and the Generation of Culture*. New York and Oxford: Oxford University Press. 19–136.
Trivers, Robin. 2011. *Deceit and Self-Deception. Fooling Yourself the Better to Fool Others*. London: Allen Lane.
Turner, Frederick Jackson. 1893/2008. "The Significance of the Frontier in American History". In Turner 2008: 1–38.
Turner, Frederick Jackson. 1910/2008. "Social Forces in American History". In Turner 2008: 89–115.
Turner, Frederick Jackson. 2008. *The Significance of the Frontier in American History*. London et al.: Penguin.

Turner, Mark. 1987. *Death Is the Mother of Beauty. Mind, Metaphor, Criticism*. Chicago and London: University of Chicago Press.
Turner, Mark. 1991. *Reading Minds. The Study of English in the Age of Cognitive Science*. Princeton, NJ: Princeton University Press.
Turner, Mark. 1996. *The Literary Mind*. New York and Oxford: Oxford University Press.
Turner, Mark (ed.). 2006. *The Artful Mind. Cognitive Science and the Riddle of Human Creativity*. Oxford et al.: Oxford University Press.
Turner, Victor [W.]. 1982. *From Ritual to Theatre. The Human Seriousness of Play*. New York: PAJ Publications.
Turner, Victor [W.]. 1986. "Dewey, Dilthey, and Drama: An Essay in the Anthropology of Experience". In Victor W. Turner and Edward M. Bruner (eds), *The Anthropology of Experience*. Urbana and Chicago: University of Illinois Press. 33–44.
Tuttle, Howard N. 1976. "The Epistemological Status of the Cultural World in Vico and Dilthey". In Tagliacozzo and Verene 1976: 241–250.
Uexküll, Jakob von. 2010. *A Foray into the Worlds of Animals and Humans* with *A Theory of Meaning*. Trans. Joseph D. O'Neil. Minneapolis and London: The University of Minnesota Press.
Vaihinger, Hans. 1925/2009. *The Philosophy of 'As if'. A System of the Theoretical, Practical and Religious Fictions of Mankind*. Trans. C. K. Ogden. New York: Harcourt, Brace and Company / London: Kegan Paul, Trench, Trubner & Co.
Valdés, Mario J. 1992. *World-Making. The Literary Truth-Claim and the Interpretation of Texts*. Toronto, Buffalo and London: University of Toronto Press.
Veivo, Harri, Bo Pettersson and Merja Polvinen (eds). 2005. *Cognition and Literary Interpretation in Practice*. Helsinki: Helsinki University Press.
Verdonk, Peter. 1990. "Poems as Texts and Discourse: The Poetics of Philip Larkin". In Roger D. Sell (ed.), *Literary Pragmatics*. London and New York: Routledge. 94–109.
Verene, Donald Phillip. 1981. *Vico's Science of Imagination*. Ithaca, NY, and London: Cornell University Press.
Verene, Donald Phillip. 1994. "Vico's Education". In Danesi and Nuessel 1994b: 135–146.
Vermeule, Blakey. 2010. *Why Do We Care about Literary Characters?* Baltimore: The Johns Hopkins University Press.
Vico, Giambattista. 1708–09/1990. *On the Study Methods of Our Time*. Trans. Elio Gianturco. Ithaca, NY, and London: Cornell University Press.
Vico, Giambattista. 1744/1984. *The New Science of Giambattista Vico. Unabridged Translation of the Third Edition (1744) with the addition of "Practic of the New Science"*. Trans. Thomas Goddard Bergin and Max Harold Fisch. Ithaca, NY, and London: Cornell University Press.
Villanueva, Darío. 1992/1997. *Theories of Literary Realism*. Trans. Mihai I. Spariosu and Santiago García-Castañón. Albany, NY: State University of New York Press.
Vonnegut, Kurt. 1977/1982. "Self-Interview". In *Palm Sunday. An Autobiographical Collage*. London et al.: Granada. 89–120.
Vorobyova, Olga. 2005. "'The Mark on the Wall' and Literary Fancy: A Cognitive Sketch". In Veivo et al. 2005: 201–217.
Walsh, Richard. 2007. *The Rhetoric of Fictionality*. Columbus: The Ohio State University Press.
Walton, Kendall. 1990. *Mimesis as Make-Believe. On the Foundations of the Arts*. Cambridge, MA, and London: Harvard University Press.
Warnock, Mary. 1972/1978. "Introduction". In Sartre 1940/1978: ix–xvii.

Warnock, Mary. 1976. *Imagination*. Berkeley and Los Angeles: University of California Press.
Warnock, Mary. 1994. *Imagination and Time*. Oxford and Cambridge, MA: Blackwell.
Watkins, Calvert. 1995/2001. *How to Kill a Dragon. Aspects of Indo-European Poetics*. Oxford and New York: Oxford University Press.
Watt, Ian. 1957. *The Rise of the Novel. Studies in Defoe, Richardson and Fielding*. London: Chatto and Windus.
Webster's Encyclopedic Unabridged Dictionary of the English Language. 1989. New York: Portland House.
Wellek, René and Austin Warren. 1948/1956. *Theory of Literature*. 3rd ed. New York: Harvest / Harcourt, Brace & World.
Werth, Paul. 1999. *Text Worlds. Representing Conceptual Space in Discourse*. Harlow, Essex: Longman.
West, M. L. 2007/2010. *Indo-European Poetry and Myth*. Oxford et al.: Oxford UP.
White, Alan R. 1990. *The Language of Imagination*. Oxford and Cambridge, MA: Basil Blackwell.
White, Hayden. 1973. *Metahistory. The Historical Imagination in Nineteenth-Century Europe*. Baltimore and London: The Johns Hopkins University Press.
White, Hayden. 1978/1987. *Tropics of Discourse. Essays in Cultural Criticism*. Baltimore and London: The Johns Hopkins University Press.
White, Hayden. 1999/2000. *Figural Realism. Studies in the Mimesis Effect*. Baltimore and London: The Johns Hopkins University Press.
Whyte, Iain Boyd. 2006. "Anglo-German Conflict in Popular Fiction, 1870–1914". In Bridgham 2006: 43–99.
Williams, David. 2012. *The Trickster Brain. Neuroscience, Evolution, and Narrative*. Lanham, MD, and Plymouth, UK: Lexington Books.
Wittgenstein, Ludwig. 1953/1991. *Philosophical Investigations*. Trans. G. E. M. Anscombe. Oxford: Basil Blackwell.
Wolf, Mark J. P. 2012. *Building Imaginary Worlds. The Theory and History of Subcreation*. New York and London: Routledge.
Wolf, Werner. 2007. "Description as a Transmedial Mode of Representation: General Features and Possibilities of Realization in Painting, Fiction and Music". In Wolf and Bernhart 2007: 1–87.
Wolf, Werner and Walter Bernhart (eds). 2007. *Description in Literature and Other Media*. Amsterdam and New York: Rodopi.
Woolf, Virginia. 1928/2000. *A Room of One's Own*. London et al.: Penguin.
Woolley, Jacqueline D. and Victoria Cox. 2007. "Development of Beliefs about Storybook Reality". *Developmental Science* 10.5: 681–693.
Worthington, Heather. 2005. *The Rise of the Detective in Early Nineteenth-Century Popular Fiction*. Houndmills, Basingstoke and New York: Palgrave Macmillan.
Wollheim, Richard. 1984. *The Thread of Life*. Cambridge, MA: Harvard University Press.
Yacobi, Tamar. 2000. "Interart Narrative: (Un)reliability and Ekphrasis". *Poetics Today* 21.4: 711–749.
Yates, Frances. 1966/2014. *The Art of Memory*. London: The Bodley Head.
Zarrilli, Phillip B., Bruce McConachie, Gary Jay Williams and Carol Fisher Sorgenfrei. 2010. *Theatre Histories. An Introduction*. 2nd ed. Ed. Gary Jay Williams. New York and London: Routledge.

Zerubavel, Eviatar. 1997/1999. *Social Mindscapes. An Invitation to Cognitive Sociology.* Cambridge, MA, and London: Harvard University Press.

Zerweck, Bruno. 2001. "Historicizing Unreliable Narration: Unreliability and Cultural Discourse in Narrative Fiction". *Style* 35.1: 151–178.

Zunshine, Lisa. 2006. *Why We Read Fiction. Theory of Mind and the Novel.* Columbus: The Ohio State University Press.

Zunshine, Lisa. (ed.). 2015. *The Oxford Handbook on Cognitive Literary Studies.* New York and Oxford: Oxford University Press.

Zwerdling, Alex. 1986. *Virginia Woolf and the Real World.* Berkeley, Los Angeles and London: University of California Press.

Electronic Sources

amazon.com
english.lem.pl (Stanislaw Lem – The Official Site)
fsgbooks.com/classicalchinesepoetry
global.britannica.com
litimag.oxfordjournals.org
metrolyrics.com
nobelprize.org
oru.se (see Skalin n.d.)
riddles.com
scholar.google.com
uqtr.uquebec.ca/AE (see Pettersson 1999b)
wikipedia.org (en.wikipedia.org/wiki/Star-crossed)

Index

This index includes names as well as the titles of works whose authors are anonymous or which have been compiled by a team of collaborators.

Abel, Reuben   29, 115
Abhinavagupta   94, 244
Abrams, M. H.   42 f., 52
Achebe, Chinua   105
Ackroyd, Peter   104, 187
Aeschylus   132, 182
Aesop   58, 170, 172, 263
Ahmadian, Moussa   256
Akutagawa, Ryonosuke   99 f.
Alain de Lille   142
Alber, Jan   43
Aldiss, Brian   69
Alexander, Gavin   235
Alexander the Great   209
Alm-Arvius, Christina   158
Althusser, Louis   19
Altieri, Charles   236
Altman, Charles F.   27
Ānandavardhana, Rājānaka   94, 136, 244
Anderson, Benedict   210, 211
Anderson, Marsten   233
Anne of Bohemia   141
Apuleius   81, 96, 106
The Arabian Nights (see also *One Thousand and One Nights*)   58, 107 f.
Archilochus   30
Aristophanes   129, 132, 256, 264
Aristotle   3, 6, 11–14, 26, 33, 38
Ariwara no Narihira   156
Armstrong, Paul B.   102 f.
Ashbery, John   198
Attar, Farid ud-Din   256, 262, 264 f.
Auerbach, Erich   2, 5, 42, 47, 51 f., 65
Augustine of Hippo [Saint Augustine]   12
Austen, Jane   127, 200, 218
Auster, Paul   129

Bachelard, Gaston   30, 39
Bacon, Francis   13 f., 24, 35
Bakeless, John   214 f.
Baker, Nicholson   130, 202–206

Bakhtin, M. M.   22, 118, 126, 274
Bal, Mieke   3, 42, 111, 155
Banfield, Ann   3
Banville, John   92–95
Barnes, Julian   63, 200
Barnstone, Willis   231 f.
Barth, John   60, 255, 257
Barthes, Roland   19
Bashō, Matsuo   53, 130, 156
Bateson, Gregory   48, 85, 112, 199, 244
Beaumarchais, Pierre   210
Beckett, Samuel   44, 55, 117, 133, 169, 177
Beecroft, Alexander   45
Bell, Michael J.   22, 27
Bely [Belyi], Andrei [Boris Nikolaevich Bugaev]   59
Berlin, Isaiah   24 f., 30
Berlusconi, Silvio   80
Bernaerts, Lars   157
Berndt, Catherine H.   268, 270 f., 273
Berndt, Ronald M.   268, 270 f., 273
Beroul [Béroul]   255
Betjeman, John   95, 136
Bharata Muni   248
The Bible   39, 208, 239, 264
Biebuyck, Benjamin   163
Bindman, David   166
Biven, Lucy   274
Blackwood's Magazine   222, 225
Blake, William   38, 41, 125, 130, 163–168, 172 f., 187–189, 196 f., 199, 275
Bloch, Ernst   67, 147
"Bo Is Brave"   54
Boccaccio, Giovanni   58, 108, 141
Bod, Rens   271 f.
Boethius [Anicius Manlius Severinus Boëthius]   141
Boitani, Piero   141, 143
Bonaventura   12
The Book of Songs [*Shijing*]   54, 122, 240, 245 f.

Booker, Christopher   117
Boone, Daniel   213–218, 220f., 227, 229, 233
Booth, Wayne C.   26, 81f., 84, 208, 236
Borges, Jorge Luis   134
Botton, Alain de   203
Bourg, Tammy   85
Bowers, Faubion   130
Boyd, Brian   29, 48, 117, 242–244
Brann Eva T.   10
Bråten, Stein   20, 112, 158
Brautigan, Richard   130
Brecht, Bertolt   44, 210
Bremond, Claude   185
Brentano, Franz   9, 17, 30
Brett, R. L.   39
Bridgham, Fred   225f.
Bristow, Michael Jamieson   211
Brock, Timothy C.   211, 241
Brontë, Charlotte   96
Brooke-Rose, Christine   5, 60, 65, 67
Brown, Andrew   203
Brown, Fredric   1f., 134, 273
Brown, Richard Harvey   29
Browning, Robert   94f.
Bruner, Jerome   120, 153f., 159
Bruno, Giordano   13, 22
Bryan, Daniel   214f., 217
Bryant, Mark L.   128
Buber, Martin   16, 61
Buck, Pearl S.   181
Bulgakov, Mikhail   59
Bulwer-Lytton, Edward   209
Burke, Johnny   32
Burke, Kenneth   17, 27, 151f., 161
Burke, Michael   29
Burton, Richard Francis   258
Butler, Christopher   237
Butler, Octavia E.   134
Butler, Samuel   178, 209
"The Butterfly Lovers"   136, 257, 259, 261
Buxton, Richard   249f.
Byron, George Gordon, Lord   217

Calderón de la Barca, Pedro   148
Callois, Roger   244
Campbell, Joseph   116, 136

Cao Xueqin   56
Caracciolo, Marco   40
Carlyle, Thomas   147
Carroll, Joseph   29, 236f., 244
Carroll, Lewis [Charles Lutwidge Dodgson]   128
Carroll, Noël   22
Carruthers, Mary   273
Carter, Angela   128
Carter, Rita   25
Carver, Raymond   70, 105
Casares, Adolfo Bioy   256
Cassirer, Ernst   17, 20f., 118, 158, 161f., 273f.
Castoriadis, Cornelius   21
Cavendish, Margaret, Duchess of Newcastle   267–271
Cawelti, John G.   216f., 219, 227
Cervantes, Miguel de   52f., 56, 58, 108, 185
Chamowitz, Daniel   274
Chan, Shelley W.   232
Chandler, Raymond   71, 178
Chang [Zhang] Liang   33
Chase, Richard   20f., 52
Chatman, Seymour   157f., 164, 201f.
Chaucer, Geoffrey   55, 58, 108, 140–143, 148, 184, 256
Cheever, John   63
Chekhov, Anton   127, 274
Chesney, George Tomkyns   222–229, 233
Chesterman, Andrew   29
Chesterton, G. K.   134
Childers, Erskine   226
Chopin, Kate   127, 169, 261
Christ (see *Jesus Christ*)
Christie, Agatha   103f., 170
Churchill, Caryl   210
Cicero, Marcus Tullius   79, 140f., 143
Clark, George Rogers   216
Clark, Herbert H.   85
Clarke, Arthur C.   134
Clarke, I. F.   222, 225, 227f.
Cohn, Dorrit   48, 87, 156
Cole, Michael   30f.
Coleridge, Samuel Taylor   15f., 35–39, 112f., 161

Collingwood, R. G.   2, 12, 17, 25, 27
Collins, Christopher   29, 112, 244
Collins, Randall   17
Collins, Suzanne   259
Colston, Herbert L.   85
Confucius [Kongzi]   45, 122, 239
Connery, Sean   227
Conrad, Joseph   74
Cooder, Ry   80
Cooper, Gary   219
Cooper, James Fenimore   216–219
Corballis, Michael   20
Corneille, Pierre   131
Cornoldi, Cesare   30
Cosmides, Leda   29 f.
Cox, Victoria   111
Crane, Stephen   224
Crisp, Peter   166–168
Croce, Benedetto   17
Crockett, Davy   218
Crumbley, Paul   192
Csicsery-Ronay, Istvan, Jr.   64
Culpeper, Jonathan   156
Cunliffe, Richard John   251
Currie, Gregory   26, 113, 236
Curtius, Ernst Robert   142

Damasio, Antonio   29, 154
Damrosch, David   53
D'Andrade, Roy   30
Danesi, Marcel   24, 129
Dante Alighieri   262
Darwin, Charles   75
Davies, Stephen   29, 244
Davis, Dick   255, 262
Davis, Todd F.   26, 236
De Jong, Irene J. F.   250
de León, Elizabeth   73
de Maistre, Xavier   202 f.
Deacon, Terrence   21, 158
Defoe, Daniel   51, 81, 102, 108
Delany, Samuel R.   185 f.
DeLillo, Don   60
Deng Xiaoping   230
Dennett, Daniel C.   28
Depp, Johnny   106
Derrida, Jacques   19

Descartes, René   12, 14 f.
Dewey, John   13, 26
D'haen, Theo   53
Diamond, Cora   236
Diamond, Jared   60
Díaz, Junot   66, 72–76
Dick, Philip K.   70, 91 f., 101, 134, 257
Dickens, Charles   60, 119
Dickinson, Emily   190–192, 196 f., 277
Dilthey, Wilhelm   16 f., 23 f., 28
Diski, Jenny   108 f.
Disney, Walt   263
Dissanayake, Ellen   17, 21, 29, 48, 86, 114, 122, 158, 236, 244
Doležel, Lubomír   116, 119
Donald, Merlin   19 f., 31, 46
Doody, Margaret Anne   53, 63, 117, 252
Dostoevsky, Fyodor   62, 89 f., 102, 129
Doyle, Arthur Conan   48
Droysen, Johann Gustav   28
Dryden, John   212
Dumas, Alexandre, père   132
Dundes, Alan   179
Durix, Jean-Pierre   65
Durkheim, Émile   20
Dutton, Denis   29, 244
Dylan, Bob   219

Easterlin, Nancy   29, 244
Egan, Kieran   10, 12 f., 20, 22
Eggers, Dave   63, 136
Eichenbaum, Boris   173
Einstein, Albert   2, 22, 227
Elias, Norbert   9, 17, 20 f., 29, 158
Eliot, George   180 f.
Eliot, T. S.   54, 59, 106, 129 f., 193 f., 196 f.
Ellis, Bret Easton   102
Ellis, Ralph D.   11, 19, 28
Ellmann, Richard   155
Emmott, Catherine   49, 85, 121, 133, 153
Engel, Susan   158
Enkvist, Nils Erik   168
Enright, D. J.   95, 136
The Epic of Gilgamesh (see *Gilgamesh*)
Epstein, Mikhail N.   269
Esrock, Ellen J.   19
Esslin, Martin   44, 210

Euripides 182
Everyman [*The Moral Play of Everyman*] 152

Fagles, Robert 249
Faragher, John Mack 214f., 217
Fauconnier, Gilles 153, 160
Faulkner, William 59, 89, 96
Feagin, Susan L. 113
Felski, Rita 64
Feng Zhenluan 51
Fenollosa, Ernest 124f., 155
Fernandez, James W. 154
Ferris, Marc 212
Fichte, Johann Gottlieb 18, 21
Fielding, Henry 51, 206
Fields, Kenneth 81
Filson, John 213–221, 227–229, 233
Fisch, Max Harold 24
Fischer, Steven Roger 124
Fiske, John 27
Flaubert, Gustave 127, 169, 180
Fleming, Ian 227
Fletcher, Angus 76, 162, 166f., 171
Flint, Timothy 217
Fludernik, Monika 3, 43, 49f., 67, 72, 74, 156, 163
Flynn, Gillian 104, 133
Fokkema, Aleid 114, 125, 184
Forceville, Charles 162
Ford, Ford Madox 102f., 185
Forster, E. M. 63, 226
Foucault, Michel 19
Fowler, Alastair 65, 201
Fowler, Karen Joy 100, 134, 149
Franssen, Paul 184
Frayn, Michael 88, 104
Freeman, Margaret H. 168
Freud, Sigmund 17f., 22, 25, 33
Freytag, Gustav 176
Frow, John 66f., 126, 199f.
Frye, Northrop 38f., 116f., 162, 167
Furniss, Thomas 94
Furst, Lilian R. 43
Fussell, Paul. 28
Fussell, Susan R. 30

Gadamer, Hans-Georg 16, 74
Gaige, Amity 93f.
Gaiman, Neil 134
Galsworthy, John 181
Gao E 56, 254, 259
García Márquez, Gabriel 59
Garst, Jennifer 211, 241
Gautama Buddha, Siddhārtha 239
Gautier, Théophile 237
Gavins, Joanna 118
Gebauer, Gunter 41, 45
Geertz, Clifford 23, 29f., 120
Gelpke, Rudolph 256
Gendlin, Eugene T. 29
Genette, Gérard 4, 41f., 66, 110, 116, 176, 184, 202, 250
Germer, Rudolf 194
Gerrig, Richard J. 85, 112–114
Gesta Romanorum 58
Geyh, Paula 182
Gibbons, Alan 66, 72, 75f.
Gibbs, Raymond W., Jr. 19, 29, 84f., 153, 160, 162, 173
Gibson, William 66, 70, 72, 75f.
Gilgamesh 106f., 131f., 239
Gill, Harjeet Singh 257
Girard, René 178
Goethe, Johann Wolfgang von 17, 53, 180, 209, 251
Goffman, Erving 199
Gogol, Nikolai 59, 81, 90f.
Goldblatt, Howard 91
Goldman, Jane 145
Goldman, L. R. 20
Goldman, Merle 229f.
Gomez, Jewelle 200
Goodheart, Eugene 102f.
Goodman, Nelson 118–120
Gopnik, Alison 25, 46, 85
Gorgani, Fakhraddin 255, 261
Gottschall, Jonathan 209
Goudsblom, Johan 9
"The 'Great Preface'" [to *The Book of Songs*] 246
Green, Melanie C. 211, 241
Greene, Graham 63
Gregory, Derek 27

Greimas, A. J.   116
Grimm, Jacob   240
Grimm, Wilhelm   240
Grisham, John   128, 225
Groom, Winston   89
Gu, Ming Dong   34, 45, 122, 124
Guillaume de Lorris   142
Gutenberg, Johannes   58

Haddon, Mark   85
Haley, Alex   209
Halliwell, Stephen   41, 45–48, 197
Hamburger, Käte   87
Hamon, Philippe   67
Hansen, Per Krogh   81
Harding, Chester   217
Hardy, Thomas   60, 176
Harrington, Brooke   81
Harris, Joanne   101
Harris, Joel Chandler   58
Harris, Paul L.   25, 85, 101, 111–114
Harrison, Harry   63
Hart, F. Elizabeth   159
Haslett, Adam   99
Haugeland, John   29
Hawking, Stephen   27
Hawkins, Paula   104, 133, 186
Hawthorne, Nathaniel   62, 98
Hayot, Eric   6, 117 f.
The Hebrew Bible   208, 239
  "Heer Ranjha"   257
Hegerfeldt, Anne C.   65
Heidegger, Martin   273
Heisenberg, Werner   22
Hekmat, Shahrukh   256
Heliodorus   56, 117
Heller, Joseph   181
Herman, David   87, 110, 114, 118 f., 157 f., 164, 166, 186, 202
Hernadi, Paul   121, 208, 236 f.
Hertzberg, Lars   29
Hester, Marcus B.   174
Heyman, Michael   136 f.
Hinton, David   123 f., 245 f.
Hippocrates of Kos   141 f.
Hirn, Yrjö   244
Hitchcock, Alfred   72

Hitler, Adolf   209
Hjort, Mette   113 f., 236
Hobbes, Thomas   13
Hochman, Baruch   58, 125
Hoenselaars, Ton   184
Hogan, Patrick Colm   94, 117, 131
Holberg, Ludvig   148
Holm, David   131, 229
The Holy Bible (see *The Bible*)
Homer   51, 105, 107, 249–251
Horace   45, 235, 238 f., 243
Horgan, Terence   30
Hühn, Peter   108
Huizinga, Johan   244
Hume, David   15
Hundert, Edward M.   31
Husserl, Edmund   17 f., 28 f.
Hustvedt, Siri   267–271
Hutcheon, Linda   121
Hutcheon, Pat Duffy   20, 31

Ibsen, Henrik   210, 233
Idema, Wilt L.   259
"In the Wilderness Is a Dead Deer"   245 f., 250
Ingalls, Daniel H. H.   136, 244
The Ise Stories [*The Tales of Ise*]   156
Iser, Wolfgang   26, 185
Ishiguro, Kazuo   83
Iversen, Stefan   43

Jackendoff, Ray   150
Jackson, Andrew   218
Jacobsen, Thorkild   54, 122
Jaén, Isabel   114, 153, 159
Jahn, Manfred   150
Jakobson, Roman   28, 44, 152 f., 174
James, D. G.   38
James, E. L. [Erika Mitchell]   104
James, Henry   63, 76, 90, 98–100, 105, 113, 127, 133, 169, 178, 185
Jay, Martin   21
Jean de Meun   142
Jesus Christ   39, 92, 147, 190, 192, 239
Jiang Qing   230
Jin Ying   228

Johansen, Jørgen Dines 159–161, 166, 171, 236
Johnson, Adam 98, 102
Johnson, Anthony W. 19
Johnson, Dominic 123
Johnson, Mark 10, 13, 15, 19, 24, 29–31, 37f., 153f., 157
Joughin, John J. 237
Journey to the West 131, 258
Joyce, James 63, 168
Jullien, François 175
Juvenal, Decimus Junius 72

Kafka, Franz 59, 61, 169f., 181
The Kalevala 106
Kālidāsa 240, 246–248
Kant, Immanuel 9, 13–16, 21, 35
Karadžić, Vuk 211f.
Karlsson, Bernhard 245
Karlsson, Jonas 209
Karttunen, Laura 186
Kasten, Madeleine 76, 162, 166
Katz, Alfred N. 30, 153
Kearney, Richard 10, 13f., 16, 18f., 30f., 162, 274
Keats, John 41
Keen, Suzanne 236
Kellogg, Robert 51f., 63f.
Kelly, Grace 219
Kelvin, Lord [William Thomson] 147
Kennedy, George A. 78
Kennedy, John F. 79, 221
Kenny, Anthony 12
Kerouac, Jack 129
Key, Francis Scott 212
Keynes, Geoffrey 165, 168, 188
Khoshbakht, Maryam 256
Kibler, William W. 256
Kierkegaard, Søren 16
Kimmel, Michael 163
King, Stephen 69, 104, 133
Kirk, G. S. 250
Kivi, Aleksis 242
Klapuri, Tintti 274
Klinkmann, Sven-Erik 23
Knight, Sabina 91
Koch, Sigmund 29

Koestler, Arthur 157, 209
The *Kokinshū* 156
Kosinski, Jerzy 89
Kouyaté, Djeli Mamoudou 107
Kövecses, Zoltán 154
Krausz, Michael 208
Kreuz, Roger J. 30
Kristeva, Julia 19, 22
Kuan Han-ch'ing 55
Kubizek, August 209
Kuhn, Thomas S. 22
Kurosawa, Akira 99
Kushner, Tony 210
Kuzmičová, Anežka 40

La Fontaine, Jean de 58, 260f., 263
Labov, William 185
Lacan, Jacques 19
Lakoff, George 15, 19, 24, 29, 31, 37f., 153f., 156, 158f.
Lamarque, Peter 47, 111
Lane, Richard J. 53
Langer, Susanne K. 17, 21, 158, 161f.
Langland, William 240
Lanham, Richard A. 120
Lao-Tzu [Laozi] 239
Larkin, Philip 197
Lattimore, Richmond 248
Lau, Joseph S. M. 124, 245
Laughlin, Charles 233
Laver, Sue 113f., 236
Lawson-Tancred, Hugh 12
le Carré, John [David John Moore Cornwell] 69, 225
Le Goff, Jacques 22
Le Queux, William 225–227
LeDoux, Joseph 14
Lee, Ang 254
Lee, Harper 89, 209, 218
Lehtimäki, Markku 130
Leidl, Christoph G. 152
Lem, Stanisław 43, 59, 129, 134, 146–149
Lennon, John 131, 137
León-Portilla, Miguel 34, 122, 268, 270, 274
Leonard, Elmore 71
Lerner, Laurence 168

Levin, Harry   168
Levin, Samuel   110–112, 114
Levine, Stephen K.   272
Levinson, Jerrold   114
Levitin, Daniel J.   19
Lévy-Bruhl, Lucien   20
Lewis, Sinclair   181
Lewis, Tyson E.   263
Lichtheim, Miriam   260
Lieberman, Philip   20
Ligotti, Thomas   267–271
Lindberg-Wada, Gunilla   53
Liu Xie [Hsie]   33 f.
Ljungberg, Christina   158
Lloyd, G. E. R.   150, 154, 175, 250
Locke, John   13
Lodge, David   271 f.
Longinus, Cassius   38
Lotman, Yuri M.   118
Lovecraft, H. P.   268
Lovell, Julia   228, 231 f.
Lu Xun   91, 228–234
Lucian   107, 126, 268
Ludlow, Noah   218
Luhmann, Niklas   21
Lynch, Kathryn L.   140 f.

McCartney, Paul   131
McCormick, Paul   82
McGann, Jerome J.   188
McHale, Brian   64, 98, 120, 125, 134, 198, 205
McInerney, Jay   169
Macrobius Ambrosius Theodosius   141
Madsen, Deborah L.   170
The Mahābhārata   56 f., 61, 132, 182, 240, 247 f.
Mailer, Norman   130
Makkreel, Rudolf A.   16
Malpas, Simon   237
Mamet, David   210
The Manyōshū   94, 155, 240
Mao Zedong [Tse-Tung / Tsetung]   228–233
Marcus Aurelius   204
Martens, Gunther   163
Martin, George R. R.   45, 104
Matlock, Teenie   162

Matthiessen, C. M. I. M.   19
Maupassant, Guy de   90 f.
Mee, Jon   165
Melville, Herman   62, 98
Mencius [Mengzi]   39, 239
Mendlesohn, Farah   64
Mennell, Stephen   9
Mercier, Vivian   177
Metres, Philip   269
Meyer, Stephenie   200, 259
Miall, David S.   29, 37, 39, 85, 114
Michelangelo di Lodovico Buonarroti Simoni   193, 196
Mikkonen, Kai   260
Milech, Barbara H.   192
Miller, Arthur I.   27
Miller, J. Hillis   236
Mills, Magnus   163, 168–173, 178, 202, 227
Milton, John   239
Miner, Earl   5, 44 f.
Minford, John   51, 61, 124, 245
Miss Manners [Judith Martin]   102
Mitchell, W. J. T.   104, 189
Mithen, Steven   30, 41
Mo Yan   61, 132, 232, 234, 257–259
Molière [Jean-Baptiste Poquelin]   44, 84, 129
Möllering, Guido   80 f., 85
Montaigne, Michel de   32
Moore, Alan   66, 72, 75 f.
Moore, Steven   53
More, Thomas   209, 268
Moretti, Franco   53
Morrison, Toni   60, 63, 182, 200
Muhammad   239
Munro, Alice   92
Murasaki Shikibu [Lady Murasaki]   57–60, 156
Murray, Nicholas   61
Murrin, Michael   166

Nabokov, Vladimir   81, 84, 92, 169, 243
Napoleon III   222 f.
Nash, Ogden   95, 136
The Nātyaśāstra   136, 244 f., 248
Newman, John Henry [Cardinal Newman]   38

Niane, D. T.   107
Nichols, Shaun   2, 236
Nielsen, Henrik Skov   43
Nietzsche, Friedrich   16
Nixon, Richard M.   79
Nizami [Nezami] Ganjavi   255f., 261
Nolan, Christopher   257
Noonuccal, Odgeroo   268, 271
Norrman, Ralf   105, 158, 177f.
Norton, David L.   10, 30f.
Novitz, David   22, 26, 49
Nuessel, Frank   15, 23f., 116, 158
Nünning, Ansgar   82f., 108, 149, 157, 202
Nünning, Vera   81–83, 120f., 149
Nussbaum, Martha C.   26, 31, 236

Oatley, Keith   48, 83, 85, 94
O'Clair, Robert   155
O'Flynn, Siobhan   121
The Old Testament   208, 239
Olsen, Stein Haugom   47, 51, 111
Olson, David R.   30, 123
One Thousand and One Nights (see also *The Arabian Nights*)   60, 239
Ong, Walter J.   123
Opie, Iona   128, 134
Opie, Peter   128, 134
Ortony, Andrew   153
Orwell, George [Eric Arthur Blair]   58, 132, 209, 263
Ostriker, Alicia   188
O'Sullivan, Maureen   81
Outlaws of the Marsh [*Water Margin*]   132, 230, 257
Ovid   121, 253f., 256, 261
Owen, Stephen   34, 246
Owen, Wilfred   234

The Pañcantantra   58, 61, 130, 339, 256, 263
Panksepp, Jaak   274
Parker, Dorothy   95, 136
Parkinson, R. B.   260
Patterson, Annabel   263
Pavel, Thomas G.   116f., 119
Peer, Willie van   157
Perrault, Charles   240, 263

Perrotin, Henri Joseph Anastase   68
Perry, Menakhem   96–98, 104
Pettersson, Bo   6, 16, 27–29, 31, 43f., 48, 59, 63, 81f., 86–89, 95, 104, 127, 130, 154, 156f., 159, 169, 172, 195, 200, 203, 208, 212, 272
Pfister, Manfred   44
Phelan, James   43, 51f., 64, 81f., 92, 95, 97, 116, 173, 236
Piaget, Jean   25, 158
Pico della Mirandola, Gianfrancesco   12f., 31
Pico della Mirandola, Giovanni   12
Plato   11f., 41–43, 47, 66, 108, 202, 208f., 268
Poe, Edgar Allan   59, 62, 81, 128, 268
Poems on Life and Love in Ancient India (see *Sattasaī*)
Poetics Today   156
Polanyi, Michael   29
Polichak, James W.   113
Polidori, John   200, 258
Polvinen, Merja   40
The Popol Vuh   270
Popova, Yanna B.   159
Popper, Karl R.   25
Posner, Michael I.   19
Potolsky, Matthew   47
Pound, Ezra   124f., 155, 243, 245f.
Powys, T. F.   152
Pratchett, Terry   152
Prince, Gerald   185f.
Propp, Vladimir   116
Protagoras   29, 115
Proulx, Annie   254
Proust, Marcel   63
Pu Songling   50f., 61, 240
Pullman, Philip   59, 127, 201
Pushkin, Alexander   242
Pynchon, Thomas   181, 200

Quintilian   38, 120, 151f., 166, 202
The Qur'an   239, 265

Rabelais, François   59
Rabkin, Eric S.   71, 76
Racine, Jean   56, 124

Radcliffe, Ann 128
Raglan, Lord [FitzRoy Richard Somerset] 116
Raichle, Marcus E. 19
Rajan, Chandra 58, 258
Ramanujan, A. K. 240
Rank, Otto 116
Ravenscroft, Ian 236
Ray, Sukumar 136
Reagan, Ronald 72, 76, 80, 221
Reardon, B. P. 56
Reed, Jimmy 169
Rees, Thomas R. 196
Reiss, Tom 222, 225, 227
Remarque, Erich Maria 129, 170
Remington, Frederic 221
Resnais, Alain 257
Reza, Yasmina 177
Rhetorica ad Herennium 120, 151, 202
Rhys, Ernest 137
Rice, Anne 200
Richard II, King 141
Richards, I. A. 32, 35–39
Richardson, Alan 3, 19, 37, 39, 113
Richardson, Brian 43
Richardson, Nicholas 250
Richardson, Samuel 51
Ricoeur, Paul 16, 21, 37f., 45, 49f., 74, 156, 158, 160–162, 167, 171–174, 176
Ridley, Aaron 17
Rieder, John 227
Riffaterre, Michael 202
The Rig Veda 122, 128
Riggan, William 81, 89f., 106
Ritvo, Harriet 27
Robbe-Grillet, Alain 257
Roberts, Frederick, Lord 226
Robinson, Gillian 21
Roche, Paul 138
Rodi, Frithjof 16
Roosevelt, Theodore 221
Rose, George 165
Rosenberg, Bruce A. 28
Rousseau, Jean-Jacques 263
"Row, Row, Row Your Boat" 49, 86f., 106, 112, 148
Rowling, J. K. 104, 201

Rubinstein, Lev 267–271
Rumi, Jalal al-Din 265
Rundell, John 21
Runeberg, Johan Ludvig 212
Rushdie, Salman 246
Russell, Bertrand 227
Ryan, Marie-Laure 4, 49, 185, 205
Ryder, Arthur William 258
Ryle, Gilbert 12, 18, 32

Saarinen, Esa 19
Saler, Michael 48
Salinger, J. D. 81, 181
Saltzman, Arthur 203
Sandbacka, Carola 23
Sanford, Anthony J. 49, 85, 121, 133, 153
Sartre, Jean-Paul 17–19, 24, 30
Sattasaī [Hāla's *Sattasaī*] 94, 240
Savage-Rumbaugh, Sue 31
Sayers, Dorothy L. 103
Scaliger, Joseph Justus 235, 238
Schaeffer, Jean-Marie 29, 47–49, 119f.
Schauer, Frederick 79
Schiaparelli, Giovanni 68
Schleiermacher, Friedrich 9, 16, 23f., 31
Scholes, Robert 51f., 63f., 71, 76
Schön, Donald A. 161
Scipio Aemilianus 140
Scipio Africanus 140f., 143
Scott, Ridley 70
Scott, Walter 218f.
Scruton, Roger 26
Sebeok, Thomas A. 24
Sedaris, David 130, 260, 264
Segal, Erwin M. 40
Segal, Robert A. 116
Seidensticker, Edward G. 57, 130
Seitel, Peter 126
Sell, Roger D. 197
Semino, Elena 118, 156, 162
Service, Robert 204
Shakespeare, William 55, 84, 121, 131, 133, 144f., 183, 218, 240, 248f., 253f., 261, 269
Shelley, Mary 62, 126, 128, 200
Shelley, Percy Bysshe 35f., 38
Shklovsky, Viktor 2, 36, 185, 206

Shore, Bradd 30
Shorris, Earl 34, 122, 268, 270, 274
Short, Philip 10, 232
Shulman, Robert 218
Sidney, Sir Philip 56, 235 f., 238
Silk, Michael 174
Silliman, Ron 188
Simon, Julien Jacques 114, 153, 159
Sinatra, Frank 32
Sinding, Michael 163
Śivadāsa 128, 258
Skalin, Lars-Åke 106
Sloterdijk, Peter 272 f.
Slotkin, Richard 217, 221
Smith, Henry Nash 220 f.
Smith, John D. 57
Smith, Roger 272
Snow, C. P. 28
Soja, Edward W. 27
Somadeva 61, 240
Sophocles 137–140, 182
Soyinka, Wole 210
Spenser, Edmund 41
Spinoza, Benedictus de [Baruch] 14
Stallybrass, Peter 22
Stanzel, F. K. 52
Steen, Gerard 162, 168
Steinbeck, John 89
Stern, J. P. 59, 67, 81
Sternberg, Meir 96–98, 104, 116
Sterne, Laurence 182
Stevenson, Robert Louis 60
Stockwell, Peter 118, 156
Stoker, Bram 200
Stoppard, Tom 149, 183 f.
Storey, Robert 29, 244
Stowe, Harriet Beecher 209
Strange, Jeffrey J. 50, 61, 89 f., 211
Struck, Peter T. 42
Su Hui 124
Suddendorf, Thomas 9, 19, 25, 30
Sundiata (see Niane, D. T.)
Suvin, Darko 67, 134, 147
Svensson [Ekström], Martin 45, 245 f.
Swain, Tony 268, 273
Swift, Jonathan 59, 209, 214

Swirski, Peter 22, 29
Szilárd, Leó 227

Tagliacozzo, Giorgio 24
Tagore, Rabindranath 136
The Tale of King Cheops' Court 242
The Tale of Sinuhe 154
The Tale of the Shipwrecked Sailor 107, 260
Tallis, Raymond 149, 237, 251
Tan, Shaun 125
Tate, Aaron 169
Taylor, Mark C. 15, 19
Tecayehuatzin of Huexotzinco 34, 182
Thomas Aquinas 12
Thomas of Britain [Brittany] 255
Thurber, James 204, 264
Tienson, John 30
Tiptree, James, Jr. [Alice B. Sheldon] 99, 105, 134
Todorov, Tzvetan 116, 158
Tolkien, J. R. R. 48, 59, 73, 104, 117, 201
Tolstoy, Leo 30, 132
Tomasello, Michael 10, 20, 25, 30, 85, 158
Tompkins, Jane 219
Tooby, John 29 f.
Torrance, Nancy 30
Trivers, Robin 78, 92
Trujillo, Rafael 73
Trumbull, John 215
The Tso Chuan [*Zuo Zhuan*] 257
Tulchinsky, Tatiana 269
Turner, Frederick Jackson 219–221
Turner, Mark 19, 29, 153, 156 f., 159–161, 220 f., 244
Turner, Victor 17, 21, 23, 158, 244
Tuttle, Howard N. 24
Twain, Mark [Samuel Langhorne Clemens] 62, 81, 83, 125, 181, 217, 262
Tylor, Edward 116
Tzara, Tristan 137

Uexküll, Jakob von 274
Updike, John 255

Vaihinger, Hans 11, 48
Valdés, Mario J. 118

Veivo, Harri 174
Verdonk, Peter 197
Verene, Donald Phillip 24, 31
Vermeule, Blakey 59, 112 f., 125
Vico, Giambattista 15, 23–27, 29, 31, 115 f., 151 f., 158
Victoria, Queen 33, 225
Villanueva, Darío 65
Vine, Barbara [Ruth Rendell] 133
Virgil 212, 262
Visnu Śarma 58, 239, 263
Voltaire [François-Marie Arouet] 89
Vonnegut, Kurt 59, 134, 178, 234
Vorobyova, Olga 145
Vultur, Ioana 47

Wagner, Richard 209
Walsh, Richard 40
Walton, Kendall 113, 244
Waris Shah 257
Warnock, Mary 10, 13, 15, 18, 30
Warren, Austin 3
Water Margin (see *Outlaws of the Marsh*)
Waters, Sarah 89 f.
Watkins, Calvert 60, 135
Watt, Ian 51–53, 56, 76
Webster's 10, 84, 161, 242
Wellek, René 3
Wells, H. G. 59, 62 f., 66–70, 75 f., 225–227, 256
Werth, Paul 118, 160, 162, 209
West, M. L. 128
Wharton, Edith 127
White, Alan R. 10 f., 13, 18 f.
White, Allon 22
White, Hayden 27, 151
White, Patrick 180 f.
Whyte, Iain Boyd 222, 225 f.
Williams, David 106 f.
Williams, William Carlos 243
Willingham, Bill 260
Wilson, H. W. 226
Winterson, Jeanette 63
Wister, Owen 71, 218 f., 221
Wittgenstein, Ludwig 9, 18, 40, 174
Wodehouse, P. G. 226
Wolf, Mark J. P. 118
Wolf, Werner 202
Wollheim, Richard 27
Womack, Kenneth 26, 236
Woolf, Virginia 63, 99, 103, 143–146, 269
Woolley, Jacqueline D. 111
Wordsworth, William 36
Worthington, Heather 62
Wulf, Christoph 41, 45

Yacobi, Tamar 81 f., 163
Yates, Frances 273

Zarrilli, Phillip B. 60, 239
Zeami Motokiyo 44
Zeckhauser, Richard 79
Zerubavel, Eviatar 10, 30
Zerweck, Bruno 83, 106
Zhou Enlai 230
Zhou Yang 230 f.
Zhuangzi 61, 149, 232, 239
Zunshine, Lisa 2, 114, 153, 158, 236
Zusak, Markus 108, 152
Zwerdling, Alex 145

www.ingramcontent.com/pod-product-compliance
Lightning Source LLC
Chambersburg PA
CBHW030606230426
43661CB00053B/1869